Community and Regional Planning

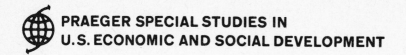 PRAEGER SPECIAL STUDIES IN
U.S. ECONOMIC AND SOCIAL DEVELOPMENT

Community and Regional Planning

ISSUES IN PUBLIC POLICY

Melvin R. Levin

Introduction by George Blackwood

FREDERICK A. PRAEGER, Publishers
New York · Washington · London

The purpose of the Praeger Special Studies is to make specialized research monographs in U.S. and international economics and politics available to the academic, business, and government communities. For further information, write to the Special Projects Division, Frederick A. Praeger, Publishers, 111 Fourth Avenue, New York, N.Y. 10003.

FREDERICK A. PRAEGER, PUBLISHERS
111 Fourth Avenue, New York, N.Y. 10003, U.S.A.
5, Cromwell Place, London S.W.7, England

Published in the United States of America in 1969
by Frederick A. Praeger, Inc., Publishers

Library of Congress Catalog Card Number: 68-55012

Printed in the United States of America

For Jo-Anne

ACKNOWLEDGMENTS

This collection of studies prepared and assembled over a period of almost three years owes much to the author's callous presumption on past friendships. My colleagues at Boston University, George Blackwood, Norman Abend, and Joseph Slavet have been mercilessly exploited for review, criticism, editorial assistance, and ideas. Their patience and forbearance have been much appreciated.

My secretaries have been confronted with a challenging task. Mrs. Alice Petrescu and Mrs. Nancy Thompson, who suffered through thousands of pages of typing and retyping, surely deserve my deepest sympathy as well as my profound gratitude.

Reflections such as these on government organization inevitably tend to take on an autobiographical tinge. In those cases where discretion seemed to be called for, names of persons and agencies have been carefully omitted out of kindness and cowardice. Nevertheless a number of anonymous benefactors, some of whom may read this book, deserve my thanks for their unwitting assistance.

Finally, acknowledgment is due to the following four journals that gave permission to use articles which first appeared on their pages: *The Journal of the American Institute of Planners* for permission to use a revised version of "Planners and Metropolitan Planning," which appeared in the March, 1967, issue and "The Big Regions," which appeared in March, 1968. The editorial comments and encouragement of the journal's editor, Ralph Gakenheimer, were most helpful. The Boston University *Graduate Journal* has kindly permitted use of "On the Poverty Front: The Expendable Executives," which appeared in the Winter, 1966-67, issue and "Public Entrepreneurship in Distressed Areas," which appeared in the Spring, 1967, issue. Acknowledgment is also made to *Urban Affairs Quarterly* for use of "Economic Development Districts: New Planning Regions," which appeared in the February, 1968, issue of that publication. A somewhat shorter, revised version of "Poor No More: Unemployment Rates and Convalescing Areas," appeared in *Land Economics,* the March, 1968, issue, under the title "New Criteria for Distressed Areas."

As a last note, the author wishes to assume full responsibility for errors of fact, poor judgment, and bad temper that may offend the learned, wise, and sensitive reader.

Boston   M.R.L.

CONTENTS

	Page
ACKNOWLEDGMENTS	vii
LIST OF TABLES	xiii
LIST OF ABBREVIATIONS	xiv

INTRODUCTION by George Blackwood
    Planning: From New Nationalism to Great Society   1
    Notes   15

Chapter

1   INTELLECTUALS IN STATE GOVERNMENT   17

    Government by Rejects?   17
    In the Firm: The House Intellectual   22
    Project Staff: King for a Day?   24
    How to Be a Rich Consultant   32
    A Concluding Note: E Flat   37
    Notes   37

2   YARDSTICKS FOR GOVERNMENT: THE ROLE OF PPBS   39

    The New Super X-Ray Calipers   39
    The Temporal Temptation: Planning for the Millenium?   44
    How Much Commitment?   46
    Design for Geniuses?   52
    Who Killed Cock Robin?   58
    Notes   61

3   COSTS, BENEFITS, AND SOCIAL INDICATORS   64

    Do Great Society Programs Have a Future?   64
    Cost-Benefit Analysis: *Déja Vu?*   64
    Social Indicators: The Big Picture   68
    Pechman-Heller, or an Exposé a Day   72

The Problem of the States: Massachusetts, for Example   74
Notes   80

4   ON THE POVERTY FRONT: THE EXPENDABLE EXECUTIVES   83

Introduction   83
ABCD Organization   85
Critical Problems   85
ABCD's Internal Administration   87
The Office of Economic Opportunity   90
Inadequate State of the Art   98
Conclusion   100
Notes   101

5   THE PERILS OF PROJECTIONS   108

Introduction: Projecting for Fun and Profit   108
Metropolitan Boston: Laggard to Prototype   112
Projections and Revisions   119
Conclusion   123
Notes   124

6   PLANNERS AND METROPOLITAN PLANNING   127

Alternative Approaches   127
Metropolitan Government   130
New State Role?   133
The Planner's Role   138
Conclusion   141
Notes   143

7   TRANSPORTATION FACTORS IN HUMAN RESOURCES
    PLANNING   148

Introduction   148
Planning for Community Colleges   150
Nursing Homes and Area Planning   156
Conclusion   165
Notes   167

8   THE ECONOMIC DEVELOPMENT DISTRICTS: NEW
    PLANNING REGIONS   169

New Directions in Area Development   169
Background of the Area Redevelopment Act   171

Chapter		Page
	ARA's Problems	173
	Economic Development Districts	175
	The Staffing Problem	183
	Notes	184
9	POOR NO MORE? UNEMPLOYMENT RATES AND CONVALESCING AREAS	187
	Introduction	187
	Basic Problems Unresolved	191
	Characteristics of Massachusetts Redevelopment Areas	191
	Unemployment Causes and Trends	195
	New Targets for Redevelopment Areas	199
	Notes	200
10	PUBLIC ENTREPRENEURSHIP IN DISTRESSED AREAS	202
	Introduction	202
	The Lost Golden Age	204
	The Schools: Community Mirror	208
	Urban Renewal Expenditures: A Measure of Public Entrepreneurship	212
	The Improving Climate	216
	Conclusions	217
	Notes	218
11	TALENT MIGRATION: DISTRESSED AREA DILEMMA	220
	Migrant Types and Migrant Problems	220
	Skimming Off the Cream	224
	Why They Leave	229
	Employment Barriers and Migration	235
	Automation and Future Manpower Needs	236
	Notes for a Government Policy	237
	Broadening the Talent Base	240
	Notes	241
12	THE BIG REGIONS	245
	The Big Regions and America's Future	245
	Historic Roots	249
	Appalachian Analogue	251
	How to Run a Surplus: The Case of New England	256
	Eight Criteria: A Bad Fit?	259
	Outmigration and the Regions	261

Chapter		Page
	Conclusion: New Regions Equal New Arenas	264
	Notes	267
13	SUMMING UP: ONE SMALL CANDLE?	271
	Background Information	271
	The Universities and the Future of Federalism	279
	The Universities and the Evaluation of Government Programs	281
	Notes	283
	SELECTED BIBLIOGRAPHY	285
	INDEX	303
	ABOUT THE AUTHOR	307

LIST OF TABLES

Table   Page

1   Summary of Problems and Goals in Economic Development Areas   177

2   Economic and Social Indices--Boston vs. Massachusetts Redevelopment Areas, 1950-66   192

3   Massachusetts Unemployment Rates, 1949-66   197

4   Selected Data for the Thirteen Largest Cities in Massachusetts, 1955-65   210

5   Educational Statistics in Massachusetts Areas, 1950 and 1960   233

6   Appalachia and EDA Regions, 1967   247

7   The New England States' Shares of Major Allocated Federal Expenditures, 1957 and 1963   258

8   Outmigration of Youth in New England and Selected States, 1950-60   263

LIST OF ABBREVIATIONS

ABCD	Action for Boston Community Development
ACIR	Advisory Commission on Intergovernmental Relations
ADP	Automatic Data Processing
AEF	American Expeditionary Force
AIP	American Institute of Planners
APAC	Area Planning Action Council
ARA	Area Redevelopment Administration
ASPO	American Society of Planning Officials
BLS	Bureau of Labor Statistics
BPR	Bureau of Public Roads
BRA	Boston Redevelopment Authority
CAP	Community Action Program
CED	Community for Economic Development
CRP	Community Renewal Program
DES	Division of Employment Security (Massachusetts)
DOD	Department of Defense
EDA	Economic Development Administration
EDD	Economic Development District
ESEA	Elementary and Secondary Education Act
EYOA	Economic and Youth Opportunity Agency
FAA	Federal Aviation Administration
HEW	Department of Health, Education, and Welfare
HHFA	Housing and Home Finance Agency
HUD	Department of Housing and Urban Development
MBTA	Massachusetts Bay Transportation Authority
NASA	National Aeronautics and Space Administration
NRPB	National Resources Planning Board
NYC	Neighborhood Youth Corps Program
OCS	Officer Candidate School
OEDP	Overall Economic Development Program
OEO	Office of Economic Opportunity

PPBS	Planning, Programming, Budgetary System
R & D	Research and Development
ROTC	Reserve Officers' Training Corps
SMA	Standard Metropolitan Area
SMSA	Standard Metropolitan Statistical Area
SSRC	Social Science Research Council
TVA	Tennessee Valley Authority
USES	United States Employment Service
VISTA	Volunteers in Service to America

Community and Regional Planning

INTRODUCTION
by
George Blackwood

PLANNING: FROM NEW NATIONALISM TO GREAT SOCIETY

Throughout the history of the United States, we have paused now and again--all too infrequently as it turns out--to appraise how well the spirit and purpose of our society is working out in the machinery of government. The ends of such examinations are evident: modifications, improvements--new directions if you will--for a new generation. The underlying assumption is that there must be a series of progressive changes to meet conditions that are shifting here as rapidly as anywhere in the world, if not as spectacularly.

In this book, Melvin R. Levin, with the background and perspectives of the planner, examines social trends and needs within American society. In a series of chapters concentrating on specific aspects of governmental relationships with society during the last third of the twentieth century, he elaborates three central themes:

Firstly, hesitantly, and up to this point without adequate and skillful use of its most vital resource--brains--the national government and to a much smaller extent state and local governments have begun to recognize and adapt to the pressing needs of society. This has come about amid much conflict, and difficult transitions in thinking lie ahead. But the needs are now beginning to be recognized; and Dr. Levin suggests that the tools are at hand at least to meet the most urgent.

Second, there is a very substantial gap, and therefore a very real dilemma for democracy, between a leadership elite that grasps the necessities of planning or experimentation with the new urban forms and ideas and a large although restless mass that is not at all sure precisely which actions it should endorse. All too often, programs for actions have been presented on paper--and then left there. Planners, economists, and social scientists in general have observed, analyzed, and criticized, but all too often they have presented grandiose and unrealistic schemes that have not respected politico-economic realities. The relationship between talent and pragmatic common sense has therefore all too often been inverse and one that creates disillusionment and frustration. Careful management of programs by agencies concerned with the quality of life in the United States can help close the existing gap.[1]

1

Third, the kind of inflated rhetoric so often encountered in public affairs makes coordination more difficult, especially when combined with a bureaucratic orientation that stresses quantity of governmental personnel in a neat organizational chart rather than quality of staff and administrative practices. The lack of adequate foresight in planning and the frequent resistance to intelligence and innovation, as for instance the failure to properly use universities as sources of ideas and talents, has fostered a "deadlock and drift" type of psychology within the governmental structure and among clients of government agencies. Certain social trends (such as talent migration) strip some areas of their capacity to act intelligently and forcefully even though such failures are often obscured by the cloud of rhetoric and the fog of bureaucracy.

The author of this book is especially concerned with the rise of a number of new professions that are vital to the future, and he stresses the role of education in American society. To planners, he addresses a special plea: It is now almost universally recognized that narrow economic and land-use perspectives are not sufficient, and a "social planning" dimension is as inevitable as it is overdue.

One caution to the reader before he proceeds further: This book is concerned with America's domestic future, and those who seek answers for our international problems should look elsewhere. American democracy, especially since World War II, might be thought of as a giant sandwich, in which a thin slice of bread at the top covers a rich variety of foods supported by another thick slice of bread at the bottom. The thin slice is the elite or leadership; the thick, of course, the general populace; the foods in the middle, public policies of all types. What the author has done is cut down the middle of the sandwich, separating domestic matters from international and examining the state of the former.

Basing his assertions on a wide-ranging knowledge of recent developments in federal and state governments, Dr. Levin suggests that the present era in domestic affairs can be considered the reverse of (yet somehow parallel to) the Great Depression. Then, as now, positive political-economic action was necessary as traditional patterns proved inadequate. Then, as now, experimentation on a broad scale seemed to be warranted. The difference is more than a generation in time, however. The problem of an affluent society may well be that it thinks in simplistic Depression terms, that scarcity of talent (combined with a viscous bureaucratic machinery) has replaced scarcity of employment as a basic social ill. Since the Depression, we appear to have learned a great deal about what *not* to do and only a little about what *to* do.

However, some recognition has begun among social thinkers of what A. F. K. Organski has called the "politics of abundance"--greatly increased productivity in a peacetime economy, better technology and economic organization for warmaking, generally high scales of living surrounded by pockets of poverty, and an economy that requires a labor force possessing increasing and diversifying skills.[2] The implications of the revolutionary economic changes that have taken place are not fully grasped by many people inside *or* outside government. For example, the structure of American Federal Government is fundamentally the same as it has been for many years, but the *substance* today is different; we still have sharing of power between the central government and the state governments, but the actual workings of their relationships are vastly different today from 1933, for example. This has been brought about largely by the pressure of social needs translated to political realities. It is not the result of a "conspiracy in Washington"--no matter how much Birchites and their fellow travelers swear to the contrary.

Awareness of the kinds of problems to which this book addresses itself is not new. In the early 1900's, Herbert Croly, later the founder and first editor of the *New Republic*, wrote: "The way to realize a purpose is not to leave it to chance.... The problem belongs to American national democracy, and its solution must be attempted chiefly by means of official national action."[3] The problem to which he referred was how to bring the "promise of American life" --abundance for all, the good society standing on the bedrock of freedom--to fruition. His suggestion was that the government needed to substitute purposive planning for the drift which he believed to be its main characteristic. Croly's doctrine of the positive state moving to meet social problems as they arose was adopted by Theodore Roosevelt as the theme of his 1912 campaign for the Presidency and put forward under the theme of the "New Nationalism." Essentially, this embodies the idea of the reconstruction of society through strong governmental intervention in the economy. The general idea had been advanced by Lester Frank Ward in his *Dynamic Sociology*, and it penetrated the Progressive Movement and its thinking; but Croly (and Roosevelt) had pinpointed the place where action needed to be inspired most--Washington, rather than the state capitals which were the focus of much Progressive thought.

In 1912, Roosevelt confronted not only the incumbent President, William Howard Taft--whom contemporary historians regard as not nearly as "stand-pat" as his associates did--but Woodrow Wilson. Wilson, the ultimate winner, stood staunchly on the traditional Jeffersonian platform of small government for small action. But within a brief time of his inauguration he began to take halting steps toward the Rooseveltian ideals--so much so that Croly turned from skepticism about Wilson to a mild enthusiasm. Still, however, Croly felt that planned action by the Wilson administration was lacking and he wrote: "The planning department of the democratic state is created for action.. ..It plans ahead as far as conditions permit or dictate. It changes its plans as often as conditions demand. It seeks above all to test its own plans, so as to discover whether they will accomplish the desired result."[4]

By this test, Wilsonianism was deficient. But if this was the case with the Wilson administration, the 1920's were a positive disaster, at least from the standpoint of government action. Furthermore, the gap between the social sciences and practical applications to society widened rapidly. Social scientists and planners, like most intellectuals, found themselves increasingly in what seemed to be an alien land;[5] but rapid advances were made in internal organization of the social sciences, in new theoretical concepts, and progress was made on the development of planning as a coherent discipline within the general framework of the social sciences.

There had, of course, been fragmentary and somewhat abortive efforts to use the techniques of governmental analysis to improve existing government machinery, the most notable private group being the Institute for Public Administration in New York. A significant step forward came in 1924, when Charles E. Merriam founded the Social Science Research Council (SSRC), a federation of various academic societies covering the major social sciences: economics, political science, psychology, sociology, and history. As a recent study points out, Merriam's basic hope was "to place academic research at the disposal of the government."[6] This hope was not to bear fruit for some years; but one accomplishment of the SSRC was as a force in helping to persuade President Herbert Hoover to appoint a Research Committee on Social Trends in 1929. The report of this committee, on which the noted sociologist William Fielding Ogburn served as chairman with Merriam as vice-chairman, resulted in little concrete action, but, it demonstrated in exhaustive detail to what extent research techniques in the social sciences (in some cases, with such tools as computers and input-output analysis not yet available, rather rudimentary) might be used by governmental agencies to gather information.

However, most concrete advances in the thinking and techniques of the social sciences in terms of adaptations to society, as of 1930, had taken place on the local level rather than the national. A significant breakthrough toward thinking on a broad national scale, with due attention to the problems of governmental units at all levels--federal, state, and local--came with the founding of the Public Administration Clearing House in 1931. This organization, with Louis Brownlow as its director, soon became a major center not only for information about governmental administration, but it also became the core of a cluster of organizations specializing in governmental research and advice in policy-making. This cluster of groups, often known as "1313" from its street address--1313 E. 60th Street in Chicago--soon began to play a role as a significant source of expertise in government which has continued down to the present.

At about the same time, planning as a conceptual field of analysis and training had begun to "jell" as an aspect of the social sciences. As in the field of governmental analysis and public administration--where the first significant advances had been in the formation of municipal bureaus of research, an American invention which by the 1930's had spread as widely as Japan and Ireland[7]-- planning had first of all concerned itself with the city. Between 1920 and 1930, as Robert A. Walker points out, the leaders of the planning movement had made important contributions to city planning, and by the latter year, practically all the larger cities in the United States had official planning agencies (on paper at least).[8] Practitioners of planning were numerous enough by 1917 so that the American City Planning Institute (now the American Institute of Planners) was created, and the first school of city planning was founded at Harvard, in 1929. For the most part, city planning at this time was not only narrow in focus but tied closely to landscape architecture as a field of study in the few institutions that had created academic programs. One broadening step was taken in the late 1920's, when regional planning for urbanized areas began to come into focus. Governor Alfred E. Smith initiated a subregional planning study for New York state; by 1929, the Committee on Regional Plan of New York and Its Environs, working closely with social scientists at Columbia University, published a series of volumes dealing with population movements, industrial development, public services, and many other facets of the various regions within the state. These pioneering efforts stood alone, however, until well into the 1930's.

The coming of the Great Depression brought about a major shift in the position and perspectives of planners, economists, political scientists, and other social scientists. Participating in a series of social experiments during the New Deal, they were perhaps more scorned that applauded. But from the vantage point of the present day, it is clear that much of the criticism was misdirected. The real problem of the New Deal was a lack of broad-gauged coordination, a failure to develop and use the talent at its disposal with sufficient skill. Nonetheless, the 1930's marked a distinct step forward in the relationship of the new techniques and perspectives of the social sciences to government.

For one thing, planning began to break out of the straitjacket of city (or more accurately, simple land use) planning toward new horizons that were of course still limited. In retrospect, perhaps the most important measure of the New Deal was the creation of the Tennessee Valley Authority. Going beyond the production of electric power, flood control, rural electrification, and related goals, the act carried the significant language that the TVA was to advance "the economic and social well-being of the people living in the said river basin." There has been much debate about the accomplishment of the TVA, but as Dr. Levin points out in his chapter entitled "The Big Regions" it provided a domestic pattern--an aborted pattern, but one which was to be revived and extended in the 1960's--for future development of regions concerned with long range economic and social planning.

The role of planning in government developed rapidly in other respects as well. Unfortunately, a substantial part of the development was verbal rather than substantive, and for a time the word "planning" was as romantic for thinking Americans as "resistance" was to be for adventurous Frenchmen a few years later. "Planning" was everything; accomplishment, nothing. For a brief Indian Summer in the 1930's, forty-seven of the forty-eight states had created planning boards (a number seem to have had primarily a paper existence) concerned with the best use of state resources. Over 1,000 city planning departments could be found, and 400 counties could boast planning boards. One of the early activities of one of the "1313" agencies, the Council of State Governments, was to sponsor commissions on interstate cooperation. Twenty were in operation by September, 1937, and it was assumed that planning would have a high priority on interstate agendas. Already, regional planning boards stretched across state boundaries, including the Pacific Northwest Regional Planning Commission, the New England Regional Planning Commission, and the Ohio Valley Regional Planning Commission. These commissions, however, seemed to enjoy little popular or legislative support and understanding; in 1938, for instance, a modest request from Governor Charles F. Hurley of Massachusetts for $10,000 to be allocated to the work of the New England Regional Planning Commission was quickly sliced out of the state budget by the hostile Legislature, which was angered at the Governor for other reasons.[9]

Within the national government, the National Planning Board, established by Executive Order in 1933, became the National Resources Board in 1934 and the National Resources Committee in 1935. Even with these changes in name and much uncertainty of functions, this body marked a signal change of direction in Washington. Originally concerned with the preparation of a national public works program under the direction of Secretary of the Interior Harold L. Ickes, the National Resources Committee by 1935 was engaged in some aspects of comprehensive national planning. Since it was evident that federal programs required cooperation from the states, it was decided that state plans could be financed from federal funds available for emergency relief. The result was that with the exception of Delaware every state set up an official planning agency, which usually had some power over public-works projects in the state. In many instances, these agencies had just begun to function, carrying on research and planning some assistance to local governments, when the federal momentum caused by the Depression began to slacken. By 1939, several states had quietly cut back their planning agencies, and by 1942 very little was being done across the country. Significantly, in a number of instances state planning boards merged with agencies concerned with industrial development.[10]

The National Resources Committee was in a strategic enough position within the governmental structure in 1935 so that when Charles Merriam and Louis Brownlow suggested a study promoting more effective organization of the Executive Branch, the committee's approval was essential in arousing President Roosevelt's interest.[11] The recommendations that were made as a result of the study included strong emphasis on planning through a permanent National Resources Board. Brownlow, the chairman of the committee appointed by the President (the other members were Merriam and Luther Gulick), assembled a group of social scientists as the research staff; the general desire of the committee and the staff was to set up an agency that would "serve as clearing house of planning interest and concerns in the national effort to prevent waste and improve our national living standards," and they asserted that "the universal aspiration for economic security and the increasing enrichment of human lives may be forwarded by substituting the results of careful scientific study for uninformed judgment and political expediency as the basis for the formulation of government plans."12

The committee's proposal to establish a National Resources Planning Board--together with most of its other proposals--encountered a difficult time in Congress. The Army Corps of Engineers stoutly resisted incursions on its domain of river and harbor development, and western senators succeeded in inserting a provision that two of the five members of the board come from west of the Mississippi. Conservatives were openly fearful of a dictatorship through planning via a New Deal sovietism. The result was a rather weak board located in the Executive Office of the President from 1939 to 1943, when it was quietly abolished.

During World War II, other facets of applying the social sciences to governmental activities came to the fore, while planning faded. Economics had undergone a rapid evolution in the 1930's, with the two most important developments (which were related) being the impact of the thought of John Maynard Keynes and the rise of a new system of national accounting centering on "input-output analysis." Keynesianism provided the theoretical base for the national-accounts system devised by Simon Kuznets and others, a system to measure the aggregate content and the changes in national production. This was now applied by government economists, who used as a base the summary figures of gross national production. One economist active in this endeavor later wrote that the new system of economic analysis was a weapon whose "bearing on victory was considerably greater than that of atomic energy," because in England and the United States it was much clearer than in Germany what was being produced, what proportions were going to military and civilian use, and how resources were allocated between immediate use and investment.13 This meant that the Germans were simply mobilizing economic resources less wisely than their major opponents, despite the vaunted efficiency of Nazism.

Two other wartime developments should also be noted: The immense growth of technology and productivity demonstrated that the country could mobilize its resources to achieve hitherto undreamed levels of living if it so desired; and the central organizing mechanism, carrying on in a different way the fight against the Depression, was the federal government. The vast expansion of the federal government indicated another step in significant alteration of state-federal relationships. At the same time, however, there was also a trend toward deterioration in the quality of government personnel that appears to have begun during or shortly after World War II; this was noted by James M. Landis in late 1960.14

Under President Harry S. Truman, wartime economics techniques were institutionalized under the aegis of the Council of Economic Advisers, created by the Employment Act of 1946 and designed as a central mechanism in governmental planning for the stabilization of the economy. Another area in which the Truman Administration moved was in expanding the role of the Bureau of the Budget; this bureau, through increased powers of decision-making for the President, became in a limited sense the "allocation planner" for the energies and activities of the government.

Since the administrative structure of the government had expanded enormously under the impact of depression and war, much attention was concentrated in the 1940's and 1950's on efforts to "streamline" and reorganize it. The First and Second Hoover Commissions and the Kestnbaum Commission were the most ambitious attempts to do this--with limited success, especially with respect to the Kestnbaum group in 1955. Probably more important, at least in its subtle effects, was the fact that major elements of American business came to accept the concept of economic and (to a limited degree) social planning on the part of the government. The major instrument in this "reconciliation" of business and government was the Committee for Economic Development (CED), a group of about two hundred corporate executives and educators who have sponsored numerous studies to help formulate policies leading to "full employment at higher living standards." Sometimes described as "progressive conservatives," CED leaders formed a seminal group around President Dwight D. Eisenhower: Robert Anderson, Marion Folsom, James D. Zellerbach, Meyer Kestnbaum, and others. All had been chairmen of the CED, and even Eisenhower himself had been a trustee of the organization while President of Columbia University.15

Although many liberals felt frustrated during the Eisenhower years by what seemed to them to be a stultification of progress in the meeting of national problems, legislation that bore great import for the future was passed. In the field of housing, for instance, the Housing Act of 1954 introduced the "urban renewal" concept. This extended the principle of the Housing Act of 1949, which provided funds for public housing and redevelopment conforming to planned programs for entire communities. The 1954 act included neighborhood conservation and rehabilitation as well as redevelopment. It required the submission of comprehensive plans by eligible communities in the form of "workable programs" before they could qualify for federal financing. A most important part was Section 701, which provided funds (on a matching 50-50 basis) to state planning agencies for assistance to smaller communities or for planning work in metropolitan and regional areas. This still did not provide planning aid for the larger cities, but later amendments broadened the act.

Another area of public policy affected by the Eisenhower Administration was highways. The Highway Act of 1956 provided billions of dollars for a 41,000-mile system of superhighways crisscrossing the country, with the federal government paying 90 per cent of the cost. A little-noticed section of the act expanded 1934 highway legislation setting aside up to 1.5 per cent of the combined state-federal highway expenditures for use in nonengineering planning studies in connection with road building, to relate economic and social patterns to the new roads. As was the case with housing legislation, the highway acts were fundamentally narrow-gauged in dealing only with one area of public policy and ignoring the far-reaching ramifications for society of a sudden thrust in one specific segment of the national economic policy.

On the state level during the late 1940's and 1950's, similar trends were evident. While rapid urbanization was taking place, state and regional planning lagged behind. Perhaps the only type of planning that could be readily grasped by executives and legislators (or at least financed in proper fashion) was that related to economic development--especially the attraction of industry. This type of "smokestack" planning (which also embraced the tourist) usually stressed colorful promotional efforts; because not a great deal was done to study the appropriate relationship between a planning agency and a development, the latter tended to overshadow the former. One result, however, was all to the good: The competition for "smokestacks" meant an increasing demand for persons with a number of different types of skills such as industrial geography, market analysis, population movements analysis, and transportation expertise. The trend toward fragmentation increased, but there was at least the unifying theme that state and regional planners engaged in industrial development could tap a broader range of talents.[16]

With the inauguration of John F. Kennedy, social scientists and planners assumed new importance in the federal government. Spencer Parratt pointed out at an American Society for Public Administration convention that "the people who are doing the most for metropolitan planning are sitting in Washington," and he stated a confident belief that the near future would witness greater federal activity.[17] Kennedy's acceptance of Richard Neustadt's concept of strong presidential leadership is well known as well as his rapport with many intellectuals. Soon after his inauguration, Kennedy proposed several measures advocated by various types of social scientists, and two were passed in 1961. The existing program of federal aid to housing was broadened, with an expanded urban-renewal program, subsidies for private rehabilitation of slums, additional public housing, and more aid for metropolitan planning, open-space development, and community facilities. The other major Kennedy innovation was legislation providing aid to urban and rural areas with substantial unemployment rates. This proposal, first put forward by Senator Paul Douglas of Illinois (the only professional economist in Congress) in 1955, had attracted Kennedy's interest with special intensity during his campaign in West Virginia. For such areas, federal loans and grants became available to build or reconstruct industrial buildings, modernize water systems, and establish training programs for workers with no skills or outmoded ones. Subsistence for the workers during the training period was also provided. The legislation was later broadened into the Public Works and Economic Development Act of 1965 and included public works project authorizations for areas with chronic unemployment and provision for planning on a broader regional scale.

In 1962, Congress passed the Manpower Development and Training Act; this directed the federal government to assess national manpower needs and to develop training programs to equip unemployed or underemployed workers to fill the needs. After Kennedy's death, several of the projects he initiated came to fruition. In 1964, the Economic Opportunity Act was passed; it provided for the Job Corps, work-study programs, the "Domestic Peace Corps" or VISTA, and community action programs, sometimes called the heart of the fight against poverty in the United States. Community action programs were to be designed locally, with representatives of the poor being enlisted in planning and operating the programs.

The Appalachian Regional Development Act of 1965 provided $1.1 billion in federal funds, four fifths of it to be used for highways in the region, the remainder to be used for such varied projects as multicounty health centers, mining area restoration, and vocational education facilities. Perhaps the most important tool in the program was the one that cost the least--the Appalachian Regional Commission. With a rather small staff, this commission is headed by a federal member appointed by the President and a state member elected from among the twelve Appalachian governors. Projects were to be designed by the states, approved by the regional commission, and executed with federal funds. In general, the approach underlying the Appalachian bill was not to meet the region's immediate needs for money but rather to improve the economy of the region. The people of the region were to increase their purchasing power through basic economic development rather than through welfare. The theory and its explanation by President Lyndon B. Johnson and his associates were attractive enough to Congress that a program covering only twelve states received the votes of at least one senator or representative from forty-eight states; the bill passed 62-22 in the Senate and 257-165 in the House.[18]

In March, 1965, when the act was passed, per capita income in the area was almost 40 per cent below the national average, and unemployment was about 50 per cent greater. The region as defined by the act extends from Lake Erie to northern Alabama; with 17 million people in 182,000 square miles, it is roughly the same size and has about 10 per cent less population than California. The difficulties and achievements of the Appalachian Commission are significant for observers of so-called creative federalism. While still too early to render a judgment, the hope is that new patterns of cooperation between the federal and state governments and combination of resources beyond the boundaries of single states will emerge.

While Appalachia represented a new concept of federal-state relations on a regional basis, urban renewal and redevelopment represented a novel federal-local planning enterprise. Initially authorized under the Eisenhower Administration in 1959, the Community Renewal Program (CRP) became a major factor in such planning in 1962, with about a hundred communities receiving federal grants covering two thirds of their cost. The general idea of CRP was comprehensive planning for city renewal rather than the project-by-project approach previously followed.

From the academic standpoint, the most important developments of the 1960's lie in the rapid growth of urban specializations within the social and behavioral sciences. The new field of urban economics has emerged, generated in large part by the Ford Foundation's supported group, Resources for the Future, which has also stimulated research into "regional accounting." Sociologists and political scientists more critically and analytically began to examine phases of urban and metropolitan life; among them might be accounted Edward Banfield, Robert Dahl, Herbert J. Gans, Nathan Glazer, Scott Greer, Daniel Patrick Moynihan, and Robert C. Wood. Computer Science also developed into a major tool for the social scientist concerned with the type of problems dealt with in this text.

By the mid-1960's, the trends were clear: Concerns at all levels of government with overriding urban and regional problems were combined with new techniques and tools of social scientists and planners. Two new cabinet departments, housing and urban development, and transportation, were set up in 1965 and 1966 respectively. In analyzing the evolution of public policy with respect to urban renewal, Lowden Wingo, Jr. wrote that the policy focus has moved

> . . . from the slum area to the neighborhood, the central city, and ultimately the region; from limited policy power concerns with the lower housing strata to the total housing stock and currently to the state of the physical plant of the region; from a policeman-and-policed relationship between local governments and parts of the private housing sector to an intricate net of intergovernmental public-private relations into which are drawn neighborhood organizations, financial institutions, welfare agencies, local interest groups, and the complex array of housing, planning, land use, and transportation agencies from every level of government.[19]

It is within this contextual background that this volume must be placed. As indicated previously, there are several themes which run throughout the text. One point that has not been touched as yet, but which arises a number of times in the book, is the relationship of the planner or technician to political leaders or policy-makers. In the chapter entitled "Intellectuals in State Government" the author discusses state government as a great intellectual wasteland of modern America and the role of the intellectual as "martyr" to conspicuous inefficiency and traditional ineptitude. Planners and others with social science training often find themselves subordinate to incompetents whom they must-- in order to achieve even limited objectives--suffer gladly.

A related perspective on this question arises in the chapter on "Planners and Metropolitan Planning," where the author suggests that there is some hope in planning coordination through the office of the state governor while he also points out that professionalization of planning at the state level has been a slow process. On the local level, this has been an even more severe problem in certain areas, highlighted in the chapter on "Public Entrepreneurship in Distressed Areas." The mediocrity so frequently found in political leadership in these backwashes of American life is paralleled by the substandard performance of technicians available for redevelopment areas, with well-qualified persons finding and using opportunities to participate in the "talent migration" which is pinpointed in another chapter as central to the plight of these areas. This theme, the planner-politico relationship as vital element in adaptation to the future, is implicit and occasionally explicit at several other points in the chapters printed here.

Another and closely related theme that emerges at several points is the continual (sometimes productive, more frequently not) friction which exist at a covert and occasionally overt level within the framework of government. Almost all textbooks in the field of public administration go into detail on the importance of coordination between agencies and their integration under an executive, and there are certain classic studies of "bureaucratic conflict."[20] Two major instances dealt with in this text arise in the context of new programs of poverty and economic development. The "expendable executives" are victims of the "war on poverty" in an unusual sense, and the case study offered here covers a community action program known as Action for Boston Community Development (ABCD) and its executives, some of whom became casualties in the conflict with the Office of Economic Opportunity and other agencies as they attempted to respond to the demands of a fragmented clientele. Less spectacular, but perhaps more representative of the troubles of bureaucratic conflict, are the challenges posed by the organization of Economic Development Districts that require coordinating action by a variety of local, state, and federal agencies. As is pointed out in the chapter on "The Economic Development Districts: New Planning Regions," overlapping regions used by different federal agencies, interagency squabbles over legislative grants of power, funding problems, and a whole galaxy of controversies create difficulties. In addition, as the model cities program comes into operation, these difficulties will be roadblocks to achievement of the program's objectives.

It is perhaps desirable at this point to briefly discuss each chapter consecutively. As indicated previously, the opening chapter deals with the challenges of state government to "intellectual martyrs." Needless to say, the United States is not going to abolish or even alter its basic form of government in the near future; this being the case, the states will continue to be important and face staggering challenges for which they will need all the talents they can muster. However, the plain fact is that such state capitals as Augusta, Columbus, Bismarck, Jefferson, Lansing, Olympia, and most others are minor league; with Washington the place "where the action is," competent persons have continuously moved as though magnetized.

In the second chapter, one of the major new tools available for long-range planning and programatic action is discussed. Planning-Programming-Budgetary System (PPBS), especially as developed by the Department of Defense, bids fair to extend through the federal government and then, with some delay, into state and local governments as well. Operations research, cost-benefit analysis, and systems analysis are other new techniques as grounds for decision-making. In the succeeding chapter, "Costs, Benefits, and Social Indicators," the author discusses other new techniques that are emerging, foremost among them the idea of a council of social advisers to devise a system of social indicators through which progress and problems in national social policy can be evaluated. This chapter stresses a theme mentioned previously: the role of the intellectual (planner or social scientist, in most cases) in relation to government. A special facet of this relationship is the "lack of capacity in state and local government not only to exploit the opportunities opened up by PPBS and other approaches but even to muster sufficient expertise to handle their current operations satisfactorily." In conclusion, the author suggests that it may be easier to respond to exciting new ideas by adopting them in form rather than in substance.

The following chapter is a case study of the expendable executives on the poverty front and demonstrates the problems of setting up new agencies and creating harmonious liaison between federal agencies and their counterparts on the local level. The result is that "heat shields" are needed and are found in the form of high priced and temporary personnel who serve as expendable administrators when public pressures and internal conflicts grow.

The next two chapters deal with some hazards and pitfalls of the planning profession. The first discusses the occupational hazard of trying to forecast the future and reviews such unpredicted elements as the shift in population trends that disrupt the projections of planners. The other chapter sets forward four concepts that have been developed about the future of metropolitan planning and examines each in turn. Each of the four alternatives--a review agency with advisory powers, metropolitan government, strengthened state planning, and coordination of federal metropolitan programs--poses some difficulties.

"Transportation Factors in Human Resources Planning" examines the role of highways and public transportation systems in drawing up plans for a network of regional community colleges and nursing homes. The chapter suggests that transportation factors have been greatly overrated as determinants in site location and that a good transportation system provides a loose framework within which a variety of locational patterns can be created.

"Poor No More? Unemployment Rates and Convalescing Areas" sets forward a critique of the use of unemployment ratios as a measure of economic distress and suggests broader measuring sticks for federal aid. The current national prosperity that in early 1968 established a record for longevity may have temporarily solved many of the problems of distressed areas, but in order to make long-range progress, it is desirable to establish ways of measuring the total environment of these areas and not merely to look at month-to-month unemployment.

This chapter is, in a sense, an introduction to the next four: on public entrepreneurship, talent migration, economic development districts, and the big region concept. The emigration of talent from depressed areas is a specific and quite alarming instance of what the author means when he stresses the total environment in such areas. The best people in an area of persistent stagnation, low income, little education, and little challenge tend to move away, winding up in larger metropolitan areas where there is more diversity, greater stimulus, and substantially more opportunity. For America, it is no longer a question of "keeping them down on the farm" but rather keeping brains spread across the nation. The chapter on "Public Entrepreneurship in Distressed Areas" points to a closely related factor; while it is the young talented who migrate from a distressed area, it is the mature untalented who remain. Thus, these areas tend to become what the author styles "Caliban territory," suitable primarily as sources of low-grade labor and low-grade enterprise. Deficient leadership in distressed areas seems to show gradual signs of improvement, however, particularly as educational levels rise and as experience is gained with federally aided programs; the clearest signs seem to be in the efforts of such areas to improve their educational systems.

Two recent developments in federal activity with respect to economic development are discussed in the chapters entitled "The Economic Development Districts: New Planning Regions" and "The Big Regions." The original response of the Kennedy Administration to the problem of depressed areas, the Area Redevelopment Act, was broadened into the Public Works and Economic Development Act of 1965. The Economic Development Administration (EDA) has changed its policies so that it no longer assists a large and scattered number of redevelopment areas but rather groups them in Economic Development Districts. The author, using Massachusetts examples in this chapter as in some of the others, analyzes the problems in implementing this approach; again he finds the difficulties entailed in interagency integration a major obstacle to progress. Under other recent federal legislation, the example of Appalachia has been followed in setting up large regions reaching across state lines. These big regions provide an interesting new concept in creative federalism and hold substantial promise for application in various parts of the nation.

Finally, the author reflects upon the relationship of universities to social problems, with an emphasis upon the academic atmosphere as a center for constructive thought. For the social scientist, he recommends a type of alternating rhythm: activity within the public arena for a time, then immersion in the academic atmosphere. This kind of pattern, now becoming somewhat more evident especially in the urban-centered university, may well provide new dimensions for American "town-gown" relationships.

One final note may be added to this already lengthy introduction. Because the text looks toward the last third of the twentieth century, it should be noticed that the author lays much stress on the role of the young within society. This is part of the point about the colleges and universities--they are places where to a surprising extent the young teach the old (although it is presumed to be vice versa). Those in constant contact with youth know that each generation of college-going youth look with new eyes and new ideas at the world around them. As is evident in several of the chapters presented here, a major task of the social sciences in our society is to teach young people realistically about the obstacles in the path of immediate constructive change--without dimming their enthusiasm for progress. This is a noble goal and difficult of accomplishment. But the young are, of course, not only the key to the future but the best road to an understanding of the present, because society shaped them to its own ends while supposedly training them for productive future careers. The migration of talented youth from backwaters to scenes of action, the need for careful structuring of educational patterns in order to provide a broad cultural base while creating fruitful specialized skills, the need for society to keep the channels open so that the economy and the policy can be geared to incorporating the talents of youth--these are only a few of the points that can be made about the role, relationships, and needs of the younger generation within our society. In a real sense, therefore, the underlying theme of this book is a constant invocation to keep the young in mind in framing policy and implementing programs.

NOTES TO INTRODUCTION

1. For some cases applying this general principle, see Robert Morris and Robert H. Binstock, *Feasible Planning for Social Change* (New York: Columbia University Press, 1966).

2. A. F. K. Organski, *The Stages of Political Development* (New York: A. A. Knopf, 1966), pp. 186-91.

3. Herbert Croly, in *The Promise of American Life,* Arthur M. Schlesinger, Jr. (ed.) (Cambridge, Mass.: The Belknap Press of the Harvard University Press, 1965), p. 24.

4. Herbert Croly, *Progressive Democracy* (New York: The Macmillan Company, 1914), pp. 370-71.

5. Richard Hofstadter, *Anti-Intellectualism in American Life* (New York: Vintage Press, 1963).

6. Richard Polenberg, *Reorganizing Roosevelt's Government* (Cambridge, Mass.: Harvard University Press, 1966), p. 12.

7. John M. Gaus, Leonard D. White, and Marshall E. Dimock, *The Frontiers of Public Administration* (Chicago: The University of Chicago Press, 1936), p. 24.

8. Robert A. Walker, *The Planning Function in Urban Government* (rev. ed.; Chicago: The University of Chicago Press, 1950), p. 35.

9. *The Boston Post,* September 4, 1937; *The Boston Herald,* April 3, 1938.

10. Albert Lepawsky, *State Planning and Economic Development in the South* (Report No. 4; Washington, D.C.: National Planning Association, Committee of the South, 1949).

11. Louis Brownlow, *A Passion for Anonymity,* Vol. II of his autobiography, (Chicago: University of Chicago, 1958).

12. U.S., President's Committee on Administrative Management, *Report of the Committee* (Washington, D.C.: U.S. Government Printing Office, 1937), p. 28.

13. John K. Galbraith, *American Capitalism* (Boston: Houghton Mifflin Co., 1952), p. 80.

14. James M. Landis, *Report on Regulatory Agencies to the President-Elect* (Washington, D.C.: U.S. Government Printing Office, 1960), p. 11.

15. R. Joseph Monsen, Jr., and Mark W. Cannon, *The Makers of Public Policy* (New York: McGraw-Hill Book Company, 1965), p. 47.

16. Council of State Governments, *Planning Services for State Governments* (Chicago: Council of State Governments, 1956), p. 27.

17. *The New York Times,* March 26, 1958.

18. U.S., *Congressional Quarterly Weekly Report,* March 13, 1965.

19. Lowden Wingo, Jr., "Urban Renewal: Objectives, Analyses and Information Systems," in *Regional Accounts for Policy Decisions,* Werner Z. Hirsch (ed.), (Baltimore: The Johns Hopkins Press, 1965), pp. 7-8.

20. See, e.g., Marshall E. Dimock, "Expanding Jurisdictions: A Case Study in Bureaucratic Conflict," Robert K. Merton, *et. al.* (eds.), in *Reader in Bureaucracy* (Glencoe, Ill.: The Free Press, 1951).

CHAPTER 1 INTELLECTUALS IN STATE GOVERNMENT

GOVERNMENT BY REJECTS?

Shortly after government in America began to be tolerated as a necessary evil--about the time of the Revolutionary War--it became necessary to staff the growing bureaucracies. At the upper reaches, there was some continuity with the all-star cast of intellectuals who had drafted the noble set of documents and laid the solid conceptual foundations for the world's longest lived, large democracy. Below the very top layer, some of the staff was conscious of being involved in a gentlemanly, leisurely calling. Hawthorne's and Melville's stints as civil servants were very much in the international tradition; the civil service had long been an unwitting patron of the arts and numbered among its successful authors Dante (government shipyard), Kafka (unemployment compensation), Trollope (postal service), and Chaucer (customs service), among many others, past and present.[1]

In an era of modest responsibilities it was not surprising that government employment came to be regarded as a sinecure for the privileged, a storehouse of good, steady jobs that should be opened to the masses. By the 1830's, victorious Jacksonian democracy was able to act on the belief that sound common sense rather than formal education was qualification enough for a government position. Following the native Jacksonian precedent, succeeding waves of immigrants, with the Irish often in the vanguard, conquered the municipalities and moved on to penetrate many state and federal government strongholds.

Up to the New Deal 1930's, the civil service, below the very top echelons, fully reflected the background of its employees and the low esteem in which it was held by the middle and upper classes. Most government jobs paid badly, but they offered the security treasured by new immigrants and the more impoverished segments of the domestic population. They were not scorned by the Negro, the poor white, or many of the newly arrived Europeans. To a degree, this sentiment still prevails. There seems to be an endless supply of applicants for jobs that hardly qualify as prestige laden in the context of the late 1960's (such as street cleaners).

17

The New Deal was clearly a watershed in civil service as it was in so many other aspects of the nation. Excitement, idealism, ambition, decent pay, and security were all obtainable in government agencies. In contrast, the private sector seemed stodgy, ingrown, dull, and the corporations were not doing much hiring. As a result, for over a decade, the civil service at all levels of government was able to skim off much of the cream of the college graduates. After World War II, however, there was a significant fork in the road. By and large, the federal civil service succeeded in preserving continuity with the 1930's; despite reductions in force, McCarthyism, and an unfriendly press, federal agencies were able to inject a steady stream of bright young people into the bureaucracy. On the other hand, except for a few mutants like New York, Wisconsin, California, and a handful of others, the states, along with most municipalities, regressed a good deal of the way back to the practices of the 1920's and earlier. As a result, in many state and local bureaucracies the thin layer of depression-era talent was nearing retirement in the 1960's, and below them was darkness.

Two explanations for the difficulty in attracting well-qualified professional talent to government service were advanced by de Toqueville in the 1830's. The first is the tendency to pay relatively low salaries for relatively scarce and hard to obtain upper-echelon jobs as opposed to comparatively generous pay scales obtainable at the lower levels that are within reach of the voting majority. The second is that historically in the United States, private employment consistently offered much greater opportunity for the ambitious man than did the government service. De Toqueville was accurate and prescient in his observation that only during depressions, when commerce and industry are checked in their growth, does "place hunting" become generally followed.[2] To a very great extent, this remains a valid description of the current situation in state and local civil service. What makes this situation dangerous as well as absurd is the growing responsibilities confronting these levels of government--solutions to problems of the schools and the cities among others. Major sums to improve the environment and the quality of life can be made available by intelligent and hopeful people in Washington, but the cutting edge of the programs is often blunted in the states and cities. De Toqueville could virtually ignore state government, but a century and four decades later, this was no longer a realistic possibility.

Thus, the return of the intellectual to state government, after the hiatus of the 1940's and 1950's, is a subject worthy of exploration. It is beyond dispute that weaknesses in the staffing of state and local agencies is a major handicap in implementing programs, particularly the innovative, pioneering efforts that call for substantial competence. Of course, this picture should not be overdrawn. There is no doubt that some states are well equipped to play an equal partnership role with the federal government. Unfortunately, the majority do not have the talent-in-depth to act as anything other than passive, clumsy responders to federal initiatives.

One facet of the problem deserves careful study, namely the frictions, difficulties, and general expendability of intellectuals employed in state government either in a staff capacity or as hired consultants. While this discussion by no means purports to present a full statement on the situation in all states, in the generation of the mid-1940's a large proportion of the states, municipalities, and county governments have tended to be rather inhospitable to college-trained professionals.

There is some dispute over the causes for the unfortunate condition of state civil service, but there is a general consensus that standard party labels have little relevance to the problem because neither long-term domination by Republicans or Democrats nor a change in control of the state house seems to have much correlation with the quality of government employees. One authoritative view ascribes many of the difficulties to the outworn rural small-town ideology prevalent among state political leaders. The gerrymandering that dominated state legislative apportionment in past years was thought to reinforce a "consecrated negativism" dedicated to simplicity, conventional wisdom, and a mistrust of trained professionals.[3] A slightly different approach is the distinction that has been drawn between the immigrant ethos focused on patronage, job security, and hostility toward many professional standards with the "middle class," "public-regarding" ethos centered on efficiency, reform, high quality of services, and friendliness to trained specialists.[4]

Both views seem to be deficient as explanations. Hostility to professionals and a high regard for tenure at the expense of quality are as prevalent in states that have barely seen a foreign immigrant as they are in the northeastern quadrant of the nation. Many rural courthouse gangs, thoroughly native in ancestry, that traditionally have dominated political life in the South and Midwest, are equally adept at hanky panky, and their government appointees are fully as incompetent as the civil servants in northeastern cities and urban states. Nor can the answer be found in nostalgically clinging to an outworn, small town ideology. If one is searching for true parochialism and paranoid contempt for the professional, he can find it in full bloom in the central cities among our urban villagers.

Perhaps a more useful dichotomy may be found in conflicts between town and gown, traditional to communities containing sizable universities. There one finds the political machinery and the civil service dominated by the townies who are unsympathetic to college radicals, immoral smart alecks, and snobs, and they are generally uninterested in such college-type concepts as reform and the public interest. There are obvious grounds for friction--conflicts over collegiate highjinks, parking spaces, and taxes. But these rather minor *casus belli* are only outward evidence of a wide chasm between two antipathetic life styles. The collegiate community mistrusts townie politicians, despises most local government employees, and is thoroughly frustrated by what it sees as a stupid, regressive governmental structure. On their part, the townies view the collegians as overeducated, overpaid, impractical, radical, immoral, and parasitic.

It may be suggested that, in a sense, much of the conflict in American government can be explained as a tense, prolonged struggle between town and gown life styles. This is far from an income or class phenomenon--there is much overlapping. A number of wealthy contractors, lawyers, undertakers, bar owners, realtors, professionals, and businessmen, many of them college graduates, are found in the town camp, while among the gown people there are members of relatively poor folk. Some of the latter are in temporary poverty (such as graduate students), but some (such as school teachers) may earn less than townies in the building trades. Obviously, the differentiation is sometimes hazy, but this categorization does seem to present a recognizable view of reality, particularly in state and local government where gown types tend to be as identifiable as albino Congolese.

There are clear differences between the townie civil servant who is probably not a college graduate and the gown-oriented government employee. The former has no (or believes he has no) alternative employment available, and partly because of this entrapment he often evinces much verbal loyalty to the system. He has found a haven, and, as a rule, he is not actively looking toward professional advancement on the outside. Rather, he hopes for gradual escalation through tenure and/or political influence within the existing framework; consequently, he is violently resentful when degree-holding outsiders or "foreigners" are recruited. The latter are viewed not only as threats to the townie's promotion but as an insult to the way of life he has chosen. On the other hand, the intellectual-professional marches to a different drummer. His employment horizons and ambitions usually transcend agency and system, and he reaches out to his professional peer group. Since the 1950's, the number of alternative opportunities has been steadily growing, and he feels that his future lies in an adherence to professional standards. This tends to create certain frictions with the townies. As a result, the gown people tend to become disillusioned quickly and move on to friendlier climes. The agency is thereby left in the care of the townie who has nowhere else to go.

At this point it is useful to clarify a few definitions. For present purposes, an "intellectual" is defined as a college graduate who holds a responsible professional position with a life style that differs significantly from most state employees in terms of job horizons, professional standards, speech patterns, reading habits, and thought processes. The existence of such an identifiable disparity in state and local government may surprise persons familiar with federal agencies or corporations, organizations in which the upward bound collegian and even the master's degree are commonplace. However, a prevalent, nonintellectual environment among executives still exists in certain lagging, corporate enterprises in which men promoted from the shop or other holders of diplomas in the school of hard knocks remain dominant.

In the 1940's there was much discussion of whether an ambitious young man helped his career more by spending four years in gaining practical business experience or in going to college. For the most part, the question is no longer asked because the issue has ceased to exist. Even in a few quaint industries such as some of the railroads and various family concerns, collegians are "in" and ungrammatical, old shoe types are "out." It gets harder every year to find executives in private industry who boast about their lack of college education. At their executive levels, state and local governments therefore possess authentic antique qualities.

If there were a market for governmental memorabilia, a dealer could become a wealthy man by stuffing, preserving, and auctioning off the quaintly preserved tableaux in state house and city hall that have remained steadfast under the inroads of college-trained executives. There is a reason for this paralysis: It has proved possible to create a new breed of university townie. A generation of people with college degrees has moved into state and local government, but their interests, outlooks, and life styles are close to the old-guard staffers. The source of this new breed of college graduates who manage to retain a considerable share of working-class orientation is the larger third-rate colleges and universities in the big cities and their backwater brethren in small, parochial communities. In faculty, course orientation, and student body, these institutions have reproduced, on a slightly more intellectual plane, the accent and outlook of local high school systems. They faithfully reinforce rather than challenge the inbred background of their students. This is, of course, an exaggeration, since in recent years, at any rate, intellectual stirrings are very much in evidence even in the remotest institution or the most insulated college. But it nevertheless is a fact that the two societies--along with much fence jumping-- embrace two different kinds of college input. Town and gown are often matters of allegiances, aspirations, and reading habits, rather than of class, income, or amount of formal education, but there are relatively few graduates of first-class institutuions among the townies.

The built-in friction between town and gown types is as much in evidence at the national level as at other governmental echelons. Secretary of Defense McNamara's experience with certain congressmen, angered, baffled, and yet unconvinced by his smooth intellectual performance, is an excellent example. Although he is surely far less abrasive, obnoxious, and openly contemptuous of inferior intellects than others in the Kennedy stable were, there were enough rough edges to irritate the townies:

> His [McNamara's] habit of marshalling a dazzling array of statistics to support his case in Congressional testimony has dismayed and irritated the Southern Conservatives on the Armed Services Committees. Many of these men . . . are anti-intellectuals and superpatriots who have vigorously resisted changes and who have been particularly disturbed by McNamara's unceasing efforts to reform and modernize the Reserves and the National

Guard. "They listen to him rattle off all those facts and figures which they can't comprehend and they can't answer and they say to themselves, 'you smart son of a bitch, you're too god-damn smart. I'm going to take you down a peg,' " one associate of McNamara's said. "And when they try and they don't succeed, they get a little bit madder."

What the Secretary's colleague did not mention is that the anger is sometimes justified when the Congressmen later discover they have been hoodwinked by McNamara's tactic of supporting a weak argument with an adroit combination of statistics and sophistry.[5]

Having established a working definition of town and gown, the intellectual in state government can be examined from three standpoints: employment as regular, permanent staff; employment as "temporary" project staff; and employment as a consultant-firm contractor. It is recognized that the dividing lines are often blurred individuals often move out of project jobs into staff positions and vice versa. Nevertheless, the distinction is generally valid; the inert mass of long-service employees who occupy most of the chairs in the state and local agencies can easily be differentiated from the three types of intellectuals.

IN THE FIRM: THE HOUSE INTELLECTUAL

Reference has been made to the injection of talent into state and local government in the 1930's. Insights into the problems of the gown wearer can be gleaned from the history of these pioneers. Many have had notable careers in government either at the state or local level or after moving into the federal agencies. A substantial number apparently regretted their career choice and either left government service in the 1940's or 1950's or retired as early as the relevant pension laws and regulations permitted. The larger share remained on after World War II. In part they were interested in protecting pension rights; counting military service, many had a ten-year investment in sizable retirement benefits. There was also the fear on the part of a depression-battered generation that the prosperity of the 1940's was ephemeral and that a recurrence of mass unemployment was just around the corner. The recessions of 1948-49 and 1953-54 were interpreted as reasons to hang on to the civil service life jacket. Also, by the late 1940's, they had accumulated seniority and status, and the thought of risking a step or two backward by moving to outside employment was unwelcome.

In general, the intellectuals of the 1930's made several types of adjustment to their surroundings. More intelligent and better educated than their seniors, the entrants of the 1910's and 1920's, and brighter than the later recruits of the 1940's and 1950's, many rose to high positions, although, as was suggested earlier, a large number quit or retired early. Those who became department and division heads adjusted, chameleonlike, to circumstances. Some became virtually indistinguishable from their superiors and employees, hiding their talents under a self-imposed discipline. The adjusters became accepted, to a degree, as right guys "once you get to know them," experts in baseball and bowling, tolerant of minor foibles, and respected by co-workers and politicians. Sometimes they were transformed into sleazy intellectual "pols," pliable hirelings who resembled nothing so much as the shyster lawyers who congregate in the men's rooms of city halls. Others have existed for years in seething frustration, witnesses to buried reports, distorted recommendations, and treatment akin to intellectual Uncle Toms, trotted out for ceremonial occasions. Often they became office sages, repositories of agency history and accumulated wisdom, respected confidants, and problem solvers for agency and personal difficulties. Their chameleon reaction to the prevailing local color parallels the career patterns of policemen with southern or central European ancestry who, after a few years of service, take on some of the Hibernian flavor that permeates many big city police departments. Many an intellectual in northeastern state and local government becomes an honorary Irishman, an occasional guest at wakes and clan picnics, and a knowledgeable participant in political tribal gossip. In the Midwest and South, they become honorary hicks and rednecks, knowledgeable sportsmen, football rooters, and basketball boosters.

Some intellectuals have sought to master their environment by imposing their own standards. They too were respected, but in their case overt deference was mingled with covert fear and hatred. Lacking political protectors, they used their brains, or more accurately, their tongues. Like the frail, elderly ladies who terrorize entire family clans unto the third generation, a number of intellectuals in government have carved out positions of power with the weapon of biting sarcasm. They are, after all, surrounded by relatively slow-witted, inarticulate people, most of whom have had traumatic experiences with sadistic schoolteachers. Under these circumstances, they can assume the waspish role of correctors of spelling errors, covering papers with vicious ridicule, singling out some unfortunate for scornful treatment. There is no need to fear resistance: Recreating powerful childhood memories can cause a man in his fifties to revert to the status of classroom dunce, the butt of his frightened colleagues in the atmosphere of apprehension, thankful at having been temporarily spared. Bullying, toadying, flunking examinations, and subordination can be re-created in a government office. The masterful, pungent individuals capable of reducing their colleagues to a state of palpitating terror tend to be rarities, however. As a rule, the house intellectual risks developing bleeding ulcers under the day-to-day psychological abrasion involved in the wrenching conflicts and compromises demanded by an alien, often hostile, environment. In contrast, the aforementioned graduate of the third-string college is immediately at home among a family of friends, peers, and colleagues.

In the late 1950's and early 1960's, however, the picture changed substantially in one respect. Taking into account the utter hopelessness of getting much done with the regular troops or of upgrading the civil-service structures, the states and localities were allocated federal funds to employ large numbers of technical mercenaries in the form of project staff or consulting-firm personnel.

PROJECT STAFF: KING FOR A DAY?

The passage of the 1954 housing act was a landmark in intergovernmental relations. Although the practice was far from new, the 1954 legislation marked the initiation, on a large scale, of the use of federal matching money in combination with local funds for the purpose of undertaking complex planning and renewal tasks. Many communities performed the job with regular staff while others hired consulting firms. Much of the planning, however, was conducted with the use of temporary project staff, employed for a one- or two-year period at premium salaries. The justification was the big push theory. There is no reason to expand the permanent payroll to undertake a single massive job, it was argued--far better to hire highly skilled technicians, even at high salaries, to complete the job quickly and then move on without benefit of tenure, pension rights, or civil-service protection.

This argument loses some of its force when short-term projects stretch on into three years, five years, or longer. Many projects can be classified as temporary only by the loosest stretch of the imagination, particularly when some project personnel may be employed for longer periods than many regular staff. Moreover, the existence of a permanent group of highly paid project personnel offers a constant source of friction with the relatively poorly paid regulars. An additional distraction is the weak borderline between the regulars and the temporary personnel where there is much shifting back and forth as permanent staff enlist in projects for a stint year or two at a higher pay, and project people are taken on into the ranks of the regulars.

The federal government has had serious second thoughts concerning the use of project staff. While well-trained project professionals can usually get a job done in the sense of turning out the stipulated paper work, there is no guarantee that they will leave much in the way of permanent residue. If the project is separated and insulated from the existing structure, it is not likely to produce a post-project staff of regulars versed in the planning process, capable of carrying project recommendations, and updating plans as time and events require. For this reason, the federal agencies have tried various techniques aimed at involving regular staff in temporary projects. One method is personnel matching.

In the past, states and municipalities have been encouraged to use a barter system to pony up the local share of urban-renewal projects. Public improvements, including construction by nonprofit institutions, have been used to pad out the local share. Taking this approach a step further, regular staff salaries can be allocated, in fact or fiction, and in whole or in part, to provide the local matching share for comprehensive planning operations of various types.

This means that an official who cannot rely on his permanent staff to under-take difficult tasks can match the salaries paid to his force of incompetents, at a two-for-one ratio, to obtain federal funds to hire competent project person-nel.

There is one minor danger--the regular staff must be certified as actu-ally participating in the operations to which their work time or a portion of their time has been pledged. Revolts in the mortuary have been known to occur. Staff regulars ordered to stay out of the way have refused to be party to a fraud; that is, on moral grounds they will not agree to sign in as matching project participants until they are bribed with promotions and pay raises.

By and large, the hope that project staff would educate the regulars in the course of the project has not been realized. The two groups are oil and water, differing in everything from pay scales to background and speech pat-terns. The project and its attendant staff tend to be regarded as a necessary evil, but fortunately, a transient one. Like the old-time regular army noncoms who cordially detest the disruptions of wartime, including the officers produced by the ROTC and OCS, the permanent staff eagerly awaits the return of peace and normality.

The hostility of the regular staff toward project personnel is one of the causes for subsequent disappointment with the temporary projects. The well-paid consultant, often a foreigner (from out of state), is regarded as an overpaid alien, short on common sense and primarily interested in extending his period of lucrative employment. Before ascribing all of this cynicism and bitterness to ill-mannered envy, it must be admitted that on more than one occasion project staff hired with attractive advance billing have proved to be poor performers, weak in pragmatic, administrative, and technical skills, naive and inept in the political arena, and purveyors of windy, expensive inanities disguised as learned research. There are instances when project staff have insisted on displaying the accuracy of Mark Twain's adage concerning certain collegians to the effect that one can send a jackass to forty universities and load him with degrees, but on his deathbed he will bray. In short, as in the case of McNamara and the Senate, there is, unhappily, ample cause for mutual disenchantment.

Setting aside the problem of the peripatetic project nitwit, there can be serious obstacles to accomplishing much even with an outstanding project staff. The project staff's path is strewn with hazards as it attempts to intrude new, unsettling concepts involving sensitive policy and operating issues into a recal-citrant, skeptical, or downright hostile bureaucracy. The prospects are far from favorable in many federal agencies, but subject to many exceptions, the num-ber of unfriendly Yahoos increases proportionately with hierarchical distance from Washington. In some states and smaller cities, the figure approaches near unanimity with barely a glimmer of intelligence in evidence.

There are two ways in which the project staff person may find himself in hot water. After an initially warm reception from a representative of the top echelon that he is subsequently likely to feel is composed of intellectual giants compared to middle management, project staff may fall afoul of the bureau chiefs, old-time technicians and in-grown professional cliques. A special problem arises from the resistance of strong, professional, in-grown groups--educators, generals, welfare workers, or physicians--to outside evaluators. There are frequent charges that the aliens have failed to grasp the elusive essence of a program, are incapable of understanding prevailing local mores, and otherwise are unqualified to perform services that in effect entail judging the performance of the controlling insiders. In addition, the old line agency regulars tend to interpret each probing question by project staff as a threat, a judgment on their past and present performance, a risk to their chances of promotion, and a potential loss of power over their empire. For these reasons, the agency administrator is clearly of two minds in welcoming the intrusion of potentially unsettling project operations. Any project worth its salt involves a hard look at existing agency operations, but as Peter Rossi suggests: "Practitioners and policymakers are apprehensive; they want evaluations of program effectiveness, but they are afraid of what might be shown."6

There is further cause for disquiet in that a project is seldom narrowly defined; with comprehensive planning very much in fashion, the fact that the project staff is employed by one agency will not prevent it from analyzing interface areas involving the activities of other agencies. The latter are frequently competing for funds and power with the agency to which the project staff is under contract and understandably tend to react with hostility and alarm to those on the payroll of a rival. The project staff finds itself in sticky situations in which its agency employers vacillate between supporting and disowning its efforts, depending on which counsels predominate at the moment.

Another type of problem arises when the project staff is involved in internal program evaluation and research. Funding for such inhouse research efforts has been made available by the federal Office of Economic Opportunity, among other agencies. Given a mandate to forage around the agency, to establish performance measurements, and to produce critiques of their colleagues, the project researcher is likely to find himself regarded with about as much affection as a police commissioner's personal investigating team assigned to ferret out corruption in the vice squad. But there is a further problem involved in that the investigators are also looking into the commissioner's activities; it is difficult to confine a research professional to scrutiny of subunit performance.

The requirements of objective research and analysis may be difficult to sustain within the context of a fast-moving action program. The in-depth gathering of material considered necessary by the project staff to provide an adequate basis for program formulation may involve substantial costs and lengthy delays. Furthermore, as suggested, there may also be a basic internal friction within the agency because of the very different orientation between the administrator and the program planning and evaluation staff. The experience in one major poverty operation is indicative:

> . . . research directors chafed at the inconsistency and inco-
> herence of much that was done, the programme directors were
> equally impatient of pretentious methodology and theoretical
> preoccupations which failed to answer their needs. In practice,
> if not in theory, the claims of research and action were hard to
> reconcile.[7]

The researcher involved in an evaluation project can ordinarily expect
to uncover much disturbing information. He will discover that the process of
program review and feedback is tenuous at best and tends to conclude that the
project staff has a sacred and unique mission to complete a task that the regular
agency personnel cannot possibly undertake.

A research director will argue that:

> . . . there will be no genuine analysis of program impact un-
> less the researcher leads the way [and that] once the impact
> model is formulated, the researcher must continue to remain
> within the environment, like a snarling watchdog ready to op-
> pose alterations in program and procedures that would render
> his evaluation efforts useless.[8]

Permanent program personnel are usually allergic to this type of autonomous and uncontrollable research empire within the agency. Furthermore, the agency regulars are rarely in a position to preserve the purity of social science experiments or to tolerate delays to slow moving research processes. The research project effort must either result in immediate payoffs in
terms of providing guidance for pressing, unpostponable decisions or else be
relegated to a low-priority status. The project researcher, on the other hand,
has a divided loyalty--fidelity to professional standards as well as a commitment to his employer. Also, by temperament he is more often contemplator
than man of action. There is, therefore, considerable possibility for mutual dis-
regard between jarring points of view that may either negate or vitiate the value
of the project or lead to a premature termination of project-staff contracts.

From a program standpoint, there is something to be said on both sides.
The task of satisfying intermediate and long-term project research objectives
cannot be permitted to overshadow the administrator's need for immediate
help in choosing between alternatives, bringing to bear such information as can
be secured with a reasonable investment in time and cost. The project staff must
decide between retaining its scientific purity or engaging in action-oriented
research that may be "disreputable" from a scientific and professional standpoint. On the other hand, most government agencies find it difficult to mount
a significant program evaluation effort under the pressures of day-to-day agency
needs and the frequent crises that absorb the limited talent at their disposal.
Though project staff researchers are usually uncomfortable in recommending

action without a full panoply of research studies, Marris and Rein propose a compromise. The agency project staff should be less a "snarling watchdog" protecting the sanctity of its domain, poised for departure the instant its prerogatives are threatened, than an amiable retriever at the service of the administrator, "uncovering whatever he can usefully use." The project staff "should and can, if necessary, improvise a well-informed evaluation."[9]

Another if not immediate dimension to the problem of divided loyalties arises because the project staff tends to include a few intellectuals who write for publication. There are temptations to publish frank, critical memoirs and scathing analyses of agency operations. In contrast, it can be assumed that a career official is aware that the publish or perish relationship may have a different sequential link in government service as compared to the university. The intellectual, employed on a temporary project arrangement, may feel he has a duty to his profession, but his enraged former hosts may consider him a hypocritical, unethical ingrate if he broadcasts inside information. One must be aware that this is one of the reasons that the intellectual is regarded with suspicion in some quarters. While oral gossip and newspaper speculation are the meat and drink of government, an intellectual on the staff is regarded as an individual who is continually tempted to kiss-and-tell for the sake of scholarly prestige and/or financial reward. Few governmental units are willing to permit access by scholarly blabbermouths to sensitive information if this material is likely to be translated into permanent print for history books or periodicals.

Another source of danger to the project intellectual is negative reactions emanating from hypersensitive client groups. Adverse criticism from the Negro community cut short Kenneth Clark's activities as a program "participant-observer" in Harlem.[10] Similarly, Daniel Moynihan's report stressing the weaknesses of the Negro family was violently attacked by Negro leaders as well as some civil rights liberals.[11]

Moynihan has identified one of the dilemmas that confront a social scientist whose research may provide ammunition for his enemies and the enemies of his allies and clients.

> Knowledge is power, and in contemporary society social scientists are often in the position of handling power in an almost absent-minded way. Professional ethics, at least as ideally defined, can lead them to hand out the very best arguments to those whom they would consider the very worst contenders. . . . all concerned with the development of a system or urban social indicators [must] be prepared in advance to find themselves accused of having been betraying some of the very causes with which they have been most allied.[12]

It should not be thought that vicious attacks on researchers are the prerogatives of seething minority groups. Peter Rossi adds some sobering thoughts on the limited possibility of implementing unpopular recommendations even by supposedly highly intellectual and rational organizations. He notes that when the report of the National Opinion Research Center concluded, contrary to the sponsor's belief, that fellowships and scholarships had no appreciable effect on either the student selection of field of study or in deterring promising Ph.D.'s from entering a field:

> The first reaction of the sponsors was to attack the sponsor's methodology leading to the coining of the aphorism that the first defense of an outraged sponsor was methodological criticism. Policy remained unaffected. I do not know of any action program that was put out of business by evaluation research, unless evaluation itself was meant to be the hatchet.[13]

The intellectual retained by a governmental agency to undertake the delicate task of pioneering in the sensitive area of goals and performance measurement (opposed to service as advocate or executioner) will probably be required to display almost superhuman qualities of patience and understanding. He may in fact discover that the continual reassurance and therapeutic counseling that his clients seem to require absorb a larger share of his time than the technical task for which he was ostensibly hired. However, even if his temperament is unusually resilient, he may conceivably find himself regarding his clients with some small measure of distaste, especially when he discovers himself abandoned on an unsupported limb. There is an understandably human but nevertheless regrettable tendency for agency chieftains to renege on verbal agreements and to deflect criticism from themselves by forcing the temporary project staffer who has faithfully been carrying out their instructions to defend their decisions against subsequent outside attack.

Is the project staff as helpless as all this sounds? In most cases one would have to give an affirmative answer: The agency belongs to the people who live with it rather than the visitors, no matter how intelligent they may be. This is not to suggest that project staff, particularly the director, is a forlorn object of scorn and a passive target for his enemies. On the contrary, if he dares to play them he actually has extremely strong cards in his hand. First and foremost he is the key to the federal treasury. With federal grant-in-aid programs surpassing $15 billion yearly, the cities and states have intensified their search for effective public entrepreneurs. There is a wide gulf between such cities as New Haven and Boston that captured $500 to $800 per capita in federal urban renewal funds by the mid-1960's and equally deserving cities that have managed to qualify for only a fraction of this amount. Persons who can, in William Lee Miller's vivid phraseology, forage for the cities "through the nation's bureaucratic jungles, extracting the meat from Titles I and II are rare specimens. It is not enough that the Federal government pass city-helping laws; there must also be hunters for the city who can make their way through the Titles I and Titles II to find the meat."[14] But finding sustenance is not enough. Administrators who can cook the meat when they bring it home are rarer still.

If by some mischance, however, the federal tap is turned off and a project director can no longer perform the feats of financial legerdemain that have insulated him from the local long knives, he may find himself playing the lead role in a nine-part scenario. With local variations, the following sequence of events is observable in a number of federal grant-in-aid programs:

1. A strong project director makes a favorable impression on federal agencies, secures wide local backing, and receives a large federal grant.

2. But the executive has moved far and fast, his salary is large, and he has made local enemies. Unhappy with some aspects of his program, local rivals and detractors journey to Washington to demand that the flow of future federal funds be made contingent on a radical alteration in agency policy that strips the administrator of much of his power. This disturbs the project director.

3. He is alarmed by the extent of local opposition and even more by the favorable hearing his opponents seem to be receiving in Washington. The director canvasses for backing among his political masters. He does not find it because he is regarded as a political liability. He also discovers that he is no longer regarded as a favorite son by his federal sponsors.

4. The federal executives have arrived at a new consensus; their erstwhile favorite is now viewed as an empire builder, a trouble maker, a Czar who is misusing or who may misuse federal largesse to ride roughshod over his clients and peers. He is also receiving too much personal publicity for operating their program. Lower echelon regional and headquarters staff whom he has bypassed in securing Washington approval for his program agree that he must be taught a lesson and made aware that his behavior has fallen below federal standards.

5. A furor follows when the press gets wind of the story. Press coverage stresses the element of conflict. Media sympathies do not lie with the local executive who has offended local interests, who threatens the flow of federal funds, and who offers a convenient peg for a stream of behind-the-scenes stories emanating in part from his enemies and in part from disgruntled staff.

6. At this point, faced with the prospect of no federal money for program commitments, the local executive discovers that all of the local politicians have deserted him; from the chief executive on down, their overriding objective is a minimum of fuss and a maximum of federal funds. In addition, townie politicians have made demagogic capital from his out-of-state origins, and his alleged arrogance and callousness to local interests. The director has become a lightning rod to absorb punishment and a source of embarrassment to his political superiors.

7. This is the moment of truth when the director approaches the critical choice: a threat of resignation that he may be called on to make good or knuckling under to pressure. If he chooses to do battle, the coalition of enemies usually collapses; the federal bureaucracy gives him his funds. More often he surrenders, partly out of loyalty to "his" program, partly out of hope of better times--vindication when his enemies hang themselves with federal rope.

8. If he compromises, the director usually discovers that partial surrender is the first step to removal. Sensing weakness, federal officials, local enemies, and the mass media move in for the kill. A broad consensus develops: His removal is alleged essential for the progress of the program. The director's powers grow weaker; he is blamed for all the misadventures of his staff (who rush to desert his sinking career) and for the accumulated and inherited errors of federal, state, and local government.

9. If this occurs, his position becomes intolerable, and the director resigns.

It may be submitted that this sequence of events is descriptive of a number of bloody dramas in the war on poverty where executive casualties have been inordinately high and of other grant-in-aid operations as well. Moreover, it can be predicted with gloomy confidence that the advent of the model cities program and the growth of other experiments in creative federalism will engender increasing numbers of similarly depressing episodes. In short, there is a fundamental tension inherent in pioneering programs that is directly correlated with the dynamism of the local executive responsible for implementation. Rapid change creates local rebellion, and federal agencies are repeatedly faced with the alternatives of continuing to finance the chosen commander of the local army or choosing instead to support the disgruntled guerrillas who seek to overthrow him. Often, despite claims to the contrary, the federal executive seems ill at ease in the presence of strong, independent talent. Like social workers who are alleged to reinforce dependency by stifling individuality and judgment among their clients, some federal executives seem to prefer passive, mediocre, local executives--safe men who make no waves, neither causing discomfort to federal guardians of program funds nor producing much of consequence. In contrast, strong local administrators pile up a host of federal as well as local enemies in their whirlwind progress. Predictably, local opponents will journey to Washington to sever the financial administrator's jugular, and often Washington executives, irritated by the local baron, seem eager to wield the scalpel. However, experience suggests that executions on living organisms require a relatively helpless victim--an executive who chooses to submit rather than fight. Those who dare to risk all in a test of nerve may emerge stronger than ever, dictating terms to a chastened federal bureaucracy and to sullen, but no longer dangerously mutinous, local opponents. In time, however, disenchanted with what they view as ingratitude, disloyalty, and needless wear-and-tear on the nervous system, it is not surprising to find that forceful executives seek alternative employment and leave the field open to residual talents. Indeed, if their antennae are sufficiently sensitive, they may leave before the cheering stops, aware that stormy seas lie just over the horizon.

The project staffer who proceeds to undertake a task on the basis of what he regards as logic, intellectual honesty, and faithful adherence to professional standards may unwittingly raise storms all around him. At worst, his services may be abruptly terminated; at best, his recommendations may be heavily diluted if not relegated to the graveyard maintained by every agency, in fact if not in name, to bury unwise, untimely, or dangerous suggestions.

HOW TO BE A RICH CONSULTANT

Unquestionably, consulting is the least effective of the three methods of injecting expertise into state government. As compared to either permanent or project staff, the consultant is usually an instrument rather than a crafts-man--a tool of power rather than a wielder of power. (The reference here is to consulting firms that work on temporary contracts, rather than to individuals who may be employed as consultants on long-term personal service contracts for periods of time comparable to regular civil service staff.) There are certain defects in using consultants to solve agency problems. From the agency's view-point, the studies are frequently expensive; they are often conducted by per-sons unfamiliar with local conditions; and much of their value is lost in transla-tion because the agency often lacks the requisite staff capability to follow con-sultant advice. The difficulty is that consulting is often misused as a substitute for rather than as a supplement to agency personnel. After the consult-and-run operation is completed and the final report submitted, there is often little per-manent residue in the form of augmented staff expertise, persons who have mastered the research substance and are fully capable of implementing study recommendations. These widely known deficiencies in the consulting-firm ap-proach have led some federal and state agencies to adopt a jaundiced view to-ward use of consulting firms as a means of avoiding employment of permanent or project staff.

Yet agencies are still tempted to hire consulting firms partly because a good staff is not easy to assemble. The consultant approach has another advan-tage: It is a means of decelerating agency empire building because it permits large jobs to be tackled without adding to permanent staff. Equally important, the consultant presumably has a qualified organization in readiness to complete projects on schedule. Agencies attempting to take on sizable projects are often faced with serious time and staffing problems. Presumably the consultant has reserve personnel capacity or, if he does not, he can more easily hire new peo-ple because he can offer them the prospect of continued employment on other projects while the agency can offer only a limited period contract to attract project staff. For these reasons, more and more consultant firms are being hired by government agencies.

The above may suggest that the title of this section has been used in a playful spirit of irony. This is not the case, however, for the fact is that consultants, like staff, come in two main varieties; there are pet consultants, friendly firms chosen in a back room more for their connections than for their talent, who can indeed wax fat on contracts with government. A state agency can have at its disposal a stable of consulting corporations with anonymous, generic names implying a worldwide practice from Lhasa to Monaco but actu-ally with only one captive client. Such firms here have been known to charge top prices for their used stencils, purveying canned products, warmed over slightly, for repeat sales. A "political" architect can place the same blueprints on the block perhaps a dozen times over, charging a standard fee for each building. Under these conditions, consulting can be a profitable trade, but in states where this kind of arrangement is customary, it tends to generate certain problems for the other, second variety of consultant--the firm that enjoyed a substantial professional reputation before that unhappy day when it decided to devote its talents to uplifting the quality of state (or local) government.

In areas where "consultant" has become a synonym for crooked incompetence, the professional firm finds itself the object of instant suspicion; it risks being crucified between two thieves. If the agency that has recently hired the firm has had a long, dismal, and well-publicized record of employing shady, third-rate firms, the day may come when a legislative investigating team takes over the files, and the newspapers print long alphabetical lists of consulting firms, some of which have been previously accustomed to being singled out in public solely for praise and prizes.

The traumatic impact of the press allegations is exacerbated by a press that appears all too ready to gloat over the plight of the razzle-dazzle, hot-shot professional and by a public which is always prepared to see rich, smart aleck brains get their comeuppance. Moreover, the consultant-on-the-griddle can expect little sympathy on the part of colleagues whose conscience has been troubled by his selfrighteous moralizing. This latter point requires explanation.

In the initial honeymoon phase of its labors, the professional consulting firm that has recently signed a state contract is prone to preachments on the moral rectitude of working for necessitous state agencies rather than restricting one's talents to federal and private clients. Other firms that have not followed this noble example tend to be skeptical, but quite often their conscience has been disturbed. Subsequently, when trouble develops, the thankful, nonparticipating firms loose a chorus of muted "I told you so's" mingled with a trace of *Schadenfreude* at the discomfiture of their friends and rivals. A vow by the consultant to avoid similar hazards in the future is by no means unusual--with a resultant diminishing of the pool of talent available to the states.

The consultant--second category--may experience extreme difficulty in getting paid. Although agencies may retain a consulting firm, they do not have to cooperate with it or pay it; by virtue of incompetence and/or misrepresentation, an agency can delay payment and processing contracts until the consultant is close to bankruptcy.

As a rule, the firm does get its money, in time, but it may have to finance its operations on IOU's for many months, absorbing the bank-interest payments as part of its lesson on choosing clients. There can be several reasons for delay in payment: An agency shell-shocked by legislative investigations may simply hold up all payments; the staff may feel, that under the circumstances, approval of outgoing checks entails a degree of risk and that, because the agency cannot be sued for lethargy, administrative caution is preferable to adherence to a stipulated contract time schedule. Added to administrative timidity, "Floogles Law" may also be operative. This law (i.e., anything which can go wrong, will go wrong) was once thought to govern out-of-town tryouts of Broadway plays and ill-fated military adventures. However, variations of this law have been discovered in many fields. In the present instance, for example, consultant bills can be wrongly routed, lost, returned for verification, or otherwise snarled in the machinery.

The mundane but vital matter of payment has been alluded to rather briefly. Like the sex of the hippopotamus which is chiefly of interest to other hippos, payment schedules for consulting firms are a matter of concern only to other consultants. However, it does assume a wider importance by contributing to the pervasive distaste for taking on state contracts. The point is that the threat of bankruptcy is added to the trauma of public insult.

Consultant in Action

It is no secret that consulting resembles other professions, and particularly the law, in its wide range of extra-contractual services. Just how broad the scope of activities for the consultant can be is a matter of conjecture. For example, in terms of the state client, a senior consultant may find himself practicing psychiatry without a license as he listens to insoluble woes and offers advice on careers and human relations which the client is totally incapable of adopting.

Frequently, a consultant finds himself employed as a hired audience, regaled for hours with anecdotes and philosophy by clients who have apparently been starved for intelligent conversation. If the consultant contract calls for a payment on a per diem basis, being transfixed as a captive listener may eventually become nothing more than an irritant. However, this role may have a disastrous impact on a consultant's earnings if he is paid for a product and the chitchat interferes with the progress of his research.

Other unobvious burdens are heaped upon the consultant's shoulders. Unlike project staff or civil service regulars, a senior consultant is expected to look intelligent and rather prosperous--unless he chooses to look intelligent and tweedy and moderately seedy which he may do if he is a college professor. In part, he has been hired as an ornament, a token of the agency's entrance into the great world. News of private opinions and advance information on unpublished research, secret information, gossip retailed by the *cognoscenti* but concealed from the masses are all part of the unstipulated services that the agency may think it is purchasing from its consultants. To a degree, this orgy of name dropping and alleged information leaks can be manipulated as both threat and promise. In corporate counseling, one financially successful operator used his hypothetical connections with the New York "money men" and what they allegedly did or did not view with favor to browbeat simple-minded Midwestern clients. Variations of this practice are not unknown in government consulting.

It is, however, apparent that the senior consultant has one enormous advantage over other types of intellectuals in state government: He need not strike a mucker pose. An interest in books, sailing, skiing, the theater, and even ballet is wholly acceptable, even desirable, as long as he does not exhibit signs of being weird or queer. After all, he does represent a tangible prestige item for the official who selected him. The savage, ulcerating struggle to empathize, communicate, and live with the townies is not part of his job. For this reason, one must temper one's sympathy for his plight. The intellectual in permanent service or on a long-term project is the deserving case; the soldier who holds the line is more worthy of sympathy than the visiting correspondent who writes eloquently of the mud and blood.

In some respects, consulting for state government is not much different than consulting for private enterprise. For example, the consultant more often than not finds himself a white chip in a high stakes poker game. He is thrust on stage in a minor supporting role, a player in a half-understood melodrama full of strange passions and ferocious infighting. The consultant normally experiences an adverse reaction to playing a bit-part in an obscure, squalid, and unpleasant scenario in which his technical counsel has the most marginal relevance to events and decisions. The consultant is frequently used to reinforce his employer's position, to second guess a previous consultant whose work is regarded as suspect or whose recommendations were unacceptable. The consultant may be a weapon of offense or defense, prompted by his employer to add weight to decisions already agreed upon and that lack only the consultant's imprimatur or to challenge another faction of another agency. In this highly charged atmosphere, the consultant may find himself wooed by opposing parties eager to capture or at least neutralize him. Whatever his personal qualities, the consultant discovers that he has more than a few enemies, some inherited from his employer and others conjured up in the research process as his probing questions succeed in generating alarm and dismay.

Only adequate financial remuneration can compensate the consultant for his mounting irritation and frustration. One particular cause for dismay is the dawning suspicion that he and his study are being used as an outright smokescreen, with barely a nod in the direction of professional counsel. Initiating a high level consultant study is a common ploy to placate an irate press and public and to head off brutal savaging by political wolf packs. Not infrequently the baying wolves will be tossed a bone or two in the form of minor research studies in lieu of meatier substance. Subsequently, the forebodings prove justified; the consultant discovers that a clause in his contract, written in invisible ink, calls for him to serve as a layer of asbestos, insulating employers from the hot blast of criticism. The consultant may be especially angered to find, that as the fires grow hotter, he is disowned by his employers despite the fact that he has faithfully followed their written and verbal instructions. Prior to his service with the state, he may have thought that the expendable employee who ascends in trial balloons is a prerogative of the Presidency, but alas, it is not. The consultant finds that minor bureaucrats in minor agencies expose their hired men to vicious, undeserved attacks to save themselves minor embarrassment. A consultant may be fully capable of swimming in dangerous waters, and when matters of great import are involved, he may be willing to risk his professional skin. Often, however, he may begin to doubt the necessity of scuba diving among the state piranhas when he may be sacrificed for inconsequential reasons.

The consultant soon learns that others besides himself question the need for service under the state banner. On occasion, he discovers that idle discussions initiated by his agency employer concerning the rewards and hazards of consulting tend to evolve into an ill-disguised attempt at job hunting. If the consultant is an academic off on a foray into consulting, the agency bureaucrat may make overt, wistful, embarrassing attempts to penetrate the professorial elysium as a nonpublishing faculty member. In either case, the consultant must express his high regard for a client whom he nevertheless feels is lacking in the essential qualifications for crossing the consultant barrier.

The amount of admiration for his client's abilities may decline precipitously if the consultant discovers that his firm has been retained to undertake a last ditch, desperate effort. The consultant experiences premonitory qualms as his smallish research study is more and more frequently referred to by his employer as holding the answer to all sorts of accumulated agency ills. The call for miracles may occur in the case of an agency that has frittered away virtually all of its financial reserves and is facing a deadline with a major report still to be produced and little money left in the till. It will seek to employ a prestigious, productive consultant to undertake instant salvation, the agency naturally absolving itself of blame for any weaknesses in the final report. This situation can arise in federally financed, lethargically run projects that call for a massive final publication. The bulk of the project funds can be drained away by unqualified and/or political consultants, expended on unproductive staff, or misused by allocating a competent staff to urgent nonproject duties. The consultant is then asked to take the compost heap of ill-assorted materials dredged up by his predecessors and to spray the manure pile with an opaque deodorant material bearing his professional signature.

It is rumored in the consulting world that somewhere there exists a well-organized client who, when honestly baffled by a problem, proceeds to hire a qualified consultant. In a brisk and clinical fashion, the consultant signs a contract, proceeds with the study, produces recommendations, and lives to see his advice either accepted or rejected on plausible professional grounds. No accurate statistics, however, are available concerning the relative prevalence of this type of client in various levels of government, or in private corporations for that matter, but they are by no means common.

A consultant who sees his role simply as an impersonal purveyor of expert opinion is likely to be disappointed by state government, but it is a matter of degree; the smoothly running organization that knows how to choose and use consultants is rare in any sphere of activity. The problem is that the potential for being run through the meat grinder for no significant purpose seems to be so much greater in state government than in other areas.

A CONCLUDING NOTE: E FLAT

State government can be viewed as an underdeveloped nation of the kind that has baffled the United Nations Technical Assistance Program and the successive American foreign-aid agencies. Sorely in need of technical aid, the states are not properly equipped to absorb it because they do not have adequate staff and cannot make good use of in-house or outside consultants. The future of the states rests in large measure in their ability to change their spots. As inhospitable places for intelligence--barring a few notable exceptions--the states will remain ciphers in the creative federalism equation unless they can somehow offer a lot of bright young men promising long-term careers and attractive service as short-term project staff. The states will also have to become the kind of clients that interest the consultant who has sufficient reputation to be selective. In brief, the states cannot hope to be taken seriously as social laboratories, or as effective governments for that matter, until they make substantial progress in closing the intelligence gap.

NOTES TO CHAPTER 1

1. Some of the authors bit the hand that fed them all the way up to the elbow. Dante's Hell bore an uncomfortable resemblance to the shipyard, Kafka's works portraying labryinthine bureaucratic nightmares drew heavily upon his experience, while Trollope's pictures of government agencies provided ammunition for demanding deep budget cuts. Perhaps an international civil service federation should take certain appropriate steps.

2. Alexis de Toqueville, *Democracy in America,* II (New York: Vintage Books, 1954), 263-64.

3. See Charles Press and Charles Adrian, "Why State Governments Are Sick," *The Antioch Review,* Summer, 1964.

4. Edward C. Banfield and James Q. Wilson, *City Politics* (Cambridge, Mass.: Harvard University Press and M.I.T. Press, 1963).

5. Neil Sheehan, "You Don't Know Where Johnson Ends and McNamara Beings," *The New York Times Magazine,* October 22, 1967, pp. 131-32.

6. Peter Rossi, "Evaluating Social Action Programs," *Trans-Action,* June, 1967, p. 51.

7. Peter Marris and Martin Rein, *Dilemmas of Social Reform,* Institute of Community Studies (London: Routledge and Kegan Paul, 1967), pp. 181-207.

8. Howard E. Freeman and Clarence C. Sherwood, "Research in Large Scale Intervention Programs," *Journal of Social Issues,* January, 1965.

9. Marris and Rein, *op. cit.,* p. 101-2.

10. Kenneth Clark, *Dark Ghetto: Dilemmas of Social Power* (New York: Harper and Row, 1965).

11. See Lee Rainwater and William Yancey, *The Moynihan Report and the Politics of Controversy* (Cambridge, Mass.:   M.I.T. Press, 1967). The Moynihan study, like other research which generated an unexpected amount of protest, was eventually disavowed by political superiors.

12. Daniel P. Moynihan, "Urban Conditions: General," *The Annals,* 371, May, 1967, 160-61. See also his article, "The Moynihan Report and Its Critics," *Commentary,* February, 1967.

13. Peter Rossi, *op. cit.*

14. See William Lee Miller, *The Fifteenth Ward and the Great Society* (New York: Harper and Row, 1966), p. 154.

CHAPTER	**2**	YARDSTICKS FOR GOVERNMENT: THE ROLE OF PPBS

THE NEW SUPER X-RAY CALIPERS

It is said that once upon a time, a truth-obsessed beauty-contest judge resigned in disgust because he would not be party to a fraud. It was impossible, he said, to reach definitive conclusions on the basis of exterior evidence. Forbidden to probe down to the fundamentals, His Honor refused to be forced to lend his good name to a potentially inflated royalty.

Under certain circumstances, it is conceivable that absolute verification could be obtained to satisfy the rigorous standards not only of the learned bench but of the losing contestants. The situation becomes much more complicated when the object to be measured is a government program, complete with history, promises, varying levels of staff performance and impact, and obscured in mists of raw data and self-praising reports. It is, in fact, the growing suspicion that the visible dimensions of many programs are synthetic and illusionary that has prompted much of the interest in various types of program biopsies. These include the traditional standbys, the legislative investigation, the budgetary review, the audit by a central agency, and more recently, a systematic effort to match investments and results known as Planning Programing Budgeting System--PPBS.

In practical terms, the movement toward clarifying objectives and measuring results has not come too soon. Judging from the vigor of the Congressional trouncing given to the model cities and poverty programs, the widespread attacks on urban renewal and in-town expressway construction, pure rhetoric is losing its utility in securing continuing support for governmental programs, even from long-standing, liberally oriented allies. The tendency to subject these programs to informed criticism has demonstrated their vulnerability to iconoclastic Ph.D. candidates, let alone to dour, rural-oriented appropriations committees. In short, more plausible proofs of performance are now required than has been the case in past years, particularly when the annual budgetary moment of truth rolls around.

In recent years, the Department of Defense (DOD) has made well-publicized progress in the direction of relating goals to quantifiable measures of achievement. Under prodding from the Bureau of the Budget, the techniques pioneered by large private corporations and successfully adapted by the DOD are beginning to percolate through the federal establishment. In August, 1965, President Johnson announced that the PPBS developed by the Department of Defense would be extended through the other federal agencies. By early 1966, the Bureau of the Budget issued appropriate instructions to the executive departments. The system was to be applied immediately in the twenty one largest agencies and eighteen other agencies were "encouraged" to adopt formal systems.[1] In practice, progress has been slow: PPBS is easier to discuss than to apply.

PPBS (and such allied decision-informational technologies as operations research, cost-benefit analysis, systems analysis) represents an attempt to develop a flow of useful information about programs that center on whether discretely measurable and presumably attainable objectives were in fact achieved. However, as we shall see, the road has been fraught with obstacles. The most serious are attributable to the fact that highly sophisticated techniques such as PPBS call for cadres of talented technicians and sympathetic and decisive executives. Not surprisingly, these are in extremely short supply at every level of government, and the few who are capable of formulating and implementing PPBS are usually hard at work on day-to-day program management and the normal run of agency crises.

According to reports, the processes of formulating goals, measuring performance, and arriving at choices on the basis of the results have been highly successful at DOD. Applying the technique to the civilian agencies is another matter. It is interesting to note that doubts as to just how effective PPBS actually *is* in the Department of Defense seem to grow in proportion to the amount of strenuous grappling with this technique on the part of the other federal agencies. However, having tasted the fruit of the PPBS and finding it good, or at least potentially tasty, the movement to translate generalities into measurable units in civilian programs is on its way. There is no returning.

It has been argued that performance standards in government agencies can serve as a partial substitute for the market mechanism that weeds out the inefficient businessman or the test of combat that eliminates weak military leaders. Forays by legislative investigations or press exposés on vulnerable government agencies are the traditional means of forcing agencies to change direction because bureaucracies tend to find self-analysis and overhauling difficult to contemplate, much less to effectuate. Changes, when they do come about, are small and incremental unless the heat is on from legislature, chief executive, and/or the communications media. PPBS offers a continuing, rigorous, and systematic method of improving agency performance without the violent upheaval of the Congressional investigation and the Presidential directive--in short, improvement without trauma. This movement to clarify, measure, and evaluate government operations may have certain real dangers to the public safety in addition to its implicit threat to complacent bureaucrats. The vagueness, imprecision, and inconsistencies that abound in private enterprise and familial life as well as in governmental programs are not solely attributable to dullards or incompetents. Secrecy as to salary levels, wills hidden in lawyers' offices, and program-reporting systems that fail to make a full disclosure of their impact share an important characteristic. A little fuzziness around the edges provides the insulation between interest groups, heirs, and employees; cloudiness tends to muffle dissent when people are not entirely clear about responsibilities, rewards, and punishments.

In contrast, precise identification of controversial issues and extreme clarity in analyses of program impact can sometimes be an invitation to conflict. To cite one outstanding example, a substantial amount of bureaucratic inefficiency and legal entanglements can mute class and race disputes by miring potential contestants in a glutinous sea of red tape. It can be argued that perfect knowledge of governmental inconsistencies, inequality before the law, and differential treatment for communities and neighborhoods augment rather than diminish intergroup suspicions. Positive verification of exactly how various groups are shafted--and by whom--is not likely to promote community harmony. Knowing in detail just how badly one is treated as compared to one's neighbors can have lethal consequences.

While an absence of hard facts can be dangerous, the high-minded verbiage of the type found in preambles to new legislation and political speechmaking has traditionally served as a placebo for impatient zealots. This is not necessarily the cynical process that it appears. Flowing rhetoric has been deliberately used on occasion as an effective method of placating agitators while avoiding immediate struggle on too many fronts, meanwhile preserving the reformer's political capital for a riper, brighter day when successful action becomes feasible. In brief, for several valid reasons, lofty expressions of good intent and vigorous verbiage are indispensable to the workings of democratic society.

The fact that the layers of fine words are being stripped away from administrative operations may therefore offer some cause for alarm by exacerbating societal conflicts. This is a policy question that will be confronting us more frequently as we learn more about how our programs actually work. Clearly, the intrusion of slide rules that measure or purport to measure the effectiveness of government operations can have a devastating effect on the administrative equilibrium, and not all administrators have been enthusiastic about innovations in goal setting and program evaluation. Some have reacted negatively, suggesting that numbers are soulless, meaningless, or misleading because they fail to capture the intangible, vital spirit that animates a meaningful program. The attacks on McNamara's "whiz kids" in the DOD launched by disappointed generals and admirals fall into this category. However, this objection has been countered by demands that the bureaucrats get to work on standards of performance which *do* have meaning. And this is precisely the point at which the trouble begins.

To begin with, there is room for long and inconclusive wrangling at every stage of the process, over goals, performance criteria, the nature and quality of the judges, and measures of achievement. The agency administrator is likely to be extremely sensitive on each of these issues. He may feel that PPBS can help him in bringing a sprawling agency operation under control (like McNamara at the DOD) but it also entails the risk of exposure. The immediate defense to criticism is to ascribe all the recently discovered agency ailments to one's predecessor. However, only up to a point can bureaucrats blame dunderheads in the previous administration; this tactic tends to wear thin as time passes and the new appointees can no longer evade responsibility for error.

Despite the administrator's natural and wholly understandable reluctance at venturing into those stormy seas, the voyage is inescapable. The point is that systematic analysis of government programs is here to stay. Although computers are popular and important, there is far more involved than simply new technology. There is a pervasive dissatisfaction with the choice of goals, with the allocation of priorities, and with the apparent difficulty in translating objectives into reality. Most of all, there is irritation, frustration, and resentment over requests for more funds for programs that do not seem to be working very well. The public and the Congress seem to echo Lincoln's response to General McClellan's demands for more troops. Under McClellan's leadership, giving the Army of the Potomac more troops was "like shoveling flies across the room"--a most descriptive comment on men and programs that seem to be, in equal measure, insatiable and unproductive. Certainly the bureaucrats' belated ex post facto admissions of ignorance on such basic matters as the reason why the educational process is operating so badly in slum schools, how a reasonable urban land use and transportation pattern can be achieved in a nation married to the automobile, or how many Negro unemployed there are in city ghettos have not diminished the growing skepticism. In short, as has happened before in history, public sentiment and technological innovation have come together to make life miserable for government agencies that have been operating comfortably and quietly on the basis of hitherto unquestioned assumptions.

New Tools: PPBS

The technique of introducing an energetic new broom to clean out old stables is as old as history. Faced with a complex, ectoplasmic mess, the traditional approach is to locate a strong-willed, effective administrator and to turn him loose. What PPBS offers is a possible means of economizing on virtuosos. It offers a new way of systematizing program management.

PPBS is a method for analyzing programs in terms of outputs as related to expenditures.[2] Properly designed, it can be an important tool in the selection of alternatives because it can help to evaluate relative results from different kinds of public investments. The design of an effective system is predicated on two very critical assumptions. The first is that a substantial, reliable flow of timely information, probably through a computerized system, will be available to program administrators. The second and even more basic prerequisite is the existence of a program design that organizes information in a meaningful framework for decisions because it is of little consequence to have access to a vast amount of marginally relevant material that cannot be put to use in answering critical questions. One can be sympathetic to those who suggest that the problem is not generating more information because administrators are already swamped with more data than they can profitably absorb and that, anyway, most important decisions are political and judgmental.[3] However, while there is obviously far too much statistical trivia on hand and the computers will generate a lot more, there remains a clear need for reliable *relevant* information on program impacts. Further, there is insufficient accurate followup information on programs in which the payoff is necessarily delayed as, for example, in education and health. Just as important, there is inadequate data that can be used to weight various programs designed to achieve similar objectives, as, for example, alternative manpower training programs. A critical distinction must, therefore, be made between masses of marginal data and the important information, much of which is not currently available and must either be forcibly excavated from a reluctant bureaucracy or generated through new research. As one observer suggests, we generate much data, but, at least in the vital field of education, it doesn't tell us what we want to know.

> When we survey the voluminous, yet unsuitable, data now available for assessing the products of education, we must conclude that practically none of it measures the output of our educational system in terms that really matter (that is, in terms of what students have learned). Amazement at the revelation of the tremendous lack of suitable indicators if almost overshadowed by the incredible fact that the nation has, year after year, been spending billions of state and local tax dollars on an enterprise without knowing how effective the expenditures are, or even if they are being directed to stated goals.[4]

One prerequisite of PPBS is that program objectives must be clearly defined, and the questions to be answered and the measures of performance must be part of a plan extending over a period of several years in the future. While there should be no suggestion that dubious programs be permitted to run on and on in the hope of long-term results or even worse, of doubling expenditures for unproductive programs on the ground that results will then surely follow, PPBS does not eliminate the need for a strong common-sense judgment on what constitutes a reasonable input of time, funds, and effort. Given this vital prerequisite--good sense--PPBS offers a way to evaluate systematically the relationship between ends and means. Properly used, it offers the possibility of escaping some of the biases injected when information is filtered through the prisms of existing agencies and current programs. For the administrator, PPBS can be an almost unprecedented method of clearing away, conceptually at least, the dense accumulation of underbrush that often obscures the paths between present programs and possible goals.

Despite these obvious advantages, there is an important caveat. If it can be said that the navy is a machine "designed by geniuses to be run by idiots," PPBS is still very much at the genius stage. The technique is not yet routinized to the point where it can be managed by persons of modest competence; in its present, pioneering stage, PPBS calls for remarkable qualities of objectivity, thorough grounding in operations, and a creative intellect. It is clear that the federal government will have to set the pace simply because there are more intelligent executives in Washington than in most of the state and local agencies. In time, a diluted, vulgarized, simplified version of PPBS will filter out through the federal establishment and down to state and local government.

Up to this point, our discussion has largely focused on the potential benefits of PPBS. If we are honest, we must squarely face some of the inherent limitations of the technique, the dangers in its use, and the difficulties in converting it into a form suitable for wide consumption. The interesting and, on the whole, melancholy history of the abortive attempts to inject cost-benefit techniques developed for water-resource projects into such other government operations as urban renewal may be remembered. Other extremely attractive innovations have foundered on the rocks of inherent but not fully recognized rocks and shoals.

THE TEMPORAL TEMPTATION: PLANNING FOR THE MILLENIUM?

While it is impossible to identity all of the problems likely to be encountered in applying PPBS techniques at the various governmental levels, we can begin to delineate a few of the more outstanding obstacles. Experience suggests that many future problems cannot be anticipated, but even a brief analysis suggests that the PPBS approach will encounter a full quota of obstacles as it wends its painful way through the government agencies.

One of the specific reasons for the increasing enthusiasm to stretch public agencies on the PPBS rack is the difference of attitude toward the passage of time between most political leaders and many bureaucrats. The pat distinction-- between statesmen (good) who allegedly plan for the next generation and politicians (bad) who are concerned exclusively with winning the next election-- loses some of its meaning when it is recognized that, like the politician, the

statesman's career is a painstaking, step-by-step affair in which immediate problems must be overcome if one is to be permitted to work on grand designs
with long-term impacts. It may be recalled that Abraham Lincoln numbered
among his many gifts a remarkable ability to manipulate postmasterships and
popular generals to win elections. The inherent incompatibility between long-
term, comprehensive plans and the pragmatic "project" orientation of the politician has been discussed at some length by Alan A. Altshuler and Edward C.
Banfield, among others.[5] PPBS does have the benefit of isolating program elements for inspection, and hence escapes some of the odium (and futility) attendant on large-scale, slow moving, closely interwoven, comprehensive plans that
tend to be pretty much ignored.

This preamble is by way of suggesting that one of the chief problems in
arriving at reasonable goals and translating them into reality with the help of
PPBS relates to different time scales. PPBS is supposed to have required four
years from design to fruitful results in the DOD and may take even longer in
other agencies. The politician and his upper-echelon appointed executives must
think in terms of efforts that yield perceptible, publicly demonstrable progress
within a year or two. This is not to say that they are opposed to programs
aimed at achieving medium- and long-term objectives, but they are confronted
with an unending series of crises calling for immediate action. As a rule, an elected official has relatively little time or attention to devote to those who plan
vast operations that may or may not bear fruit in his successor's administrations
but that obviously have only a marginal relevance to his current problems--not
the least of which is his re-election.

This sense of political urgency is usually shared by the appointed executive at the highest level to almost the same degree as the elected official. At one
conference, for example, a senior administrator remarked that a junior planner,
disillusioned by the futility of long-range planning, had remarked that henceforth the planning profession should concentrate on short-range efforts. The
young man subsequently explained that by "short range" he meant five years.
The senior official suggested that this time span, while an improvement on
some previous programs that moved at glacial pace, was still far too extended
for political utility. He argued, that from the viewpoints of the voting public,
the President and Congress and appointed supergrade executives like himself
who are charged with implementing legislation, five years is a political lifetime;
half a decade may embrace a change in control of the Senate, two Congressional elections, and a turnover in the Presidency. If there were no substantive payoff within two years, the planning operation was not likely to secure much
support, he observed.

The matter of timing is crucial to any number of government programs
ranging from the Supreme Court's variously interpreted "deliberate speed" for

racial integration of school systems to the surfeit of hastily drawn program requirements and preposterous deadlines that have confounded the local poverty program administrator. Determining the point at which a digestion problem arises in assimilating new legislation, at which a transient political opportunity for reform must be exploited despite the risks of overloading a frail administrative structure, and the point at which cautious delay may fade into indefinite postponement calls for delicate exercises in judgment. Critics of the politicians' and reformers' penchant for haste may be reminded that passion more often than prudence makes the political world go round. Waiting for plans to be perfected is usually an exercise in theological patience rather than practical politics. Successful politics and administration are largely matters of seizing fleeting opportunities. PPBS will have to adjust to this builtin urgency if it is to have much significant impact on policy. This means that with or without PPBS, program planners and administrators must be prepared to offer judgments and recommendations on the basis of incomplete information, half-finished matrices, and subjective hunches because events refuse to wait until the last word in research and program evaluation has been spoken.

If it can be assumed, as a general rule, that more progress may be achieved by launching a leaky administrative vessel than by waiting for the waters to recede, PPBS does offer a method of testing for hidden holes below the waterline, both prior to and after embarkation. There would seem to be no reason why a preliminary PPBS (like cost-benefit) analysis should not be required as a prerequisite to justify proposed new endeavors as well as to test existing programs. The danger would seem to be in the misuse of half-baked PPBS as another handy method of formulating plausible rationalizations for shoddy programs. A false aura of scientific objectivity can be enlisted to sell more than patent medicines.

HOW MUCH COMMITMENT?

If there is one central problem in implementing reform legislation and injecting controversial new techniques, it is the combination of underlying resistance to change by vested interests and the minimal support at the crucial moment vouchsafed by those who had previously been lavish with friendly rhetoric. It takes a lot of pushing to penetrate the layers of inertia and hostility, and unless there is genuine and real muscle to back up the speeches, the result is frustration and disillusionment.

The phrase "lip service" is used to denote verbal commitment to an objective unaccompanied by any real efforts to achieve it. Accusations that those in power are freer with promises than with action are of ancient vintage, and doubtless, cave drawings will someday be discovered attacking the probity of some clan chieftain who solemnly promised happier hunting but failed to deliver on his pledged word. This gulf between words and deeds was perhaps a major key to the domestic credibility gap of 1967-68. It has been charged, for example, that at the 1967-68 level of expenditures, the war on poverty was no more than a series of skirmishes, and that the bold promises of clean rivers, pure air, and slumless cities would not be redeemed by minimal budgetary allocations. In neither instance was the administration's budgetary request nor the subsequent dehydrated Congressional appropriation consonant with either the stirring rhetoric of the legislative preambles or the eloquent Presidential messages.

It should by no means be suggested that skimping on money is the only way of slowing progress on a program like PPBS that promises to upset many bureaucratic applecarts. Belief in good intentions may be severely tested. The administrative saboteur who wishes to give the appearance of cooperation and open-mindedness or indeed the politician who is not committed to his platform beyond election day or is simply short of budgetary funds has a wide choice of weapons. The PPBS movement may be slowed to a walk by solemn and protracted bickering on details and concentration on tangential or irrelevant issues. Defensive bureaucracies and powerful client groups can agree on selecting policy and implementing committees that offer a combination of incompatible views, clashing temperaments, and feeble administrative sense. One step beyond, artistic undercutting can be managed by relegating the program to unsympathetic, weak, and/or captive administrators certain to decelerate forward movement.

Even progress designed to achieve ostensibly noncontroversial goals are susceptible to blockage at the operating level. For example, community development programs aimed at the presumably consensual objective of improving the local economy are so much the rule that the city which openly opts for the economic status quo is a rarity. Yet, although all communities affirm their verbal adherence to efforts aimed at stimulating new economic growth, for various corporate or personal reasons, leaders in some communities have been fertile in devising techniques that halt every concrete step in this direction. When adherence to a common goal is barely skin deep, a cynic might suggest that opponents can think of a problem for every solution.

While it is not difficult to discover any number of instances in which practice is not consonant with ideals in the city hall or the state house, skepticism can be exaggerated to the point of paranoia. PPBS can play a significant role even in its early stages by examining, clarifying goals because goals possess a force of their own, even if long unachieved. The exposure of hypocrisy is often an effective method of squaring current reality with accepted objectives.

As Gunnar Myrdal correctly predicted with respect to America's treatment of the Negro, a moral commitment to a goal, even if long unfulfilled, can in time be a powerful weapon in securing passage of corrective measures.[6] By linking program achievement to goals, PPBS can be a significant lever for social change. It can document, in detail, our modest progress in moving toward accepted goals. PPBS may, as one of its by-products, provide copious ammunition for basic reforms.

Conflicting Goals and Priorities

At bottom, PPBS assumes that meaningful goals exist against which programs can be tested and evaluated. This is quite an assumption. Certainly there is no shortage of goals and objectives, but there is considerable difficulty in assigning priorities between them.

The financial limitations placed on great-society programs in fiscal 1967-68 point up two most serious problems. The first and most obvious involved finances. Escalation of the American involvement in Vietnam, a conflict that has been assigned priority over domestic programs, had absorbed the financial reserves for the projected expansion of great-society programs. Appropriations for the war on poverty, model cities, aid to education, and antipollution measures reflect this budgetary malnutrition. The rhetoric remained unchanged, but the money was not there, nor was it likely to be forthcoming within the next fiscal year. Widespread racial rioting during the summer of 1967 did not elevate priorities for the city slum population to the damn-the-deficit level that has historically been accorded only to overseas conflicts.

Were the lavish resources that are being expended in Vietnam available for civilian use--perhaps $30 billion in 1967--the situation might be far different. To place this figure in perspective, it has been estimated that perhaps a $12 billion annual subsidy would raise all of the nation's poor above the poverty line. As things are, a series of difficult choices were forced on the administration and the Congress in 1967. The primary reaction to stringency was to fund fully only politically popular programs while small poultices were applied to social inflammations. In the first category, the Appalachian Regional Commission received virtually all it requested, and the poverty program and aid for elementary and secondary education were funded at roughly the level of the previous year. In the second category, only $75 million was allocated for summer jobs in a spectacularly unsuccessful attempt to head off disturbances in the Negro slums; the model cities program was drastically truncated in the House of Representatives, and the House laughed to death the famous rat control bill before reversing its stand after the 1967 summer riots.

Should military expenditures continue to claim a similar or growing share of the gross national product, more strains on civilian programs can be anticipated. The revolution of rising expectations may, in fact, result in an intensification of internecine struggles by warring interest groups, all of whom can reasonably claim that a budget reduction would jeopardize an important national goal. Such battles might pit rural and urban areas against each other and could stimulate conflicts between programs designed to aid the aged as against efforts to help dependent children and lead to demands that funds be allocated to public transportation against pleas for more highways. The struggle could easily spread to include civil wars among urban, ethnic, and racial groups as well as choices between equally valid national and international goals. Perhaps the bitter struggles for poverty funds among neighborhoods of some cities are ominous omens of coming disturbances. Paradoxically, limitations on funds may force the pace of moves to introduce PPBS and other program soul searching by the federal agencies. It will not be the first time an ill wind has blown a little good.

For Motherhood or Flag?

It would be an error to suggest that goal setting for PPBS can be translated into a simple matter of financial priorities. Were this in fact the case, a cutback in overseas commitments and subsequent release of a major share of the federal surplus would eliminate problems of choosing between alternate goals and priorities by permitting a massive advance on a broad program front; virtually all significant budget requests could be honored. But there is obviously much more involved in achieving goals than a doubling or redoubling of appropriations. There are implicit conflicts between various goals. To cite a specific example, massive intown highway construction to provide easy access for a dispersed population to their work places and other destinations (as perhaps desired by a voting majority) is in conflict with other urban goals such as neighborhood stability and efficient urban development patterns. An across-the-board green light that includes heavy allocations for more urban expressways is therefore likely to diminish the possibility of achieving other, equally accepted objectives.

There is a more significant problem: Experience has proved that higher appropriations in themselves may not yield the desired results. In fact, it has been charged that appropriations may have precisely the opposite effect for which they were intended. To cite one example, Scott Greer has charged that the net result of an expenditure of $3 billion in urban renewal funds was a net reduction in the number of housing units available to low-income families.[7] Others have pointed out that funds allocated to regulatory agencies may end up as a kind of supplemental budget for the industries supposedly being regulated. Furthermore, there is often a matter of outright wastefulness of various types, including some programs that have outlived their usefulness, others that make no visible impact on their clients, and still others that leap from one costly, abortive experiment to another. It is hardly necessary to point out that a weak or stubbornly foolish bureaucracy wedded to obsolete ideas and practices can dissipate very large sums without commensurate product.[8] The Middle Eastern sheikdoms are not the sole instances where funds have been squandered with little resulting public benefit. There are instances in which additional funds may make a bad situation worse. Allocating new money to the old men may perpetuate and reinforce rather than remove the problems that the input of funds was supposed to solve. On the other hand, a prime argument for PPBS is that very often much can be achieved with little in the way of new allocations. Within urban areas, for example, training and recruitment programs for the police, better selection and promotion policies for the schools, and more effective housing-code enforcement may be undramatic, but a realistic PPBS may discover that modest improvements like these--aimed at doing better with what we have--may be of more lasting benefit than some massive, costly programs.

The idea that progress is purchasable, that military victory and social progress can be achieved by more lavish spending, is not purely American, but it would be fair to say that Americans seem to be especially prone to suggestions that in larger budgetary allocations can be found the answers to intricate domestic and foreign problems. One reason for the surge of interest in PPBS is that faith in this simple-minded approach may be waning; at least a limited awareness that less money and more hard thinking may provide part of the answer is slowly creeping through the federal establishment. Success in this endeavor may compensate for temporary, less than hoped for funding of domestic programs.

It is clear that one of the basic problems with the selection of goal and program priorities which must provide the basis for effective PPBS is that the nation seems firmly committed to just about everything good--slum-free communities with healthful, attractive environment, and moral uplift, high-paying jobs for the employable, and livable incomes for welfare recipients. It is entirely possible that within a generation or two, when the gross national product doubles and trebles, it will be feasible to provide the trillions of dollars needed to achieve these goals. Meanwhile, as has been suggested, choices must be made not only between the clearly vital programs and the obvious marginalia but between a number of efforts that are normally accorded high-priority status. If this were not sufficient complication, there is evidence that some goals may be in direct conflict with other, equally cherished objectives.

It may be useful to cite a case that caused much concern in the mid-1960's, the improvement of housing conditions for Negro slum dwellers. Each avenue selected or recommended to achieve this highly desirable goal seems to be in actual or potential conflict with other goals and values:

1. Fair housing programs to provide access to relatively affluent suburban communities for Negroes able to afford such housing seriously deplete the thin leadership stratum in the ghetto. Open housing of this type may defeat the objective of strengthening stable Negro community leadership.

2. Programs aimed at large-scale dispersal of the ghetto to white areas through rent supplements, creating pockets of public housing or other means, may lead to early, violent conflict in previously orderly white working-class and

lower-middle-class communities.9 These strata of the population seem to be afflicted with disproportionate amounts of insecurity and bigotry that often take overt physical expression. Similar although less explosive opposition may be encountered in moving large numbers of low-income Negroes into close proximity to middle- and upper-income groups. There may also be some resistance to the dispersal concept from advocates of black power who view the ghetto as a political base and see its dilution as reducing Negroes to a permanent political minority status among Caucasian majorities.

3. Improving housing within the ghetto through construction of public housing and/or large-scale renovation and rehabilitation will tend to perpetuate housing and school segregation and the economic and social divisions that breed mutual fear and hostility. On the other hand, requiring public-housing projects (or other housing under direct government control) to be fully integrated may alleviate the pervading pattern of segregation to only a limited extent because the net result is likely to be the creation of socially unstable oases in the midst of all-Negro areas.

4. Permanent improvement in housing conditions for slum residents will require a fundamental change in living habits of many disadvantaged families. There is no hard data on the proportion of low-income Negroes in the ghetto who differ from the white and Negro middle class only in their lack of money, sharing similar values and aspirations. Many Negroes are moving each year into the middle class and it is apparent that more would do so if the path could be made easier. In contrast, a substantial, although undetermined proportion of Negroes and Caucasians apparently do not share middle class and/or (even) working-class values, as, for example, a moderate respect for property and cleanliness. A minority of building residents who are not yet housebroken can reduce a new public housing structure or a private apartment building to a shambles in short order. Effecting a significant large-scale improvement in slum housing may therefore require isolating and possibly retraining hard core vandals under close supervision and/or selecting and segregating slum residents who can be relied on not to wreck the building in which they live. However, this kind of supervision can easily be labeled a bigoted, callous move to create racial or low-income concentration camps.

This example may suggest some of the limitations of PPBS. The technique can indicate progress and program impact, but it cannot reconcile the irreconcilable. Perhaps it is wisest to agree with the conclusion that its principal usefulness is educational: It will force agencies to do some unaccustomed, rigorous, systematic thinking about their programs.10

This is not to suggest that PPBS will revolutionize the ways in which goals are formulated and implemented. The United States (and perhaps most nations) seems to develop goals through some mysterious organic process. A climate of opinion is gradually established in the press, in the articulate portion of the community, among business leaders and among a few bellwether reformers in the Congress. Gradually, as this process of subliminal educational exposure percolates into the lairs of the Philistines, it becomes transformed into legislation and thence settles firmly into the political landscape.

A classic example of the osmotic process of goal formation is discernible in the field of public higher education. In the late 1950's and early 1960's, a decision seems to have been taken in a number of states to provide every qualified high school graduate with an opportunity for a low-cost college education at a public institution located within commuting distance of his home. This frightening outline, is now an accepted, unchallenged feature of the political environment. The same is discernible with respect to a variety of programs that have undergone the same process.

DESIGN FOR GENIUSES?

Perhaps none of the problems that surround the injection of PPBS into the governmental bloodstream is more crucial than the supply of trained, or trainable, technically capable manpower. The belated realization that shortages of qualified manpower rather than shortages in funds are crucial obstacles to program implementation has already been reflected in evaluation programs, funded by the Office of Economic Opportunity, the Department of Housing and Urban Development (HUD), and Health, Education, and Welfare (HEW), among others. It is also reflected in legislation introduced by the U.S. Civil Service Commission (the Intergovernmental Personnel Act of 1967), by Senator Edmund S. Muskie, and by HUD and HEW to expand the supply of trained professionals. In addition, some federal agencies have begun to tap outside manpower to conduct critiques of major programs, a form of independent evaluation that was almost unthinkable only a few years before.

Whatever corrective measures are under way or in prospect, the current situation is far from promising. The Joint Economic Committee looking into federal human resource programs found, for example, that although its queries did not call for "the extensive analytical effort, special studies, detailed program examinations, and financial tabulations" that are required by the Bureau of the Budget, the questions bearing on economic impact "referred to types of information which apparently were unfamiliar to some of the Government personnel who were called upon by their agency heads to prepare the replies."[11] Only a few agencies were able to prepare an effective response (that is, the Social Security Administration, the Office of Manpower Policy, Evaluation, and Research, and "several" units of the DOD). But the committee expressed its hopeful belief that such difficulties will "gradually be overcome by the disciplines of the formal PPBS which carries its own internal sanctions" but it "anticipated a transitional period of incomplete analyses and shallow analyses of costs and benefits." The Joint Economic Committee concluded on a grim but realistic note, calling attention to the immensity of the task:

> Either there is a scarcity of penetrating analysis in many program operating units or the assignment to prepare responses was often given to persons who were not familiar with program analyses. . . Much work needs to be done in the clarification of objectives and concepts, the formulation of analytical techniques, the explanation of procedures to individuals called upon to produce the necessary studies, and the definition of criteria for the interpretation and evaluation of findings. This will require a continuous process of examination and instruction throughout the executive branch.[12]

It is possible that the committee was somewhat naive in its initial expectations. Douglass Cater has quoted a Brookings Institution study to the effect that the Congress has done little to strengthen the top-level civil service. The top 3,000 or more career executives who head the various bureaus and divisions were found to be "predominantly inbred. . . . Many had started in government service at a lower level, had risen through the ranks by concentrating on specialties and are frequently indifferent to the larger problems of government."[13]

As noted previously, staffing problems encountered at the federal level are multiplied exponentially in most state and local governments. One can agree with George C. S. Benson that "in some states the personnel is superior to federal personnel,"[14] and still hold with Charles R. Adrian that, of the three levels of government, "The states have been slowest of all to professionalize and this has crippled the administrator at that level in his attempts to share in the decision-making process."[15]

Assuming that competent staff can somehow be located to operate PPBS in government agencies, questions arise as to the orientation and direction of this staff. PPBS is not a neutral, value-free process. The measurement techniques selected can have a powerful influence on goals and priorities. PPBS cannot itself define benefits, nor can it determine what kind of weights should be given to alternative results affecting different income groups and different, conflicting objectives.

It must be understood that while PPBS can be useful in re-examining old prejudices, it is no guarantee against new forms of snobbery. To cite a specific example, critical problems may arise because the program-design assignment is virtually certain to be relegated to holders of college degrees whose middle-class outlook will undoubtedly be reflected overtly or subtly in the performance standards and targets. In effect, technicians whose orientation reflects the status and aspirations of a particular social class are called on to set standards for programs affecting lower-income people with different living patterns and often with different aspirations. This is not a new situation. It may be re-called that standard intelligence tests have aroused considerable opposition on the ground that they are formulated in a middle-class framework, and hence the test scores discriminate against working-class children. In the mid-1960's, one of the basic questions was whether the poor or the redevelopment areas were or should be evaluated on the basis of their progress in effecting a transition into the national, middle-class mainstream.

Obviously some amount of class bias is inevitable in any program because a substantial amount of conformity to middle-class standards is usually a prerequisite for admission to the ranks of the goal setters and program designers. However, it is vital to recognize that either by calculation or simply because certain values are assumed as "givens" by the planners, unless great care is taken, PPBS, or indeed any system of performance evaluation, reflects and measures a relatively narrow spectrum of activities closely linked to the background of the designers. This may suggest that impartial, independent opinion should be brought into the design phase. More than likely, in time there may be demands for "maximum, feasible participation of the poor" in designing goals and performance measures for welfare, education, housing, and other programs. This may entail equipping the various client groups with the technical assistance advocates needed to protect their interests in program design and performance measurement. From the viewpoint of dissenting client groups, whenever controversial matters are involved, no panel of savants and/or corporation presidents is likely to produce a satisfactory consensus in assigning program priorities or in deciding exactly what it is that should be measured.

This brings us, of course, to the inevitable question: Should programs be geared to the tastes, abilities, and aspirations of the majority, or should goal setters and administrators continue to assume a paternal responsibility for re-molding the masses in a middle-class image?

Much can be and has been said on both sides of this issue of mass and class. In recent years, there has been considerable attention to the need for re-dressing the traditional, quasi-elitest thrust of government operations by according greater weight to the opinions and values of the public as a whole or of major and minor elements of the population. The evils of government-by-expert and government programs designed by small groups of relatively affluent and articulate persons imposing their standards on the inarticulate majority, on the unorganized, the politically inarticulate, the currently unpopular, and the minority groups have been given wide currency.

Unfortunately, because government rests on a foundation of successful communication and manipulation of expertise and money, there is no easy solution to this dilemma. One obvious response is to ensure that every group has its capable spokesmen to give its interests adequate representation not only in the political arena but also in technical disputes. This would entail that some planners, economists, and sociologists join the legal professions in preparing partisan briefs for clients, a development which in any event seems to be well on its way in some new fields, particularly city planning.16 But it would be a mistake to limit attention to the organized or potentially organizable.

Provision must also be made to guarantee adequate protection for submerged segments of the population. The question is how to achieve this objective for groups (like children on welfare) who cannot communicate easily or perhaps at all. There is also the problem of securing representation for groups who are obviously able to make themselves heard but who cannot or will not devote sufficient attention to complex operations in the face of competing issues that demand their attention. It is often difficult to secure meaningful responses from interests like downtown businesses--organizations which one would believe wholly capable of participating fully in the process of setting goals and performance standards. Even the goals established for a discrete and manageable area like the Minneapolis Central Business District evoked little comment from the downtown businessmen whose interests were presumably most directly involved. In fact, the detailed planning subsequently undertaken to implement goals evoked little reaction in Minneapolis until the plans were subsequently simplified in highly specific terms that clearly indicated the potential impact on traffic, or parking patterns, or on individual business establishments.17 If PPBS design is to avoid charges of backroom manipulation and dictatorship-by-technician, it will obviously be necessary to translate a highly technical process into bread-and-butter terms meaningful to potential clients.

The experience in Minneapolis suggests that preparation of generalized goals is a task congenial to politicians, civic and business leaders, but involving them in a continuing dialogue with professionals is likely to be frustrating. Few nonprofessionals can devote the time and effort necessary to master a technical subject, and most groups are unable to employ a capable protagonist, nor are they willing to empower a technician to commit the organization to significant planning proposals. Because few interests are in a position to employ qualified lobbyist representatives, the result is that it usually falls to the technician to seek out meaningful responses from many of his client groups, particularly those without the technical knowledge or funds to employ professionally trained spokesmen. This, of course, does not place an unusual amount of responsibility on the professional but rather recognizes a situation that has always existed.

As John Dyckman observes, "most social planners have at least a modified caretaker orientation."18 Leonard J. Duhl sees the planner-forecaster as an agent of social change acting as a kind of ombudsman, "returning the franchise" to the people partly by serving as a communications link with the "invisible colleges" of intellectuals and partly through conscious efforts as a political manipulator.19 It is incumbent on the technician involved in PPBS design to develop a concept of short-run and long-run client interests. If he is to engage in this perilous activity, he cannot attend the luxury of technically neutral detachment. As Dyckman suggests, he will not be handed a ready-made packet of goals in the form of a set of well-ordered preference functions, and the task of discerning "latent" goals will take great patience and much interpretation.

It should be made clear that the relatively restricted technically support-ive role suggested for the PPBS staff is at variance with other views on the func-tion of the program-planner in government. A more exalted pivotal role is identified by John Friedmann, who underscores the potential of the researcher-planner as an agent in effecting social change, and implicitly, in assuming a major responsibility in selection of goals and programs. In his articles on "inno-vative planning"[20] Friedmann differentiates between the cautious creatures engaged in sanctioned, gradualist planning with its emphasis on effective alloca-tion of resources within a system of incremental change, and the innovative planner. The latter seems to be a cross between a swashbuckler and an *eminence grise* who has deliberately chosen to become an engineer of rapid change in per-forming a planning, advisory, and manipulative role, working closely with top-level executives.

The innovator seeks to legitimize new social objectives by concentrating on main points of leverage and, like a bold staff Saul Alinsky, he seeks to "or-ganize dissatisfied creative minorities to translate general value propositions in-to new institutional arrangements." Concentrating his efforts on making maxi-mum use of all available resources by focusing on areas likely to produce the greatest changes, he eschews comprehensive planning in favor of strategic ac-tions based on what he interprets as demonstrable results. Because innovative planning is associated with periods of crisis and change (like the present), Fried-mann feels that it is currently more prevalent than the conservative, allocative variety.

While it may be argued that in playing this free-wheeling semiconspira-torial role, the planner arrogates responsibilities which are, or should be, in the province of the elected official, it can be countered that he functions as the chosen instrument of the politician. If he operates under a loose rein, it may be presumed that either he possesses the full confidence of his boss and has the sense to check sensitive decisions with his elected superiors or that his tenure will be short lived. Further, it may be assumed that this *modus operandi* has considerable attractions for the results-oriented politician, provided the planner stays out of too much hot water. Under varying job descriptions, most incum-bents number practicing bureaucrat-planners-researchers among their trusted subordinates. These are people who can be relied on to get a job done without bothering their superiors and without making too many waves. They are usual-ly prepared to serve as loyal expendables; if things go wrong, they deflect the blame from the man who appointed them whether or not the trouble arose from bad luck or faithful adherence to orders. In fact, because a considerable amount of friction from change-resisters is inevitable, the turnover among inno-vators may be substantial. For this reason a quick, thrusting, hit-and-run strat-egy is clearly in order rather than the incremental type of planning associated with planners who have hopes of retiring on the job.

Whether this description is accurate or indeed whether it is a role that planners and administrators should deliberately choose is open to question. Clearly, some have found this a congenial role, working as a trusted lieutenant to an imaginative executive. In any case, the innovator seems to be more suitable for the executive's personal staff rather than to the staff of technicians committed to long-term service with a permanent agency. Furthermore, he must recognize that his enlistment may be drastically curtailed unless he possesses remarkable personal gifts and a great deal of good luck. The planner who attempts to manipulate the facts, control the news, and engage in behind-the-scenes social engineering is likely to end up in a pot of hot water, particularly if he discusses his role openly with friendly reporters. It can probably be taken for granted that social planning will be an uneasy, hybrid mixture of open plans openly arrived at and the kind of high-minded conspiracies described by Friedmann.

Whatever the particular mix in a particular time and place, there are areas in which wholly objective tests can be developed as for example, such indisputable yardsticks for health programs as the infant mortality rate or family income patterns, the occupational distribution of minority groups, and the proportion of college graduates in various communities and population groups. But there remains a wide latitude for bitter disputes on the type of performance standards to be employed in measuring progress on such basic issues as the status of the Negro in America or the quality of life in our cities. The fact is that such performance measures as exist in these and other areas are traditionally established in societies by a small group of cultural pacesetters. This returns us to the original dilemma: Do we set standards that satisfy the current tastes of the electorate or are there overriding professional standards? If purely mass standards were to serve as the criterion, the outlook for a host of subsidized activities ranging from parks and universities to operas and educational television would be bleak indeed. It would appear to the author, at any rate, that adoption of Philistinism in the guise of a modern-day slogan of *vox populi, vox Dei*, represents an abdication of responsibility rather than, as some argue, a progressive step in the direction of democratic freedom.

The danger of bowing uncritically to popular sentiment shows up most clearly in relation to racial and religious issues. If local referenda were to be the guide, anti-Negro prejudice would be certain to bar progress on civil rights in many areas, North as well as South. While it is perfectly true that it is all too easy for middle- and upper-class residents (or PPBS designers for that matter) to prescribe racial balance for working-class areas because *their* neighborhoods escape most of the potential hazards to life, schools, and property,[21] even if it is admitted that there is some rationale for white backlash, abject surrender to popular bigotry is hardly the answer.

To a degree this mass-class argument is, in every sense of the word, academic. Whatever the technique in vogue for measuring the popular will--elections, polling, or revolution--in the end, most decisions are made by elites.

Decisions may be modified or influenced by systems that accord greater weight to wider strata of public opinion, but the number of persons actually involved in decision-making is almost always very small. Nor is there any indication that mass education and mass communication have fundamentally enlarged the proportion of the population which has a significant influence on decisions. The civil rights movement, like the earlier successful efforts aimed at securing legal and political equality for labor unions and women, has enlarged the spectrum of clienteles who must be taken into account in formulating and administering public policy. As government and society grow more complex, the distance between technician, administrator, and politician can be bridged only in part by mass media, opinion polls, periodic elections, sporadic disorders, technical interpreters, advocates, and ombudsmen. Demonstrations are a method of calling attention to a cause, not a consistent approach to influencing day-to-day program operations. For this reason, the burden of representation of much of the public will continue to fall in great measure to program designers and administrators. There must be an awareness of this extremely important responsibility.

The person at the upper echelons in government also has broader responsibilities. He must not be contented with programs and efforts good enough to satisfy his clients but short of what he knows is desirable and possible. Moreover, he is, or should be, an educator rather than either a bureaucratic calculating machine or a pliable professional survivor. He has a duty to the spirit and substance of his program rather than solely to generate laudatory comments in the legislature and the press. PPBS, if he uses it properly, can serve him as an effective teaching aid. On the other hand, if he misuses it or promises too much from its use, the result is likely to be growing cynicism and suspicion on the part of client groups convinced that a new black art has been developed to justify unpopular decisions.

WHO KILLED COCK ROBIN?

Like military combat, the challenges entailed in mounting a genuine PPBS operation cannot be fully appreciated until one has actually been in the field. From its inception through its inescapable revision, the designer is called upon to render a series of judgments involving interpretations of legislative intent, community values, and professional standards.

One of the thorniest problems in measuring impacts is disentangling programs from their environmental context. It is necessary to identify the role of each layer of government, of each relevant program, and of other societal factors that may have an equally important influence on events. Moreover, since the sum is often greater than the total of the individual parts, the combined impact of various programs must also be examined.

In attempting to isolate the effects of any single government program in the field of health or employment, for example, it is extremely difficult to determine, with certainty: (1) which changes occurred as a direct result of a particular program, (2) which changes can best be classified as indirect or corollary impacts, and (3) which changes are attributable to exogenous factors. A manpower-training operation, for instance, can exhibit a combination of all these: A group of trainees may be hired as a result of a good literacy campaign, because of an unanticipated increase in the gross national product, success in a local area development effort, or a modification of union rules or company policy. The inherent merits of program design and execution may have little relation to success in locating good jobs for the trainees.

Tracing the indirect impact of a program or its effects in combination with other programs is often a tricky affair. One example may be cited: the relationship between poverty programs, singly and in combination, and the violent disorders that erupted in the Negro ghettos during the summer of 1967. In the spring of 1966, officials in poverty agencies claimed that the constellation of programs financed and administered by the Office of Economic Opportunity (OEO) had been instrumental in taking the steam out of riots by providing hope, tangible accomplishments, and employment for potential agitators. During the summer outbreaks, critics subsequently suggested, with somewhat tenuous logic, that, on the contrary, racial disorders occurred in some measure because poverty programs had titillated but not satisfied the aspirations of the poor. In partial agreement with this stand, Sargent Shriver later pointed out that poverty funds represented only a fraction of the amounts requested by the riot cities, indicating that larger allocations might be more effective in muffling violent protests. From a slightly different perspective other observers suggested that the modest improvements introduced by the poverty programs and related efforts by the mid-1960's had accentuated social disequilibrium by breaking through the thick crust of despairing passivity that had kept the slums passive under worse conditions (such as the 1930's Depression).

Obviously identifying cause and effect is far from an easy task under these conditions. Programs do not operate in a vacuum, and it is not always possible to state with certainty that effect B was caused in part or in whole by program A.

There is a further problem in creating defensible yardsticks for evaluating programs: Assessing highway beautification, open space, historic preservation, the impact of placing utility lines in urban areas underground, of cultural development, and other programs in purely monetary terms is ridiculous. How is the quality of life to be measured, and who is to do the measuring? How can emotions like pain, grief, humiliation, anger, and happiness be converted into comparable dollar units? Costs and emotions are often related, but it is hard to enter them on the same balance sheet even after the linkage has become obvious. The decades of humiliation and despair that exploded in the 1967 racial disorders have had measurable consequences running into hundreds of millions in property damage. However, the anger and hatred that led to the arson and robbery are *not* quantifiable.

There is also an obvious temptation to expend many years and much money in assessing the probable, possible, and conceivable, and the immediate, middle-range, and long-term relationship between programs and consequences both in the so-called pure and applied categories. An affluent nation can pursue all kinds of research avenues that might be of value and it is feasible to feed the entire pack rather than run the risk of starving one of the hounds that might have caught the quarry. The difficulty is that much time and effort may be expended in belaboring the obvious. The ancient give that a sociologist is a man who spends $100,000 to locate a brothel has more than a glimmer of truth in it. On a more sophisticated level, there is the danger of overconcentration on one or a few enticing aspects of a problem to the exclusion of other, possibly more promising, research areas. The results may make a good deal of sense but they may divert attention if the study suffers from tunnel vision that fails to take account of the major dramas on the periphery. In short, while research is needed to identify the relationship between specific programs and their impact, it is just as hard to formulate useful research studies as it is to design effective programs.

In formulating program design for PPBS, it must be recognized that the information received in the form of impressive print-outs and charts may, nevertheless, be superficial and misleading. Any number of key items may be missing, as, for example, confidential information on program impact in slum areas or sensitive data pointing to administrative lapses. There is also the question of how far to rely on self-justifying statistics furnished by separate agencies with similar or identical missions. Substantial knowledge is necessary to reach behind the budget and performance data when attempting to measure the relative effectiveness of different but overlapping programs such as the OEO's Neighborhood Youth Corps, which is six times more expensive per trainee but is also relatively six times more productive. On the other hand, there may be corollary, nonmonetary benefits (such as a fresh perspective for trainees) that compensate for the higher costs.

To summarize, PPBS offers a number of extremely attractive prospects. It may shed new light on tired programs and demonstrate just how much we do not know about government and the society in which we live. On the other hand, overselling or overrelying on PPBS would be tempting fate. Quite probably the by-products of the intellectualization of government represented by PPBS will be a species of technical warfare between warring advocates, each of whom can point out the fallacies in assumptions, values, and techniques of his opponents, their programs and their recommendations. In brief, PPBS may become a new arena for informed but nonetheless deadly conflict.

At the risk of appearing tiresome, it must be noted that one critical shortcoming appears glaringly obvious when we consider introducing new and intricate programs. PPBS calls for outstanding intelligence in the design and evaluation phase and solid competence in its operation. It cannot conceivably be made a foolproof, self-adjusting mechanism. Surely the technique is beyond the current capacities of many government agencies, particularly in state and local government. Ideally, the process should be delayed until there is assurance of adequate staffing, but government does not work in a simple, logical progression. Realistically, the best that one can probably hope for is that parallel, strenuous efforts will be made to enlarge the supply of trained staff as PPBS is diffused through the governmental structure. After much preliminary floundering, people competent to handle the mechanics of the system will be available, and we can proceed to the next plateau. On these Plains of Abraham to be scaled in the 1970's will be waged interesting technical battles involving ideological and value issues that reach into the heart of government.

NOTES TO CHAPTER 2

1. U.S. Bureau of the Budget, *Bulletin No. 66-3, Planning-Programming-Budgeting,* Washington, D.C., 1965; and *Supplement to Bulletin No. 66-3,* Washington, D.C., 1966.

2. For an excellent, very short, but authoritative description of PPBS, see statement of Charles L. Schultze, Director, Bureau of the Budget, *Hearing Before the Subcommittee on Intergovernmental Relations,* "Creative Federalism," 90th Cong., 1st Sess., Pt. I, pp. 388-419.

3. See the comments of Professor Charles A. Reich, Hearings Before a Subcommittee of the Committee of Government Operations, House of Representatives, *The Computer and Invasion of Privacy* (Washington, D.C.: U.S. Government Printing Office, 1966), pp. 22-42.

4. Wilbur J. Cohen, "Education and Learning," *The Annals,* issue entitled *Social Goals and Indicators,* Vol. 373 (September, 1967), pp. 87-88.

5. See Alan A. Altshuler, *The City Planning Process, A Political Analysis* (Ithaca, N.Y.: Cornell University Press, 1965), chaps. 4-6. Also Edward C. Banfield, *Political Influence* (Glencoe, Ill.: The Free Press, 1961), chaps. 8, 9, and 12.

6. For opposing views on this critical matter, see C. Wright Mills, *The Power Elite* (New York: Oxford University Press, 1956); Floyd Hunter, *Community Power Structure* (Chapel Hill, N.C.: University of North Carolina Press, 1953); and Edward M. Banfield, *Political Influence* (Glencoe, Ill.: The Free Press, 1961). Also Gunnar Myrdal, *An American Dilemma, The Negro Problem and American Democracy* (New York: Harper and Bros., 1946).

7. Scott Greer, *Urban Renewal and American Cities: The Dilemma of Democratic Intervention* (Indianapolis: Bobbs-Merrill, 1965), p. 3.

8. See Senator Edmund S. Muskie, "Manpower: The Achilles Heel of Creative Federalism," *Public Administration Review,* June, 1967.

9. See Herbert Gans, *The Levittowners* (New York: Pantheon Books, 1967), especially pp. 427-28.

10. See William Gorham, "Notes of a Practitioner," *The Public Interest,* issue entitled *PPBS, Its Scope and Limits* (Summer, 1967), 408.

11. U.S., Joint Economic Committee, Subcommittee on Economic Progress, *Federal Programs for the Development of Human Resources,* I (Washington, D.C.: U.S. Government Printing Office, December, 1966), 31.

12. *Ibid.,* p. 31, p. 92.

13. Douglass Cater, "The Fourth Branch," *Power in Washington* (New York: Vintage Books, 1964).

14. George C. S. Benson, "Trends in Intergovernmental Relations," *The Annals,* issue entitled *Intergovernmental Relations in the United States,* Vol. 359, May, 1965, 5.

15. Charles R. Adrian, "State and Local Government Participation in the Design and Administration of Intergovernmental Programs," *The Annals, ibid.,* pp. 36-37.

16. Paul Davidoff, "Advocacy and Pluralism in Planning," *Journal of the American Institute of Planners,* XXXI (November, 1965).

17. Altshuler, *op. cit.,* pp. 235-90.

18. John Dyckman, "Social Planning, Social Planners, and Planned Societies," *Journal of the American Institute of Planners,* XXXII (March, 1966), 70-71.

19. Leonard J. Duhl, "Planning and Predicting: Or What to Do When You Don't Know the Names of the Variables," in *Daedalus,* issue entitled *Toward the Year 2,000: Work in Progress* (Summer, 1967), pp. 779-88.

20. John Friedmann, "Planning as Innovation: The Chilean Case," *Journal of the American Institute of Planners,* XXXII (July, 1966).

21. William Lee Miller, *The Fifteenth Ward and the Great Society* (New York: Harper and Row, 1966), chap. 6, pp. 99-111.

3

COSTS, BENEFITS, AND SOCIAL INDICATORS

DO GREAT SOCIETY PROGRAMS HAVE A FUTURE?

A provocative, question-begging heading demands immediate clarification. The burden here is that we can pass a flood of new legislation, fund it generously, and then find to our dismay that it does not do the job it was supposed to do. Obviously, one reason for disenchantment is faulty conception. Spending in some cases was totally inadequate in relation to the size of the problems, and too many hopes were loaded on rather modest programs. In putting together the voting coalition to pass new housing, area development, and poverty legislation, it is fair to say that the Congress and the public were promised too much for too little. But excessive fervor and the kind of insulated millenialism prevalent in Washington during the first half of the 1960's were not the only reasons for the growing disillusion with government programs.

While most of the new programs were reasonably sound in design, we lacked the people to administer them properly. The desperately mistaken assumption of the early 1960's was that an enormous reserve supply of competent cadres of federal, state, and local administrators existed to staff the new, massive programs and successfully adapt them to local needs and changing circumstances. Typically, perhaps, the initial response to poor administrators was not prompt action to increase the supply and quality of administrators but an attempt to develop increasingly sophisticated management techniques valuable in highly experienced hands but totally beyond the ken of the typical mine-run bureaucrat available for program operations. All this would not be so tragic and ludicrous if we had not had ample warning, albeit on a lesser scale, at least a decade earlier. To cite one example, the 1960's attempt to infuse the government structure with advanced PPBS techniques is far from dissimilar to the enthusiasm of the 1940's and early 1950's for cost-benefit analysis.

COST-BENEFIT ANALYSIS: *DÉJA VU?*

Youthful enthusiasts for PPBS are sometimes appalled by the cautious reserve of their elders toward promising innovations. It may be that some of this skepticism is attributable to past experience with such devices as cost-benefit analysis. Like PPBS, the cost-benefit approach attempts to develop a systematic and orderly relationship between total investment inputs and total expected outputs. Ideally, the system produces a simplified statistical balance sheet listing all costs on one side and anticipated results on the other, with the relationship between the two reduced to a simple arithmetic ratio. A range of alternatives can be compared with ease and dispatch by the busy executive and politician and, *ceteris paribus,* the investments with the best ratios--the highest yields in relation to costs--are then given high priority.

Developed and systematized for use on water-resource projects, cost benefit generated considerable scholarly interest in the 1940's and 1950's. As is currently the case with PPBS, there was much talk of applying the technique on a wholesale basis to transportation, housing, education, and other programs. And, if historical parallels may be pursued a step farther, as cost benefit was considered for such wider uses, probing questions began to be asked regarding its alleged triumphal progress in guiding dam building and irrigation projects.

On closer examination, the technique was found to have serious disadvantages. For example, it was discovered that there is a tendency for decision-makers to ignore textual addenda and prologues and explanatory footnotes, and, instead, reach their choices solely on the basis of grossly simplified, consolidated balance sheets--provided these were in agreement with political necessities. In the cost-benefit analyses prepared for water-resource projects, it was found that "scientific" ratio statistics could be, and were, manipulated to secure desired results, and that, as always, political log rolling usually guided the decisions. Equally important, cost benefit provides a beguiling but misleading common denominator permitting inaccurate comparisons between actions that may differ tremendously in characteristics and impact. One study concluded that:

> Comparisons of governmental programs in terms of expenditures is deceptively simple and can be misleading as a basis for public policy choices. This is not only because the figures, with their appearance of precision, gloss over numerous difficulties, discrepancies, and ambiguities that inevitably beset the compiler. That kind of shortcoming--a common attribute of analytical and accounting data--is serious enough. But the principal reason that expenditure comparisons are an inadequate basis for policy preferences is that they necessarily treat equal dollar expenditures as though they were equal contributions to the solution of various problems when, in fact, the problems may be quite dissimilar in quality, resources marshaled for different purposes may be quite varied, and the effects of equal expenditures may differ in intensity as well as kind.[1]

A variation of cost benefit is the cost-revenue study that enjoyed considerable popularity in the 1950's. In their crudest form, such studies elaborated on a rather obvious truism: Slums cost more in tax expenditures and yield less in tax revenues than other neighborhoods. This reasoning was used (and in fact is still used) in support of proposals for urban renewal and related programs on the tenuous assumption that slum areas can be changed by improving the quality of the housing. More sophisticated studies in the mid-1950's were concerned with alternative tax returns and costs generated by decisions on various types of urban land development, expenditures for public services, and tax policies.[2]

The overriding problems with the cost-benefit technique are not only the tendency to slight unquantifiable essentials but the consistent failure, until recently, to evince much interest in obtaining critical social data bearing on program operations. In fact, it is only when cost benefit is broadened into PPBS that we have come to realize just how much little the scholars know and, surprisingly, the extent to which this ignorance is shared by the operating agencies.

Bertram M. Gross and Michael Springer suggest that "among the weakest links in benefit-cost-output analysis" is the lack of comparable, systematic, and periodically gathered social data. They maintain that "no conscientious budget-examiner could rely uncritically on the data presented on education, mental illness, crime, delinquency, transportation, and urban problems by scores of competing bureaus anxious to justify budget proposals."[3] Thus, not only is there not enough of the right kind of data but the statistics that are developed and presented for legislative action are often self-serving and suspect.

Currently, extremely crude cost-benefit comparisons are freely offered to guide major expenditures of government funds. Appropriations for the Job Corps have been solicited, to cite one of many examples, on the basis of comparisons between per-trainee costs in Job Corps camps that has been running as high as $12,000 annually as compared to the amount required to support and guard a prisoner in a federal penal institution. In a burst of political hyperbole, President Johnson charged that opponents of the administration's urban reform and poverty programs were "helping to produce convicts." The President wondered "why some people are willing to sit idly by and are willing to take the more expensive route--the delinquency route, the jail route, the penitentiary route."[4]

A certain amount of simplification is inevitable in politics, but serious problems may develop when sweeping judgments are habitually used in justifying or, for that matter, in attacking particular programs and proposals. At the very least, when better information becomes available, attacker and defender can engage in bloody combat with more plausible weapons systems. Partly for this reason, a study on the human problems of technology has called for a system of social accounts to measure performance in achieving goals. A system of social accounts would be created to measure the social costs and net returns of innovation, to assess social ills, to create performance budgets in areas of defined social needs, and to develop indicators of economic opportunity and social mobility.[5]

As was suggested above, one reason for the failure of cost-benefit analysis as a planning tool is the difficulty in assigning adequate weight to unquantifiable factors. This point is underscored in James C. T. Mao's theoretical framework for measuring the costs and benefits to society derived from a residential slum-clearance project.[6] While it is feasible to assign dollar values to changes in land values, to measure tax returns and savings in public programs, and to identify various project costs, assessing project impact on the community's social fabric, on esthetics, and on the strengthening or disruption of neighborhood coherence is an extremely hazardous undertaking. Boston's West End project that was attacked at great length by Herbert Gans[7] is a net gain in some accounting systems. Gans and others like Jane Jacobs[8] have stressed the debit side of the ledger in this massive project in terms of human costs and the destruction of a stable Italo-American neighborhood that offered a satisfactory environment for its residents.

The cost-benefit equation becomes even more complicated when problems arise in allocating limited amounts of funds to alternative methods of meeting the same social need. For example, poverty administrators have experienced much difficulty in assigning priorities to projects designed to help: (1) preschool children, (2) teen-agers, (3) family heads, (4) neighborhood organizations, (5) manpower training, (6) health programs, or (7) programs designed to assist the aged.

Martin Rein and S. M. Miller point out that if one takes into consideration long-term, second- and third-stage benefits, this inevitably leads to a bias in favor of child-oriented programs as opposed to efforts aimed at assisting the elderly.[9] Unless other goals and values are taken into consideration, cost-benefit analysis is likely to reinforce the emphasis on child-centered and youth-centered expenditures observable in the poverty program. A workable system of cost-benefit analysis that would help to determine the proper weight to be given each component of the poverty program would be most welcome. Realistically, this goal is probably unattainable.[10]

On a practical level, it would not appear that cost benefit or any other technique is going to be of much use in a close race. Most of the underpinnings, the inputs, goals, values, and assumptions are much too debatable to permit honest choices between the front runners.[11] Assumptions with respect to future interest rates, consumption patterns, occupational distributions, and income levels are particularly vulnerable to manipulation and attack, but even a factor as innocent and technically neutral as population projections rests on uncertain, hard-to-defend foundations. It is difficult to escape the conclusion that cost-benefit analysis can function as a quasi-administrative spectroscope ordering material into tidy, measurable components only so long as it remains unchallenged. By changing a few assumptions, the informed critics are able to revolve the lens again and again so that the instrument begins to function like a kaleidoscope, presenting patterns and results pleasing to the operator.

What cost benefit can be used for, aside from its invaluable assistance in injecting fresh perspectives into policy and operations, is to help rule out the worst projects, the proposals that are patently outrageous. If this limited role is visualized as a principal contribution to government decision-making, we may approach a situation in which a prestigious legitimizing technique is used by administrators to fend off proposals that unaided common sense indicates are ridiculous or to justify actions that the administrator is convinced are necessary. Perhaps an analogous situation occurs with respect to civil rights legislation that provided liberal-minded administrators with a handy excuse for taking action which they had wanted to take previous to the legislative enactment. In short, cost benefit, like PPBS and other techniques, is helpful in aiding the administrator and legislator not only in arriving at decisions, but in the last analysis, in validating the subjective, informed, and partly intuitive judgment that has been and will remain the key to goals, priorities, and measurement.

SOCIAL INDICATORS: THE BIG PICTURE

One of the attractive possibilities opened up by PPBS and cost-benefit analysis is their use in formulating and operating a system of social indicators. The keystone of this approach is the creation of an observation post at the summit, a federal council of social advisers.

In 1967, Senator Walter F. Mondale of Minnesota introduced legislation to establish a council of social advisers; paralleling the Council of Economic Advisers' report on the economic state of the nation, the new council would be assigned the responsibility of devising a system of social indicators to advise the President and to help in evaluating national social policy. The President would be required to submit to the Congress an annual social report, indicating progress, identifying future goals, and delineating policies for achieving these goals. The new council would construct yardsticks to measure the nation's progress toward social goals, and, implicitly, the impact of the various government programs in achieving that progress.

For the most part, the Mondale proposal would create an agency whose function would closely parallel the functions of the present Council of Economic Advisers. For example, a third component of the legislation calls for the creation of a joint committee of Congress to review the presidential report, just as the Joint Congressional Economic Committee exercises a similar responsibility over the President's report.

Social indicators will, in effect, represent a kind of report card for the nation. On the "macro," national level they can provide part of the framework for PPBS--cost-benefit analyses for many of the individual agencies measuring overall progress in achieving social goals. The indicators can be used by both the council and the agencies as a reference point for measuring overall progress and as a first step in evaluating the contribution of each agency toward achieving national goals. The proposal to extend the indicators on a subarea basis would add a further dimension to the analysis as well as enormous headaches in program design. There is no reason why the indicators could not be carried a step farther; it would appear logical to develop indicators for social classes and ethnic groups. In a fairly crude way, this effort has been going on for some time with respect to distressed areas and Negroes; in both instances, indices of family income and unemployment as well as educational welfare and health indices have long been used to chart progress and to bolster proposals for various programs.

The historical origins of the nation's first attempts to create social indicators (i.e., Thomas Jefferson in the 1800 census) and the potential benefits and very difficult problems involved in their design and use are discussed at considerable length in the seminal volume edited by Raymond A. Bauer.[12] Including contributions from six outstanding authors and running to almost 350 pages, the reader is warned that this massive effort does not do much more than scratch the surface of what promises to be a lengthy and complex as well as rewarding task.

The authors literally point to scores of unanswered questions and complications entailed in the process. They include many of the problems that bedevil PPBS and cost-benefit analysis: the lack of much useful data, the tendency to concentrate on quantifiable statistics to the neglect of other vital information, and the temptation to seize on measurable symptoms (e.g., poor housing) as a surrogate for more basic problems. There is also pessimistic inflationary bias on the part of designers that may make the situation look much worse than it is. Furthermore, there is the possibility that the close investigation required to develop valid indicators may in itself actually change situations. The information uncovered in the process of examining social ills is often a political weapon. Some conservatives have long feared that the federal government would one day create a center of unrest and dissatisfaction under the guise of research. The Council of Social Advisers may be it.

It can be predicted that, if passed, the new legislation can have a significant impact on the federal establishment, and subsequently, on the states. Many of the latter have, with varying degrees of success, indulged in their traditional weak mimicry of federal initiatives by creating councils or boards of economic advisers. Whether state boards of social advisers will be much more than paper organizations, symbolic of adherence to fashion rather than a genuine expression of reform, remains to be seen.

If the history of the economic advisers can be used as an analogue, a federal Council of Social Advisers would function as a semiautonomous body engaged in pioneering research, clarifying public policy issues (e.g., improving the ghetto vs. dispersing the ghetto) and adding fresh perspectives on existing programs. It would probably not, as some of its proponents hope, revolutionize government operations by guaranteeing the injection of hitherto neglected social considerations and the social sciences into the decision-making process.[13] Instead, again based on the experience with the economic advisers, it would open up a new field of technical disputes in an area presently governed by all sorts of implicit assumptions and dominated by partly understood and/or inadequate data.

Following the trail blazed by the economic advisers, the social advisers would be one authoritative voice among many that claim equal or greater wisdom. The social science equivalents of the Federal Reserve Bank, the Brookings Institution, and university departments of economics and sociology will doubtless be available to challenge the findings and recommendations of a new council. Moreover, substantial overlapping in responsibilities, research and program advice between the economic and social advisers, is virtually certain to ensure disagreements on socioeconomic issues. Treading on unexplored, controversial areas, the new council will present an enticing target for Congressional, journalistic, and professional criticism. In Albert D. Biderman's phraseology, there has been a demonstrated tendency for social indicators to develop from "social indicators" to "social vindicators," depending on the orientation of the designer and consumer.[14] The dispute in the mid-1960's concerning the pace of Negro progress in urban areas offers only one example to suggest that the possibilities for argument on the basis of interarea, interclass, and international comparisons are endless.

A basic difficulty in the use of the indicators is that the central thrust of national policy seems to veer away from readily quantifiable indices like income, housing starts, or dead Vietnamese. Increasingly, problems seem to involve exploration into spongier areas involving community morale and environmental livability; the Negro problem has moved away from simple, measurable demands for equal housing opportunities, voting rights, and jobs onto psychological terrain involving motivation, alienation, and pleas for recognition of dignity and manhood. By all quantifiable standards, enormous progress in solving Negro problems has been made, but the figures can be deceiving; victory or even interracial tranquility has proved elusive.

The recommended creation of a council of social advisers is closely allied to other developments that are likely to result in more searching critiques of goals and program operations. (PPBS and cost-benefit analysis have already been discussed at some length.) There is also the proposal offered by Senator Abraham Ribicoff of Connecticut to create an office of legislative evaluation to determine the extent to which federal legislation achieves its intended goals and the proposal by Senator Fred Harris of Oklahoma to create a new national social science foundation. Whether or not such legislation is passed in 1968 or 1969 is of less consequence than the trend that these bills represent. Moves to identify goals, to weigh alternatives, to measure program impacts, and, in general, to subject government to a broadening spectrum of critical evaluation will be reflected in new federal law and internal administrative changes within the next few years.

As was suggested earlier, if there are separate councils of economic and social advisers, one of the difficulties in social indicators may be their separation from economic indicators. Are poverty and the lagging redevelopment area social problems or economic problems? Whose analysis and recommendations are to prevail? Which indicators are most significant? What makes good economic sense from the standpoint of efficiency may not have desirable social consequences. A given amount of investment in a flourishing metropolitan area will usually yield more than an equal amount allocated to a distressed area, which, like the underdeveloped nations, is often weak in capability, labor skills, and infrastructure. Despite special legislation aimed at providing special help for redevelopment areas, it is not surprising to find that, through the workings of normal economic and social processes, the thriving metropolitan areas receive more government aid on a per capita basis than most distressed areas.

An examination of available indicators raises some important issues concerning the nation's choice of values and goals. As an example of things to come, it may be useful to examine one economic indicator that borders on the social--per capita incomes. It can be assumed that one consistent objective in a sometimes conflicting pattern of national goals will be further action to diminish interarea disparities in incomes and living standards. It is not at all difficult to develop a broad series of indicators that can be used for measuring the qualities vital in area progress: community leadership, worker motivation, social frictions and factions. It is perhaps instructive that as we become more sophisticated and disillusioned with our accustomed indices of change, more and more of the informative research on the problems of the poor is coming from psychiatrists and social psychologists rather than economists. To cite one example in which quantitiable indices offered a mixed reading even to the sophisticated analyst, in early 1967, statistical "radar screens" failed to pick up advanced warning of the forthcoming summer of ghetto riots, but instead turned up indications of slum-area unemployment and delinquency that differed not very much, if at all, from earlier, less turbulent years. As in the case of the larger redevelopment areas, social indicators in urban distressed areas provide masses of conflicting data on symptoms and progress. What the indicators can help us to do is to raise the level of ex post facto argument to an informed, technical, and possibly less heated level. Moreover, the technique inevitably leads to a searching self-examination on just what are the nation's goals and priorities. But it is also clear that hard, interpretive analysis which goes well beyond, or more accurately, behind, under, and around the figures, is crucial if the social indicators are to be satisfactory policy instruments. The consolidated tables themselves can or should only be regarded as the tip of the iceberg; one can only hope the other seven eighths will receive the attention it deserves.

PECHMAN-HELLER, OR AN EXPOSÉ A DAY

Cost benefit, PPBS, and social indicators are attractive, complicated techniques. A chronic shortage of professionals even capable of asking the proper questions, let alone providing plausible answers, raises some doubts concerning their use in the federal establishment. One's skepticism multiplies geometrically if the burden of adaptation to the new world is to be placed on the frail shoulders of state and municipal staff.

A special facet of the problem of injecting sophisticated management techniques into state and local government is their lack of capacity not only to exploit new opportunities opened up by PPBS and other approaches but even to muster sufficient expertise to handle their current operations satisfactorily. Access to quantities of free money is not the simple answer to structural incapacity. It is ironic that side-by-side with mounting evidence of their painfully slow progress in mastering complex advances in management, there are simultaneous efforts in progress to vastly increase state responsibilities.

Since the 1950's, there has been a recurring cycle of innovative government programs, followed, at diminishing distances, by scathing criticism. Formerly most of the attacks were linked to financial scandal, but more recently they have been focused on inefficiencies and on the disappointing gap between promise and performance. The time period between high-level hearings, instant, laudatory press releases, and the first virulent exposés seems to be becoming increasingly truncated. For example, while the blasts against the urban renewal program required an elapsed time of five to ten years, the poverty program became a target for liberal as well as right wing critics in less than a year. It may be possible to further accelerate this pattern of initial huzzas followed by bitter disenchantment if program control is transferred to state and local governments.

There was a growing tendency in the mid-1960's to decry centralization in government. The Pechman-Heller proposal to turn over a share of unearmarked federal tax revenues to the states, suggestions for a more local federal-state partnership in urban development,[15] and recommendations for a stronger state and local role at the expense of a rigidified federal establishment[16] are only a few manifestations of a change in climate that may result in significant changes in the structure of federal-state relations. (This assumes that the end product will be more meaningful than the Eisenhower-era Kestnbaum Commission that labored in vain in efforts to transfer federal programs to the States.)[17] The parallel and conflicting demands that the cities, rather than the states, be given direct access to federal tax revenues for urban renewal and other programs may also meet with some response. Legally, cities are creatures of the states, and many city problems require action on a metropolitan or state level. Whether the main thrust is in city or state government, the outcome may be predictably dismal, at the very least passing through a difficult transitional period.

Given a working knowledge of the programs, the available alternatives, and the orientation and limitations of the cast of characters, it is possible to begin writing the first exposés before the shift in operational responsibility away from the federal level takes place. It requires no power of clairvoyance, for example, to predict the main thrust of state controlled programs in the deep South that involve racial issues. Although there are likely to be a number of surprises when some local governments take hold of programs currently under tight federal supervision, it can be anticipated that observers will conclude that most state and local governments are poorly equipped to do an adequate job. Whether flexible approaches can be developed that permit a wide variation in federal control depending on local capability is another question. Such arrangements do, in fact, exist on an administrative *ad hoc* basis, but it is doubtful if they can be codified into law without considerable wrangling from states and localities that have the will but lack the means to perform competently without close federal scrutiny.

The shift in management responsibility and funds to state and local government will most likely represent an exacerbation rather than a departure from the pattern of program innovation and deterioration noted in federal agencies. Considering the well-documented weaknesses at these governmental levels, we can anticipate early scathing attacks from liberal elements on the ineptitude, callousness, and impenetrable stupidity of many state and local goverments. On the other hand, attacks from the conservative right may be delayed because of the importance of grass roots in the conservative political ideology. Within a few years, however, a substantial swing in the pendulum is likely; even conservatives will not be able to stomach the results of giving a green light and a full purse to utterly incompetent bureaucrats. In particular, conservatives are likely to declare open season on the blunderers appointed by the opposition party. Ammunition for the barrages will undoubtedly be supplied, in profuse quantities, by federal bureaucrats who have little faith in local competence and who deeply resent their loss of authority, by enterprising journalists, and by disgruntled elements on the local scene. In addition to maladministration, the possibility of substantial pilfering at the state and local level, a minor problem in the federal bureaucracy, cannot be discounted. All in all, lively times may lie ahead.

While the preceding discussion has focused on a broad panorama of state weaknesses, the picture, it must be emphasized, is a generalization. The pattern of incompetence not only varies from state to state, but, depending on circumstances, programs, and staff, from agency to agency and even from division to division of the same agency.

In one agency, a third-echelon federal official of modest abilities may be seen in action on the average of once each month, strutting past tiers of cringing, slow-witted executives who are terrified by the awesome shadow of federal power. Fifty feet away, on another floor, his status undergoes a radical change. He is the picture of humility in a sister bureau of the same agency that

is headed by an intelligent, ruthless chief who has developed close ties to the
Washington headquarters of his agency. Not only would Chief 2 not entertain
the notion of catering to the whims of a lower-echelon federal errand boy, but
he has used federal funds to hire the project staff he needs to strengthen his
hand against the federal professionals. This tale of two bureaus is illustrative:
A few key appointments can change the pattern of agency competence almost
overnight. It is not surprising that the pecking order in intergovernmental relationships is constantly changing and that consequently there is more than a ray
of hope for the creative federalism optimists.

THE PROBLEM OF THE STATES: MASSACHUSETTS, FOR EXAMPLE

Some political scientists are hopeful that increased responsibilities will
improve state and local competence by attracting more able men into their
bureaucracies. They begin by assuming more responsibility and offering higher
salaries. Others, perhaps more prudent, demand that minimal federal program
standards should be imposed before Pechman-Heller cash is made available. A
blank check to simply too dangerous a temptation. One step of major significance is action to relieve the desperate staffing problem. Senator Muskie, President Johnson, and others have recommended greatly enlarged federally assisted
programs to train people for public service along with other incentives such as
salary subsidies for highly skilled personnel serving in state and local government. But it must be recognized that this should have been done a decade or
two earlier. Training staff is a long-range, or at best, a middle-range solution for
the problems that afflict states and municipalities. Even if large-scale programs
were in operation by the late 1960's, an extended period of painful, sometimes scandalous, transition can be anticipated while we wait for state and local
government to develop adequate capability.

The preceding discussion should not be construed as an indictment of
either the humanitarian intentions or the capacity of even the most backward
state to carry forward a few effective programs. If there is room for believing
that a transition to broaden state responsibilities need not have horrendous
consequences, it lies in the remarkable record of the majority of the states in
such vital areas as public higher education.

Some of the enormous problems inherent in the process of federal decentralization can be ascertained by examining the current situation in Massachusetts. With a population of 5.5 million and with per capita income somewhat above the national average, the Massachusetts state government ranks
among the large middle bloc of states in size and financial resources and in
being governed with modest competence. It is obvious by this time that the injection of a technique as sophisticated as PPBS or social indicators into the federal government process is far from a simple task. A few of the booby traps and
inconsistencies in goals, standards, and performance measures that call for an
enormous input of fresh, hard, and clear thinking on an unprecedented scale

have been identified in the previous discussion. However, it is apparent that if progress has been painful in the federal establishment despite a civil service equipped with reasonably[18] well-paid and well-trained executive cadres, the strain on the bureaucracies in state and local government will assume awesome dimensions. It may be useful to sketch a few of these problems in a fair-to-middling state government--Massachusetts--to provide a useful perspective on this crucial aspect of federalism.

One basic problem in Massachusetts is a limited capacity to undertake in a systematic manner the analysis, design, and implementation of program elements and to conduct intensive program evaluation. Planning staffs at the agency level are, with few exceptions, weak or nonexistent. Moreover, past experience indicates that modern managerial and planning techniques are beyond the capabilities of present staff. For this reason, advanced techniques cannot readily be imposed by federal fiat as minimum criteria for grants in aid. The prerequisite is a major, preliminary, conceptual effort predicated on a basic reform in the quality of staff in state government. In the absence of such reform, Massachusetts is limping along, responding as best it can to federal initiatives and increasingly complex federal program requirements. It is not that the state does not know what is needed: Sweeping reform measures have been enacted in transportation, education, and finance, to cite the major examples, but the follow-through is missing. Reforms have had a nasty habit of being vitiated by weak appointments in the upper-management echelons and equally feeble lower-echelon staff. Personnel reform is exceedingly difficult because the state civil service system that gives absolute preference to veterans (in Massachusetts, reformers are against civil service) discourages inputs of talent. Setting aside Massachusetts' unusually retarded civil service, however, the state is not much different from most of the others. Most simply do not have the quality of people they need to operate present programs. Whether or not an influx of new federal funds would improve matters cannot be predicted.

Massachusetts, like most other states, has engaged in periodic "Baby Hoover Commission" exercises, the latest example of which was completed in 1965.[19] Some of these recommendations have resulted in changes in administrative structure, but the fundamental weakness confronting Massachusetts and other states, the shortage of talent in depth, has not been effectively attacked. An upgrading in personnel will not be meaningful or lasting unless corollary action is taken to improve the defective Massachusetts decision-making machinery. In theory, most of the framework for improvement in state government presently exists. In Massachusetts government, the Executive Office for Administration and Finance has the legal authority to coordinate and implement policy and program planning. But there is a gulf between theory and practice. For example, a budgeting system has been in operation for many years, but the current pattern can perhaps best be classified as first generation, using the categories developed by Allen Schick.[20] The period roughly between 1920 and 1935, the first stage in modern budgeting, Schick suggests, was dominated by efforts aimed at developing an adequate system of expenditure control. From the mid-

1930's to the early 1960's, the second or New Deal stage focused on the movement for performance budgeting. The emphasis was on improved management, work measurement programs, and the focusing of budget preparation on the work and activities of the agencies. The third and most recent stage has witnessed the mergence of PPBS linked to modern information technology. This third generation is only beginning to have much of an impact even in the most advanced states. Massachusetts, like many or possibly most states, seems barely to have crossed from stage one to stage two and is obviously a long distance from stage three. For this reason, one is forced to the conclusion that recommending or requiring PPBS and other highly sophisticated techniques be adopted by a typical administratively backward state (or local government) seems analogous to assigning open-heart operations to barber-surgeons who have barely become aware of the limitations of leeches.

Massachusetts' inability to keep abreast of the times in its central budget operations is reflected in a similar failure with respect to its capital improvement programs. Most building construction for Massachusetts' state agencies is handled by the Bureau of Building Construction, which is part of the Division of Central Services of the Executive Office of Administration and Finance. Major lacunae in its jurisdiction include the Metropolitan District Commission which retains responsibility for the installation of metropolitan Boston's water and sewer facilities, the state higher education building authorities responsible for self-financing projects such as college dormitories, and the Government Center Commission which is responsible for the construction of the State Office Building and other state agency facilities in Boston's Government Center. Perhaps more important, the Massachusetts Bay Transportation Authority and the Department of Public Works, the Massachusetts Port Authority, and the Massachusetts Turnpike Authority, agencies responsible for the larger part of the state's transportation operations also formulate and implement capital outlay programs independently of the Bureau of Building Construction. Thus, major agencies responsible for major expenditures and having a vital impact on the state and its regions operate as semiautonomous empires with their own legislative constituencies and their own patronage arrangements. Insofar as they exist, the plans and goals of these agencies are formulated on a quasi-independent basis without either effective interagency coordination or close integration into overall state operations.

There is much that is wrong even with the limited area of construction which does come under central control. As of August, 1966, the Bureau of Building Construction was processing approximately $250 million in construction, renovation, and architectural projects--but little planning was in evidence. Instead, the bureau's relatively small planning unit was almost entirely engaged in current project development and administration; no staff was assigned to long-term policy and program planning.

To sum up, there are major deficiencies in the Massachusetts capital budget process:

1. The exclusion of agencies responsible for major capital outlays limits the scope and effectiveness of the system,

2. Although state law requires the development of a long-term construction program, only a one-year capital budget is prepared and enacted into law,

3. Although some staff is ostensibly assigned to long-range planning, urgent tasks in supervising construction-in-progress and related activities divert them from this vital function,

4. The capital budget is handled separately from the operating budget at both the executive and legislative stages, a separation which impedes assessment of their relationships and impacts.

The second crucial element in a modern decision-making process, an effective Automatic Data Processing (ADP) operation, is in an equally rudimentary stage. For the most part, advanced-generation ADP equipment in Massachusetts is currently used to speed handling of routine data formerly processed by unit-record installations. The state's principal computer applications include the processing of unemployment compensation claims, motor vehicle registration and licensing, state tax administration, payrolls and accounting, public works engineering and management, and the manipulation of education data.

Although some of this routine data can have considerable relevance to state budgeting and program evaluation, most of it is not in usable form for such purposes. This is partly due to the fact that the data are being collected, stored, and processed in a form suitable only for each agency's specialized, routine needs. Extraction of potentially useful data is also hampered by the fact that state ADP installations have been designed and are operating under piecemeal and uncoordinated arrangements involving a variety of equipment and machine language.

In short, while there are individual exceptions, ADP development for the state government as a whole has been retarded. In 1965, the Governor's Management Engineering Task Force found

> . . . an almost total lack of professional competence in information systems management. By business standards the state is twenty-five years behind the times in its ability to cope with paper work. We find serious cases of duplication of . . . information processing functions, with almost no organizational capability for coping with this problem.[21]

Meanwhile, there is no overall state plan to meet current and future state requirements for data processing systems. As a result, individual agencies cannot realistically plan to fit their data-processing activities into a state framework. In some cases, operations are inadequate to meet growing needs, and in other cases, well-conceived plans have not been implemented largely because of a shortage of systems analysts and programmers. At the same time, increasing pressures of work volume are leading each level of government and each aspiring agency either to install an inhouse computer system or to make extensive use of outside computer services. Over and above the ADP problems in the regular agencies, there are further complications arising from the temptation for large short-term projects and for newly emerging regional and metropolitan planning agencies to place great stress on ADP.

Much of the data useful for planning is generated through various special projects. The data developed through such short-term projects is often relevant to longer term planning; but since it was accumulated to meet urgent objectives, relatively little attention was given to the requirements of continuing planning and the common data needs of other agencies. The result has been a proliferation of piecemeal ADP installations, overlapping and duplication of data gathering and storage, needless increases in costs, and aggravation of the manpower scarcity in this field.

Some problems at the state level have been inflamed rather than alleviated by the federal programs. One good example is the mushrooming of data processing in state government that has been stimulated by the federal agencies. Growing amounts of federal funds have been available for special ADP oriented projects in an increasing number of areas. For this reason, and despite the pious strictures emanating from Washington concerning the needs for close coordination of interagency data handling, some of the ADP empire building among the agencies is traceable to a flagrant lack of coordination at the federal level. (As is suggested elsewhere in this text, notably in the discussion on economic development districts, federal agencies that cannot manage to coordinate their interagency relationships are sometimes tempted to shift the burden of interagency program integration to other levels of government.)

The task of mediating between, let alone coordinating, activities of two or more federal agencies along with their state counterparts is not a job for the faint hearted. It requires talented staff, thoroughly conversant with a range of information well beyond the scope of the average bureaucrat. What is striking about the area of data processing at the state level is not only the absence of this extraordinary level of skill, but the seemingly inability to do a creditable day-to-day job on many agency programs. In the Massachusetts data-processing operation, as elsewhere in state government, much of the failure is attributable to inadequate staff. The extreme difficulty in recruiting and retaining experienced ADP personnel was the most frequently mentioned problem encountered in interviews through the state's ADP installations.[22]

A special facet of the serious staffing problem is the generational gap that separates the mature administrator, who knows his program but is relatively unfamiliar with ADP, from the young ADP specialist with limited knowledge of governmental policy and program problems. Administrators who possess a rather sketchy knowledge of ADP may be unable to detect misuse or to direct younger administrators with impressive expertise in the new technology but little program background. Unfortunately, it may be predicted that the introduction of PPBS will exhibit this same divergence between enthusiastic young specialists and their irritated, uncomprehending seniors.

Given the pervading weaknesses in staff capability, it is hardly surprising to find that the things which are wrong with data processing can be found elsewhere in most areas of state government. In short, the defects apparent in state budgeting, capital outlays, and ADP operations are symptomatic rather than isolated. There are, for example, equally serious deficiencies in the area of agency planning. Major problems in this area include the following: (1) Few agencies have completed meaningful comprehensive plans; some agencies clearly regard comprehensive planning as a token exercise useful only in satisfying federal requirements for grants-in-aid, (2) In some fields, there are overlapping, unintegrated plans--in higher education, for example, at least three separate agency plans are being developed to guide policy and programs, (3) There is no central guidance or framework on which to base agency plans; there are no consistent population or employment projections, to cite a glaring example.

In the absence of overall state guidelines, the agencies tend to operate and to plan in a policy vacuum. Although agency plans may satisfy the requirements of their federal funding agencies, plans, programs, and operations are not related to each other within an overall policy framework in which relative priorities are assigned and scheduled.

There is considerable variation in planning operations from agency to agency. A survey of state agencies aimed primarily at determining the extent and nature of statewide and regional comprehensive planning activities[23] revealed that agencies whose federal counterparts place strong emphasis on planning prerequisites for funding were found to be committed to both long- and short-range planning activities. With some exceptions, agencies without federal counterparts or sponsoring federal agencies place much less emphasis on long-range planning. In this category are most of the authorities established by the state legislature that have no current access to federal funds or other connection with federal agencies. There is not much interest in comprehensive planning in other agencies as, for example, in public welfare which is responsible for expenditure of large sums of money but which has limited functions in construction of capital improvements. In brief, although many agencies can wave thick documents about, duly certified in Washington as acceptable master plans, it would probably be accurate to conclude that no major area of the Massachusetts state government can be characterized as operating in accordance with a well-conceived, comprehensive plan.

As a footnote to the situation respecting state planning, it may be useful to point out that in 1964 Massachusetts created a Board of Economic Advisers. Although the board's functions were supposedly to provide Massachusetts with the expert economic counsel available to the federal government through its Council of Economic Advisers, this has not, in fact, proved to be the case.

The appropriation has been insufficient to employ professional staff, and, as a result, the board's output has been limited to producing annual reports, to sponsoring a conference on state data needs, and to conducting occasional small-scale research projects. In this, as in other instances, a state has followed the federal example in outward form rather than in substance.

This rather gloomy picture of state government in general and Massachusetts in particular can be overdrawn. It is conceivable, although hardly probable, that the states will rise to the occasion and that the decades of abdication and irrelevance can be quickly ended when responsibility is thrust on them along with the cash to hire the staff they so badly need. Frankly, one is entitled to have serious doubts that this happy situation can or will occur. The defects of the states, the legislative resistance to modernization and change, and the backwardness of entrenched bureaucracies will take much time and effort to correct. With hard work, the quality of state government has been improving, and perhaps in time most of the states will be able to assume the partnership role to which they aspire. Until they do a better job in meeting their present responsibilities, it seems reckless to entrust them with new areas to administer. In fact, it is quite possible that one of the by-products of moves to apply PPBS in the states will be to expose rather than to cure the profound weaknesses of state government. After examining a few of the problems that the federal agencies have already encountered with PPBS, social indicators, and other assorted Chinese puzzles, one can hardly expect most of the states to rack up an impressive record.

NOTES TO CHAPTER 3

1. U.S., Joint Economic Committee, Subcommittee on Economic Progress, *Federal Programs for the Development of Human Resources*, I (Washington, D.C., December, 1966), p. 28.

2. See Ralph M. Barnes and George M. Raymond, "The Fiscal Approach to Land Use Planning," *Journal of the American Institute of Planners* (Spring-Summer, 1955); and William L. C. Wheaton and Morton J. Schussheim, *The Cost of Municipal Services in Residential Areas*. Prepared for the Housing and Home Finance Agency (Washington, D.C., 1955).

3. Bertram M. Gross and Michael Springer, "A New Orientation in American Government," *The Annals*, issue entitled *Social Goals and Indicators in American Society*, I (May, 1967), 10.

4. *The New York Times*, June 22, 1967, p. 3.

5. Report of National Commission on Technology, Automation and Economic Progress, *Technology and the American Economy* (Washington, D.C.: U.S. Government Printing Office, 1966).

6. James C. T. Mao, "Efficiency in Public Urban Renewal Expenditures Through Benefit-Cost Analysis," *Journal of the American Institute of Planners,* XXXII (March, 1966), 95-106.

7. Herbert Gans, *The Urban Villagers: Group and Class in the Life of Italian-Americans* (Glencoe, Ill.: The Free Press, 1962).

8. Jane Jacobs, *The Death and Life of Great American Cities* (New York: Random House, 1961).

9. Martin Rein and S. M. Miller, "Poverty Programs and Policy Priorities," *Trans-Action* (September, 1967).

10. For penetrating analyses of some of the problems involved in calculating the net returns from health, education, and other programs, see U.S., Joint Economic Committee, *Federal Programs for the Development of Human Resources, op. cit.* See also Theodore W. Schultz, ed., "Investment in Human Beings," papers presented at a conference called by the National Bureau Committee for Economic Research in *The Journal of Political Economy,* LXX (October, 1962), supplement; and Robert Dorfman, ed., *Measuring Benefits of Government Investments* (Washington, D.C.: Brookings Institution Studies of Government Finance, 1965).

11. See Aaron Wildavsky, "The Political Economy of Efficiency," *The Public Interest,* 8 (Summer, 1967), 30-48. Wildavsky makes a plea for examination of political costs and benefits in program planning.

12. Raymond A. Bauer, ed., *Social Indicators* (Cambridge, Mass.: M.I.T. Press, 1966).

13. See the editorial by Irving Louis Horowitz and Lee Rainwater, "Social Accounting for the Nation," *Trans-Action* (May, 1967).

14. See Albert D. Biderman, "Social Indicators and Goals," in Bauer, *op. cit.,* p. 78.

15. See Norman Beckman, "For a New Perspective in Federal State Relations," *State Government* (Autumn, 1966), pp. 260-70. Beckman is fully aware of the current inadequacies of state government but in his article discerns many hopeful signs of reform.

16. See Richard N. Goodwin, "The Shape of American Politics," *Commentary* (June, 1967). See also James Q. Wilson, "The Bureaucracy Problem," *The Public Interest,* VI (Winter, 1967), 3-9.

17. The Kestnbaum Commission (1955-59) and the Joint Federal-State Action Committee (1957-59) were created to reverse alleged overcentralization. The latter, after much huffing and puffing, in the end recommended transfer of two small programs involving 2 per cent of total federal grants in 1957. Neither recommendation was accepted by the Congress. Morton Grodzins, "The Federal Systems," *Democracy in the Fifty States,* edited by Charles Press and Oliver P. Williams (Chicago: Rand McNally Co., 1966); President's Commission on National Goals, *Goals for Americans* (Washington, D.C., 1960).

18. The word "reasonably" is used advisedly. See Douglass Cater's discussion of the Federal bureaucracy, *Power in Washington* (New York: Vintage Books, 1965), Chap. 6. Cater quotes a Brookings Institution study to the effect that the Congress has done little to strengthen the top-level civil service. The top 3,000 or more career executives who head the various bureaus and divisions were found to be "predominantly inbred." Many had started in government service at a lower level, had risen through the ranks by concentrating on specialties and "are frequently indifferent to the larger problems of government."

19. Commonwealth of Massachusetts, Governor's Management Engineering Task Force, *Survey Report and Recommendations* (Boston: May-August, 1965).

20. Allen Schick, "The Road to PPBS: The Stages of Budget Reform," *Public Administration Review* (December, 1966), pp. 243-58.

21. Commonwealth of Massachusetts, Governor's Management Engineering Task Force, *op. cit.,* p. 147.

22. Report prepared by Policy Management Systems, Inc., for the Massachusetts Department of Commerce and Development, *ADP in Massachusetts* (MSS July, 1965).

23. "State Agencies and Regional Development: A Study Prepared for the Massachusetts Department of Commerce and Development" (unpublished manuscript, Area Development Center, Boston University, October, 1966).

CHAPTER **4** ON THE POVERTY FRONT:
THE EXPENDABLE
EXECUTIVES

INTRODUCTION

One of the more interesting displaced persons is the veteran wounded or slain in the war on poverty. This growing fraternity owes its existence to lost battles at every level of the program, not excluding agency headquarters in Washington. The casualty rate among upper-echelon officials has been frightful, despite the remarkably attractive salaries offered by the program and its inherent interest for many public service personnel. Perhaps this brief analysis of the problems of a single local poverty agency may help to supply a few of the reasons for executive decimation which, in the case of Action for Boston Community Development (ABCD), amounted to a 50 per cent attrition in less than two years. This chapter suggests that a major reason for attrition is the tendency for such executives to be ground to powder between the millstones of uncertain federal agencies with wavering Congressional support and conflicting and frequently unsatisfiable client groups. There is a direct parallel in Scott Greer's description of the executives who head up city renewal agencies:

> The men who head these agencies are appointed officials. . . usually well paid by governmental standards, but they often have no strong rights to tenure. They are, along with their key line officers, soldiers of local political fortune. Like the city managers, they hold their jobs by the will of the political leaders and, like them, they exercise such power and influence as they can generate through their multiple commitments and alliances . . . the public entrepreneurs at the local level must satisfy the requirements of their jobs through accommodating two sets of pressures--those from the local community and those from the federal agency.[1]

This analysis is based on a brief examination of one part of one local poverty agency, the Community Action Program (CAP) of ABCD. Materials that have appeared from time to time on the administration of local poverty programs suggest the variety of problems and frustrations which confront the CAP administrators. From Los Angeles, a novelist describes the Economic and Youth Opportunity Agency (EYOA), as "bizzare, confused, ever in flux,

strangely ineffective. EYOA hardly sees a day go by without somebody resigning, or being fired, or making an accusation or answering one."[2]

The situation in New York is similar, as is suggested by the following:

> Whenever workers in the city's antipoverty program search for a
> literary allusion to explain their problems, they invariably come
> up with the same author: Franz Kafka. Kafka's portrayal in *The
> Trial* of a maze-like government where no one can find out who
> makes the decisions comes immediately to mind they explain,
> because the effort to aid the poor has created an almost direc-
> tionless bureaucracy, with overlapping and ill-defined programs
> and agencies, sudden shifts, and a complete lack of planning.
> The built-in problems, they add, have been compounded by the
> struggle of established social welfare agencies to protect their
> vested interests; the near paranoid belief of local groups that the
> city is plotting against them--and the acts by the city to support
> that belief; personal and political ambitions; confusion and
> bungling.[3]

Despite ABCD's substantial head start in antipoverty activities,[4] and
despite its advantages over a program like New York's in terms of size and
manageability, CAP has faced problems similar to those of New York and Los
Angeles but far less explosive in character. In every city, the CAP is in a uniquely vulnerable position. At the local level, it is caught between the civil-rights
revolution and internecine feuds among factions of the organized poor on the
one hand, and its responsibility for the inarticulate poor on the other. It has
also fallen heir to accumulated and often insoluble grievances created in part by
actions of the mayor and various agencies. Most of these difficulties have been
compounded by wavering, sometimes poorly conceived federal and local policies, and, often, by weak administrative organization of the federal funding
agencies.

ABCD suffers from all of the ills typical of the war on poverty programs: limitations on funds and executive talent: the inadequacy of the state-
of-the-art in this field; internal administrative difficulties; and the great complexity of the social, human, and political problems that are revealed as the
program proceeds. While the advent of the war on poverty offered the opportunity for great expansion in the original ABCD program, it tended at the same
time to increase drastically the administrative tasks confronting the agency. The
extreme rapidity with which the enlargement and reshaping of the program occurred in 1964, the improvisational and experimental nature of the Office of
Economic Opportunity's planning and funding procedures, the repeated changes in personnel and outlook of the New York OEO regional office, and certain
limitations and uncertainties of the Youth Employment and Training Program
of the federal Department of Labor added new dimensions to the agency's
tasks. Finally, the unexpected 1966 cutback in funding related to the escala-

tion of the war in Vietnam generated a special category of urgent problems in allocation among programs and neighborhoods.

ABCD ORGANIZATION

The ABCD organizational structure consists of a self-constituted, non-profit corporation that selects a board from a combination of representatives of public and private agencies and delegates from local planning councils. It would be fair to say that the membership is composed of persons of moderate views acceptable to the city administration. The board selects an executive director who nominates professional staff for approval by an executive committee composed of board members. Under the director is a deputy director as well as two major program divisions, the Community Action Program and the Demonstration Program. The latter branch conducts research projects primarily in the field of education but also undertakes social, work-oriented, multiservice centers and legal service programs. The Demonstration Program is funded by a combination of national and local foundations as well as federal and school department funds.

The ABCD-Community Action Program (CAP), the subject of this study, was responsible for the expenditure of approximately two thirds of total ABCD funds in 1965-66. In addition to the Neighborhood Youth Corps, CAP operations include Headstart, student remediation and enrichment programs, and a skid row program. OEO provides most CAP funds, but part of its operations are also funded by the U.S. Department of Labor. As compared to the Demonstration Program of ABCD, CAP operations involve relatively more work with community organizations, and in consequence, as this analysis indicates, offer considerably more potential for disputes and frictions.

CRITICAL PROBLEMS

The principal problems that confronted the Community Action Program operated by ABCD in the late winter of 1965-66, can conveniently be grouped under five major categories: (1) shortage of funds for fiscal 1966-67, (2) internal difficulties with ABCD administration and staffing, (3) problems with OEO and other agencies, (4) conflicts with community groups and community organizational problems, and (5) the undeveloped state of the art in antipoverty planning.

Shortage of Funds

In the confident expectation of a major increase, perhaps a doubling in federal poverty funds, throughout most of 1965 local poverty agencies were encouraged to develop imaginative (and expensive) proposals for enlarging existing programs and for funding new programs. Proceeding on this assumption, in consultation with the director of the New York regional OEO office, Community Action Program officials stimulated proposals from neighborhood organizations and consultants that, when combined, would have required expenditure of $8-$10 million in federal funds. In addition, ABCD's CAP operation was encouraged to initiate a number of short-term (three-to-six month) projects in the expectation that longer-term OEO funding would subsequently become available.

The escalation of the war in Vietnam wrought a material change in the federal budgetary picture. OEO appropriations were decreased slightly, falling from $1.7 billion in fiscal 1965-66 to under $1.6 billion in fiscal 1966-67. Moreover, the number of local antipoverty agencies requiring funding increased substantially during the year. The result was that Boston received approximately the same amount of money in 1966-67 as in the previous fiscal year. This means that $3.22 million was available for CAP programs in Boston in fiscal 1966-67. Since some funds are allotted for ABCD central administration costs, only $2.92 million was available for actual program costs.

In consequence, instead of allocating additional money to new and/or enlarged programs, ABCD was in the unhappy position of having to allocate a limited, less-than-anticipated amount of funds among competing programs and neighborhoods. One of the agency's major priority tasks was, therefore, to identify programs which, under the circumstances, could be considered expendable.

Another difficult set of decisions related to neighborhood allocations. The Roxbury, North Dorchester, and South End areas, largely populated by Negroes, together total less than a third of Boston's welfare cases and less than a quarter of its adult male unemployment and low-income families. In 1965-66, these areas received a combined total of 60 per cent of total CAP allocations. CAP faced the problem of redressing the balance, a task which embroiled the agency in conflict with Negro organizations. The Negro-populated areas that had been given priority status under Boston's urban-renewal operation were relatively well organized, highly sensitive to governmental decisions, and fairly sophisticated in bringing pressure on governmental machinery.

The difficult questions posed by the less-than-anticipated funding for 1966-67 were somewhat alleviated by the city school department's assumption of special education responsibilities for children from low-income families. However, the allocation of U.S. Office of Education funds to Boston's school department rather than to ABCD was opposed by neighborhood leaders from Negro areas who had battled the school committee over the *de facto* segregation and school-bussing issue. To satisfy this objection, the ABCD staff recommended the creation of an ABCD Citizen's Educational Committee to "ensure an effective community voice in the planning and use" of funds provided through the federal Elementary and Secondary Education Act (ESEA).[5]

It was also decided not to create additional, fully staffed, multiservice centers (such as those operating in Charlestown and Roxbury) in areas that did not yet have such centers. Instead, CAP decided to place increased emphasis on "neighborhood action centers"; the latter are to make maximum use of community aides, volunteer organizations, self-help activities, and referral to the existing ABCD service network of other agency resources, where appropriate. The decision to postpone establishment of full-scale multiservice centers, made necessary by financial stringency, created substantial ill will for ABCD, particularly in the Italo-American areas of the North End and East Boston.

Another CAP decision, the redirection of program emphasis on citywide programs operated out of the central office instead of through neighborhood organizations, was prompted by the need to serve the one third of Boston's poor who are not in poverty target areas but who instead live in small poverty pockets in more affluent parts of the city. This raised a number of fundamental questions on the relative weight to be given to the spokesmen for the organized poor--most of them were concentrated in sizable neighborhoods as compared to the equally needy unorganized poor, most of whom were dispersed throughout the city.

ABCD'S INTERNAL ADMINISTRATION

The recognition of the problem of poverty as a suitable target for large-scale government action was quickly followed by the decision to develop new antipoverty organizations at the federal and local level rather than to use existing agencies as the vehicle for the new program. The latter were not considered suitable mechanisms for a bold, innovative attack on poverty because they were regarded as "careful, dull, unimaginative and bureaucratic" and because they were governed by a narrow professionalism that had "coexisted too comfortably with poverty."[6]

The rapid creation of a sizable federal poverty agency and a host of community poverty agencies engendered a number of difficulties in attracting and retaining adequate staff and in developing suitable administrative structures to operate, supervise, and control rapidly expanding programs involving large numbers of poorly educated and sometimes hostile clients. These inherent difficulties were intensified by the problems of interagency coordination, stresses within the community, and the inadequate knowledge and expertise existing in the field.

In 1965, ABCD experienced particular difficulty in exercising close supervision over the Neighborhood Youth Corps program (the NYC). The "crisis" involved a moderate amount of payroll padding but was greatly exaggerated by the local press, the federal labor department, and OEO; it primarily involved newly hired field staff and amounted to only a tiny fraction of program expenditures. However, ABCD experienced a continuing fall-out from its NYC operation; it included resignations from the ABCD director and a key deputy.[7] Unfavorable publicity regarding NYC in the summer, fall and winter of 1965-66 led to investigations by Federal agencies and the Ford Foundation and to delays in processing ABCD program applications.

Four major administrative and staffing problems confronted the agency in 1965-66:

1. *Lack of strong, continuing leadership to develop a cohesive structure.* ABCD shares with other poverty agencies a laudable desire to avoid excessive administrative rigidity. One result of adopting this loose approach to organization has been operation on an insufficiently integrated interdivisional basis. There is inadequate reporting of divisional activities, poor communication between divisions (The Ford Foundation's supported ABCD program operates on a virtually autonomous basis.) and lack of supervision through the chain of command. In addition, many of the agency's current organizational difficulties can also be attributed to an OEO decision in the late winter of 1965, in response to pressures from civil-rights organizations, not to fund any ABCD programs, including the administrative grant for CAP programs, until the ABCD board was completely reorganized. In effect, this OEO decision resulted in a series of program dislocations as funds were exhausted or withheld. It also prevented the agency from hiring its new upper-echelon CAP staff cadre for a minimum of six months.

For this, among other reasons, CAP staff operated in a crisis atmosphere from the summer of 1965. The problem was compounded by the fact that OEO approved approximately $1.5 million in program funds for ABCD but did not grant concomitant funds for administration and supervision. In fact, OEO did not release sufficient funds for central office accounting and program-auditing operations until April, 1966.

2. *Stresses in personal relations between staff at various levels.* Some staff conflicts have emerged to light in resignations, but others remain to create special problems in communication and supervision. Long hours, the frustrations inherent in being able to cope to only a limited degree with the urgent problems of poverty, inconsistent pressures from federal agencies, conflicts with neighborhood groups, and flare-ups in the press have tended to magnify latent strains in interprofessional relations. Also, much to the dismay of their superiors, some staff members have tended to view themselves as emissaries from the poor to a suspect, alien power--ABCD--rather than as agency employees. Mixed staff loyalties are in some measure related to a tendency apparent throughout the poverty program, the practice of offering executive jobs to community leaders qualified as successful agitators or self-designated spokesmen for the poor. The technique of putting mildly paranoiac, modestly charismatic slum dwellers on the payroll not only did not head off trouble in the neighborhoods but tended to transfer some of the hurly burly of the streets to the poverty agency offices.

3. *Recruitment and staffing problems.* In the poverty programs as a whole, shortages of qualified personnel combined with the temporary nature of poverty assignments has tended to raise salary levels for staff positions[8] without eliminating the problems of attracting and retaining talented people. ABCD salary levels and salary increases, while lower than in some large city poverty agencies, have nevertheless been sufficiently high and have become a target for protesting political and civic representatives.[9] As social work executives can testify, relatively high professional salary levels are often vulnerable to criticism when the clientele is extremely poor. Along the internal, intra-ABCD differences of opinion, the availability of attractive alternative employment offering similar salary levels, less wear and tear on the psyche, and more home life has been a serious factor in draining away the agency's cadre of experienced administrative personnel.[10]

4. *Problems with OEO and other agencies.* Rarely has an agency whose origins were marked by controversy and whose actions and approaches have been seriously questioned received more favorable attention than the Office of Economic Opportunity.

For example, difficulties that have erupted in Job Corps camps and in a number of cities were minimized as "an overblown myth" by Representative Adam Clayton Powell, while criticisms have been muted by repeatedly singling out Operation Headstart for special praise.

The decision to establish an entirely new agency to mount and coordinate the attack on poverty created unusual opportunities and problems. Under the heading of successful exploitation of opportunities, the federal agency was able to select talented staff from other agencies and from outside the government service by offering many challenging jobs in upper-salary levels, including the 16-18 supergrades.[11] Unfortunately, some of these highly creative people have proved to be poor administrators, short of common sense and prone to succumb to untested, sometimes inconsistent fads and theories. A primary cause of the turmoil in the poverty program was the unusual nature of the executives gathered under its banner. OEO for example, seems to attract more than its share of romantic dogmatists who blend a consciousness of moral rectitude with naive Machiavellianism.

Daniel Moynihan, a principal critic as well as a supporter of the program, suggests that the "muddle, trouble and dismay" is caused by the fact that the enterprise has been "flawed from the beginning" by radical differences of understanding within the federal government. He points to four different, partly incompatible definitions of what constituted "community action": the efficiency concept of the Bureau of the Budget, the conflict objective of the Saul Alinsky followers, the Peace Corps provision-of-services concept, and the political-effectiveness principle embraced by the original task force that drafted the program. Each faction is well represented in agency decision-making, sometimes simultaneously, sometimes serially.[12] Moynihan unaccountably overlooked one major faction, the fast-moving, recently promoted careerists who tarried briefly in the agency on their way to positions that offered equally attractive pay scales but fewer risks.

The combination of high motives and pragmatic responses to pressures and opportunities has several consequences. As is often the case with academic, religious, and eleemosynary institutions, the nobility of the objective is used to excuse behavior that would (and sometimes does) shock a ward politician. Criticism tends to be interpreted as the outgrowth of reactionary ideology or lack of understanding. Furthermore, vertical and horizontal loyalties are in short supply; critics are deflected to other members of the agency who fail to share the respondent's intelligence, sensitivity, or motivation. OEO seems unique among Washington agencies in that from mailroom to the upper echelon, the finger of blame is unerringly pointed in some other direction. Given this unwillingness to accept responsibility for mistakes, it is not surprising that selection as a sacrificial victim is a principal source of executive turnover.

THE OFFICE OF ECONOMIC OPPORTUNITY

OEO's administrative problems have multiplied because of constant changes in budgets, political pressures, and concepts. Moreover, the line agencies on whose functions OEO encroached have in some cases given less than their full cooperation. With the help of Congressional and press criticism, agencies such as labor and health, and education and welfare have begun to amputate the more attractive OEO functions, aimed at leaving that hapless organization with vulnerable operations like the Job Corps camps.

The stresses encountered by the Office of Economic Opportunity, some of which are obviously beyond that agency's control, have had a serious impact on local agency operations. From the viewpoint of the ABCD program, OEO-related problems include the following:

1. *Faulty budgetary planning.* OEO's encouragement of local agencies to develop new programs and to expand existing programs backfired on ABCD when the Vietnam escalation sharply curtailed anticipated OEO allocations. It is extremely significant that it is local agencies like ABCD rather than OEO that bore the brunt of community displeasure. While the recalcitrance of Asiatic adversaries was unexpected and OEO must be absolved from censure on this account, the federal agency apparently erred in stimulating local agencies to initiate large numbers of short-term projects that the OEO seems to have failed to annualize in designing its 1966-67 budget. However, some local problems are beyond OEO control. For example, ABCD finds it difficult to engage in long-term programing simply because OEO cannot normally commit funds for more than one year.

2. *Administrative inconsistency.* OEO retains the air of improvisation and experimentation that marked its beginnings. The agency by design is wide open to civil-rights pressures and is under fire from Congress and the press when the programs it has funded explode in demonstrations or financial scandal. It is not surprising that under these conditions the agency has vacillated in policies and commitments.13 OEO executives have sometimes reneged on verbal understandings and have taken evasive action (e.g., holding themselves incommunicado) when an infruiated applicant demands action on overdue promises. Furthermore, partly for federal protective purposes, OEO has increased the burden of paper work on local agencies to awesome proportions.

The catalogue of complaints is unending. Local agencies claim that OEO officials have often displayed reluctance to commit themselves in writing. Poverty agencies charge that senior staff can deliver assurances but not final federal approval on important matters. Regional and lower echelon OEO executives find it difficult or impossible to secure a rapid affirmative from their superiors who are apparently fully endowed with negative powers; poverty agency program requests, applications, and other materials have been frequently and repeatedly returned for revision, often on the basis of verbal rather than written communications.

3. *Regional hurdles.* Local agency irritability regarding the shabby treatment they claim to receive from regional offices of federal agencies is by no means an unusual phenomenon. Nevertheless, the situation respecting the OEO New York regional office seems to present a special constellation of frictions. From ABCD's experience, it appears that some of the trouble is attributable to rapid turnover; in 1965-66 there were seven different regional administrators in the course of a single year, each of whom had a particular view of his responsibilities and of the proper nature and conceptual approach of the program. In addition, OEO liaison procedures between headquarters and regional offices have not yet been perfected; for example, in the period 1965-67, the New York regional office was not always consulted or even informed in advance by Washington with regard to important policy decisions.

4. *OEO's failure as a clearing house.* As part of its responsibilities in the war on poverty, OEO has sponsored considerable research, has collected enormous amounts of data on operations, and has employed consultant firms and individuals to analyze, suggest, and improve its activities. From time to time, some of this research and evaluation is reflected in program revisions, in new regulations and procedures, in a scholarly article, or in a mass media story. Unfortunately, there is little systematic reporting of this field intelligence and research to local agencies. This failure engenders a loss of perspective and raises the danger of unnecessarily duplicating avoidable errors. Moreover, there is a sense of frustration arising from sketchy reporting on the poverty program in the mass media that inevitably focuses on scandals and conflicts. This may have a number of undesirable side effects: Recruiting is made more difficult, other agencies tend to be less cooperative, and local agencies are forced to rely on

casual personal contacts and other less-than-satisfactory sources of information
to find out what is happening to programs in other communities confronted by
similar problems. There is bewilderment when the results of costly program and
research efforts are unavailable. This is particularly the case when the agency director admits to "mistakes, poor judgment, and inefficiency," characterizes a
major community program as "confused if not sometimes chaotic," and forecasts that the war on poverty will "continue to be noisy, visible, dirty, uncomfortable and sometimes politically unpopular."[14] From the local agency standpoint, the testimony of Mr. Shriver was refreshing in its candor, but the chief
difficulty for ABCD and its sister agencies is that many of the abrasions and
contusions resulting from OEO deficiencies occur at the local rather than the
federal level.

5. *Problems with other agencies.* An article on the United States Employment Service (USES), a branch of the U.S. Department of Labor, indicated
one of the reasons for not placing major reliance on old-line agencies in the poverty war. USES officials, without naming names, were reported as castigating
some state employment services for:

> . . . failing to provide specialized counseling to meet the needs
> of unskilled workers, others for failing to coordinate job train-
> ing programs with prospective job openings, and nearly all for
> failing to seek out unschooled job-market rejects who do not
> know where to turn for help.[15]

While these comments on present deficiencies reveal part of the reason
for allocating a secondary role to the Department of Labor in the poverty program, they also point to a source of local agency resentment of federal practices. The state employment agency in Massachusetts has for some time been
attempting to secure additional funds to meet increased program responsibilities (such as the Manpower Development and Training Act program), to assist
in raising salary levels, and to undertake necessary research. Up through 1967,
however, the federal labor agency paralleled OEO practice with local poverty
organizations: Funds requested for research and administration have been denied and Washington has subsequently blamed local agencies for deficiencies
that approval of these requests might have helped to remedy.

ABCD's specific difficulties with the state employment agency include
its inadequate labor market information, particularly on the characteristics of
unemployed and on future occupational needs as well as the tendency of the
employment security agency to act as an employer's service that leaves the
problems of marginally employable labor to the poverty agency.[16]

To a lesser extent, similar frictions exist with other agencies, including
the U.S. Department of Health, Education, and Welfare, and on the local level,
with the Boston Redevelopment Authority (BRA). ABCD was established and
funded in 1961 largely as a consequence of efforts by the BRA administrator
who was convinced that the city needed a social renewal agency to complement

its extensive physical renewal program. The BRA administrator has continued to view ABCD as a useful auxiliary in weakening neighborhood opposition to renewal proposals. However, ABCD quickly discovered that close association with the BRA aroused a storm of protest from ABCD's prospective clientele. The divergence in orientation has never been fully resolved.

ABCD has inherited a legacy of mistrust and hostility. Anger at the operations of the mayor, the BRA, the police department, the school department, the welfare agency, and others find an outlet in ABCD's Community Action Program and a target in its staff. In this sense, ABCD serves as a lightning rod; it absorbs community outrage for the alleged misdeeds of local agencies over which it has no control and with whom cooperative arrangements offer the possibility of only minimal influence over policy and programs.

6. *Improving performance of the funding agencies.* A local agency funded almost entirely by federal sources is in a difficult position in urging reforms. dence of local weakness rather than federal inadequacies. Grass-roots protests serving as a buffer for its federal counterpart. It seems clear that unless federal may be slightly more effective if they are presented by a number of communities, and an areawide or intercity approach may be helpful. Another alternative avenue, calling on local political leaders for assistance, tends to be self-defeating because it represents an open admission of agency incapacity and feebleness. In any event, this approach is likely to meet with scant success because, to an outsider, local complaints seem to concern minor technicalities and minor misunderstandings rather than serving as symptomatic evidence of deep-seated organizational and conceptual problems in the funding agency. Local agencies may achieve more results by concentrating on perfecting internal structure and staff rather than attempting to reform operating practices in federal agencies. Many of ABCD's troubles are the result of unwittingly and perhaps inescapably serving as a buffer for its federal counterpart. It seems clear that unless federal assurances are clearly recognized as possibly transitory reflections of current thinking, a local agency courts danger if it permits itself or its clients to take advanced action based on federal promises that may later be disavowed.

7. *Conflict with neighborhood groups.* Probably the most controversial aspect of the poverty program to date was the decision to seek "maximum feasible participation of the poor" in operating local (but not federal) poverty programs. The vehicle for participation is the Community Action Program. Over and above participation in OEO programs, the objective appears to be to endow the poor with sufficient political power to demand improved services, better treatment, and facilities from city hall.

There has been some criticism of this approach by those who, like Glazer, see merit in the goal of stimulating a "creative disorder" but express doubts that the way to improve the institutions of government and welfare (including the new poverty agencies) "is to finance guerrilla warfare against them."[17] Other critics suggest that the participation of the poor in Community Action

Programs is a deceptive gimmick.[18] In one city, the poverty agency dissolved itself following charges that the poor lacked adequate representation.[19] Similar accusations have been reported in San Francisco, Washington, D.C., Oakland, California, Syracuse, and Boston, among other cities. In New York City, Puerto Ricans have demonstrated to protest against what they believed to be over representation of Negroes in the Bronx board of the city's antipoverty program.[20] Judging from press reports, Boston's difficulties with community groups have been rather mild. Neither demands for immediate dissolution of ABCD nor complete rejection of poverty agency programs (as was the case in San Francisco)[21] has been seriously advocated by Boston neighborhood poverty organizations.

To a great extent, the poverty revolt in central cities is closely linked to the civil rights struggle of the Negro and to the fact that the leadership and much of the membership is often identical or overlapping. The bitterness and depth of both battles was neither expected nor perhaps predictable. The poverty program--like the 1966-68 outbreaks of racial violence--revealed the existence of a latent, apparently bottomless, reservoir of Negro ill will to the white power structure, including the mayor, the police, the schools, the welfare, employment, and redevelopment agencies, and employers.

Strained relations with Negro areas and problems of mediating between groups representing the Negro and white poor are central issues in ABCD as with other city poverty agencies. As compared to most white leaders, Negro neighborhood poverty leaders tend to be younger and more militant, and partly for this reason, the Negro sections of Boston, which contain a quarter of the city's poor, received almost half the total ABCD-CAP program funds in 1965-66. The revision of neighborhood percentage allocations prepared by the ABCD staff in the late winter of 1965-66 reflected the recognition that there were more white poor than Negro poor in Boston.

It would be a mistake, however, to view the neighborhood problems confronting ABCD solely as a racial conflict. The Negro community is internally divided between more militant and less militant factions[22] just as white power groups and leaders are often in basic disagreement on class lines and on specific issues. The white poor, too, are sometimes opposed to local poverty agencies. In the spring of 1967, a bitter dispute erupted in East Boston's largely Italo-American section between rival factions in the Area Planning Action Council (APAC); the group that lost ABCD recognition demanded OEO intervention in its favor, including sanctions against ABCD. ABCD's difficulties with the Italo-American North End target area offers another example. While the area's opposition to ABCD in early 1966 was engendered by the agency's decision to cut back previously promised Boston poverty funds, other problems, particularly the threat of large-scale urban renewal, created an attitude of suspicion and animosity.[23]

A number of issues are raised by OEO's insistence on "broadly based" organizations that included provision of "meaningful opportunities to protest or to propose additions to or changes in the ways in which a community action program is being planned or undertaken."24 In most cities, including Boston, OEO interpreted this provision as a mandatory requirement that CAP programs be approved by local neighborhood councils. Among its side effects, this insistence resulted in a delay of more than a year in launching ABCD's manpower-oriented Work Horizons Program since the neighborhood councils which were to review this program had not yet been established. Five months elapsed before this structural event took place and almost another year before the councils agreed to approve a revised version of Work Horizons. By that time, the expansion of the conflict in Vietnam had reduced the amount initially requested by ABCD and approved by OEO by almost two thirds.

It is clear that one of the difficulties in implementing programs subject to the community veto is the lack of technical experts among the poor, particularly the Negroes. Most of the recent experience (and successes) of the Negro leadership has been won in the civil-rights arena, where a straightforward, vigorous militancy has helped to redress a number of long-standing grievances. However, Negroes, like most of the poor, are less well equipped to cope with the complexities, alternative choices, staffing, and technical problems involved in administering a broad range of poverty programs. Negro suspicions of white and Negro agency staff (suspected Uncle Toms) have contributed to delays in the Boston poverty program, although, as indicated, the situation is far less serious in Boston than in many other cities.

Another difficulty is the tendency for APAC neighborhood action organizations to attempt to operate as autonomous agencies. The APACs lack sufficient technical staff and are dependent on funding through ABCD. APACs have demonstrated an understandable desire to secure a maximum amount of ABCD allocations with a minimum of ABCD supervision. In part, this problem has arisen because many representatives of the poor are not yet fully aware of the limitations of OEO and its local counterparts. Some do not yet realize that the agency cannot (1) solve all of the problems of poverty, (2) dictate policy to city or federal agencies, (3) replace the school or welfare systems, or (4) secure a blank check to finance all of the programs that ABCD and/or local groups believe are desirable.

Two other issues bedevil neighborhood relations. The first involves the question of representativeness. In most cities, less than 10 per cent of eligible poor voters have turned out in poverty council elections, and recently OEO has decided to cease financing them.25 OEO has steadily increased the proportion of "non-poor" eligible to act as neighborhood representatives; Boston now requires only that a simple majority of the APAC representatives be low-income residents of the area.26

Another issue involved the choice of technical staff to operate the program. To some extent, patronage factors are at stake since the poverty agency offers a number of jobs that pay high salaries by local standards. There is also a symbolic and actual struggle for power in the choice of key staff and in establishing lines of responsibility. Some ethnic and racial leaders in Boston, as elsewhere, have strongly urged the appointment of a maximum number of executives drawn from their group, not only to fill vacancies at the neighborhood level but also in the central office of ABCD. The war on poverty offers a substantial number of prestigious, visible, high paying, instant executive jobs that can be filled by individuals with limited qualifications. In a sense, this practice places the poverty effort in the mainstream of the historic, American political tradition.

In part, this orientation reflects the concept that the poor have developed a subculture that cannot be fully understood by outsiders. This point of view is strongly attacked in a report on a project involving Negro families in Washington, D.C. The Negro poor, the report indicates, may be ungrammatical but are fully capable of communicating with any social scientist who is willing to set aside his professional jargon.[27]

Following the separate culture theme, some suggest that native interpreters in a leadership capacity are needed to bridge the gap between the minority group and the outside world. Again, this is not solely a Negro view. Hiring of a person fluent in the Tuscan dialect and of obvious Italo-American extraction was suggested by the North End neighborhood poverty group. Moreover, most nationalities have traditionally insisted on recognition in political offices and jobs, a pattern that is reflected in the "balanced tickets" usually presented to the electorate by both parties in multiethnic areas.

In Boston, as elsewhere, demands for job patronage have long been associated with the early stages of immigrant acclimatization to an urban, democratic society. Anthony Lewis has hypothesized that "the immigrant era seems closer here than in other states, and voters more consciously think of themselves as members of a racial bloc that must watch out for its own."[28]

The orientation of the immigrant was fundamentally pragmatic, geared to food purchases and rent payments rather than to abstract concepts of efficiency. As the newest urban migrants, Negroes can be expected to share a point of view that reaches well back into Massachusetts history. Richard M. Abrams suggests that by 1912, the end of the "Progressive Era,"

The overarching cause to which the progressive movement was dedicated--the effort to maintain standards of social behavior which focused on a "larger community view" and which transcended "bread and butter objectives"--had failed in Massachusetts. . . . From his (the immigrant's) viewpoint, the leaders of his adopted land too often served up . . . principles as substitutes for enlightened social policy. . . . This seemed as true for the reformers as for the old guard conservatives. . . . Under the circumstances perhaps it *required* short-sighted, parochial, bread and butter efforts to obtain relief from conditions for which no particular malfeasance could be blamed.[29]

The poverty agency is torn between OEO's desire to assign a maximum number of poverty staff positions to the poor and OEO's simultaneous requirement that ABCD continue to meet high quality standards of efficiency and responsibility. The danger is that the agency will be badly hurt in a damaging crossfire between the "middle class" and "immigrant" standards concurrently imposed by its principal funding agency.

A constant maneuvering for control of the poverty effort has been an outstanding characteristic of the neighborhood councils that are dominated by various ethnic groups. For example, a series of year-end reports submitted by staff to the director of the Community Action Program[30] identified the following areas of contention in the organization stage: (1) Whether community organizers should report to the CAP executive director or the neighborhood program directors, (2) The degree of priority or exclusivity to be given to neighborhood residents in filling neighborhood staff positions, (3) The extent to which ABCD's central office can allocate funds without neighborhood approval, (4) The extent to which ABCD could choose or disqualify one or more local choices for contenders for central staff or neighborhood positions, and (5) The degree of latitude that ABCD has in choosing between competing groups which claim to represent neighborhood interests.

Subsequent discussion in February, 1966, revolved around the amount of money to be allocated to each area and the choice of programs to be funded. Most of these controversies had been settled by June through a compromise that gave substantial weight to the opinions of the leaders but that reserved overall control to the central office.

To an outside observer, it appears that ABCD's relations with community groups, while frequently strained, can by no means be characterized as bitterly abrasive; the Boston pattern is far from the paralysis and civil war that prevails in other cities. It has been a painfully slow task, marked by setbacks but ABCD has achieved considerable success in working with local leadership. The approval of the revised and scaled-down manpower program and neighborhood acceptance of the proposed, diminished program for target areas is a repayment on the staff's major investment of time and unpaid overtime in working with neighborhood leaders.

Despite encouraging progress, further frictions in community relations are inevitable; the allocation of limited funds, ABCD's close links to the mayor and city agencies, and setbacks in school integration or employment can all cause serious trouble in the future. Nevertheless, there are also moderately encouraging auguries; many neighborhood leaders have advanced beyond the stage of simple opposition and are grappling effectively with program responsibilities and choices. Younger leaders are being developed and the fear and distrust of professionals is diminishing. While it is far too soon to prophesy, it now appears that ABCD's community relations may avoid the no-quarter conflicts which have beset community action programs elsewhere in the nation.

INADEQUATE STATE OF THE ART

The catalogue of complications and troubles that confront ABCD and the federal poverty agency would be far briefer and much less grim were it not for the fact that the problem of poverty is so complex. If false starts, foundering, inconsistencies, and administrative confusion characterize the program, those deficiencies reflect in part the inadequacies in the state of the art. When the program was launched, many people were certain that they possessed the keys to eliminating poverty. After only two years of experience with the Economic Opportunity Act, there seemed to be less certainty of definitive solutions, more humility, a greater recognition of the fundamental gaps in knowledge and ignorance in social engineering.

If the program has done nothing else, it has succeeded in focusing attention on a neglected topic. In the past few years, a number of publications have appeared, some polemic, some scholarly, but most in agreement that the poverty problem is substantial and complex, that much of it is difficult to solve, and that more effective government intervention is needed. There are critics who maintain that the situation of many of the poor (viz., Negroes and Appalachian whites) is akin to that of foreign immigrants at the turn of the century and that, given time, perhaps a generation or two, both groups will work their own passage into the middle class in the same manner as their immigrant slum-area predecessors.[31] This is a minority view; most observers feel that the poor of the 1960's constitute a specially intractable problem debarred by age, by family disruption, and often by color from sharing fully in the affluence of a society increasingly oriented toward advanced education and specialized skills.

One major issue concerns definitions. Who *are* the poor? The $3,000 per family standard is obviously a weak yardstick. An income sufficient for a three-person family will fall far short of the money needed by the six- or eight-person family.[32] To get around this difficulty, it has been suggested that per-capita figures be used instead, $600-$800 per person, for example. However, there have been basic attacks on the allegedly low level at which the poverty line has been pegged. Some have suggested use of Bureau of Labor Statistics (BLS) on the city worker's family budget that in most areas is above $6,000. Using the BLS formula, the per capita figure might rise to almost $1,600.[33]

It has been estimated that Negroes, who comprise about a tenth of the U.S. population (and Boston), represent a fifth of the total number of persons in poverty.[34]

What Causes Poverty?

The literature on the poverty program has identified most of the reasons for poverty: the vicious circle of broken and/or culturally impoverished families, inadequate education of the young, early marriage, blighted prospects in slum areas. Other scholars add automation, the fundamental weakness of the Negro family,[35] and racial discrimination in employment. Also frequently cited as causative factors are the deprived culture of urban and rural slums and mining hamlets, the cultural shock of migration to urban areas, and the technological changes that have reduced the need for unskilled labor and hence limited employment opportunities for the poor in the 1960's as compared to earlier decades.

Other, subtler arguments are sometimes advanced suggesting that the "work-hard-and-sacrifice-for-the-children" characteristic of earlier generations of Americans has weakened under the enervating influence of a consumption-focused, affluent society. It has also been suggested that the poor now want the fruits of affluence without the grinding labor and hardship experienced by earlier generations of slum residents who, with less government assistance, succeeded in moving from the poverty level to the middle- and upper-income strata. Still others point to what they see as a major defect in the current approach to poverty, the emphasis on youth and employment, and recommended more attention instead of beefing up welfare grants for the old and the deprived children[36] along with federal higher minimum-wage legislation.

ABCD and other local poverty agencies are now engaged in a spectrum of programs predicated on various assumptions regarding the causes and hence the solutions to poverty. The past emphasis on education and social services and the coming stress on job development indicate an alteration in these assumptions. However, field experience is not necessarily the only guide to the future; the relative lack of popularity of family counseling, for example, as compared to Headstart may indicate a temporary lag or cultural resistance to a vital program.

How to Measure the Impact of Agency Programs?

At their inception, each of the major social advances in 1966 ran into allegations that they were unnecessary, that the problem was exaggerated, and, in any case, that the overall progress of the national economy would suffice for their solution. In the case of the poverty effort, opponents added the charge that existing mechanisms rather than an entirely new program offered the most effective vehicle for getting the job done. This viewpoint is shared by many who are repelled by administrative disorder. The problem of program evaluation is complicated by the difficulty of undertaking research that requires the retention of uncontaminated control groups in sensitive social areas where deprivation of a segment of the poor may be good science but callous, suicidal politics. There are ways around this obstacle as, for example, comparisons between Headstart programs in different schools and communities. However, translating an uneasy awareness that all is not well into an effective, evaluative research effort that has a genuine feedback on programs is extremely rare among operating bureaucracies.[37]

The results of the commitment of $4 billion over three years were not fully discernible. As a penetrating study suggested, the impact of Headstart will not be measurable for some time to come because: "The senior members of this group have not yet passed their eighth birthday."[38] Some programs can be evaluated, however, and Sar A. Levitan indicates, for example, that although: "Literally it took an act of Congress for the Job Corps to develop the data which have turned out to be quite favorable for the program."[39] Sadly, however, Levitan concludes that OEO experience reveals "the difficulty of designing and administering mass projects which lead to the economic self-sufficiency of the poor."[40] It is not surprising, therefore, that much of the antipoverty funds has been expended on traditional relief measures to meet age-old problems.

It is evident that the creation of a new poverty administrative structure has had beneficial effects in focusing the attention of established line agencies on their unfinished business and neglected clientele. For example, the impending reform in Department of Labor employment service operations undoubtedly owes much to the stimulus of the poverty program.

The Department of Labor, the Department of Health, Education, and Welfare, and other established agencies have developed a feedback and evaluative mechanism that, if imperfect, still permits a relatively orderly revision of structure and operations. Over and above its consultant evaluation efforts, in 1967, OEO vigorously promoted the adoption and installation of PPBS within the central agency and at the local level. The success of this effort depends on the skills and sophistication of poverty executives. The era of administrative consolidation that usually follows hard on the heels of the initial period of innovation is just beginning in the poverty program. It may even have arrived too late to save the parent agency.

CONCLUSION

As compared to other cities, the Boston poverty agency is in reasonably good condition. It has weathered storms that have sent some agencies to the scrap heap and left others floundering. Unfortunately, in some cases a shortage of executive talent, created in part by the heavy attrition that seems to be an inescapable component of the poverty program, has hindered the process of adaptation to new complexities and circumstances. One cause of the executive casualty rate is the growing power of the client groups at the expense of the professionals, a tendency that is observable in urban renewal, model cities, welfare, civil rights, education, and other programs. The poverty agencies seem to be prime targets for Black Power militancy, a movement which may lead to the carving out of new Negro-run cities from the Black ghettos.

Many unanswered questions involve the leadership potential of the poor, a vital concern since their participation became an important element in CAP. In this respect, the auguries in Boston are not unfavorable. Occasional factionalism, initial suspicion, and hostility have been more than counterbalanced by encouraging signs of progress. Since 1965, the agency has benefited from the increasing capacity of community representatives (not all of them poor) to come to grips with difficult programs and choices, to work closely with professionals, and to contribute useful criticism of professional approaches and suggestions. This does not mean that all is serene or that the prognosis for community agency relations is rosy, but it does appear that all sides in Boston have thus far acted more rationally and constructively than has been the case in some other cities.

The outlook for antipoverty executives is less favorable. As the resignation of the second ABCD Executive Director in May, 1968, suggests, they will continue to be war casualties. The Director's parting comment after two years of service may serve as an epitaph for the fallen: "In the past month or so, I have been asking friends what's available for me--a guy aged fifty-one and beat up."[41]

Judging from the pervasive gloom in OEO and local poverty agencies during 1967-68, it can be predicted that Black Power and other conflicting, relentless pressures will continue to generate a high rate of executive resignations and replacements in OEO, its regional offices, and local poverty operations.[42] In fact there is a good chance that OEO will be dismembered,[43] its functions distributed among other federal agencies after appropriate, and on the whole, accurate eulogies.

NOTES TO CHAPTER 4

1. Scott Greer, *Urban Renewal and American Cities: The Dilemma of Democratic Intervention* (Indianapolis: Bobbs-Merrill, 1965), pp. 11-12.

2. Thomas Pynchon, "A Journey Into the Mind of Watts," *The New York Times Magazine*, June 23, 1966, p. 80.

3. John Kifner, *The New York Times*, June 14, 1966. New York City in September, 1966, announced a sweeping reorganization of its poverty program as part of a new human resources administration. This was subsequently

followed by the resignation of the new agency director in favor of a position with the Ford Foundation.

4. In the 1950's, the city of Boston embarked on a massive urban redevelopment program that entailed considerable dislocation and hardship for residents of low-income areas. The election of Mayor John Collins in 1961 marked the beginning of an enlarged renewal effort that included major attention to the low-income residential areas of Roxbury, North Dorchester, the South End, and Charlestown. Concerned with the human problems associated with urban renewal, under the leadership of the city administration, local civic leaders created an autonomous poverty organization in the city in 1961, almost three years before the passage of federal war-on-poverty legislation. In mid-1962, the organization was incorporated and given the name, Action for Boston Community Development--a charitable, tax-exempt corporation. Large-scale operations were initiated in late 1962 when a $1.9 million grant was made available by the Ford Foundation.

5. ABCD staff recommended a major increase for community organization and program development over fiscal 1965 and allocations for manpower programs. These were to rise from a quarter of the CAP total to almost a half. See Action for Boston Community Development *Staff Memoranda* (Boston, February, 1966). In part, this shift was made possible by the availability of education funds from the Office of Education. ESEA was passed in 1965.

6. Nathan Glazer, "The Grand Design of the Poverty Program," *The New York Times Magazine,* February 27, 1966, p. 69.

7. This was not the agency's first major personnel crisis. In 1964, disputes over the administration and orientation of the agency, particularly the degree of independence to be accorded to research staff, led to resignations by several professionals.

8. Because poverty agencies offer extremely long workweeks, continual administrative turmoil, no tenure, and few fringe benefits, the high salaries are partly an optical illusion. However, these unfavorable working conditions have not diminished widespread envy and criticism of ABCD staff.

9. OEO has attempted to answer some of this criticism by limiting the maximum salary increase which can be offered to new recruits to $2,500 or 20 per cent of their previous salary, "whichever is smaller," according to: Office of Economic Opportunity, "Personnel Policies and Procedures," Memorandum No. 23 (Washington, D.C.: U.S. Government Printing Office, March 3, 1966). After much discussion, Congress set a limit of $15,000 on agency executive salaries; however, amounts in excess of $15,000 can be provided from nonfederal sources.

10. Approximately 30 of the nearly 60 professional and consulting staff employed by ABCD in August, 1964, were no longer with ABCD in March, 1966. See Action for Boston Community Development, *A Report on ABCD Activities,* "ABCD Staff and Consultants" (Boston, September, 1963--August, 1964), Appendix E: p. x. By early 1968, few of the original cadre remained.

11. In the flurry of charges and countercharges surrounding the approval of 1966 poverty legislation, it was discovered that OEO not only had the highest proportion of supergrade executives of any Washington agency--jobs paying over $20,000--but that roughly a third of these positions were unfilled. There has been a steady attrition of OEO staff as a result of internal frictions, disputes with Congress, and the siren call of alternative employment. The 1966 poverty program amendments provided that no supergrade positions in OEO headquarters and its seven regional offices could be created or filled for the rest of the fiscal year. *Congressional Quarterly Weekly Report,* October 21, 1966, p. 2562.

12. Daniel P. Moynihan, *The Public Interest,* V (Fall, 1966), pp. 4-7.

13. For example, in total contradiction to the past policy of working through the poor and the poverty agencies, in March, 1966, OEO adopted a "checkpoint procedure" which required CAP programs to be approved by mayors and relevant agencies. Although these approvals are not necessarily binding on OEO, it is probable that the procedure will engender additional delays and resistance at the local level, leaving the CAP agencies in the middle, between the impatient poor and the existing power structure. U.S., Office of Economic Opportunity, Community Action Program, "Strengthening and Checkpoint Procedure," Memorandum No. 28 (Washington, D.C.: U.S. Government Printing Office, March 25, 1966).

To cite another recent example, in response to mayoral complaints, OEO prepared and distributed a "secret list" of fifteen cities and counties where local officials were granted veto powers over poverty projects to seven regional offices. As a result of Congressional pressure, the list was made public. Boston is not among the fifteen (*The New York Times,* March 25, 1966). However, OEO officials in Washington were quoted in *The Times'* story as conceding that "it was conceivable local officials in hundreds of other communities might seek and might receive veto power now that the directive had been publicized."

14. *The Christian Science Monitor,* March 10, 1966, p. 10.

15. *The Wall Street Journal,* March 7, 1966, p. 1.

16. It was partly as a result of USES failures that Secretary of Labor Wirtz suggested "an inventory of the poor be compiled" and that existing manpower-training programs should be redirected by increasing on-the-job training

in apprenticeship programs and basic training, "to meet the needs of the wholly unprepared, hard-core unemployed." *Congressional Quarterly Weekly Report, op. cit.,* March 18, 1966, p. 603.

17. Glazer, *op. cit.*

18. *The Christian Science Monitor,* March 8, 1966, p. 1. The story refers to the poverty program in Los Angeles, where, as in other cities, local poverty groups want more control over CAP programs.

19. *The New York Times,* February 10, 1966, p. 39. The story refers to Kansas City. Wisconsin reported even more serious difficulties involving the representation issue, but more important, widespread apathy even toward the nationally popular Headstart program. Projects in Milwaukee "were blocked by the regional director of the Office of Economic Opportunity in Chicago because he said the poor were not sufficiently involved." *Ibid.,* January 23, 1966, p. 42.

20. *Ibid.,* February 2, 1968, p. 14. A staff member was quoted to the effect that "this agency has always been in chaos but now the power plays and the rumors and the sense of drift are the worst they've ever been."

21. *Ibid.,* January 16, 1966. On March 13, 1966, p. 72, *The New York Times* reported that in San Francisco "ghetto leaders who wrested control of the local anti-poverty program from City Hall six months ago are still struggling to put the program into effect. [The neighborhood poverty organization] accepted five city-wide projects and rejected nine." This score was surpassed in Kansas City, where the rejection rate was 13 out of 13.

22. *Ibid.,* March 6, 1966, p. 69, reported on an internecine struggle in East Harlem involving two rival local poverty groups, a tenants' council and another agency. The latter was accused by its opponent of representing established social-work agencies, a charge which it strongly denied, contending that its program has instead reflected the influence of the poor in its planning.

23. Much of the resentment and fear of the Boston Redevelopment Authority (BRA) is traceable to the massive total clearance of Boston's old West End. Over 3,000 low rent dwelling units were removed in this Italo-American area and subsequently replaced by an unattractive luxury apartment development. The BRA inherited the ill will engendered by the West End project which had been initiated by its predecessor agency. Despite frequent protestations that the days of large-scale clearance are over and that the program has been redirected toward rehabilitation and conservation, residents of a number of Boston renewal areas (which are also poverty target areas) have been thoroughly sensitized to potential threats from the public agency bulldozer. For example, Jane Jacobs' allegation that the North End (also occupied by Italo-Americans) was slated for treatment similar to the West End (see her

The Death and Life of Great American Cities, Random House, 1961, especially pp. 8-11), has helped to inflame neighborhood suspicions in that area.
ABCD has also inherited some of the spillover from the renewal conflicts that
have simmered or exploded in other areas, particularly in the South End
(Negro) and Charlestown (predominantly Irish).

24. U.S., Office of Economic Opportunity, *Community Action Program
Guide,* "Part B, Eligibility of Applicant" (Washington, February, 1965), par. 5.

25. In his testimony before the House Education and Labor Committee,
Sargent Shriver said "he was disposed to stop financing the election of representatives of the poor to community action boards. He stressed there were
small turnouts of eligible voters in most cities where elections had been held"
including a 1 per cent turnout in Los Angeles, according to *The New York
Times,* March 9, 1966, p. 24.

26. Action for Boston Community Development, *Community Action
Program 7-30* (Boston, November 10, 1965), p. 3.

27. Hylan Lewis, *Poverty's Children* (Washington, D.C.:   Cross-Tell
[Communicating Research on the Urban Poor], Health and Welfare Council,
National Capital Area, 1966).

28. Anthony Lewis, in the last of a series of articles on Massachusetts, in
The New York Times, June 21, 1961, p. 47.

29. Richard M. Abrams, *Conservatism in a Progressive Era: Massachusetts Politics, 1900-1912* (Cambridge, Mass.:   Harvard University Press, 1964),
p. 292.

30. Community Action Program, *Staff reports,* Parker Hill-Fenway,
Charlestown, Columbia Point, Roxbury--North Dorchester, South Boston,
North End, East Boston, and Jamaica Plain target areas, submitted to Robert
Coard, Director, CAP-ABCD, December 1964--January 1966.

31. For an eloquent exposition of this viewpoint, see Irving Kristol
"The Negro Today is Like the Immigrant Yesterday," *The New York Times
Magazine,* September 11, 1966, pp. 50-1.

32. See Molly Orshansky, "Who's Who Among the Poor: A Demographic View of Poverty," *Social Security Bulletin* (July, 1965), pp. 3-32. The
median size for families below the poverty line is 4.0 persons compared to only
3.6 persons for families in the nonpoor category.

33. In 1959, it was estimated that $6,300 was needed to provide a
four-person family (husband, wife, and two children under eighteen) with a
"modest but adequate" level of living. The Boston Regional CAP Directors'

Association requested the U.S. Department of Labor to relax its criteria for Neighborhood Youth Corps enrollee families upward from the 1965 levels of $3,150 for a family of four to a maximum of $5,090 for a family of seven or more, roughly $700 per person. This is slightly higher than OEO's maximum of $4,685 for a family of seven. *Congressional Quarterly Weekly Report,* XXIV, 14 (April 8, 1966), p. 755; *The Commonwealth Service Corps News,* II, 2 (March, 1966), p. 2.

As defined by the Bureau of Labor Statistics, the city worker's family used as the basis of this estimate consists of four persons who live in a rented dwelling, and the wife is not employed outside the home; U.S., Bureau of the Census, *Statistical Abstract of the United States,* 1965, Table No. 499, p. 364.

34. The exact proportion is a matter of some uncertainty. Using 1959 census data, Herman P. Miller estimated that Negroes accounted for about one-fifth of the poor; see his "The Dimensions of Poverty," in *Poverty as a Public Issue* edited by Ben B. Seligman (Glencoe, Ill. The Free Press, 1965), p. 29. Miller suggests that "poverty in its truest sense is more than mere want; it is want mixed with a lack of aspiration (i.e., hope for themselves and their children)" (p. 27).

35. See Daniel P. Moynihan, *The Negro Family,* U.S. Department of Labor, 1965. Bayard Rustin differs with Moynihan's analysis, contending that many of the pathological symptoms exhibited by Negro families are the consequence of unemployment and low income rather than a special racial history. He cites evidence indicating that during the Great Depression, white families displayed similar symptoms of disorder; "The Watts 'Manifesto' and the McCone Report," *Commentary,* XLI (March, 1966), 33. Another dissent to Moynihan's thesis is found in Hylan Lewis, *Poverty's Children, op. cit.,* pp. 40-42. This study of low-income families funded by the National Institute of Mental Health indicates a wide variety of objectives and life styles among poor families, suggests that artificial groupings in neighborhood councils may "lead to built-in frustration," and recommends strong concentration on viable families who can be "saved at less cost to the community."

36. Alvin L. Shorr, "Program for the Social Orphans," *The New York Times Magazine,* March 13, 1966. Shorr estimates the total number of children living in poverty at 7-10 million and suggests that one in nine children lives in a broken home or in an institution. To meet this special problem, Shorr recommends increased coverage and allowances in the Federal Aid for Dependant Children program and introduction of a family allowance system based on the Canadian and European model.

37. For a useful discussion of this problem, see Peter Rossi, "Evaluating Social Action Programs," *Trans-Action,* June, 1967.

38. Sar A. Levitan, *Antipoverty Work and Training Efforts: Goals and Reality* (Washington, D.C.: Joint Publication of the Institute of Labor and Industrial Relations and the National Manpower Policy Task Force, August, 1967), p. 1.

39. *Ibid.,* p. 4.

40. *Ibid.,* p. 109.

41. *The Boston Globe,* May 22, 1968, p. 8.

42. A continual trickle of poverty agency firings and resignations is reported in the press. In early 1968, OEO, responding "to pressures from influential whites in rural Georgia" threatened to withhold federal funds unless the antipoverty agency headquarters in Athens discharged its executive director and other workers; *The New York Times,* January 13, 1968, p. 24.

43. A 1965 Presidential task force recommended spinning off most OEO functions to other agencies. In 1966, Congress transferred four OEO programs and reportedly has its eye on the popular Headstart program that was to be transferred to the Office of Education. Mr. Shriver was quoted as remaining philosophical: "When you're in the front tank in a war like this you're bound to get hit once in a while." *The New York Times,* November 6, 1966, p. 6E. To the surprise of many, OEO was in full operation, albeit in a battered condition, in early 1968. It has been suggested that its survival is related to the 1967 summer riots in Negro ghettos since OEO is regarded by some as a riot preventative.

CHAPTER **5** THE PERILS
OF
PROJECTIONS

INTRODUCTION: PROJECTING FOR FUN AND PROFIT

For many of the same reasons that astrology, palmistry, and gypsy tea-rooms retain their popularity, peering into the future with the help of modern planning techniques enjoys great popularity. An examination of some of the pitfalls in the projection business suggests that less time and effort should be devoted to this pastime. Such an approach implies lesser expenditures on fewer expensive and elaborate projections, and more humility entails less chance of erroneous clairvoyancy.

One of the more enjoyable aspects of the planning profession is the art and alleged science of preparing projections for municipalities, metropolitan areas, states, and large regions. Unlike the case in other professions, errors are apparently no bar to a planner's advancement. Although his projections may seldom be even within close range of the target and occasionally are wildly inaccurate, the planner has mastered the indispensable skill of escaping the odium for mistaken forecasts. In fact, the exposure of past errors offers a useful opportunity for learned post mortems. These excuse the departure of predictions from subsequent reality by carefully pointing out that a variety of unpredicted (and hence unpredictable) events were responsible for greater-than-anticipated deviations. Further, it is made clear that truer prophets were either extraordinarily lucky or were culpable of similar inaccuracies which, fortunately for them, had more beneficial results on their overall projection.

Also, planners change jobs frequently, and the passage of time and substantial physical distance effaces the consequences of wrong forecasts. Like doctors, planners bury their mistakes, although they use file cabinets rather than coffins to inter the remains. More often than not, time is an ally of the blunderer because new problems of such magnitude emerge in the forecast period that such gaffes are obliterated as (to cite one notable example), a 50-million or 100-million person underestimate in national population projections.

As if all this were not sufficient to obscure one's errors, planning forecasts are, at best, a nine days' wonder. Most reports, along with the projections they contain, are either unread or quickly forgotten. Finally, there are certain professional standards that tend to protect the luckless and incompetent. To return to the medical analogy, a mistake that has proved fatal to the patient is not necessarily harmful to the late patient's physician. In the planning world, a colleague is always available to point out that planning is not a product but a process, involving many unforeseen variables and requiring highly trained talent to review and revise the rather numerous errors that time and new research have uncovered in last year's expensive master plan. As in Vietnam, the battle cry after each debacle seems to be requests for more money and more staff.

The preparation of advanced, modern planning projections is by no means an inexpensive undertaking. There is, therefore, ample cause for disenchantment when, more often than not, the efforts and funds expended in developing planning projections for such purposes as economic development, population growth, and transportation prove to be a poor guide for subsequent events. But expense is partly an illusion. Large federal subsidies are available to finance the projection business. Hence, it is not uncommon to find small communities spending a disproportionately large amount for projections of various sorts, even though the forecasts bear little relationship to any economic or financial or social ventures or expenditures. At any level of government, there is often no discernible relationship between elaborate projections and decisions. Close inspection usually reveals that action is based on an intuitive judgment linked to a few rough calculations scribbled on a sheet of foolscap. Subsequent projection operations that may be conducted are more in the nature of ex post facto justification than guides for future action. In short, the vast sums expended on elaborate forecasts tend to serve as retroactive rationalizations for decisions that have already been made. Highway construction is an excellent case in point. The fancy and extraordinarily costly computer-based projections that were generated in the area of transportation studies in the early 1960's have rarely served any purpose other than to secure the planner's imprimatur for the existing plans of the highway agencies.

Most of the massive capital improvement programs in cities, metropolitan areas, and states are based principally on immediately foreseeable departmental requirements and some rough measure of future needs. These simpleminded estimates of medium- and long-range needs have two advantages: They are unpretentious and inexpensive. The fact that departmental operations are not linked to the long-term planning projections is by no means surprising. There is an understandable suspicion that the fancy projections are not much better than the horseback estimates prepared by an experienced administration.

Projections do not necessarily have to be statistical in nature. Dennis O'Harrow, former Director of the American Society of Planning Officials, took just as gloomy a view of one type of projection, the regional land-use plan. The land-use forecast and development alternatives differ from the economic or population projection by being prepared with colored pencils and being presented on a map, or, more accurately, three to five maps.

A favorite indoor sport of metropolitan planning staffs is the preparation of comprehensive regional planning alternatives. Which means constructing from three to a dozen maps on which

> are shown ingenious--or ingenuous--arrangements of residential,
> commercial and industrial land patterns, parks, greenbelts, new
> towns, urban corridors, nuclei, all laced together by hypotheti-
> cal rapid transit lines that will probably never be built.
>
> The alternatives are tested by picking great quantities of
> numbers off the maps and pushing them through a mysterious
> formula in a computer, and then further testing by exposing the
> maps to public scrutiny. . . .
>
> So long as planning for urban regions continues as it is
> now practiced, this fatuous exercise in public participation will
> continue.[1]

There seems to be no close correlation between the possibility of errors
creeping into long-term as compared to shorter-term projections. However, it is
noteworthy that demands for periodic revision and updating seem to have accelerated after disillusionment with the long-range forecasts prepared during the
1930's. During this first broad surge of interest in areawide planning in the
1930's and 1940's, preparation of a single forecast series for planning and programing periods covering 20 and even 30 years were not uncommon. The quick-
ening pace of events in the 1940's seems to have shortened the time perspective
in planning projections. Following World War II, in the late 1940's and early
1950's, the commonly accepted planning period for most area planning studies
was a slightly more realistic 20 years, usually rounded off to the nearest five-
year period for convenience.

Two further advances in projection technique became popular during
the 1950's. In many planning projects, it became the practice to identify short-
term and long-term planning goals rather than to select a single long-term goal,
as had been the practice in the past. The use of alternatives also allows a little
more room for maneuver as circumstances change. This technique was also useful in raising the important matter of priorities that had frequently been overlooked or neglected in long-range planning projects. High-priority items could
be accorded some urgency by being grouped among short-term goals.

A second important innovation of the 1950's was the step projection.
Using this technique, projections are made for a long-term period as in the past,
but interim, shorter-period projections are also prepared as part of the study.
These intervals help to establish priorities and also provide a basis for checking
the progress of a plan or program and for gauging the accuracy of its forecasts.

The transportation studies that were conducted in the 1960's to satisfy
the requirements of the Federal Aid Highway Act of 1962 have incorporated
another principle of long-range planning. There is an attempt to design data collection and analysis operations in order to facilitate updating in future years. In
actual practice, these innovations were perhaps less useful than advertised. Step
projections have been prepared on more than one occasion merely by taking
the appropriate value from the long-term projection rather than by preparing

genuine intermediate forecasts. Moreover, technicians often found that there
were so many unknowns and assumptions piled on assumptions within a planning program that their projections were rendered almost meaningless. Thus,
paradoxically, while it was believed perfectly feasible to make long-range projections, the intermediate step projections were in many cases considered less
realistic than the projection that looked twenty, thirty, or forty years ahead.
Thus, the step-projection technique tended to underscore rather than eliminate
the need for constant review and updating. As a result, in the 1960's, efforts
were concentrated on study designs that would facilitate updating with a minimum of expense, on the premise that the projections would need a thorough
overhauling almost as soon as they were published. One observer, Edward C.
Banfield, suggested:

> Change occurs so rapidly in our society that it seldom makes
> sense to try to look ahead more than five years. The importance
> of technological change is obvious . . . but changes in consumer
> tastes and public opinion occur just as fast and may be even
> more important. (Who even five years ago predicted the civil
> rights revolution?) It is impossible to provide now for the future
> as people will want it 10, 20 or 30 years from now if we have no
> way of knowing what they will want.[2]

Subsequently, Banfield's observation has been borne out by any number of carefully prepared projections that proved wildly off the mark: A notable example was the admission that in 1970 the nation would produce more
than twice as many doctoral degrees (27,000) than the 12,000 estimated by a
study group in 1954.[3]

It is becoming common practice on larger studies to keep careful records not only of the data collected but of the techniques used for projections.
This practice may be helpful in post mortems: There are so many variables and
assumptions in any of these projections that the end product may be to expose
the shaky foundations (e.g., future zoning patterns or family-size preference)
underlying the superstructure of computer printouts.

The long-range value of those second-generation studies in terms of their
money and time-saving potentials has yet to be assessed. They do represent a
hopeful development in that they recognize that the process of periodic updating is superior to the attempt to prepare one-time projections only to observe
the predictions quickly overtaken and confounded by unforeseen events. On
the other hand, they are damnably expensive.

The purpose of this chapter is to identify a few of the key issues and
problems relating to planning projections. The laboratory area selected for this
exercise is New England, with special focus again on Massachusetts and metropolitan Boston. Two particular problems are discussed, both bearing on unpredictable elements in long-range forecasting. The first considers a major change
that occurred over the past three decades. This is unpredicted transformation of

metropolitan Boston, and indeed, much of southern New England, from a decadent laggard area to a position of national leadership. The second is the problem of population forecasting in the Age of the Pill.

In the past 30 years, there was a fundamental and totally unforeseen
change in some of the Boston region's economic and social roles. In the 1950's,
the region that had been a slow-growing backwater area became an attractive
prototype area considered by other parts of the nation as a goal and a model.
This change in role was not reflected in planning projections and in fact tended
to escape notice until the transition was nearly completed. Looking ahead to
developments at the turn of the century, it is important to recognize that there
are many elements in population projections (as well as related land use and
transportation forecasts) that cannot be accurately forecast. It is necessary and
useful to prepare such projections, but as the discussion of a possible deceleration in the projected rate of population growth suggests, in the last analysis,
scientific methods of prediction are based in large measure on variation in human behavior that may change over surprisingly brief time periods.

METROPOLITAN BOSTON: LAGGARD TO PROTOTYPE

In the alteration in statewide patterns and trends over the past years, it
is useful to begin with a benchmark year. Fortunately, a point of comparison
useful for planning purposes is available in the 1936 progress report of the
Massachusetts State Planning Board, a comprehensive document covering many
aspects of state development.[4]

The distance that separates the 1936 report from our present study is
only a generation in time, but it encompasses great changes in almost every aspect of regional development. Unemployment has been reduced to a relatively
minor problem; New England's textile industry has nearly vanished and has
been replaced by such industries as instruments and electronics which were relatively insignificant or which barely existed in the mid-1930's; birth rates have
increased by over one third (but seem to be returning to Depression levels);
real incomes have skyrocketed; and motor vehicle ownership and suborganiza-
tion have proceeded at a much faster pace than could possibly have been predicted. There are, however, some striking similarities between the description
of planning progress prepared in the middle of the Great Depression and the situation in the 1960's. The similarities can be attributed in part to failures to
solve long-standing problems. Identified as critical issues in 1936, water pollution, serious slum conditions, disproportionately high electric power rates, and
traffic congestion persist as unfinished business a generation later. Other items
discussed in the 1936 report also bear a close resemblance to conditions today.
One example is recreation. By 1936, recreation and tourism had developed to
the point where it had allegedly become the state's second-largest industry.
Another is the critical importance of education, especially higher education, to
the state economy that had already become fully apparent in the 1930's. Final-

ly, the state's rates of population growth and employment expansion were well below the national level just as they are today.

In measuring the progress of the past three decades, it is essential to place particular stress on certain unquantifiable factors that had a major, unanticipated impact on economic and social development. The state's renowned private universities had been producing business and research leaders for the nation, but it was only in the 1940's and after that this function assumed a central role in stimulating area development. The extent to which this unique asset would have a direct economic spillover into the area economy only began to be apparent during World War II. Allied to these generators of scientific and business activity, there were certain long-standing assets, especially a high quality of local amenities, which created a desirable environment for management and scientific personnel.

In the 1930's and up to the late 1940's, New England, Massachusetts, and metropolitan Boston were regarded as economic museums allegedly populated by tired antiquarians and warring ethnic groups, offering excellent college educations and pleasant holidays, but unsuitable for either investments or careers. By the mid-1950's, this view had radically altered, and metropolitan Boston in particular emerged as a much envied and emulated prototype for aspiring areas throughout the nation.

In the late 1940's and early 1950's, the state experienced a basic alteration in both its inner and outer aspect: A lagging deviant became a leading prototype for the nation. The seeds of this change were already present, but as has been suggested, the forcing ground and dividing line between the two eras was World War II, with its emphasis on research and sophisticated weaponry. Although various dates can be selected for the subtle but basic alteration in role, the early 1950's, when electrical machinery employment in Massachusetts surpassed textile employment, represents an arbitrary but perhaps accurate point in time. Whatever the date, the effect has become obvious. It may be noted that in metropolitan Boston, which contains over half the state population, per-capita incomes relative to the U.S. average had declined by 28 points between 1929 and 1950, but between 1950 and 1962, the trend was reversed and the area rose by seven points.[5]

It is useful to recall the deepseated sentiments that colored the outsider's view of New England. A rigid social-class structure, the absence of significant natural resources, and the decreasing number of enterprising immigrants were thought to have created an atmosphere unfavorable to economic expansion. The region, some said, consisted largely of dying family businesses hostile to new people and new ideas, and its economy was clearly lacking in resilience and potential. Novelists like J. P. Marquand and Edith Wharton[6] helped to fix an image of an ingrown population living in an area located on a kind of economic cultural peninsula, outside the mainstream of the nation's social and economic development. Fiction spilled over into fact: The prospective industrialist and financier was often discouraged by certain real handicaps such as high electric-power rates but even more repelled by old-fashioned ways of doing business and by the reputed overly conservative investment policies of New England banks. Most important, he was usually more impressed by the availability of excellent alternative locations in other regions. Perhaps even more significant was the fact that many New Englanders had written off their region, preferring to place their capital in more promising areas; in many cases, the more enterprising younger people chose other places for their lifetime careers.

The unfavorable view of the region dated well back into the nineteenth century, and it grew stronger with the passage of time and the opening of the West. During the first decade of the present century, a New England booster felt it necessary to examine and attempt to refute allegations of regional unprogressiveness and attitudes inimical to progress. This defense was illuminating.

> The New England temper has been loath to accept optimism for its guiding motive. There has been a certain grim liking for adverse conditions in the New England character. We are inclined to be persistently stubborn in our business methods. We do not like to experiment. . . . New Englanders went out into the nation and built it up. There has been a drain of New England energy and initiative. The wholesale and continued transfusion of her best blood to the veins of the newer states could only mean the weakening of her own constitution and the limiting of her own development.[7]

Despite this preamble, the booster and the report went on to suggest that the "decadence" of New England was a "fiction." Although the outmigration of talent and the abandonment of farms were admitted as realities, the authors contended that outside allegations regarding the region's loss of manufacturing--including textiles--were erroneous or exaggerated. (A decade later, denials were no longer possible, and by the 1940's, some New Englanders were taking comfort in the fact that in "exporting" textiles to the South, the region had also transferred the problems that seem to surround that industry like a nimbus, to the areas that had sent the Dixie raiders.)

Published in 1911, this Boston Chamber of Commerce report was prescient but premature by three or four decades in its assertion that "conservation and stagnation" were giving way to progress, thanks to the "high quality of the region's schools," the "abilities and industriousness" of its workmen, and even more, to such intangible factors as an "impulse toward progress" based on moral character, receptive attitudes, and a regional tradition of cooperative efforts toward improvement. However, the report's authors anticipated later scholars who have come to recognize the critical importance of technically trained cadres, favorable work attitudes, and an unquantifiable but vital spirit of receptivity to change. The region's problem was that these assets did not become marketable commodities again until World War II.

The study placed considerable emphasis on two other aspects of life in the region that have a distinctly modern flavor, New England's amenities both for year-round living and for recreation and its major cultural attractions. The comments regarding New England's "much maligned" weather as a beneficial component of its environment are also pertinent, particularly with the increasing popularity of winter sports. But the attempt to link the area's rigorous climate to a capacity for hard work and to the sterling character of the region's labor force would doubtless be considered debatable by Californians and others.

The study quotes a Chicagoan who summarized the view of Boston widely held about the turn of the century (and for some decades beyond). Boston is, he asserted, "a fine little city--historic associations, fine educational opportunities, delightful place to visit; but you must admit you are not in the same class with us when it comes to industrial energy and all that."[8]

In refuting the midwesterner's allegations, another modern note is struck: The outsider's misconception of Boston weakness is blamed on the U.S. Bureau of the Census reports that reflected a relative decline in population and economic activity in the central city. Because of Boston's long-standing inability to annex its suburbs, city figures exclude data for the area's growth communities. It was suggested then, as in later decades, that comparisons based on data for the "500-square mile" Boston region would have been fairer and more flattering.

Among Boston's major assets half a century ago are many that remain valid today and hopefully will continue to characterize the region. In the first decade of the century, Boston and vicinity had long been known as a region where residents enjoyed a better-than-average standard of living. Then, as now, Boston was concerned about the obsolescence of its port and this resulted in great plans--and continued disappointment. The Boston area still remains the principal transportation and trade center of New England, and the city's downtown area was geared to great volumes of public transportation commuters.

One of the most up-to-date notes struck in the publication is the stress of the region's need for superior quality of production, on skilled people manufacturing high-value products from imported raw materials. Even some of the phraseology is up to date.

> What might be termed human resources, constitutes one of the most important industrial assets of Massachusetts. . . . They are the result of a century of industrial experience and the advantage of an early start. In the estimate of industrial resources, they must be reckoned of even more account than proximity to supplies of raw materials or markets. . . . The policy which will enable (us) to profit most fully from this advantage . . . To overcome the disadvantage of our geographical location and the dearth of mineral wealth, is one which will incorporate a very large amount of value in comparatively small bulk.[9]

In assessing the relative merits of suburban and central city location, the study describes the tendency of expanding manufacturing industry in need of sizable sites outside Boston but suggests, as others have done in recent decades, that the city was partly to blame for this industrial exodus because of its failure to develop adequate, intown industrial sites. The report identified the Boston waterfront as an admirable place for new, large-scale industrial growth and the city proper as the host for a variety of smaller enterprises enjoying transportation advantages and access to large pools of labor. More recent publications have hardly improved on this prescription. Modern also is the description of the two Bostons, "the poor who remain in the city" and the more affluent who earn their living in Boston but who have moved to one of "two-score bedroom" communities. The warning, too, is familiar: "Ultimately, unless the metropolitan district fuses into a single community, suburban selfishness is bound to be its own defeat, since the house is divided against itself."

The gloomy view of New England's prospects deepened during the Great Depression when one writer underscored New England's extreme pervading conservatism[10] while another suggested that New England, alas "is a dying culture. . . . In years to come, America will probably see New England's main, because more lasting, achievement in the fact that its sons are chiefly responsible for the colonization of the South [sic] and the Middle West."[11]

Between the ebullience of 1911 and the bright prospects of the mid-1960's came the Great Depression, two world wars, and the postwar transformation of the late 1940's and early 1950's. To a greater extent than the period following World War I, the second major conflict was a turning point in the economy and social patterns of the region and the nation. It would be an error, however, to suggest that the change was unrelated to the past. In fact, traditional Boston values such as superior higher educational institutions and the intangible complex of attractive living conditions were discovered to be major local benefits in an era when many growth industries were freed from reliance on local raw materials and low-cost power and were oriented instead toward a combination of universities and amenities. New England and mainly the Boston area had educated a substantial share of the nation's business, scientific, and intellectual leadership, but as late as 1952, a careful research study could report a significant "brain drain" with large numbers of native New England science graduates relocating out of the region after graduation, partly because higher salaries and better opportunities were available elsewhere.[12] The region was weak in major industrial research laboratories and secured only a disproportionately small share of research and development contracts.[13] To a great extent, these observations also applied to the Boston region which comprises roughly one third of New England's total population.

Only a decade later, the situation had materially improved. For example, in the mid-1960's, a study by the National Aeronautics and Space Administration (NASA), justified selection of the Boston area as the site of the agency's new Electronic Research Center by pointing out the area's highly competitive standing not only in the awarding of large numbers of advanced scientific and engineering degrees but also in the number of scientists and engineers at work in the area. In its study of location factors, NASA identified the proximity of "electronic research oriented graduate-level educational resources of proven high quality as being the most important criterion."[14] Boston's compactness was a significant factor in this performance rating. Although the Boston area ranked second to New York, the New York area's resources "are so scattered that it does not seem realistic to consider them as a single unit."[15]

NASA estimated that the proposed center would add 300-350 graduate-school student enrollments in nearby institutions and that many would be enrolled in doctorate-level courses in electrical engineering or physics. A demonstrated capacity to award five or six doctorates in electrical engineering and two or three doctorates in physics a year was a prerequisite for consideration.[16] (The Boston area averaged twenty-nine doctorates per year in electrical engineering and forty-five in physics in the period, 1960-62).

Other criteria (in which all of Greater Boston ranked high) included attractive amenities, a major airport, and the presence of a substantial science-engineering community, including an array of professional personnel, industrial laboratories, and related firms. The total number of electronic research and development personnel identified by the U.S. Bureau of the Census for NASA in the Boston area in 1961 was 37,800. In 1960, The National Academy of Science included 14,700 area residents as industrial research and development personnel. Only two areas exceeded the Boston area on both counts--New York and Los Angeles.[17]

In 1963, in the Boston area, there were an estimated 1,500 doctorate-degree holders and 4,700 holders of masters' degrees engaged in research development work in industries. The critical numbers that played a significant role in justifying NASA's decision were clearly quite small in relation to the Boston area's labor force of over 1 million. The element of size is even more apparent in considering the number of scientists engaged in basic research in the area-- only 1,609 in 1962.[18] It would have been foolhardy indeed to suggest in the 1930's that the presence of a few thousand engineers and scientists and the existence of universities, hospitals, banks, and other institutions that had become a customary part of the landscape would, within decades, be significant factors in reversing the area's economic trends.

One effect of the alteration in Massachusetts' role in the past generation has been to transform the state--paced by metropolitan Boston--into a major beneficiary of federal spending, particularly in the fields of defense, research, and urban renewal.

It had long been believed that because of a combination of high incomes and the effectiveness of southern and western legislators in securing federal aid for military installations, agriculture, and public works, Massachusetts was among the wealthy victims who contributed far more in taxes to the federal treasury than were returned in dollar benefits. This view is sharply contradicted by 1957-63 data which show that, far from being drained by federal taxation, Massachusetts has been the beneficiary of a relatively large and rising proportion of total federal spending.

A report published in mid-1966 indicates that, in 1963, Massachusetts received a total of $735 in per capita federal expenditures in the national-income accounts, 20 per cent above the $597 per capita for the nation and well above the levels of the Midwest, Southeast, Southwest, Plains, and Rocky Mountain regions. Only the Far West figure ($862 per capita) was higher.[19]

In 1963, federal expenditures amounted to 27.3 per cent of total Massachusetts personal income vs. 22.3 per cent in 1957. This percentage was higher than the nation (25 per cent), although somewhat lower than the South and Far West (29-32 per cent). Massachusetts personal income is so much larger ($2,800 per capita in 1963 vs. $1,800 in the Southwest) that a slightly smaller percentage represents a larger dollar amount than in poorer states. The data tend to refute the notion that federal government expenditures necessarily result in a reallocation of income from wealthy states to poor states.

The primary sources of Massachusetts federal expenditures were defense and welfare payments. In both respects--the share of the total provided by defense and federal transfer payments for welfare programs--Massachusetts is one of the national leaders.[20]

An attempt has been made to describe the transformation of the Greater Boston area during a period of rapid and largely unexpected changes. The question is, could these changes have been foreseen? Who, in the mid-1930's, could have predicted World War II and its aftermath and the opportunities presented by these events for the special assets offered by metropolitan Boston? Who, for example, could have foretold that a single major laboratory established under MIT auspices to meet the government's wartime needs in electronics and other fields would, 20 years later, "spin off" over 60 research and development (R & D) firms and provide subcontracts for over 200 R & D firms? The magnetic attraction of the major educational institutions in Cambridge and Boston, allied to the complex of laboratory and research facilities in the area, generated a substantial new industry in two decades, with over 500 private firms employing 26,000 people.[21] It was clearly impossible to penetrate through the murky gloom of the Great Depression and look ahead to the mid-1960's. Perhaps an assessment of the shape of the 1960's and 1970's was feasible by the early 1950's. However, major capital improvements are not planned 10 or 15 years ahead, but must be designed for time spans of 20 years, 30 years, or more. Rapid-transit systems, equipment, and highways, for example, are supposed to have a life span of 40 years.

The long-range planning studies of the 1930's are today curios rather than basic documents which through constant usage, revision, and updating have become working guides for continued planning and programing. The question that now arises is whether our current studies are designed for the library or the work table. Analysis indicates that in the short-term sense, two to five years, many of them will indeed be used. Highways, schools, and medical institutions will be constructed on the basis of master plans that embody a response to immediate needs in the perspective of some type of long-range projection. While there is no difficulty in identifying urgent and obvious requirements, it is in this latter area, the forecasts, that there are problems similar to those which confounded the false prophets of the 1930's.

The new planning studies in many cases do not really build either upon the studies or the lessons of the past. Instead, they refer, with a touch of humor, to their predecessors' efforts, noting the quaint ways in which they went astray. It now remains to be seen if our current efforts are likely to be much more satisfactory. In essence, the question may be rephrased: Is it possible to discern coming events or trends in the foreground or on the horizon that can have as dislocating effects on present projections as World War II and associated developments had on the forecasts of the 1930's?

PROJECTIONS AND REVISIONS

The built-in uncertainties involved in preparing population projections suggest some of the difficulties in developing and using forecasts. In this connection, a 1966 U.S. Department of Labor projection on nationwide manpower needs for 1970 notes some significant problems in looking ahead only four years:

> . . . the projections are dependent on assumptions about unemployment rates, growth in productivity, the mix of consumption, investment, government expenditures and other key economic variables. A crucial assumption underlying the projections is that the Vietnam situation will have been resolved by 1970 and that defense expenditures reduced to a more normal level.[22]

Thus, in view of international, diplomatic, and military uncertainties, it is rightly considered extremely hazardous to make firm predictions even three or four years ahead. When projections are prepared for longer periods, the results have often been wildly out of line with subsequent events.

In contrast to the U.S. Bureau of the Census, which in the 1930's predicted that U.S. population would level off by 1960 or 1970, a census projection prepared in 1943 projected a national total of almost 200 million by the year 2000. The nation surpassed this level by the end of 1967.

A high point in the bureau's projections was reached in 1964. The U.S. year 2000 population was estimated at a low of 291 million to a high of 362 million. Two years later, the bureau had lowered its sights to 280-356 million by the year 2000.[23] Quite probably, further downward revisions can be anticipated. The critical problem facing population specialists and the nation in the last third of the twentieth century is the huge potential for population growth created by the nation's present age distribution. It is difficult, if not impossible, to predict in advance the number of children families will desire in coming decades now that low-cost, effective contraceptive techniques render choice rather than accident a key factor in child bearing.

Population specialists point out that the U.S. birth rate declined from 55 per 1,000 in the early nineteenth century to 18 per 1,000 a century later, during the Great Depression. Meanwhile, in the same period, the death rate declined from 20 to 25 per 1,000 to 11 per 1,000.[24]

On the critical factor of family-size preference, there have been significant changes over the years. In the early nineteenth century, the number of children ever born to the typical, married, American female is believed to have been between eight and ten. By 1920, the number had declined to three, and in the midst of the Depression, to two. It might be noted that to keep population level stable, all that is necessary is that each adult women have one adult daughter who lives through childbearing age and whose offspring similarly survive and reproduce.

Population studies published in 1959 and 1966[25] comparing family-size preference in the past few decades indicate that the preferred two-child family of 1940 rose to a modal preference of three children by 1945, and to four children in 1955 and 1960. It is almost as if children were regarded as a luxury denied by the Depression, and larger families had become an expression of postwar affluence.

Maintaining population at a stable level requires only about 2.1 children per family. Consequently, the current downward trend toward a 2.5 level will, if it continues, probably result in a stabilized population by the turn of the next century.

Errors of similar magnitude in past decades ranged from 1929 forecasts of continuing prosperity to warnings of a recurring depression issued during World War II. In Massachusetts in the 1930's and beyond, forecasts of future highway traffic, water demand, and the need for classroom facilities have proved to be gross underestimates. Throughout the nation in the 1960's, planners erred in predicting increases in central city populations only to have their forecasts shattered by the 1960 census.

In assessing the accuracy and usefulness of projections, a clear distinction must be made between prediction and control. There has been much criticism, for example, of forecasts that appear to rest on assumptions of some type of central control over growth rates and over the distribution of population density (e.g., regional zoning) where such coordinative powers do not exist.

The possibility of making projections come true by fiat has probably been overestimated. Even totalitarian societies have found that there is wide scope for initiatives outside the scope of the plan. One of the principal areas where personal preferences confound the planners even in dictatorships is in family size. Low birth rates have become a major issue in Hungary and East Germany. Conversely, India has been considering a variety of expedients including bonuses and mandatory sterilization of fathers with three or more children to reduce its rate of population growth.

It seems possible that population trends may have in store more surprises for American planners. Short of such events as a major military cataclysm or a severe economic depression, over the course of the next 10 to 30 years, a steep decline in birth rates may be one of the principal factors in rendering current projections as ludicrous as those prepared in the 1930's. Slower population growth (or a leveling off of growth) would have a major impact on every aspect of national life ranging from housing to food production, from jobs to needs for land and water. It would be difficult to overestimate the significance of a stable population that, after 350 years of continued expansion, had at last reached its upper limit.

Up to the mid-1960's, projections for the nation, state, and Boston region generally pointed to a continuation, with some modifications, of the growth rates of the 1950-60 decade. It has become increasingly apparent that these population projections may be on the high side.

The total number of live births in the nation began to turn downward in 1961. Massachusetts anticipated this trend by a full four years: In Massachusetts, the total number of births in 1965 had declined to a point well below the level of 1957, despite the fact that the state population had grown by 50 per cent during the period. This decrease in births occurred in the face of a nationwide trend toward marriage at earlier ages and despite the "bulge" in teen-agers as a result of the sharply higher postwar birth rates during the middle and late 1940's. The relatively high birth rates of the late 1940's and 1950's may, in fact, represent transitory peaks similar to those that occurred in earlier periods. In 1950, for example, Massachusetts produced approximately the same number of births as it did in 1917 when the state's population was less than 4 million, 20 per cent smaller than in 1950.

Wide publicity has been given to the recent change in the Roman Catholic Church policy and to the pill as prime elements in the downturn of the birth rate. In past decades, we managed without either. For example, in the 1930-40 Depression decade, the national birth rate reached a point slightly lower than in

1966. The rate fell to just over 18 per 1,000 in 1933.[26] It may be useful to indicate the numbers involved in a declining population growth rate in Massachusetts, a state that has consistently tended to grow at a modest pace as compared to the nation. As is indicated by the following statistics, the population projection business is in a state of flux. In 1966, the Bureau of the Census forecasted a rate of population expansion in Massachusetts between 1960 and 1980 at close to 0.9 per cent annually, the 1950-60 annual growth rate. However, the bureau also indicated that the increase might be as high as 1.2 per cent per year.[27] Estimates of net migration over the 25-year period range from a minor loss to a small net gain. Outmigration is expected to diminish in impact on population growth trends in the two decades as compared to the 1940-60 period. Taking the 25 year period 1960 through 1985, the population increases projected in the four alternatives prepared by the bureau range from a low of about 25 per cent to a high of over 35 per cent.

The key element in the federal projection is that state's "recent level of overall fertility [births per 1,000 women, 15-44 years old] in relation to national levels."[28] A decrease in family size as reflected in a decline from the fertility levels of a three-year period centered on 1960 would obviously have major repercussions on overall population expansion. It should be noted that the bureau estimates the average annual rate of population increase in Massachusetts between 1960 and 1966 as only 0.7 per cent, well below the 0.9 per cent 1950-60 rate and below the bureau's projections for the 1960-85 period. Moreover, the bureau estimates that actual population growth in Massachusetts between 1960 and 1966 was only 4.1 per cent. If this growth rate is projected through 1980, the population would increase by only 12-14 per cent in the period 1960-80, less than half the gain projected by the 1966 census study.[29]

A key question in projecting population growth is the family-size preferences of young Massachusetts residents. Based on the 1957-67 decline in births, the bureau fertility estimates may be very much on the high side. However, continuing economic trends, prosperity, and employment accompanying growth may compensate for lower birth rates by generating a substantial influx of working-age residents and their families to the state. The Bureau of the Census apparently anticipates no such net inmigration; each of the four census projections for Massachusetts assumes a decline in the scale and significance of migration as a factor in population growth.

The reason for a careful watch on birth rate trends is clear enough. A small revision in the natural increase rate resulting from a moderate shift in birth rates can have important implications. For example, given a total population of 5.5 million in the state, a decline of only 0.1 per cent in the growth rate over a 25-year period can eliminate the need to construct perhaps 50,000 new homes, 2,000 classrooms, and 2,500 hospital beds. There would also be a similar decline in the consumption of open land, in requirements for other public facilities and services, and in the private sector of the economy. If there is a more sizable decline in the annual growth rate, perhaps exceeding 0.3 per cent, the impact would be correspondingly greater. A continuation of the rate of population growth of the 1950-60 decade would result in an expansion of over 1 million in state population during 1960-80. This total is almost twice the 1965 population of the city of Boston. Unless there is an unexpected increase in net inmigration, a continuing steep reduction in birth rates might limit population growth in the two decades to perhaps half that amount. While this is still a staggering total to house, employ, and serve, it obviously entails a lesser scale of investment and services than a population rising by another 500,000 to 600,000.

Although birth rate trends are often considered more stable than economic and employment trends, the year-to-year fluctuations in birth rates in Massachusetts have been 10 or 20 times greater than 1/10 of 1 per cent, and decade-to-decade changes in a 25-year period can be 50 to 100 times greater. The decline of the U.S. birth rate to 19.2 per 1,000 in 1965 and 18.5 per 1,000 population in 1966, slightly above the Depression low point, has led some observers to predict further steep declines in birth rates leading to a population plateau by the year 2000 not only in the U.S. but in most advanced nations.[30] Another authority is reasonably optimistic concerning the prospects for a stabilized U.S. population.[31] If this view is accurate, population expansion in Massachusetts may level off completely within the next two or three decades, a development which would have staggering consequences on every aspect of the state.

To reiterate, a change in the birth rate is the critical factor. No significant alteration in death rate is expected; reductions in infant mortality rate and anticipated improvements in health conditions among disadvantaged segments of the population are likely to be offset by lower birth rates as incomes, living conditions, and expectations all rise.

CONCLUSION

The great variations in past birth rates, and especially the recent decline, suggest the adoption of a cautious attitude in assessing population projections. The preparation of population forecasts is necessary to guide operations of public agencies, but as the evidence of the past suggests, it behooves planners to exercise extreme caution in preparing projections, in advancing claims for their accuracy, and in advocating the expenditure of large sums to prepare projections that are necessarily based on many uncertainties and shaky assumptions. The same observation is valid for economic projections. In the 1930's or even the 1940's, it would have taken divine guidance to foresee the shape of Massachusetts in the mid-1960's. There is no reason to suppose that similar surprises may not be in store for the forecasters of the 1960's who are looking through the mists to the 1990's.

NOTES TO CHAPTER 5

1. Dennis O.Harrow, "A Broad Brush With A Sharp Edge," *American Society of Planning Officials Newsletter,* June, 1967.

2. Edward C. Banfield, "The Uses and Limitations of Metropolitan Planning in Massachusetts," in *Taming Megalopolis,* H. Wentworth Eldredge (ed.), II (New York: Anchor Books, 1967), p. 712.

3. Dael Wolfle, "Can Professional Manpower Trends Be Predicted?" *Seminar on Manpower Policy and Program,* U.S. Department of Labor, Manpower Administration (Washington, D.C.: May, 1967), p. 4. An error of much lesser magnitude (15 per cent) was made on the projection on college graduates.

4. Commonwealth of Massachusetts, State Planning Board, *Progress Report,* "A Report Prepared by the Commonwealth of Massachusetts State Planning Board" (Boston, November 30, 1936).

5. U.S. Department of Commerce, *Survey of Current Business,* Table 1, (Washington, D.C.: May, 1967).

6. J. P. Marquand's *H. M. Pulham, Esquire* and *The Late George Apley* along with Edith Wharton's *Ethan Frome* exemplify the problems and quaintness of those who chose or were forced to remain, while Marquand's *Sincerely, Willis Wade* provides an excellent example of the upward mobile careerman who severed his ties with the region, liquidating a local mill in the process. Edwin O'Connor's novels about Boston have probably been less influential in this respect because of their unique ethnic and political themes.

7. This section draws on a report prepared by a special committee of the Boston Chamber of Commerce, *New England, What It Is and What It Is To Be,* George French (ed.) (Cambridge, Mass.: University Printing Press, 1911). The quotation is on pp. 3-4.

8. *Ibid.,* p. 208.

9. *Ibid.* This quotation and succeeding comments are in the chapter entitled "Boston: The Next Phase," pp. 221-32.

10. James Truslow Adams, "The Historical Background," in *New England's Prospect: 1933,* J. T. Adams, H. S. Graves, *et al.,* (eds.) (New York: Little, Brown and Company, 1931), pp. 5-6.

11. Herman Keyserling, "Genius Locii," *Atlantic Monthly,* CXLIV (September, 1929), 304, quoted in Howard W. Odum and Harry Estill Moore, *American Regionalism* (New York: Henry Holt and Company, 1938).

12. Report by the Committee of New England of the National Planning Association, *The Economic State of New England* (New Haven: Yale University Press, 1954), pp. 566-70.

13. *Ibid.*, pp. 560-66.

14. Report of the National Aeronautics and Space Administration, *Electronic Research Center* (Washington, D.C.: U.S. Government Printing Office, January 31, 1964), p. ix.

15. *Ibid.*, p. xi.

16. *Ibid.*, p. C. 6, Table H. 1.

17. *Ibid.*, Table C. 3.

18. *Ibid.*, Appendix H. Boston Area (c).

19. U.S., Committee on Government Operations, Subcommittee on Intergovernmental Relations, "Federal Expenditures to States and Regions," 89th Cong., 2nd Sess., June 29th, 1966, Table C-10, p. 134.

20. *Ibid.*, Table A-10, p. 117.

21. Anne H. Cahn and Ashok Parthasarathi, *The Impact of a Government-Sponsored University Research Laboratory on the Local R & D Economy* (Cambridge, Mass.: M.I.T. Press, 1967), tables 3 and 4.

22. U.S. Department of Labor, *Projections 1970, Interindustry Relationships, Potential Demand, Employment,* Bulletin No. 1536 (Washington, D.C.: U.S. Government Printing Office, 1966), p. 1.

23. Population Reference Bureau, "Boom Babies Come of Age: The American Family at the Crossroads," *Population Bulletin*, XXII, 3 (August, 1966), 63-64.

24. *Ibid.*, pp. 77-78.

25. Ronald Freedman, Pascal K. Whelpton, and Arthur A. Campbell, *Family Planning, Sterility and Population Growth* (New York: McGraw-Hill Book Co., 1959); and Pascal K. Whelpton, Arthur A. Campbell, and John E. Patterson, *Fertility and Family Planning in the United States* (Princeton, N.J.: Princeton University Press, 1966).

26. In 1967, the nation's birth rate declined to 17.9 per 1,000, the lowest in recorded history.

27. U.S. Bureau of the Census, *Current Population Reports, Population Estimates,* "Illustrative Projections of the Population of States: 1960 to 1985," Series P-25, No. 326, February 7, 1966.

28. U.S. Bureau of the Census, *Current Population Reports, Population Estimates,* "Interim Forecasts of Aggregate Population, Employment, and Income, 1965-2000," Series P-25, No. 326, February 7, 1966, p. 6.

29. U.S. Bureau of the Census, *Current Population Reports, Population Estimates,* Series P-25, No. 347, August 31, 1966. The census estimate is for Massachusetts State Economic Area C. Area C contained over 3.1 million people in 1960 vs. 2.6 million in the Boston Standard Metropolitan Statistical Areas (SMSA).

30. See Donald J. Bogue, "The End of the Population Explosion," *The Public Interest,* VII (Spring, 1967), pp. 11-20.

31. *Population Bulletin, op. cit.,* p. 79.

6

PLANNERS AND METROPOLITAN PLANNING

After a decade or more of hesitations, false starts, and discussion about whether it was wanted or needed, metropolitan planning is at last becoming a reality. Statutory metropolitan planning agencies are in the process of being created throughout the nation because the federal government requires them as a prerequisite for public transportation grants, among other benefits, and it has become necessary to have a comprehensive planning agency on hand to qualify for sewerage and water-system aid and other boons. Further, if Senator Edmund Muskie and the Advisory Commission on Intergovernmental Relations (ACIR) succeed in their purpose, all federal capital grants in metropolitan areas will be subject to mandatory referral to such agencies for review and advisory comment.

This federal pressure for metropolitan planning did not originate at the grassroots level with local governments or political leaders. It was clearly inspired by planners, public administrators, and federal officials, and Congressional leaders who listened to them. Metropolitan planning has attractiveness, logic, and (best of all) federal money in its favor; but it is likely to run into horrendous problems if it is to become anything more than an exercise in pageantry and charades, a "fun exercise," as Harold Wise called it.[1]

ALTERNATIVE APPROACHES

The reason for this rather grim prediction may be found when examining four alternative methods used in achieving comprehensive metropolitan planning. Two of these, the independent "floating" agency, sometimes governmental but always some distances from the dicision-making echelon, and the transportation planning agency, can now be effectively discounted. As in the outstanding case of the privately supported New York Regional Plan Association, the independent organizations can perform or sponsor valuable research, but their ties to power are generally tangential and tenuous, and their influence on the pattern of development is limited to education and persuasion rather than command. As such, they can reasonably be regarded as transitional entities whose efforts kept metropolitan planning vigorous in the lean years and whose future status, where they are continued, is likely to be restricted to problem raising and technical criticism.

The second method, which has proved to be a blind alley, is the area-transportation study. Many of these studies burst into flower in 1962 and 1963, under the impact of the provisions of the Highway Act of 1961. The act stipulated that no federally aided highways would be approved in metropolitan areas after mid-1965 unless there were in existence a comprehensive plan, a planning agency, and a planning process. Many planners had hoped that the interagency transportation study organizations created by joint stimulus of the U.S. Bureau of Public Roads and the U.S. Housing and Home Finance Agency (HHFA) would produce great results. By 1963, however, one disillusioned HHFA official stated that participation by local officials was "less than adequate," that the studies were "highway dominated," that the planning process had not "really tangled with nontransportation issues," that the planning profession had been "rendered mute and defenseless by a piece of hardware" (the computer).[2]

A year later, the disenchantment was even more profound. Another key executive in HHFA, who had also been intimately connected with the area transportation studies, delivered the following comments to an audience from the American Institute of Planners (AIP):

> The line of least resistance makes transportation planning into what is, in reality, highway planning. Comprehensive planning becomes a support function providing data inputs. Lest I appear too critical without cause, think about the studies going on today all about us . . . . Can you imagine the Montreal or Toronto subway being born out of one of our so-called "land-use transportation studies?"[3]

There remain, therefore, essentially two separate, though not necessarily exclusive, mechanisms which might be used for comprehensive planning at the metropolitan level.

The Metropolitan Review Agency

In his closing remarks at the 1964 Conference of the AIP, Victor A. Fischer, then Assistant Administrator (Metropolitan Planning) of the HHFA, outlined his vision of the future metropolitan planning organism. The planning mechanism would be divided into three parts: (1) highway planning, to be conducted by the state highway agency; (2) transit planning, by a metropolitan transit agency; and (3) metropolitan planning, by a coordinating agency responsible for land use and other planning requirements and including in its policy-making board, representatives of the highway and transit agencies and local communities. This division of planning jurisdictions is, in fact, a description of the current situation in the Boston region.

Is there a future for this kind of area coordinating agency, attempting through persuasion to knit together separate agencies with varying objectives? The question is critical because it now appears that this is the emerging pattern of area planning, roughly as recommended by ACIR and Senator Muskie and subsequently enacted into law.

The Commission [ACIR] has recommended the enactment of a
general statute which would provide that all grant-in-aid applications in the major facility programs--airports, hospitals, highways, and the like--emanating from a political subdivision within
a standard metropolitan area be reviewed and commented upon
by an areawide planning body prior to action by the federal
granting agency.[4]

Weaknesses of Review Agencies

If past experience is any guide, the prognosis is poor for reaching genuine syntheses through this type of voluntaristic planning operation. The coordinating agency is a forum, remaining an innocuous research mechanism until
such controversial issues arise as unfavorable "review and comment" on a proposed highway. At that point, it becomes an arena for playing out the competing, interlocking games described by Norton E. Long.[5] How is such an agency to make choices and impose a selection among competing alternatives? The
answer is that one obvious course is not to raise potentially embarrassing matters, to shun ticklish issues. In Charles R. Adrian's terms, the planner in a multi-
government metorpolitan area could serve as a "head-shrinker to the community's conscience, the symbolic advocate of the society's unconscious values who,
if he understands his role correctly, can avoid frustration by not confusing
rhetoric with a call to action."[6] Large-scale Negro entry into white suburbs by
open-occupancy policies, encouraging rehousing outside the central city versus
large-lot zoning and low-density ordinances designed to keep the poor and the
apartment house from darkening the suburban landscape, and a policy favoring
transit as an alternative to intown expressways are examples of issues likely to
plunge a gentlemanly forum into chaotic stalemate.

Conferring mandatory referral powers upon such an agency via Senator
Muskie's bill (S561 which was passed in 1965) will merely hasten the crisis. One
finds it difficult to imagine a favorable reaction on the part of semiautonomous
empires like the central cities, such federal agencies as the Bureau of Public
Roads (BPR), HEW, or Federal Avaition Administration (FAA), state highway
departments, and metropolitan transit agencies to "advise" and "comment"
that a major program operation was poorly conceived or that the location of a
proposed metropolitan facility was in error. After the initial shock wears off,
the offended agency would clamor for veto privileges on the policy-making
council as insurance against further indignities. Alternatively, it may simply
choose to ignore the advisers, proceeding majestically along its chosen path. One
can anticipate outbreaks of technical warfare between planners (perhaps following the precedent of disputing economists) as an unexpected by-product of
the "coordinating" alternative.

The key defeat is that the metropolitan review agency is not a governing
body. Unlike a metropolitan government, the next alternative to be examined,

it lacks a strong chief executive who is able to override the contenders and force resolution of disagreements. There is the possibility (in fact, the likelihood) of appealing to a higher court when an impasse is reached.

One method of solving the power problem is to establish single-purpose, functional organizations to handle metropolitanwide functions. For example, the Boston area has four of them: The Metropolitan District Commission (water, sewerage, open spaces, and parkways), the Massachusetts Port Authority (port, airport, Mystic River Toll Bridge), the Massachusetts Turnpike Authority (turnpike and tunnels), and the Massachusetts Bay Transportation Authority (transit and bus lines, commuter railroads). However, the special, functional district approach cannot be considered a complete answer. While authorities possess power and action, they present a frightening problem in coordination and in effective citizen control.[7] As self-regulating operations, the authorities often tend to succumb to the twin temptations of high-handed arrogance and challengeable bookkeeping procedures. Considerable effort, for example, was required to fumigate and modernize three of the four Boston area authorities in the late 1950's and early 1960's. In short, independent authorities do not solve the problems of coordinating activities within the metropolitan area, and in some ways, make it worse. Integrating the plans of a half-dozen autonomous kingdoms like the New York Port Authority is not a task for the weak, the tolerant, the poor, and the friendless--that is, the regional planner.[8] From a variety of perspectives, therefore, the prospects for achieving effective metropolitan planning by means of a review agency that does not have its own solid power base are not promising.

METROPOLITAN GOVERNMENT

The wide interest in metropolitan government characteristic of the 1940's and 1950's seems to have faded in consequence of metropolitan Toronto and Miami having found few imitators.[9] A good deal, in fact, has been written to suggest that this kind of basic change is unwanted, feared, and possibly even unnecessary in view of the American genius for *ad hoc* inventions to handle clearly metropolitan functions such as water and sewerage, parks, and transportation. The following sampling of authoritative comments in testimony presented to the Advisory Commission on Intergovernmental Relations and elsewhere, however, suggests that some opinionformers, who are perhaps less than a decade in advance of policy, are convinced of its necessity.

Commentaries on a report[10] included William L. C. Wheaton's statement that: "In the absence of metropolitan government a metropolitan planning agency would be in a weak position to make decisions on controversial issues." Guthrie S. Birkhead noted: "Effective planning must have a strong protagonist--an elected chief executive. Mandatory 'review and comment' is a long way from power." In the same report, Coleman Woodbury said: "No one should claim effective metropolitan area planning can be done in the absence of areawide government." Thomas H. Reed noted: "An elected areawide government is needed for solution of the metropolitan problem. Multipurpose authorities are not the answer." And, as quoted from Martin Meyerson: "Metropolitan planning will continue to be impotent through the lack of metropolitan government."

Eli Comay has said: "The firm conclusion to be drawn from the metropolitan Toronto record [is] that effective metropolitan planning requires metropolitan government."[11]

For the sake of balance, three dissenting opinions must also be included:

Edward C. Banfield: "Metropolitan planning can lead to nothing practical because there is no possibility of agreement on the 'general interest'."[12] Robert C. Wood: "We know of no other time when a revolution (that is, metropolitan government) occurred when the existing system was solidly established, and its citizens . . . content."[13] Charles A. Adrian: "Both professional bureaucrats and members of Congress are . . . certain in the foreseeable future to stop short of requiring metropolitan-wide government or area planning backed by effective sanction."[14]

New Federal Stimulus to Metropolitan Government?

The suggestion that metropolitan government will be defeated by the undeniable hostility of suburban communities, that it is necessarily doomed because of grass-roots opposition, may be viewed with some skepticism. Similar assertions were made prior to the passage of a whole range of great society legislation in the field of civil rights ("You can't legislate tolerance.") and poverty ("Those people can't be helped.") among others. Perhaps the era of reform may be brief; the "deadlock of democracy," which was the death knell of much reform legislation up to the accession of President Johnson, may reappear at any time and in fact showed disquieting signs of revival in 1967-68.

But recent experience does suggest that the urban environment is far more plastic than many of us had thought. The combination of forceful and highly successful Presidential leadership, a receptive Congress, and the Supreme Court's decision in Baker vs. Carr, which weakened the rural strongholds of conservatism in the states, has resulted in much being imposed on local governments that would not meet with approval in a local referendum. In short, if local sentiments can be overridden on civil rights and other traumatic issues, there would seem to be at least a possibility that soon HUD may write off the various experiments in regional advisory planning as unsuccessful attempts to run a race on crutches and propose more powerful measures. They could conceivably recommend that, after a suitable cut-off date, future federal grants be contingent on the existence of a representative, elected, metropolitan agency possessing substantial governmental power over land use, education, and other matters presently diffused among a multitude of separate jurisdictions. Then, to secure further aid, a decision-making structure in metropolitan areas would be required, alongside federal, state, and local governments. It could be argued that no such federal action would now be needed had the states assumed the responsibility of ensuring that central cities could meet this problem in the twentieth century as they did in the nineteenth, by annexing their suburbs.

If a federal decision is made to the effect that advisory councils and *ad hoc* organizations controlling some fragment of the metropolitan complex are not enough,[15] one could foresee rapid results of a kind that a reliance on local plebiscites would not produce. It can therefore be suggested that the emergence of metropolitan government is a real possibility by the early 1970's, not because of local dissatisfaction, but because a comparatively small group of persons influential in shaping federal policy may reach the conclusion that it is needed to cope with metropolitan problems.

It may well be desirable to accompany a move in this direction with a partial splitting up of the larger central cities to more manageable and less frightening size. Harvey Walker has suggested the desirability of breaking up most central cities into community units not exceeding 100,000 to 150,000 in population, both as a means of combating citizen anomie and to reduce suburban fears of central city domination within a metropolitan federation.[16] Even this figure would seem to be on the high side; if community empathy were the objective, units of 25,000 to 50,000 would appear to be more reasonable in order to afford minorities adequate representation and to permit legislators to provide close attention to their constituency.

Racial Imbalance--An Incentive to Metropolitan Government?

Finally, certain recent demographic trends, such as racial imbalance, may spur integration of units into a metropolitan government. As the Negro population increases in central cities above the halfway mark, we may see growing demands for metropolitan school systems and for housing and land-use planning on an intercommunity scale necessary to break down ghetto barriers.

Metropolitanization could be a response to the prospect of Negro political control of central cities. The critical municipal functions are police protection and local taxation of real estate. Assuming that mass evacuation of central cities by financial, medical, educational, and business operations is unlikely, the question arises as to whether the shift of power to the Negro will have major impact on the structure of multiple governments in metropolitan areas. There are some who suggest that the transfer may be no more shattering than the Irish takeover of certain central cities in the nineteenth century. Prior to their rise to respectability in the twentieth century, the Irish had similarly been excoriated for alleged addiction to vice, crime, and loyalty to alien standards.[17] It seems more likely, however, that the Negro represents a special case. The denial of full citizenship to the Negro after a century of emancipation and three centuries of settlement is a reflection of unique discrimination not accorded to other groups including the much smaller number of Japanese and Chinese Americans.

The extensive race riots of 1966 and 1967 are perhaps indicative of a depth of bitterness, alienation, and despair not encountered in previous urban immigrant groups. There is strong evidence that this violence has inflamed existing, barely latent, feelings of hostility among Caucasian majorities.

Based on past experience, a mistrusted central city majority can be prevented from controlling critical central city functions by a number of different methods. Home-rule power can be simply withheld, as in the case of Washington, D.C., or control over police and/or fiscal affairs can be transferred from allegedly irresponsible local politicians to the state, as in the case of Boston and Fall River, Massachusetts. Alternatively, the district can be gerrymandered into a minority status, a move for which there are countless precedents.

If we can assume that the federal government will provide financial incentives for moving toward a form of metropolitan government (such as metropolitan planning with review powers), the suburban majority may devise a fourth alternative. This could be an ingenious type of metropolitan government that retains local autonomy over schools, police, property taxation, and land use in the suburbs but denies similar powers to a central city under Negro control. It would involve a legal redefinition of certain central city functions and areas. For example, the central business district might henceforth be removed from central city jurisdiction and made subject to control of a metropolitan body. It is also conceivable that in the process of redistributing powers, the central city might be subdivided into smaller autonomous municipalities, a move that would eliminate the big-city mayor as a major political factor. Furthermore, if extremely serious frictions arise on such matters as hiring practices of private firms and institutions, the reaction is likely to be adoption of additional steps to weaken the coercive power of central city governments. In short, the proponents of metropolitan planning and metropolitan government may not be completely happy with their offspring's antecedents, motives, or conduct. Metropolitan government has the potential for providing a structure of power that could support effective metropolitan planning; if we have read the trends correctly, the possibilities for forming such governments are greater than past efforts would indicate.

NEW STATE ROLE?

Although planning may not yet have blossomed into a form useful to metropolitan problems, state governments have become the fastest-growing segment of the federal-state-local partnership. Between 1955 and 1964, total state expenditures more than doubled, as compared to the 50 per cent increase in federal outlays in the same period. In many cases, increases in state expenditures represent a simple-minded response to federal stimuli. For example, the state's growing role in water pollution, mass transportation, and manpower development reflects the inputs and matching requirements of federal grant-in-aid programs. However, there is a large area of expenditures that represent a

state response to public demands. Costly programs of public higher education
are initiated and financed by the state with limited federal aid used to flesh
out segments of the operation. The situation is similar with respect to public
health and mental health in which the federal role is even more restricted. Thus,
the states have proved more than conduits and echoes for federal funding and
federal programs.[18]

It would seem that the expansion and growing complexity of state government responsibilities in the great society (perhaps combined with the threat
of giving up publicity and power to the growing metropolitan planning agencies)
may provide a stimulus that state planning has lacked. In addition, the percolation of policy and program planning out of Washington may be instrumental in
improving state planning capabilities. The cost-effectiveness techniques widely
applied in private industry, used by Secretary McNamara to bring under control the sprawling U.S. Department of Defense, and now being gently urged
upon the federal civilian agencies by the U.S. Bureau of the Budget, are beginning to find their way into state government.

It is likely that the transmission of this specific set of techniques to the
states may not be focused in traditional "comprehensive" planning agencies.
For a time, at least, responsibility for policy and program planning may be centered in budget bureaus with counterpart planning units in the operating agencies. However, in the long run, the need for a strong central information and
planning agency to insure consistency will be unavoidable.

Meanwhile, the fact that a variety of state agencies are now required to
develop master plans, ranging from health, education, and welfare, to transportation and natural resources, may result in the production of a variety of unintegrated, perhaps competitive, statements of goals and blueprints of varying
quality and impact. Some consistency at least in agreeing on population projections and other basic assumptions could be effected by the state agencies
which are normally assigned the mission of producing studies on population,
land use, and economics. This minimal role leaves open the problem of policy
coordination which has to be located in the governor's office.

Most important for our purpose, however, is that some form of planning advice will also be needed in the governor's office to help resolve squabbles within the metropolitan agencies. Interagency bickering, which has been
one of the more prominent features of the genuine (as opposed to the highway-
dominated) transportation study, is likely to develop into an active branch of
unarmed combat in any metropolitan planning council which attempts to come
to grips with live transportation issues. Interagency and intercommunity dog-
fights almost always lead to appeals to higher authority in the appropriate executive and the granting federal agencies. For example, the bitter interagency
dispute over control of the Boston Regional Planning Project in 1962-63 was
finally resolved by the intervention of the governor, just as the explosive
highway-transit battle in Washington, D.C. has been repeatedly referred to the

President. It is difficult to foresee any other solution when equal powers are deadlocked.

If the metropolitan agencies evolve into problem-raising agencies, much of the job of refereeing and choosing among alternatives will fall to the governors, unless one faction seizes full control, that is, if some of the competitors are willing to surrender agency prerogatives and objectives.[19] A strong mayor allied with a highway or transit agency could grasp the reins, a move which, temporarily at least, would settle the power dispute. It should be remembered that a planning agency in dispute with anyone is often a loser; a scrap with the transportation agency or a central city mayor would be a disaster. In fact, its only chance of even partial victory in a fight with local or federal power blocs would be support from the governor and backing from a major federal agency like HUD. There is thus an important role for governors in breaking existing or incipient deadlocks. If they choose to take on this role, they will become important figures in metropolitan planning. If they do not, the conflict will be routed on to the regional and Washington offices of the affected federal agencies.

Some skeptics at the national and local levels are ready to see the states wither away; they are of the opinion, based on their experience, that the majority of states have little to contribute except red tape, useless delay, and windy obfuscation. Charles R. Adrian asserts that some of the friction between the states and federal and local agencies arises because the state level has been the slowest to professionalize its bureaucracy, and conflicts arise when the state's "opposite numbers" do not share the values and goals of other administrators.[20] One can sense a certain disillusion with state performance (and state personnel) between the lines of an AIP workshop report:

> States should be encouraged in every possible way to do better planning jobs, but federal aid in metropolitan areas should not be channeled through state agencies until they have demonstrated better understanding of local problems and local activity. In general, consensus favored state representation (in the metropolitan planning agency) if persons with adequate stature attended meetings.[21]

Apparently, some metropolitan planners have had their fill of the expendable nonentities who are sent as chair-warmers by agencies that demonstrate little interest in or respect for metropolitan planning. In the case of the urban-renewal and antipoverty programs, among others, a direct federal-local relationship has evolved which, in most instances, has reduced the state role to minor proportions. The same pattern may develop with respect to metropolitan planning, but as has been suggested, the representation of state agencies in metropolitan councils will ensure a stronger state involvement than has been true with other programs, provided the metropolitan agencies do not skirt controversial issues. Here again is an opportunity for and some pressures that may bring about more vigorous and effective participation by states in metropolitan planning.

It is difficult to generalize concerning the way states can or should function with respect to metropolitan planning. In very small, urbanized states like Rhode Island and Delaware, state planning and metropolitan planning could be virtually synonymous. In a number of states without metropolitan areas, state planning is clearly keyed to resource and economic development and low density urbanization. In larger states containing multiple metropolitan areas, the problem is more complex, particularly if, as frequently happens, metropolitan areas cross state lines and interstate treaties are required. In some cases, it may be feasible to develop state regional offices on the order of those in Tennessee, but designed to serve metropolitan areas rather than engage in small-town planning. Whatever the administrative choice, however, greater state involvement in metropolitan affairs, if only in the roles of referee, judge, and second-stage arena, appears almost certain. In its favor it should be recognized that the state, while it is as thoroughly fragmented as the metropolis, does have an established structure for arriving at decisions, settling disputes, and implementing programs. In short, there is an executive with power to lead agencies and other power centers in a particular direction. These are all lacking in the metropolitan area.

Planning and the Governor

Given that certain factors favor a more active role by states in metropolitan planning, how should planning within states be conducted to capitalize on the situation? Without reviving perennial arguments over the proper placement of the planning function, past experience suggests that while there is a vital area for a line planning agency, the major unfulfilled need is for planning input at the executive level, in the governor's office. If comprehensive planning is to become a reality, particularly if it is to embrace plans for human and natural resources and economic development, the coordinative function must be lodged within the range of an executive capable of knocking reluctant heads together. For example, although Edward C. Banfield suggests that metropolitan areas have no goals, there is no agreed method of solving their problems and in any event "coordinative planning . . . cannot be carried on without a political base," he also indicates that "the Governor must be in effect the chief executive on metropolitan area matters." He strongly urges that metropolitan planning be considered one of the governor's executive functions and that the office of the governor be strengthened in order to enable him to carry out this responsibility effectively. Banfield warns that unless the governor has sufficient technically qualified staff, presumably including planners, he will remain the prisoner of the agencies and interest groups on whom he normally depends for technical advice.[22]

There have been very few states where a professional planner has been part of the close circle of gubernatorial advisers. Planning at the state level takes on "value and effectiveness" to the degree to which the governor is able to use it.

He needs an office that is close at hand, in which he has confidence and a personal relationship and which in turn, is in close

touch with other staff services such as budget, personnel, accounting control, and public relations. . . . It is suggested, therefore, that each state consider adding an office of planning services to the executive office of the governor along with, but independent of, the budget office.[23]

At present, the chief advisory slots are filled by lawyers, public administrators, and businessmen; in virtually all states, the place that could (and in the
author's opinion, *should*) be occupied by a planner is vacant. The suggestion
that the planner participate as part of the intimate circle of an elected official
raises several issues. One concerns the continuity of planning. If the chief advocate of a set of planning studies and policies stretching beyond his term of office is defeated at the polls, does his planning adviser remain, along with the
programs he recommends? Or does his intrusion into the political struggle mean
that his head goes on the block when his boss is defeated? One answer to this
problem is to cite the record of the U.S. Bureau of the Budget, where top-level
heads may roll after the White House changes tenants, but operations and continuity can proceed unmolested. Is this change from the gray, neutral technician's role necessarily bad? Paul Davidoff suggests not, proposing further that
planners assume controversial policy-level roles by serving, for example, in established majority and minority planning staffs in the legislative branch.[24]
Subsequently, advocacy planning has been expanded to volunteer and paid professionals working for the poor and disadvantaged against the "establishment"
and its planning staff. The prospects for what amounts to an adversary planning process with experts locked in bitter combat with other experts appeared
extremely bright in the late 1960's. One interesting by-product of this trend is
its effect on publications. Agency planners are more wary of making sweeping
claims and proposing policy changes on the basis of shaky assumptions when
they are uncomfortably aware that hostile experts are waiting to pounce on
printed materials. The result is likely to be greater reticence, more humility,
and, hopefully, a better product.

This overt identification of plans and planners with parties and personalities already exists, to some extent, among planners at the local level who
have long bounced in and out of town as reform mayors entered and left office
and as the "planning climate" changed from warm to frigid. It is also true
among economists and other professionals (even including physicians), many
of whom have become identified with a particular social and political posture
without losing their scholarly credentials and professional standing.

On the other hand, the local precedent has not been followed at the
state and metropolitan levels. Metropolitan planners are just as mobile as local
planners, but they tend to leave for better opportunities or occasionally because of ferocious personal vendettas rather than because an incumbent has
lost an election.

THE PLANNER'S ROLE

The recommendation that planners pitch into the political arena also raises the issue of the role of the planner in relation to other professionals, to the politician, and to the public. In a sense, this is the familiar "high priest" versus "hired gun" argument. Should the planner be comparable to the engineer and attorney and be at ease in the role of hired expert? Should he place his talents unreservedly under the direction of an elected and politically responsible master, or does he have a special set of values and an outlook that fits him for a unique role as the guardian of the public interest? Norman Beckman raises the specter of built-in conflict because both the planner and politician see themselves as playing a similar role: Each feels responsible for integrating independent development decisions and providing leadership in "achieving the good life generally." Furthermore, because each sees himself as mediator, coordinator, and goal maker, the conflict can be resolved only by the planner reverting to the kind of subordinate role suitable for an employee who lacks an independent power base.[25]   He can express a basic difference in values by achieving an ulcer, a valedictory press conference, or a new job. Alan A. Altshuler sees the problem somewhat differently in stressing the planner's role as innovator, gadfly, and for other planners, evaluator and educator. Agreeing with Beckman, however, he fails to see a significant role for the planner in comprehensive planning.[26]

Clearly, the state planning adviser must thus possess unusual capabilities if he is to function in a complex, tension-ridden environment helping to resolve conflicts and policies at the state and, most likely, at the metropolitan level. What he does possess, as compared to his metropolitan colleague, is a governor who can act to some purpose when so persuaded. The author and others see the answer in Robert Walker's insightful observation that in the role of confidential adviser to incumbent officials lies the path for planners to contribute significantly to the government process.[27] Therein lies the prospect of influencing decisions instead of a career made up of endless frustration and marginal activities.

To Beckman's suggestion that the planner in the executive office be humble, self-effacing, and quietly loyal (but nevertheless expendable), one might add that he must be articulate, energetic, and quick to grasp issues and opportunities. One reason for insistence on state planning is that this represents one method of spreading the limited number of people with this unusual combination of talents more effectively; it may be easier to locate 50 first-quality planners than to find four times as many for all 212 metropolitan areas. Moreover, the 50 might achieve considerably more results.

Coordinating Federal Policies

Planners have been seriously concerned over the tendency of federal agencies to pull in different directions in metropolitan areas. There is one agency for highways, another for mass transit; part of HUD is stimulating suburban scatteration, and another part attempts to generate a central city revival. Conflicting federal policies have raised basic questions as to who is to coordinate development programs for metropolitan areas and where coordination is to be achieved. One answer, that, as we noted, appears wholly unsatisfactory, is to place the principal burden of coordination in the hands of the metropolitan agency. Another obvious approach, of course, is to improve coordination at the federal level in the first place.

The notion that metropolitan areas, which had little success in developing coherent intercommunity and interagency planning, are likely to have greater luck in formulating consistent plans for federal agencies is appealing but perhaps not entirely realistic. Apparently the Presidential task force came to this conclusion, since a prominent feature of the President's special message on cities involved a promise of improved federal interagency coordination through action by regional offices and in "model cities" chosen for experimental action. In the President's Message on City Development, HUD was charged with the responsibility to "mesh together all our social and physical efforts to improve urban living" and to "assume leadership among intergovernmental agencies dealing with urban problems."[28] Urban programs are to be "melded" in cities chosen for experimental action. In this connection, the views propounded by Robert Wood, as chairman of the task force, take on special significance.

> We need to think in terms of Federal leverage at critical junctures. In short, given [Federal] goals, we must devise ways and means to make them operative. We must have a single public policy which specifies the kinds of metropolitan regions the Federal government wishes to encourage. . . . What we require now is the formulation of a balanced strategy for metropolitan growth which will insure that all Federal agencies have common criteria to apply. . . . The *ad hoc* individual programs need to be reviewed at the local level by metropolitan planning agencies. . . . Coordination needs to take place first among the Federal agencies as well . . . an extension of the "workable program" to the metropolitan area at large appears now to be a feasible undertaking. It is the key concept for the next decade of public policy making.[29]

Substantial improvement in interagency policy for metropolitan areas would represent a major contribution to metropolitan planning. There are a number of obstacles, however, that must be overcome before the prospect can be translated into reality. One difficulty is the limitation on HUD's powers. Contrary to reported task force recommendations, highway transportation, the Community Action Program of the OEO, and the antipollution programs of

HEW were not transferred to HUD. Thus, the agency starts its task of coordination with substantially less scope than had been hoped. This means that HUD's coordinative activities may be the most effective in developing a consistent policy line within the agency itself. Unlike its predecessor, the Housing and Home Finance Agency, HUD has greater command of the former Federal Housing Administration and other previously semiautonomous nephews and nieces, a fact that may offer ample scope for intra-agency (as opposed to interagency) rationalization.

Sibling rivalry is a fundamental obstacle; the new agency may enjoy departmental status, but its greater prestige will not end jockeying for a place in the urban sun with other agencies that have staked out claims in human and natural resource planning, in land-use planning, in transportation, and in economic development. In fact, now that a number of federal agencies, including HEW, Agriculture, FAA, and EDA have retained planners or similar professionals, it is conceivable that a species of technical warfare may erupt in Washington as well as in metropolitan areas. This is based on the assumption that agency planners will tend to become co-opted by the agency to which they owe allegiance and hope for promotion, in the manner of service representatives in the Department of Defense, although a few may take the broader view before resigning. Thus, it can be predicted that the percolation of planners through the agencies will by no means usher in an era of interagency harmony. The results, a few years hence, may be demands to develop the type of responsiveness and coherence among civilian agencies that Secretary McNamara achieved in the Department of Defense. One can perceive the faint outlines of a basic administrative restructuring in the not-too-distant future that will go far beyond the limiting reshuffling of responsiblity proposed by the task force.

In the immediate future, arriving at coordinative arrangements is not likely to present any great problem at the upper echelon in Washington. Top-level bureaucrats are usually near enough to the summit of their agency to permit broad views, relaxed attitudes, and enhanced sensitivity to Presidential desires. Upper-echelon treaties, however, tend to be rather imprecise, generous in uplifting rhetoric, and unclear on operating details. The interagency agreements for conducting the area transportation studies indicate that it is after high-level agreements are turned over to parochial middle management that the trouble occurs. HUD may secure agreements to cooperate in Washington, but lower echelon foot-dragging can vitiate the best of intentions. The dimensions of this problem were succinctly summarized in a 1965 ACIR report:

> Functionalism, or the respondents' preoccupation with protecting and promoting the purposes of their individual programs, was the most important single conditioner of their comments. . . . The great majority of these middle management administrators, then, are unsympathetic to efforts at the national or urban field levels which are geared to interrelating federal urban development programs and to injecting a broad-gauged metropolitan viewpoint into the administration of such pro-

grams. And most of this distrust is rooted in fear--fear of change, fear of delay, fear of a dilution of individual program goals, fear of meddling by inexpert generalists, fear of dual or triple supervisory procedures, and fear of a diminution of agency autonomy. . . . Stand-pattism, or the rigid defense of traditional practices, procedures and principles, is a theme found in their answers. . . . As conservative defenders of administrative continuity and stability against innovating pressures . . . these middle management officials could hardly be expected to indicate that present practices . . . in metropolitan areas are something less than sensible and sound. . . . Indifference or the cavalier dismissal of serious questions and topics as being irrelevant or unimportant was reflected in response to every section of the questionnaire.[30]

Interagency rivalries are not the only problem HUD faces. Active coordinative efforts are likely to bring the agency to a face-to-face confrontation with elected officials at the state and local levels and with state and local agency heads. Some are likely to be hostile to a federal superpower that threatens accustomed procedures and alliances. The avowed federal objective of relying heavily on local initiative will undergo considerable strain in the tug of war for favorable rulings. Despite pious claims of nonintervention, the temptation to use federal pressures to lift a few local scalps--a practice not unknown at present--may be difficult to resist. Moreover, the local agencies and officials will, over time, adapt to the new era of technically sophisticated arguments and counter-arguments. Apparently, clear choices will increasingly become blurred and controversial, and the federal coordinator will find himself increasingly acting as referee in tangled area disputes in which all sides appear to have almost equal claims. For this, among other reasons, a very high order of judicial and technical talent will be required of federal administrators.

The supply of skilled professionals is clearly critical to the success of a coordinative endeavor. It is no secret that federal regional offices are not now liberally stocked with personnel of this calibre and that the cadre available in the central offices is by no means large enough to meet enlarged regional and metropolitan needs. Obviously, structural improvement in itself is not enough if good urban planning is to be successfully injected into the metropolitan environment by the federal agencies or anyone else. A prime requisite is a substantial number of extremely talented people.

CONCLUSION

Excluding at the outset the use of independent voluntary agencies and the area-transportation study, there are four institutional mechanisms by means of which metropolitan planning might be made more effective: (1) the metropolitan review agency with advisory powers, (2) metropolitan government, (3) an enlarged planning function within the office of state governors, and

(4) improved coordination and policy-making by federal agencies having an in-influence on metropolitan development.

The first approach is the one that is currently being followed, but at the same time it appears to be the least promising, primarily for lack of a single center of power which can break deadlocks among competing power groups. An argument can be made that the lack of effectiveness of metropolitan planning efforts up to now is in part attributable to the fact that planners do not have the kind of talent necessary to be effective in this environment. C. David Loeks' observation in 1958 remains valid in the 1960's:

> Not all the people doing metropolitan planning are planners. . . . The extent to which this is true might prove a surprise to some people. I know it was to me. Our colleagues in the fields of political science, public administration, economics, law, and so forth, have been structured in pivotal roles. . . . This is not a criticism of the [planning] programs so much as it is a commentary on the leadership and discipline we planners have been exercising in these areas.[31]

It is notable that the planner has received little of the public and scholarly attention accorded to figures in the military and political spheres, where the characteristics of important figures and the interplay of personalities are often described in great detail.[32] The planning profession, on the other hand, has seemingly concentrated on considerations relating to administrative structure and technical expertise. Perhaps planners have had far too little influence on decisions because they have just not concentrated enough attention on recruiting and training people capable of functioning effectively at the policy level. If, however, one accepts Robert C. Wood's description of the metropolitan area as consisting of "an alienated and indifferent public . . . highly diverse and unstructural sets of elites . . . highly decentralized and highly volatile patterns of influence,"[33] the challenge facing the planner with ambitions of preparing and implementing a comprehensive plan appears rather substantial. To make matters even more difficult, Wood notes the indigestible qualities in the intergovernmental mixture: ". . . in addition to the centrifugal local forces . . . . We sketch a process chronically beset with such political tensions, conflict, and diversity of participants as to be always in danger of flying apart."[34]

Assuming that this diagnosis is accurate, what is to be the prescription? Wood suggests that the planner should play a politically activist role, fashioning a strategy for the diverse interest groups, and building coalitions to implement it. It would seem, however, that the metropolitan planner is in an extremely weak position to undertake either task; he does not possess the leverage to succeed at the elaborate game of power politics needed in this highly charged environment. Without the kind of power base that could be provided by metropolitan government, or perhaps by an aggressive governor, he has two alternatives: long-term public and agency education for planning, which may pay off in five, ten, or twenty years and/or the kind of ritualistic charades which Adrian maintains is all that the metropolitan areas really want. Coalition-building in the metropolitan jungle is clearly no pathway to short-term or even longer-term injection of comprehensive planning in metropolitan areas.

Implementing metropolitan planning on an advisory basis calls for the qualities of a near-genius who is blessed with extraordinary luck. This combination seems to be in extremely short supply.

There are a few straws in the wind which suggest that greater efforts will be made to, coordinate the many federal programs that directly affect metropolitan areas. Under present administrative arrangements, however, there are many obstacles to substantial improvement here--particularly with respect to programs falling outside the direct control of HUD. Even under the best of circumstances, the coordinative approach requires the highest level of planning talent, and the federal record on this count, notably in regional office positions, has always been reassuring.

In the last analysis, it is difficult to predict with any certainty what institutional changes will occur to facilitate the effectuation of metropolitan planning or to be dogmatic as to what changes should occur. It is clear that changes must occur, but it is likely that there will be no single pattern. A metropolitan planning agency with essentially only advisory powers may do useful work in some areas, metropolitan government may be suited to others, while elsewhere, state planning will function effectively, possibly at the expense of metropolitan power. Much will depend upon the federal role in the future--whether it will seek a more solid base of power for planning within cities while continuing a federal-city emphasis, or whether, perhaps, it may place greater emphasis on the states.

It is also clear that future efforts must include a stronger emphasis upon the planning process at the policy level and the development of a much larger number of professional planners who can function effectively in the decision-making process.

NOTES TO CHAPTER 6

1. "Regional planning . . . in many cases has seemed to be a kind of fun exercise, done by nice people, for the advice of people who don't particularly want to take--nor do they have to take anyone's advice . . . . Regional planning without regional decisionmaking is a joke." Harold F. Wise, *Planning 1965* (Chicago: American Society of Planning Officials, November, 1965), pp. 48-49.

2. Frederick O'Reilly Hayes, "Urban Planning and the Transportation Study," *Proceedings of the 1963 Annual Conference* (Milwaukee: American Institute of Planners, February, 1964), pp. 112-18.

3. Victor A. Fischer, "The New Dimensions of Transportation Planning," *Proceedings of the 1964 Annual Conference* (Milwaukee: American Institute of Planners, February, 1965), pp. 97-105.

4. William G. Colman, "The Federal Government in Intergovernmental Programs," *The Annals,* May, 1965, Vol. 359, p. 30.

5. "The dispersal of power [in the metropolitan area] renders the process of government one of endless committee-ing and negotiation, the proliferation of veto groups and the relinquishment of government to the hands of the full-time bureaucracies who alone have the time and functional requisites for the enterprise." Norton E. Long, "Citizenship or Consumership in Metropolitan Areas," *Journal of the American Institute of Planners,* XXXI (February, 1965), p. 5.

6. See Charles R. Adrian, "Metropology and the Planner," *Planning 1962* (Chicago: American Society of Planning Officials, November, 1962), pp. 75-81. Adrian does not discuss one substantive function which can be performed even by the "symbolic" planner viz. long-range education aimed at achieving most of its impact ten or twenty years hence.

7. ". . . the preference for special districts already to be found in attitudes of citizens and professional administrators . . . further obscure[s] the pattern of local decision-making, to make the decision-makers less visible to the voting public and to increase the influence of the professional administrator at the local level, since special districts are usually dominated by these persons." Charles R. Adrian, "State and Local Government Participation in the Design and Administration of Intergovernmental Programs," *The Annals,* May, 1965, Vol. 359, p. 41.

8. See Edward T. Chase, "The Trouble with the New York Port Authority," in *Urban Government,* Edward C. Banfield (ed.) (Glencoe, Ill.: The Free Press, 1961), pp. 75-82.

9. The following figures are illustrative of the popular apathy and resistance to metropolitan government: Between 1950 and the end of 1961, proposals for a significant change in local government structure were introduced for action in only 18 of the nation's 212 metropolitan areas and were finally approved in only 8. U.S., Advisory Commission on Intergovernmental Relations, *Factors Affecting Governmental Reorganization in Metropolitan Areas* (Washington, D.C.:   U.S. Government Printing Office, May, 1962), p. 1. If future proposals for the reorganization of metropolitan government are to be subject to the voters of an area for a final verdict, as the ACIR recommends, the prognosis for metropolitan government is obviously gloomy.

10. Commentaries on a report by the Advisory Commission on Intergovernmental Relations, *Government in Metropolitan Areas,* Section 1 (Wash-

ington: U.S. Government Printing Office, December, 1961). Comments by Professors William L. C. Wheaton, Guthrie S. Birkhead, Coleman Woodbury, Dr. Thomas H. Reed, and Professor Martin Meyerson. Meyerson, however, is by no means an advocate of metropolitan government.

11. Eli Comay, "How Metropolitan Toronto Government Works," *Planning 1965* (Chicago: American Society of Planning Officials, November, 1965), p. 30.

12. Edward C. Banfield, "The Political Implications of Metropolitan Growth," *Daedalus*, Winter, 1961, I, 1 [of the proceedings of the American Academy of Arts and Sciences], p. 71.

13. Robert C. Wood, *1400 Governments, New York Metropolitan Region Study* (Cambridge, Mass.: Harvard University Press, 1961), p. 114.

14. Adrian, "State and Local Government Participation," *op. cit.*, p. 42.

15. At the municipal level, Banfield and Wilson point out a positive danger in planning for limited objectives: "Project planning or planning within one agency . . . will proliferate and thereby make overall or master planning even more difficult. Planning, which once was thought of as the means to coordinate all aspects of city development, has now made such coordination all the more difficult." Edward C. Banfield and James Q. Wilson, *City Politics* (Cambridge, Mass.: Harvard University Press and M.I.T. Press, 1963), pp. 201-2. This observation is even more valid at the vastly more complex and more fragmented metropolitan level.

16. Harvey Walker, *ACIR Commentaries*, Commentaries on a report by the Advisory Commission on Intergovernmental Relations, *op. cit.*, p. 49.

17. See Irving Kristol, "The Negro Today is Like the Immigrant Yesterday," *The New York Times Magazine*, September 11, 1966, pp. 50-51. Kristol feels strongly that the rise of "half-a-million Negroes a year" above the poverty level is seriously neglected in favor of a focus on lurid symptoms of social disorganization. As far as a potential transfer of power is concerned, several generations of exposure to colorful aberrations in the mass media is likely to have more impact on the white majority than the existence of a sober, industrious, Negro majority.

18. See Terry Sanford, "The States Have Done Much," *Storm Over the States,* Chap. VII (New York: McGraw-Hill Book Co., 1967).

19. Presumably state government could intervene to end the "time-consuming battles engendered by rivalries among bureaucracies" which leave area needs unfilled, noted by Mowitz and Wright in their Detroit study. Also, the state with a good planning staff could provide a means of assisting the lay

citizen (and legislator) to "challenge policies and decisions based on technical determinations of the bureaucracy." Robert Mowitz and Deil S. Wright, *Profile Of a Metropolis, A Case Book* (Detroit: Wayne University Press, 1962), pp. 632-33.

20. Adrian, "State and Local Government Participation," *op. cit.*, pp. 36-37.

21. American Institute of Planners Committee on Metropolitan Planning, *Workshop Report, Proceedings of the 1964 Annual Conference* (Milwaukee: American Institute of Planners, February, 1965), p. 288.

22. "The Uses and Limitations of Metropolitan Planning in Massachusetts," reprinted in H. Wentworth Eldredge (ed.), *Taming Megalopolis: Vol. II, How to Manage an Urbanized World* (Garden City: Anchor Books--Doubleday and Co., Inc., 1967), pp. 710-19.

23. *Planning Services for State Governments* (Chicago: The Council of State Governments, 1956), p. 46.

24. Paul Davidoff, "Advocacy and Pluralism in Planning," *Journal of the American Institute of Planners*, XXX (November, 1964), p. 335.

25. Norman Beckman, "The Planner as a Bureaucrat," *Journal of the American Institute of Planners*, XXX (November, 1964), pp. 324-27.

26. Alan A. Altshuler, *The City Planning Process, A Political Analysis* (Ithaca, N.Y.: Cornell University Press, 1965), chaps. V and VI.

27. Robert Walker, *The Planning Function in Urban Government* (1st ed., Chicago: University of Chicago Press, 1941).

28. U.S., Text of "President's Message on City Development," January 26, 1966, *Congressional Quarterly Weekly Report*, February 4, 1966, p. 8.

29. Robert C. Wood, "A Federal Policy for Metropolitan Areas," in *Metropolitan Politics: A Reader*, Michael N. Danielson (ed.) (Boston: Little, Brown and Co., 1966), p. 334.

30. A study prepared by the Subcommittee on Intergovernmental Relations of the Committee on Government Operations, "The Federal System as Seen by Federal Aid Officials," results of a questionnaire dealing with intergovernmental relations (Washington, D.C.: U.S. Government Printing Office, December 15, 1965), pp. 92-99.

31. C. David Loeks, "Where Metropolitan Planning Stands Today," *Proceedings of the 1958 Annual Conference* (Milwaukee: American Institute of Planners, February, 1959), pp. 31-33.

32. Planners, unlike architects, are also overlooked in fiction. The author has encountered only one reference to an urban planner in recent American novels. "There was Irving Sklare thumping along in his space shoes. They called him 'Irving Development' because he was a city planner. Every third word out of his mouth was 'environment'." Wallace Markfield, *To an Early Grave* (New York: Pocket Books, 1965), p. 157.

33. Robert C. Wood, *Planning 1962* (Chicago: American Society of Planning Officials, November, 1962), pp. 8-10.

34. *Ibid.,* p. 10.

CHAPTER 7 TRANSPORTATION FACTORS IN HUMAN RESOURCES PLANNING

INTRODUCTION

A period of roughly five years, beginning in the late 1950's and ending in the early 1960's, marked the start and finish of the great urban transportation crisis in the United States. In previous decades, attention in the cities had been focused on such topics as absorbing foreign immigration, on municipal corruption, and on substandard housing. Then came transportation. Before poverty, crime and race problems moved up to center stage in the mid-1960's, highways and mass transit occupied what in retrospect appears to be an inordinate share of planning efforts and funds. Like all urban "crises," it grew out of publicity. In each so-called crisis, a spotlight is focused on what is alleged to be an urgent, unpostponable problem, the solution of which is a necessary prerequisite to the revival of our urban regions, if not to national survival. In point of fact, the entire transportation affair seems to have been related to the fact that in the late 1950's, a batch of commuter railroads decided that it was time to quit hauling local passengers. There was also a great deal of hullabaloo concerning the impact of interstate highways through densely settled urban neighborhoods. Equally important, for a few years, highwaymen and planners had reached a transient consensus on the notion that urban transportation systems planned in conjunction with land-use development could be the key to a significant improvement in urban regions and that the time was ripe for large-scale, intergovernmental projects.

Now that other problems have moved into the spotlight, it would be tempting to say that it was all a mistake. Possibly, co-existence, or at best an uneasy *detente*, is the best we can hope for between such antipathetic interests as North and South, East and West, Turk and Greek, highwayman and planner.

Looking back, it now seems that once a reasonably dependable system is in being, transportation is chiefly important in increasing the range of regional development alternatives. The thesis of this chapter is that transportation is not necessarily a determining factor in all aspects of regional development. Rather, a reasonably operable urban transportation system provides a broad framework within which a wide range of choices can be made, although, in highly specialized cases, transportation does represent a major determining element. In many programs, including the case studies in social planning examined here, the primary role of transportation as a major determinant disappears once the system is operating satisfactorily.

148

This leads to a corollary hypothesis: The tendency to inject impressive transportation data and graphics into decision-making processes in which transportation is not particularly significant serves as either a smokescreen concealing other basic factors or as a bit of marginalia, not much more important in many types of social planning than water or sewerage systems would be.

The areas in which transportation is a vital component are well known. New highways obviously have a major impact on structures and neighborhoods directly in their path. Transportation systems also have intrinsic values and development possibilities. At times, transportation projects can be deliberately designed to attack a social problem. For example, highways may in fact be located to remove slum housing. Highway construction is relatively expensive and, until recently, resistance to the routes laid down by highway engineers was minimal. Situations like that portrayed in a science-fiction novel in which a traffic engineer is employed by a hypothetical Latin American nation to prepare a highway plan that would blot out some of the urban-squatter hovels defacing the capital are not unknown in the United States.[1] The city of Fall River, Massachusetts, not only made use of an interstate expressway to cut a swathe through some of its slums but also managed to eliminate its obsolescent city hall in the process. (There was a prior agreement to build a modern city hall on air rights over Route I-195 with the use of federal funds.)

There are other circumstances in which the crucial role of highways and public transportation systems is readily identifiable. Sometimes the impact occurs in cycles. The case of elevated transit lines in New York, Chicago and Boston is a good example. Soon after they were constructed, property values along the elevated lines rose only to fall as time, grime, and gloom took their toll. Subsequently, many of the old "Els" were removed and the values of contiguous property rose once again. As a rule, subway extensions in residential areas usually have been associated with the construction of high-density housing along the lines, with clusters of commercial development at the stations. In earlier decades, suburban commuter railroads were frequently associated with pockets of residential and business development surrounding the stations. In contrast, suburban highways were similarly associated with low-density residential development, along with a new type of manufacturing center, the low-density, suburban, industrial park.

In each of these instances, there was clearly a close linkage between some type of change in land use and/or in property values associated with the construction or elimination of a key transportation component. However, the linkage between transportation and other aspects of the urban area and the region may be less significant, as indicated by the following two case histories. Both concern social planning conducted by Massachusetts state agencies. The first is drawn from a study prepared for the Massachusetts Board of Regional Community Colleges,[2] and the second, involving nursing homes, was prepared for a division of the State Department of Public Health.[3] Judging from these two examples, transportation is an important "given" rather than a determinant in the planning process.

PLANNING FOR COMMUNITY COLLEGES

The publicly controlled community college, a modern, broader version of the junior college, is one of the nation's fastest growing types of educational institutions. Between 1955 and 1965, the number of two-year institutions in the United States nearly trebled, while the number of four-year institutions barely doubled. In the period 1960-65, first-time student enrollment at the nation's two-year institutions nearly doubled, while the increase of first-year students at the four-year institutions was roughly 50 per cent.[4]

The percentage increase in students enrolled at community colleges in Massachusetts has been far more rapid, partly because the program is relatively new. In 1958, the system was still in the discussion stage. Seven years later, nearly 6,000 students were enrolled in 9 colleges; by the fall of 1967, total enrollment had increased to almost 12,000 at 12 community colleges.

Based on projections prepared by Massachusetts community college presidents and on ratios proved valid in other states, it is probable that the total demand for community college seats in Massachusetts will exceed 50,000 by 1975. The reasons for this extraordinary growth are not hard to find. Regional community colleges offer two years of low-cost, higher education within commuting distance, and tuition charges at many of the private institutions in Massachusetts are approaching $2,000 per year. Moreover, many of the most respected colleges and universities have made the decision not to expand at the undergraduate level, or, in other cases, have decided to place an increasing emphasis on attracting out-of-state students. In consequence, public institutions of higher education are expected to assume a larger role in providing college training for Massachusetts youngsters, particularly since, in Massachusetts, as in other states, political leaders have apparently placed education at the top of the state's list of priorities.

A major function for community colleges will probably continue to be the education of transfer students. Freshmen and sophomores can complete their first two years of college at a fraction of the cost of attending a residential institution. However, the community colleges' currently rather small, adult, evening training program is likely to expand substantially as the demand for employee skills training grows and upgrading and periodic retraining of adult workers becomes virtually mandatory in many fast-changing parts of the economy. The one- or two-year, daytime, terminal training role forecasted for community colleges, however, may not grow as rapidly as some had hoped. There are several reasons for this limited expansion. There is apparently less need for new technicians than was originally believed; a very large proportion of technicians are high school graduates trained on the job or are four-year college graduates; and finally, there are alternative methods of securing technician training, ranging from vocational high schools to public and private technical institutes and programs.

The primary objective of the *Planning Component Study* was to examine potential service areas for a partially developed community college system, particularly in the densely settled Boston area, where several colleges were planned. In theory, time-distance highway travel from existing and proposed community colleges was to be a major criterion. Final recommendations emanating from the master-plan study, however, were based on more relevant issues. In a relatively small state, where travel demand is well served by highways, the time-distance factor is not a major determinant of institutional location.

Massachusetts is a state of less than 8,000 square miles, and its compactness is considerably enhanced by a good road network. Highway travel from downtown Boston to the ends of Massachusetts--Williamstown to the west and Provincetown on the tip of Cape Cod--is under three hours. Within metropolitan Boston, half an hour's driving distance will embrace a population of almost 2 million from the central city to circumferential Route 128. The time-distance relationship with respect to public transportation is far less satisfactory, but this is probably not a matter of critical importance. Even at colleges served by public transportation, most students arrive and depart by automobile. Whether Boston's public transit authority, the MBTA, can succeed in its objective of altering area-transportation habits, particularly in severing the intimate relationship between the automobile and the adolescent male, is problematical.

The report that stimulated establishment of the Massachusetts regional community college system suggested the selection of locations within "20 miles or less commuting distance of the potential student body."[5] The subsequent master-plan study revised this to 30 miles, with a maximum driving time of 45 minutes from home to school.[6] However most students will be in the twenty- to thirty-minute category. Any reasonable upper-time limit in commuting is more likely a matter of local tradition; many residents of major metropolitan areas regularly commute for 1 hour to 1½ hours to work or school under conditions that would appall most of the nation. It was assumed, however, that one of the principal attractions of metropolitan Boston was the relative ease in moving from place to place. The highway system makes it feasible to serve the state effectively on the basis of substantial regions rather than a large number of small service areas.

As a general practice, the methodology used for estimating future enrollment in community colleges is based on a given population ratio. The community college is designed to provide adult education and adult vocational training as well as freshman and sophomore college courses. Thus, use of the general population figure seems reasonable.

The rule-of-thumb ratio, which has proved accurate as a method of forecasting demand, is 75 to 100 full-time, day, community college students per 10,000 population.[7] Thus, in states where public higher education is dominant, community colleges are constructed in the expectation that enrollment will constitute about 1 per cent of the total population. For a number of reasons, including the presence of fast-growing alternative public and private institutions, it would appear prudent to use the lower ratio in Massachusetts, 75:10,000 or ¾ of 1 per cent of the population. A ratio of 75 community college students per 10,000 population by 1975 would result in an enormous increase in student population, as noted above.

Three statistical guidelines were developed by the Massachusetts Board of Regional Community Colleges to govern size and location decisions: (1) The acceptable *optimum* size for new colleges after ten years of operation was to be 2,000 students. On the basis of the 75:10,000 ratio, this suggests that a service area should have a population on the order of 250,000 persons. Most of the existing and proposed community college service areas are in the 200,000-500,000 range. (2) The *maximum* size for a community college outside the densely settled Boston core area, but within Route 128, was to be 5,000 students, a figure that suggests a maximum service area population of perhaps 700,000. This standard presents no special problem; aside from Massachusetts Bay Community College, none of the existing or proposed regional areas exceeds 550,000 in 1965 population. (3) The *maximum* size for a community college within the core area was not to exceed 7,500.

The board's decision to create a large number of community college districts in the state precludes the necessity for long-distance commuting except in rare instances. The 1963 Census of Transportation showed nationally that over 75 per cent of the nation's total employees require less than 36 minutes to commute.[8] In the professional and managerial class, this figure rises to over 80 per cent. Portal to portal commuting times to downtown Boston frequently approach and exceed an hour, because of long walking distances between downtown parking spaces and offices and also between rapid transit stations and offices. In the larger office buildings, time spent in walking through the buildings, waiting for elevators, and travel in elevators must also be considered as part of the total commuting time. Thus, a longer commutation to downtown destinations is to be expected.

Except for travel to the Boston Central Business District, however, a full hour commutation period is considered excessive in Massachusetts. A recent study made in a major manufacturing and research complex in a northwest suburban location shows average employee commuting time between 25 to 30 minutes, with few trips below the 15 minute mark, and few requiring more than 45 minutes. The portal-to-portal increment in these cases is small. Thus, for most community college regions, a 30-minute service area seems a reasonable standard.

In addition to pure travel considerations, other factors relating to community college planning were found to be of vital importance, including size, class, and race. The Board's decision to place relatively low enrollment ceilings on the colleges had a number of extremely significant ramifications. The creation of one or more very large campuses in the central portion of Boston would have been entirely feasible from a commutation standpoint; perhaps two thirds of the metropolitan area population can reach the downtown area in less than a half hour. Moreover, all of the low-income areas in Boston, Cambridge, and other core communities are accessible via existing public transportation lines. Further, a decision to concentrate on one or two large campuses would have resulted in economies of scale, including the prospect of providing a greater variety of courses at less cost and closer physical proximity to the area's primary cultural and employment resources. It would also dictate a heightened degree of intermingling of classes and races which a system of suburban colleges would be likely to discourage.

There was one exception to the rule: Access to public transportation was considered important to Boston's low-income Negro population. The board tentatively selected a college site outside the Central Business District on the borderline between Boston's Negro district and the adjoining high-income town of Brookline. Because Brookline has a good school system, it is likely that most students from this community will enroll elsewhere, rather than attend a racially mixed college with much of the enrollment drawn from the Boston schools.

Several reasons were advanced for the decision to construct many smaller colleges rather than one or two major institutions. The first was an attachment to smallness. Amherst, Williams, Smith, and similar high-prestige colleges apparently provided the model that governed suburban enrollment ceilings. A student body of roughly 2,000 was believed to be the optimum number that would permit close ties among faculty, administration, and students. The enormous California-style community colleges of 10,000 to 15,000 students were believed to entail an unacceptable risk of alienation by all participants.

A second element in the size decision involved the goal accepted by many community college planners of a close identification between area and college. One tendency toward educational localism is based on the safety-in-the-streets and psychological arguments that are advanced in favor of the retention of neighborhood elementary schools. Community college orientation stresses the area service mission of an institution designed to assist local industries as well as residents, adults as well as teen-agers.

One or two large Boston institutions serving 1 or 2 million people would obviously violate two canons of the community college creed. The institutions would be larger than thought desirable, and they would remove the possibility of creating area institutions to serve special local needs throughout the metropolitan area. There was also a vision in the minds of many community college administrators and board members of a quiet, tree-shaded, suburban campus rather than an urban skyscraper surrounded by concrete, traffic, and jarring neighbors. The decision to build on urban sites indicates that the board was not wholly bound by this image. The board took its responsibility for creating area service institutions quite seriously. Nevertheless, there seemed to be an obvious reluctance to place all of the college eggs in one or two large urban baskets, regardless of time-distance ratios and alleged social benefits. The area service function, as well as the possibility of a full, outdoor athletic program, was advanced to justify the suburban schools, but undoubtedly, a clear and strong mental picture of a grassy campus had some influence on the final decision. The obvious consequence of this decision was the creation of homogeneous suburban institutions mirroring the income and class characteristics of surrounding towns. Over time, it is likely that a hierarchy of colleges will emerge, each reflecting the special qualities of the area population. To a considerable extent, one or two larger colleges in Boston may serve as cross-cultural melting pots, but as suburban schools open, the overall income level from which the central city community college population is drawn may decline. Moreover, given the central city location of most of Boston area's Negro population, it is likely that the proposed community college system of small regions will reinforce racial and social segregation patterns. In fact, it does not seem that the racial segregation issue received much attention. It was apparently assumed that under an enrollment system with at least two community colleges located within easy access to both white and Negro neighborhoods, the chosen pattern of smaller area colleges would combine the advantages of modest scale and close relations with residents of the surrounding community.

Two other arguments were apparently involved in the little regions decisions. The first is the local economic advantage to be derived from a new college. Cities like Boston and Cambridge may complain of land takings by institutions that create traffic problems and yield little in the way of taxes, but there can be little doubt that a substantial educational institution of higher learning offers significant benefits for area economy. Older industrial communities in Greater Boston are well aware of this fact, although precise measurement of this influence is difficult because of the nature of the components and variables involved, not all of which are quantifiable in any meaningful sense.

In one respect, the community college represents a vehicle for preventing economic losses rather than a new input to the area economy. Were it not for the community college, some hundreds of local residents would spend their freshman and sophomore years elsewhere. Others would either receive no educational or vocational training or would use alternative institutions. Neither of these possibilities creates the type of economic gain represented by institutions that attract substantial numbers of out-of-area students.

Based on a study of the economic impact of higher education, it is possible to develop a tentative estimate of this component of community colleges. Given an enrollment of 2,000 students and assuming that half, or 1,000, would otherwise have left the area for their schooling, the community college results in a retention of about $800 per capita or a total of $800,000 per year in student expenditures.[9] Much of these expenditures are apparent in retail stores, such as restaurants, drugstores, book and record stores, and gas service stations. As compared to retail expenditures generated by manufacturing payrolls, the 1,000 "retained" students are the equivalent of perhaps 200 factory workers employed at an annual wage of $5,000 to $6,000.

Aside from these "retained" benefits, the community college is the source of two types of economic inputs identifiable as additional gains. First, at an average of $4,000 per student[10] in land, equipment, and building-construction costs, there is the $8 million expended for construction of a 2,000-place college and the additional monies required for upkeep and maintenance. The employment stimulus of construction contracts is estimated at 223 man-hours per $1,000 of contract cost. An $8 million building is therefore estimated as the equivalent of a year's work for almost 1,000 men. Approximately one third of the total is on-site man-hours, with the remainder in various stages of manufacturing, mining, trade, and transportation.[11]

A second type of benefit is derived from the employment of faculty or administrative staff attracted from out of the area. One such person is employed for every eighteen students, resulting in a payroll of about 100 for a 2,000-student college.

At an average salary of $8,000 per year, these 100 staff people represent the equivalent in payrolls generated of 160 factory workers paid $5,000 a year; an annual payroll on the order of almost $800,000 can be anticipated. An additional 60 nonprofessional persons may be employed as clerical and maintenance workers. Based on 1965-66 data for the Massachusetts regional community college system (i.e., an average salary of $4,200 per year for clerical and custodial staff), the total payroll for this category is likely to be about $250,000 annually.

To summarize, the immediate cash benefits of a 2,000-student community college include: (1) $8 million in construction expenditures plus continued operating, maintenance, and renovation expenditures, (2) $800,000 a year in "retained" student expenditures, (3) an annual professional payroll estimated at $800,000, and (4) an annual nonprofessional payroll estimated at $250,000. Finally, over and above these ideological, educational, and economic considerations, apparently certain pragmatic advantages accrue from the creation of many smaller colleges; more colleges mean more college presidencies.

There were some observers who argued that the decision to keep enrollment ceilings relatively low reflected a desire to maximize the number of presidential openings.

Finally, it is clear that a good highway system permitted a wide latitude for decisions governing the size and location of Massachusetts' burgeoning community colleges. Within the broad limits of half-an-hour's commuting time, the board established a pattern of class and race segregation or integration, depending on the set of values that it preferred. For the most part, location decisions were based on other than transportation considerations, despite the rather restrictive travel-time standards adopted as a general guide.

NURSING HOMES AND AREA PLANNING

The typical nursing home resident in Massachusetts is an elderly woman on welfare whose stay lasts about two years, until her death.[12] Most of the nursing homes are small--under 50 beds--and are located in older, converted buildings. Almost one third of the state's 730 nursing homes are over 50 years old, and only 1 in 7 was constructed within the last 20 years. For reasons that are largely obscure, a substantially higher proportion of Massachusetts' aged population is in nursing homes than in neighboring New York and Connecticut. In spite of the relative liberality of public welfare standards in these states compared to Massachusetts, families are apparently more reluctant to place their parents in nursing homes primarily catering to patients on public assistance.

Nursing home payments under public welfare in Massachusetts are generally considered inadequate: The $55 per week available for such patients in the mid-1960's was over one third lower than the weekly payment in Connecticut. Thus, the fact that nursing homes are a highly profitable investment raised serious suspicions in many quarters regarding the treatment, feeding, and facilities accorded to residents. In Massachusetts, as elsewhere, nursing home operations have occasionally erupted into scandals ranging from nasty fires in converted wooden tinderboxes to outright neglect of patients, and charges that underworld money was being attracted to this lucrative business.

Some improvements are clearly in evidence. The new nursing homes, built in the period 1955-65, average over 60 beds as compared to only about 30 beds in older homes. Facilities are newer, buildings are fire resistant, and staffing is not as minimal.

About 60 per cent of the nursing homes in Massachusetts are privately operated for profit; only 1 bed in 10 is located in a nursing home run by non-profit organizations. The dominant form of operation is the proprietary corporation, a pattern that prevails in the nation as a whole. In the past few years, hospitals have indicated increasing interest in sponsoring affiliated or directly operated nursing homes partly as an adjunct to teaching and research functions.

For purposes of state hospital administration and planning, Massachusetts has been divided into 68 hospital service areas by the state Department of Health. Each of these service areas is centered around one or more general hospitals. In some instances, the hospital service areas are virtually identical with the 1960 Standard Metropolitan Statistical Areas established by the U.S. Bureau of the Census. For the most part, however, there is a stronger degree of localization centering around communities too small (under 50,000) to qualify as central city by census criteria. Until such time as a comprehensive, medical services plan could be completed for the state, the study prepared for the Division of Adult Health recommended that existing hospital service areas be utilized as the basic unit in nursing home planning, rather than attempting to establish special nursing home service areas.

In 1965, the Division of Adult Health was confronted with a critical, pressing problem: the approval or disapproval of applications for the construction of new nursing homes containing approximately 6,000 nursing home beds. The U.S. Department of Health, Education and Welfare has established a ratio of 3 beds per 1,000 population as a reasonable standard. This appears to be on the low side for Massachusetts, where the proportion of aged population is substantially higher than the national average (11.1 per cent of the population vs. 9.3 per cent for the nation in 1960). The study prepared for the Division of Adult Health suggested that a more reasonable state ratio might be between 4 to 5 per 1,000, the proportion being somewhat lower in the Boston suburbs, where there are smaller proportions of older people, and with higher proportions in Cape Cod and other areas where the proportion of aged persons exceeds 12 per cent of the total population. Furthermore, if the Medicare and Medicaid programs result in a permanent, substantial increase in the demand for nursing home beds, the ratio might well be increased to the 6 per 1,000 level.

Although the location of nursing home beds tends to correlate positively with population distribution, there are very substantial differences between various hospital service areas. Many of the state's hospital service areas were well above the federal 3 per 1,000 standard in 1965, but significant deficiencies appear to exist in a number of service areas, some of them located within the Boston SMSA.

If all the applications on file in 1965 were approved and the proposed nursing homes were placed into immediate operation, most of the state would be well above minimum federal levels; but in some areas, most of them in southeastern Massachusetts, the bed-to-population ratio would still be below the federal standard.

It should be borne in mind, in evaluating existing and future deficiencies, that these ratios were based on continued operation of all existing nursing home beds. In mid-1965, the Division of Adult Health recognized that approximately 50 small nursing homes housing 1,000 patients would not be able to meet proposed new standards being considered by the division. It appeared likely that an additional but undetermined number of beds would be ruled substandard on the basis of stricter federal minimum criteria developing out of the 1965 Social Security amendments. For example, it was estimated by state and federal officials that more than 75 per cent of existing nursing home beds would not meet federal Medicare requirements, although it is probable that a substantial number can be successfully upgraded by expanding and improving medical and related services. Any significant reduction in the number of approved beds would create a need for construction of replacements. However, the possibility of releasing beds by restorative treatment of patients,[13] returning them to families, rest homes, or making other arrangements for their departure from nursing homes, would substantially reduce the number of beds required by nursing home patients. However, the patient profile described above limits these possibilities.

In addition to population growth trends and program revaluation and changes that will affect future bed requirements, other trends may exert an appreciable influence on future needs for nursing home beds. There is, for example, a reported tendency to transfer elderly, long-term patients from mental hospitals to nursing homes after age has made younger, unruly patients more docile. Depending on trends in psychiatric care and public policy, the mental hospitals can become a significant source of additional demand for nursing home beds. On the other hand, there are several factors that may depress future demand. These include increasing affluence, particularly higher pensions and improved medical insurance (which, among other results, will permit more elderly Massachusetts residents to migrate), and medical research and programs that will reduce the incidence of sickness among the elderly and hence decrease the need for costly care facilities. For example, incentive payments for families, relatives, or other persons may be effective, in conjunction with out-patient care, in reducing the number of older patients in nursing homes.

How Many Beds Needed?

At present, there are a number of imponderables whose future impact on nursing home needs cannot be accurately foretold. It is assumed that some factors tending to increase or decrease the need for nursing home beds will counterbalance each other and that further study will undoubtedly make it possible to estimate the effect of such factors with greater precision. It is clear, however, that a substantial increase in approved, high-quality nursing home beds is needed. Unless presently unforeseen factors intervene, by 1975, the state will require over 30,000 beds in nursing homes that offer a high quality of nursing care. Of this total, up to 10,000 additional qualifying beds may be required before 1970, depending on: (1) the impact of Medicare and Medicaid, (2) realignments in patient care between nursing and rest homes, and (3) the number of beds ruled substandard in terms of comprehensive nursing care criteria. For the purposes of this estimate, it is assumed that nursing homes with less than 30 beds can be assumed to be substandard. There are about 250 nursing homes caring for 6,000 patients in this category. All but two of these homes are located in converted frame buildings. Assuming a replacement need for 6,000 beds and a minimum of 1,500 beds to satisfy population expansion and medical needs, up to 1,800 new, standard, quality beds a year may be needed in between 1966 and 1975.

The projections of beds needed in Massachusetts may be compared to the estimates presented in the state of New York. In its 1963-64 plan, the New York State Department of Health indicated that 4 out of 10 of the 786 nursing homes in the state were in nonfire-resistive structures. To receive federal aid, nursing homes that are adjuncts to general hospitals are required to have at least 30 beds. Nursing homes located apart from such a hospital must have a capacity of at least 60 beds and be affiliated with a general hospital. Under existing conditions in 1965, if this 60-bed criterion were adopted in Massachusetts, it would eliminate over 80 per cent of the nursing homes and about two thirds of the nursing home beds in the state.

Aside from the minimum-size standard, the physical criteria of structures adjudged fire-resistive, physically safe, and therefore suitable for long-range planning resulted in classifying 40 per cent of existing beds in New York (17,550 out of 42,100) as unsuitable.[14]

Patient Distribution

An analysis of patient origin and current location by community indicates that the service areas of nursing homes are relatively small. The figures show that between 70 per cent and 80 per cent of beds within most sizable communities are occupied by residents. For example, in Boston, the percentage is 81 per cent, and in other Massachusetts communities, the figure is roughly the same. Where there are one or two smaller nursing homes in a small suburb of a large city, the percentage is much lower, but it rises rapidly if residents originating in adjoining communities are included.

Boston, the largest city in the commonwealth, does not show any substantially different pattern of patient origin than smaller centers in the state, such as Worcester and Springfield, or smaller metropolitan centers, such as Fitchburg and Lawrence. The same pattern of patient distribution is evident, with most of the patients originating from the central city and most of the remainder from abutting towns.

The relocation pattern of residents from metropolitan centers is similar to the flow-in pattern. There are very few patients who relocate outside of their own town to a nursing home. In the case of Boston, for example, only Brookline attracts any large number of patients, and a few other nearby suburbs attract smaller numbers. Accounting for the remaining patients, however, does demonstrate a wide scattering of patients throughout the entire state. It must be assumed that this wide distribution of a minority of patients is accounted for by personal preference, family situations, and other conditions that affect the selection of a nursing home.

The conclusion that can be drawn from this analysis is that the nursing home service areas are reasonably definable. By the same token, the relatively small potential service area of most new nursing homes can also be delineated with some precision. Thus, it becomes possible to evaluate a proposed nursing home on the basis of its potential service area and its current service level. This, of course, does not apply to a nursing home that serves a special category of patient, such as a religious institution, or to nursing homes designed to care for patients with similar types of disorders.

It would appear that the choice of the proper location and size of a nursing home within a particular community should be largely determined by local factors, such as the extent of the local market, land use, zoning, and street patterns. Relationship to the statewide network of highways or transportation facilities does not appear to be a significant element.

Staffing Needs

It is estimated that in 1965, the equivalent of 4,500 full-time staff were employed by nursing homes to care for 29,000 Massachusetts nursing home patients. In the future, higher standards of care, a restructuring of nursing home functions to weed out less seriously affected, restorable patients, combined with more comprehensive care, could result in a ratio of one employee for every three patients.

A standard that involves one staff employee for every three patients would require substantial increases in all categories of nursing home employees, ranging from janitors and orderlies to therapists, recreation workers, and physicians. Moreover, aside from the need for additional staff to provide comprehensive services, the need for staff would increase as the patients grew in numbers. Another factor that must be taken into account in calculating personnel needs is attrition; staff turnover, particularly among lower-echelon employees, is extremely high. For some occupations, it is reported to exceed 10-20 per cent annually. Also, an estimate of the need for training must consider the necessity of upgrading managerial and other key staff now engaged in the operation of nursing homes. It is generally agreed that serious deficiencies exist in this area in Massachusetts as elsewhere in the nation. However, it must be recognized that a substantial proportion, perhaps two thirds of nursing home employees, require little formal training. Janitors and maids, orderlies, laundry and restaurant workers, and yardsmen can be trained on the job. Other employees, including clerical personnel, therapists, nurses' aides, practical and registered nurses, administrators, and other specialized sub-professional and professional personnel require varying degrees of vocational training, ranging from high school level courses to professional degrees. It is assumed that other professional inputs will be provided (and in fact expanded) through close association with outside physicians and hospitals.

Relationship to Land Use and Zoning

Nursing homes have not been a subject for thoughtful consideration in land-use planning. This neglect has apparently been general throughout the nation. A report prepared by the American Society of Planning Officials (ASPO) was hard put to discover a significant number of zoning bylaws and studies reflecting special consideration of nursing home locations and community impact. Moreover, aside from problems created by parking, transportation access and similar factors have apparently caused little concern in nursing home location. Since most existing nursing homes are converted older structures, many of them former single-family structures, most nursing home locations reflect the availability of deteriorating Victorian mansions.

The location of newly constructed nursing homes tends to differ from the location of older, converted structures. For the most part, new nursing homes are two-story brick buildings of undistinguished appearance, located on traffic arteries zoned for multifamily or commercial use. However, a number of suburban homes are found on comparatively isolated sites in districts zoned for single-family residences. Part of the reason for the scarcity of nursing homes in newer, single-family residential areas lies in the fact that most Massachusetts zoning bylaws and ordinances permit location of nursing homes in single-family districts only with approval of the local zoning board of appeals. Here again, access to public transportation or other transportation factors appears to be unimportant in location. Site availability is the major factor.

In 1964, ASPO devoted one of its special research studies to the topic of nursing homes, canvassing and analyzing planning and zoning practices related to nursing homes in a number of communities through the nation.[15]

Parking space standards varied considerably, ranging downwards to one space for every six beds up to one parking space for every two beds. This relatively high ratio of one to two is currently required in Worcester, Massachusetts, Fort Lauderdale, Florida, and Ithaca, New York. The American Nursing Home Association recommends one parking space for every four beds, the same standard suggested by the Massachusetts Department of Public Health.

Various recommendations for outdoor recreation space, walks, shrubbery, and screening walls were included in the reports and ordinances analyzed by ASPO. Aside from prescribed setback and frontage provisions, however, recommendations for screening and outdoor recreation areas tended to be general in nature with requirements based on such subjective terms as "adequate," "sufficient," "ample," or "necessary."

The ASPO report bears out a major conclusion reached in the course of the analysis and inspection undertaken in the planning study for the Division of Adult Health: Old or new, nursing homes appear to have a minimal impact on the areas in which they are located. Currently found in all types of neighborhoods, nursing homes appear to be among the most inconspicuous types of development, often blending almost unnoticed into their surroundings. When a considerable amount of physical isolation on a suburban site exists, a nursing home tends to be even more of an "invisible neighbor" than is the case in settled urban areas. The general mediocrity of their design seems to have an advantage of assisting them to fade almost unnoticeably into their environment.

The ASPO report indicated that requirements for nursing homes have not been carefully considered in many communities. On the whole, the general public seems to expect that nursing homes should be located in high-density, multifamily, and commercial districts, but ASPO indicates a trend toward greater diffusion of nursing homes throughout residential areas. It is not clear how this trend accords with the reported desirability of locating nursing homes "near the center of community activities" as suggested by the U.S. Public Health Service.

The principal Public Health Service publication on nursing home problems and standards concentrates on medical care and service facilities, but it does include recommendations relating to site planning and location.[16] The report refers to the need to provide adequate space for outdoor recreation and to the need for screening this space for privacy. The principal locational recommendation of the Public Health Service was that nursing homes be placed at quiet sites within reasonable distance of public transportation, and, as indicated above, "near the center of community activities."

Building and Site Standards

The Division of Adult Health of the Massachusetts Department of Health suggests that a gross-floor area of 180 square feet be provided for each bed. For a 100-bed nursing home, this would involve a total of 18,000 square feet of building space. Up to August, 1965, the ground area covered by the structure could apparently vary between a 1/2 an acre and 1/7 of an acre. The removal of the two-story maximum in 1965 reduced the building requirement to as little as 5,000 square feet, a postage-stamp size that the division believed to be consonant with high-quality land prices of intown areas.

The thrust toward improving the standards of nursing home care has had a direct impact on parking-space requirements for more staff. On the basis of current estimates, the total staff required to provide adequate services for a 100-bed nursing home is about 25. An increase in standards to California levels, a development that can probably be anticipated in coming years, would increase the total staff to 35. Fewer than 25-35 parking spaces are needed for staff purposes, however, because employees work on a three-shift basis.

In addition to employee parking, additional parking spaces must be provided for delivery trucks and other vehicles. Currently, one parking space for every four beds is considered adequate for this purpose. This ratio would involve the allocation of only 7,500 square feet of parking space for a 100-bed nursing home, using the commonly accepted ratio of 300 square feet per automobile.

Traffic Implications

One of the questions that has seriously concerned neighborhood residents is the burden which might be placed on local streets if a major traffic generator is located in their area. In general, a 100-bed nursing home does not constitute such a traffic generator. During the peak hours of the journey to work and return (7:30-9:30 A.M. and 4:00-6:00 P.M.), total traffic to and from such a nursing home would essentially be limited to ten to twenty employees traveling in each direction, in addition to an occasional delivery truck or service vehicle. Most visitor traffic to a nursing home occurs during the evening hours and on week ends. Lesser amounts of visitor traffic may occur in off-peak weekday morning and afternoon hours. Finally, most deliveries and service vehicles arrive during off-peak hours. In summary, it would appear that as far as traffic is concerned, a nursing home probably generates less activity in the crucial peak hours than most other types of urban development.

Transportation

With a few exceptions, the nursing homes in the commonwealth are all within half an hour's driving time to a general hospital, although peak-hour driving time in congested areas may add ten to twenty minutes to the total. The same half-hour time-distance relationship holds true for staff and visitors to most nursing homes. There are, however, a number of residents living in nursing homes at considerable distances from their home communities either as a matter of personal choice or by virtue of a family decision.

In cases where complex medical treatment is required that is not available in the locality, relocation from the home community is mandatory. Similarly, as the minimum economic size of nursing homes increases to 60, 80, or 100 beds, many residents of thinly populated communities will find relocation necessary. However, unless more than 20-30 miles are involved, relatives can visit them with little difficulty with half an hour of driving time.

One question that has concerned persons involved in establishing standards for nursing home location involves access to public transportation. The aged population is generally considered part of the captive market for mass transportation, and it has been thought desirable to situate nursing homes on bus and transit lines, to permit ambulatory residents freedom of movement and visits from aged friends. The proportion of nursing home residents reported to be fully ambulatory in the Boston College Study was 47 per cent while only 6 per cent of the patients were fully bedridden.[17] However, while many patients can move freely within a protected environment, the percentage capable of using public transportation is probably extremely small. Since nursing home residents are by definition sick persons requiring custodial care, few are willing or able to travel via bus or subway. On the other hand, it is probable that rest homes which tend to house relatively well older people (as distinct from nursing homes) should be located on sites where such transportation is available.

Proximity to public transportation does appear to be significant in one respect. While professional staff and patients' relatives can be expected to own or have access to automobiles, this may not be true of the nonprofessional staff required by nursing homes. Hospitals and nursing homes located in suburban areas reportedly have encountered difficulty in filling nonprofessional positions because the principal labor market for this type of low-paid service occupation is found in core cities. With time, however, as automobile ownership becomes more diffused, some of these personnel recruitment problems may be alleviated, although they are unlikely to disappear.

Relationship to Hospitals and Medical Personnel

To a considerable extent, the reduction of travel time through expressway construction reduces the importance of immediate proximity to hospitals, medical facilities, and personnel. It would seem vital, however, to husband limited resources by locating patients requiring complex care that is available only in a few locations to the sources of care as is feasible; even the modest amount of time lost in travel by medical personnel can significantly diminish the time available for patients.

The Boston medical complex appears to be the major key to patient care in much of Massachusetts. An examination of the residences of physicians and other medical personnel and facilities indicates the premier role played by Boston as a regional, national, and international medical center.

Aside from the differential between the Boston area and other areas of Massachusetts, another type of geographic differential has caused some discussion. Like other middle- and upper-income patients, physicians and skilled nurses prefer to live in suburban communities, although much or most of their working lives are spent in core areas. If nursing homes are to be located near physicians and nurses, there is an obvious choice: They can be sited in proximity to medical work places (primarily hospitals, but also downtown medical offices), or they can be sited in the suburbs where most doctors and many nurses reside. At the present time, the core areas are clearly dominant in the nursing home field. For example, no fewer than 5,000 beds, over 1/6 of the state total, are in nursing homes in Boston. Overall, about 80 per cent of nursing home beds are located in large communities in various parts of the state, with the remainder in suburban or, infrequently, in rural communities. Part of this central city orientation is attributable to the location of welfare patients.

Over 70 per cent of the commonwealth's welfare patients lived in core communities before entering a nursing home.

Up to mid-1965, there appeared to be no pronounced tendency for the kind of core-to-suburb relocation of welfare patients or of urban poor families that has been characteristic of industrial plants, shopping centers, and business executives. In fact, the elderly poor are becoming more concentrated in central cities as financially better-off young families move to the suburbs. The growing stress on close ties to hospitals, embodied in Medicare legislation, may help to strengthen the existing central-area orientation of many of the aged.

It is obvious, however, that suburbanization is to have a significant if belated impact on the nursing home pattern. An examination of pending applications for almost 6,000 nursing home beds reveals that about 70 per cent were to be located in suburban locations. Part of the reason for the increased emphasis on suburban locations can be found in population and income trends. Most nursing homes are operated by private entrepreneurs, and many hope to serve the $70-$100-a-week suburban market and to keep the number of low-paying patients to a minimum.

There is also the site-cost factor to consider. Well located, intown sites may cost $40,000 or more for the half-acre site required for a two-story nursing home with adequate off-street parking, minimal set backs from property lines, and probably much more. In contrast, a suburban site will usually cost no more than one quarter to one half that amount; one-acre sites can be secured for a maximum of perhaps $10,000 to $20,000. Thus, to some extent, the two-story limitation has tended to stimulate suburban nursing home location because of high intown site costs.

It is assumed that one of the principal goals of nursing home planning is to develop closer links with hospitals. The Medicare program, which makes explicit provision for close ties between hospitals and nursing homes, represents a clear statement of a hitherto largely unmet and obviously desirable objective. It is clear that a coordinated planning effort is required to bring together various types of regional and local medical facilities. Existing transportation systems permit a variety of medical care patterns. In short, as in the case of the community colleges, transportation provides a framework within which widely differing objectives can be sought. Nevertheless, other factors appear to be of greater significance.

CONCLUSION

There are parts of the nation, mainly, urban slums, in which transportation is critically deficient. To cite one problem that is receiving increasing attention, the absence of good access to suburban jobs may become a significant obstacle to achieving substantial reductions in ghetto unemploy-

ment. In this sense, adequate transportation--as long as it remains unavailable--
is a key element in social planning.

The social planning cases discussed in this chapter are probably representative of a wide range of instances where transportation factors are not of
great significance; transportation access does not present particular difficulties
for most people in most areas. Consequently, once the system exists, it tends
to assume the same taken-for-granted, backdrop role of public water or sewerage systems.

The key locational decisions governing the delineation of service areas
for community colleges and nursing homes reflect differing concepts of client
groups affected by these institutions. In the case of community colleges, the
major factor was proximity to students. This general guideline did not in itself narrow the range of planning alternatives. The decision to limit the size of
core area colleges and to opt instead for a number of small suburban colleges
was not reached on the basis of transportation considerations but on the
grounds of prevalent notions concerning the pragmatic and intangible benefits
of smallness and close linkages between the colleges and their local service
areas.

The case of the nursing homes presented a somewhat different picture.
Until recently, the principal locational criterion was proximity to patients. In
more recent years, the trend toward suburbanization that has affected the distribution of metropolitan area population and economic activity has exercised
a growing influence on nursing home location. To a degree, this trend also reflects the predilections of upper-echelon staff, doctors, managers, and nurses,
many of them car-owning residents of the suburb. Two other counterbalancing
trends are in evidence, however. The first is the need for tapping the low-skill
labor market in the core areas. Orderlies, attendants, kitchen staff, and practical
nurses seem to be more difficult to find and keep in the suburbs. In view of the
heavy turnover in these occupations, location in or near the urban core on a
site well served by public transportation may be indicated for many nursing
homes, especially as they increase in size and staff.

Another locational trend is also exercising a growing influence on nursing home location. A stronger emphasis on providing a wide range of therapeutic services and on advanced medical care and research is associated in part with
Medicare legislation. Medicare, however, is only one element in a heightened
interest in gerontology linked quite probably to the expansion in numbers
and impact of the nation's aged population. This tendency is likely to be reflected in a further accentuation of the trend toward locating nursing homes as
adjuncts to hospitals. In this sense, the original location decision that prompted
the choice of a hospital site leads to the concept of a medical complex including physicians' office buildings, housing for medical personnel, post convales-
cent facilities, special research operations, and nursing homes. Medical facilities

clearly display some of the same characteristics as other types of locational aggregation.

This discussion hardly suggests that transportation is no longer a significant element in social planning. It does indicate that transportation is only one of a number of factors bearing on locational decisions, although partly because of its susceptibility to quantification and colorful graphic presentation, it often tends to be overemphasized.

With the major exception of the poor and other elements in the population who require public transportation, most people in the metropolitan area rely on the automobile and a highway system that permits easy access to a large swath of territory. Under these circumstances, transportation systems, especially in sizable metropolitan areas, have become a foundation element in the decision-making equation, the chessboard on which a multitude of combinations can be worked out.

NOTES TO CHAPTER 7

1. John Brunner, *Squares of the City* (New York: Ballantine Books, 1965).

2. Melvin R. Levin, Project Director, *Planning Component Study,* Prepared as part of *Master Plan Study* (Commonwealth of Massachusetts: Massachusetts Board of Regional Community Colleges, March, 1966).

3. Melvin R. Levin, Project Director, *Toward A State Plan for Nursing Homes,* Prepared for the Division of Adult Health (Boston, October, 1966).

4. U.S., Bureau of the Census, *Statistical Abstract of the U.S., 1967,* Washington, D.C., 1967, Table No. 188, p. 133.

5. Commonwealth of Massachusetts, Special Commission on Audit of State Needs, *Needs in Massachusetts Higher Education* (Boston, March, 1958), p. 10.

6. Massachusetts, Board of Regional Community Colleges, *Access to Quality Community College Opportunity: A Master Plan for Massachusetts Community Colleges Through 1975,* A Summary Report (Boston, May, 1967).

7. In contrast, the state of Rhode Island has used 36 to 50 per 10,000 population as the low and high range in estimating future community college enrollment. In view of the fact that several community colleges in Massachusetts have already passed or are approaching the 40:10,000 ratio, 75:10,000 appears to be a more reasonable working figure for Massachusetts.

8. U.S. Department of Commerce, *1963 Census of Transportation,* "Home-to-Work Travel" (Washington, D.C.: U.S. Government Printing Office, 1963), TC63 (A)-P5.

9. Francis S. Doody, *The Immediate Economic Impact of Higher Education in New England,* Education Studies No. 1 (Boston: Bureau of Business Research, College of Business Administration, Boston University, 1961), pp. 34-37. Data has been updated to reflect changes in the cost-of-living index.

10. Data supplied by Donald Deyo, Director, *Master Plan Study,* Massachusetts Board of Regional Community Colleges.

11. Claiborne M. Ball, "Employment Effects of Construction Expenditures," *Monthly Labor Review,* LXXXVIII (February, 1965), 154-55.

12. Data characteristics of nursing homes and nursing home patients is derived from Boston College, *Fact Finding Survey of Nursing Homes* (Boston, 1963), and from information supplied by the Division of Adult Health, Massachusetts Department of Public Health.

13. In a 1964 study in Maine, physician interviewers estimated that 21 per cent of nursing-home patients possessed rehabilitation potential. An estimated 9 per cent could be rehabilitated to the point where the patient could function with limited supervision or feeding and lodging. Maine, Office of Health Education, Department of Health, Education, and Welfare, *Nursing Home Patient Care* (Augusta, January 20, 1965), Table 37, p. 41.

14. New York State Department of Health, Division of Hospital Review and Planning, *Priorities for Federal Grants-in-aid for Construction of Nursing Home Facilities* (Albany: State of New York, July 1, 1963).

15. American Society of Planning Officials, *Nursing Homes,* Information Report No. 185, April, 1964.

16. U.S. Department of Health, Education, and Welfare, Public Health Service, *Nursing Home Standards Guide,* Publication No. 827 (Washington, D.C., June, 1961, reprinted April, 1963).

17. *Fact Finding Survey of Nursing Homes, op. cit.,* p. 28.

CHAPTER	**8**	THE ECONOMIC DEVELOPMENT DISTRICTS: NEW PLANNING REGIONS

NEW DIRECTIONS IN AREA DEVELOPMENT

In addition to its proposed substantive role in assisting the area economy, the new Economic Development Districts created under the Public Works and Economic Development Act of 1965 represent an experiment on the frontiers of creative federalism. The districts will serve as a yardstick of the extent to which a regional organization sponsored by one agency, the Economic Development Administration (EDA), can successfully coordinate its programs and policies within the framework of a variety of state and federal jurisdictions, sponsorships, and clienteles. Moreover, this test will occur at a time when the entire federal-state-local relationship is in ferment.[1] Cities and states are vying for federal support and power, federal and state agencies are sparring for a dominant place in the urban constellation, and political leaders of both parties are proposing a host of modified and new approaches to solving urban and regional problems. It is apparent that from their very inception, the Economic Development Districts were clearly confronted with substantial problems that would tax the ingenuity and patience of their leadership, their staff, and the federal agency which sponsors and sustains them.

The federal Public Works and Economic Development Act of 1965 places heavy stress on programs designed to make a significant impact on hard-core unemployment. In this respect, the legislation parallels concepts advanced in the Vocational Education Act of 1963, the Economic Opportunity Act of 1964, the Elementary and Secondary Education Act of 1965, and subsequent amendments of the Manpower and Development Training Act. EDA is developing administrative requirements for federal assistance that underscores this emphasis, including adequate representation of the "poor" on local economic development committees, technical assistance and other programs in selected large-city slum areas, and careful examination of the impact of local development proposals on the employment problems of disadvantaged persons.

Other modifications in federal policy for distressed areas are also embodied in the act. With respect to Massachusetts redevelopment areas, the key features of the new approach are the creation of a New England regional development commission and the selection and designation of economic growth centers within newly created multiarea economic development districts.

As in most parts of the nation, physical, economic, and human-resources planning in redevelopment areas is fragmented among agencies, between central cities and suburbs, and among various levels of government. This splitting of jurisdictions and programs creates problems of varying degrees of severity in a flourishing economy, but in a long-distressed area, it can create havoc. There, the backlog of needs is greater, the gap with the constantly improving major metropolitan areas is wider, local expertise is in short supply, and local financial resources are usually less than adequate. The obvious solution is to hire professional staff and compensate for local deficiencies by launching large-scale, federally aided programs. Unfortunately, the amount of money specifically earmarked for distressed areas is extremely limited when compared with funds available to all areas from the major grant-in-aid programs. As suggested by their relative lack of success in securing urban renewal allocations, the distressed areas often find it impossible to marshal the expertise, unity, and civic leadership needed to secure a proportionate share of federal allocations, let alone compensate for accumulated neglect. In short, the distressed area has more need but less capability to secure aid and less know-how in operating complex, federally assisted programs.

The Economic Development District, a key feature of the 1965 legislation, may be one way to escape this dilemma. The provision for federal financial aid for professional staff--75 per cent of the total cost--and the requirement that a meaningful development plan be presented as a prerequisite of receiving aid for development projects raises interesting possibilities. With this combination of incentives and painless funding, the objective is to have the distressed areas design and establish a single mechanism to formulate and implement comprehensive development plans.

While there was evidence that the Area Redevelopment Act of 1961 had achieved some positive results, most observers agreed that fundamental changes in area-development legislation were in order. The Public Works and Economic Development Act of 1965 reflects some of the modifications suggested both by domestic empirical experience and European models. Following the Appalachian precedent, the legislation contained provisions for the creation of large-scale regional commissions. Second, reacting to criticisms concerning the tendency to dilute the impact of development programs by designating too many redevelopment areas, the states are now required to delineate larger and presumably fewer economic development districts, each of which is to contain one or two designated growth centers to provide an attractive focus for economic expansion. It was recognized that not every depressed community and rural area could induce economic growth; the growth centers, it was hoped, would provide new jobs within easy commuting range, i.e., within 20 to 30 miles, thereby permitting residents of distressed areas to remain in their present residences if they so desire. However, the probability that outmigration would be

unavoidable for many residents to whom jobs could not be made available was
reflected in portions of the legislation related to manpower training and relocation assistance.

It is useful to review both of these vectors, the operations of the Area
Redevelopment Act and foreign experience, to understand the reasoning underlying this decision to indicate the kinds of results that can be expected.

BACKGROUND OF THE AREA REDEVELOPMENT ACT

During his 1954 election campaign, Senator Paul Douglas, the author of
the Area Redevelopment Act, was confronted with the economic ailments of
southern Illinois, in much the same way that President Kennedy encountered
similar problems in West Virginia seven years later. Southern Illinois, an area
known as "Egypt," containing picturesque communities such as Cairo and Kar-
nak, had long been battered by declines in the dominant soft-coal industry that
had been superimposed on a marginal agricultural economy.[2]

Better by far, the Senator reasoned, to use costly existing social-
overhead capital (i.e., schools, streets, and other public facilities) in depressed
areas than to have to replace it elsewhere if people from southern Illinois were
forced to migrate for jobs. The Senator recognized, moreover, that much of
the manpower in labor-surplus areas, particularly the older workers, was im-
mobile. The best answer, the Senator concluded, was to bring jobs *to* labor-
surplus areas.

Initially, Senator Douglas suggested that the way to achieve this objective was a combination of more public works, a modest-sized federal industrial
credit corporation, federal technical assistance, and an extension of unemployment insurance to workers willing to undertake retraining.

By 1965, he had broadened his proposal. On the theory that one of the
key problems was the lack of venture capital, the Senator proposed the establishment of a $100 million revolving fund to permit new or expanded indust-
ries in depressed areas to borrow money at low interest rates. Further, in view of
the unsatisfactory condition of many of the existing access roads and water and
sewerage systems, the Senator also proposed another $100 million revolving
fund to help construct and renovate such local public facilities. In addition, the
new bill included an extension of unemployment insurance for retraining, and
two new provisions--rapid tax write-offs for firms locating in depressed areas
and area priority for federal purchases of supplies and services.

Based on unemployment rates prevailing in the mid-1950's, assistance
was to be limited to urban areas that had experienced an unemployment rate
of at least 6 per cent for 3 years, or at least 9 per cent for 18 months.

In 1956, extensive hearings on the proposed depressed-area legislation marked out the battlefield for the coming five-year struggle. Conservatives displayed implacable hostility and suggested that the program was both useless and harmful. Any enterprising community, they asserted, could solve local problems without federal help. They warned that the Douglas legislation would sap local initiative, weaken moral fiber, and distort the healthy and natural processes of industrial location. Proponents of the depressed-area legislation, however, argued for an even bigger bill with more benefits. They cited as evidence experience in Pennsylvania and elsewhere which seemed to suggest that a limited input of local venture capital ranging from a few hundred dollars to a few thousand dollars could create permanent jobs in a depressed area. Ironically, identical case histories of local- and state-aided successes in stimulating economic growth had been used by the opposition as proof that local initiative could do the job without federal assistance.

A major impetus for broadening the coverage of the act came from southern legislators, many of whom are customarily suspicious of new federal programs, particularly those that call for large-scale expenditures in other regions. To secure needed southern support in the face of strong Republican opposition, the legislation was altered to include aid to low-income rural areas. In effect, this encompassed the entire rural South. The fateful decision to grapple with the intractable problems of the marginal farm counties created major difficulties after the legislation was finally enacted. It also helped to precipitate a battle to ensure that southerners would not use the program to industrialize their region by raiding northern industrial centers. To placate the Northeast, a special protective provision was added prohibiting "pirating," i.e., relocation with assistance from the Area Redevelopment Administration (ARA).

Another of the many ironies involved in this legislation was that its passage was helped considerably by nationwide recessions in 1957-58 and again in 1960-61. Sentiment for federal aid increased when unemployment reached the spectacular rates of from 10 per cent to 20 per cent in some urban depressed areas. Although the rural unemployed and underemployed, camouflaged on subsistence farms, tend to be overlooked in jobless statistics, their suffering did not go unrecognized by their congressmen.

It is partly because of the total impossibility of devising purely rural solutions to meet the needs of redundant farm labor that the economic development districts were created. Since farm families were already accustomed to driving considerable distances for shopping, schools, sales of farm products, and recreation, the rationale could be carried one step farther: Given federal stimuli, it was reasoned, adequate number of jobs could be generated in nearby urban centers to permit rural labor, miners, and loggers to remain living in their homes while they commuted to work with no more discomfort than that experienced by an affluent suburban executive.

President Kennedy, who was deeply impressed by the misery of West Virginia during his 1960 primary campaign in that state, had earlier been a strong advocate of the Douglas legislation. Area redevelopment legislation was given urgent priority in his first hundred days, and on May 1, 1961, almost six years after Senator Douglas had introduced his proposed legislation, the Area Redevelopment Act was signed into law.

ARA'S PROBLEMS

Sar Levitan[3] is at pains to underscore certain weaknesses in the act that he believes contributed to its disappointing impact on distressed-area problems. Briefly, his assessment is that a new and untried agency was given inadequate tools to do too big a job under unfavorable conditions.

It has been suggested that tougher standards designed by the U.S. Department of Labor would have been helpful in limiting eligible applicants to a more manageable number, but it can be argued that the legislation might not have passed unless a large number of areas could expect to benefit. Because of this need to gain wide support, programs as finally enacted often fall far short of an administrator's ideal. This deficiency is indicated to a degree in considering the modest impact of Area Redevelopment Administration operations in Massachusetts.

ARA-approved projects in Massachusetts redevelopment areas in the four-year period, May 1, 1961 through August 31, 1965, resulted in the creation of an estimated 1,095 jobs. To place this substantial number in perspective, it is necessary to recall that the total labor force in Massachusetts redevelopment areas is over 250,000 and that approximately 2,500 jobs are needed to reduce total unemployment in Massachusetts redevelopment areas by 1 per cent. Moreover, during the four-year period approximately 16,000 high school students in the redevelopment areas graduated or dropped out of school, and textiles and other industries reduced their employment by several thousand. Finally, unemployment rates nevertheless declined by 2-5 percentage points in each of the areas. It can be seen, therefore, that ARA aid made a limited contribution to reducing joblessness in these areas. It is possible that the new program, which calls for more money, more power, better organization, and a concentrated focus on growth centers, can have a more substantial impact on development trends.

Genesis of the Districts

Despite its far-reaching implications, the proposed melding of redevelopment areas into economic development districts generated little discussion in Senate and House hearings held in the spring of 1965. Instead, as in the previous decade, most of the controversy concerned federal financing of business loans. In contrast, comment on the new economic districts was both sparse and uniformly favorable. Testimony from spokesmen for Minnesota and Tennessee, for the Upper Great Plains, and for the AFL-CIO stressed the utility and applicability of the concept to semirural, mining, and forestry areas. On the other hand, statements from representatives of New England and other urban regions were strongly in favor of the proposed interstate regional development commissions and/or generally supported the proposed EDA legislation[4] without discussion of the applicability of the district concept to northern urban areas.

It had been noted that in the midst of decades of surrounding social and economic gloom, Appalachian metropolitan areas and urban centers had displayed substantial growth during the 1950's.[5] This Appalachian, quasi-rural theme dominated development district and growth center legislation.

The new legislation also reflected thinking in Western Europe, especially in France, which has made strenuous efforts to counter overcentralization in the Paris area by stimulating growth in satellite regional centers.

Lessons From Abroad

It is worth briefly examining this French pattern, because it appears to be directly relevant to the future of area development in the United States. Despite recent efforts to reverse the pattern, much of the growth in France continues to take place in the Paris region, if not in the immediate area of the city and its environs, then in an extended territory within an 80- to 100-mile radius.[6]

This drift toward the capital under the impetus of generations of past decisions and a wealth of internal and external stimuli is equally characteristic of other European metropolises such as London, Stockholm, Budapest, and Vienna. More recently, similar efforts have been launched by the Hungarian and Polish governments, fearful that unchecked expansion in the capital would result in the creation of mammoth goitres draining vitality and talent from the provinces.[7] To a limited degree, the same observation applies to Washington, New York, and other United States regional capitals such as Los Angeles, San Francisco, Chicago, Boston, Atlanta, Denver, Houston and Minneapolis-St. Paul.

At home and abroad, complaints have been registered over the generations concerning the tendency of small-town talent to migrate to the big cities, a trend that is closely associated with limited employment possibilities and the social backwardness and cultural deprivation of rural areas and small towns; the depressing effect of these conditions on sensitive, sophisticated urban spirits has been a recurrent theme in international fiction.

French regional development plans place great stress on modernizing community facilities, commercial and small manufacturing plants, and expansion of government offices and universities. Within the nation's geographical framework, the objective is to foster a better population and labor force distribution as a function of natural resources and economic activities. However, as was true in the United States, the French efforts were discovered to be spread too thinly among too many areas so that recent attention has increasingly been focused on a few key areas in Brittany, the West, and the Southwest. This policy of concentrating the geographic focus of the development program contrasts with earlier decisions (in the 1950's) to include portions of northern and northeastern France among the "critical zones" requiring major government aid.

The final verdict on some foreign distressed-area programs remains in doubt. One English study concluded, for example, that the number of jobs created by Board of Trade incentives and regulations in British distressed areas was 200,000,[8] roughly double the number that ARA claimed it helped to generate in the United States redevelopment areas in 1961-65. However, even this gain was not sufficient in England to halt the long-term drift of population to the Southeast, away from redevelopment areas.

One reason for the failure is that in Britain, as in the United States, the growth of government jobs, trades, and services has provided a major share of employment expansion; the continued postwar drift to the Southeast was partly due to the lack of control over the location of public and private white-collar employment and office construction in greater London. Not until the mid-1960's did stringent regulations on office construction, combined with mounting shortages of labor and incentives to locate elsewhere in Britain, succeed in bringing the "notorious surge of people from the impoverished provinces to the lush metropolis to an abrupt end."[9] Second, the authors question the role of outmigration in bringing about a balance between available labor and available jobs in distressed areas. In Britain, most migrants are in the middle occupation groups, and their departure does not necessarily create job openings for the unskilled, hard-core unemployed. Moreover, to date, the total volume of outmigration from British redevelopment areas has been small, amounting to only one sixth of the average number of unemployed.

ECONOMIC DEVELOPMENT DISTRICTS

As prerequisites for their formation, the Economic Development Districts (EDD) authorized by Section 403 of the 1965 Public Works and Economic Development Act require a minimum of two designated redevelopment areas and the selection of at least one "economic development center" as a principal focus of regional growth. The act offers communities and areas two principal incentives for inclusion in such districts: a 10 per cent increase in EDA grant assistance to redevelopment areas up to a maximum of 80 per cent of project cost; and full eligibility for EDA benefits, now available only to designated redevelopment areas, for the district growth centers. Some of the problems involved in applying a concept not easily applicable to the urban Northeast can be observed in Massachusetts, where six out of the state's eight designated redevelopment areas are being regrouped into two Economic Development Districts.

In late 1966 and early 1967, after consulting with potential member areas, the Massachusetts Department of Commerce and Development proposed the creation of two Economic Development Districts for Massachusetts and adjacent fringe communities in New Hampshire and Rhode Island. The first was in the Merrimack Valley, including three designated areas, Lowell, Newburyport, and Gloucester along with one nondesignated area (Lawrence-Haverhill), and eight small adjacent communities across the New Hampshire border. The second, in southeastern Massachusetts, included the Fall River, Bourne-Wareham, and Plymouth areas, the currently nondesignated New Bedford area, and a number of adjacent Massachusetts towns, including the Massachusetts fringe communities of the Providence-Pawtucket, Rhode Island area.

The formation of the two Economic Development Districts in Massachusetts involved a substantial amount of discussion primarily concerned with the willingness of certain border areas to join or remain aloof from the districts.

There appear to be three immediate issues that require future resolution: the development of priorities for district programs, alignment of district boundaries and programs with those of existing regional planning agencies, and the selection of growth centers. The choice of one or more growth centers, for example, presents unusual difficulties.

It can reasonably be assumed that EDA will require much more sophistication, planning, and implementation in such programs than was the case with the Overall Economic Development Programs (OEDP) required of redevelopment areas under the terms of the 1961 ARA legislation. More often than not, OEDP's were hodgepodges of hastily prepared statistical material dwelling at length on the area's chronic economic problems but sparse in realistic interpretation and analysis. As one study concluded: "Preparation of OEDP's normally involved only a limited thoughtful analysis of community resources and contained little that would provide a blueprint for future community economic development and thus hardly deserved the name 'program'."[10] Since OEDP's recommended action programs consisted of superficial encyclopedias, for the most part summarizing old proposals, few could be regarded as serious planning documents.

Table 1 presents a brief summary of OEDP prepared by redevelopment areas located in the Massachusetts economic development districts. Despite their lack of sophisticated analysis, they do present a reasonably accurate picture of the problems that were uppermost in the minds of the local OEDP committees.

While each of the OEDP indicated that unemployment was a troublesome problem, it is significant that all of the areas listed a variety of difficulties

Summary of Problems and Goals
in Economic Development Areas*

EDA Areas	Attleboro	Bourne-Wareham	Fall River	Gloucester	Lawrence-Haverhill	Lowell	New Bedford	Newburyport	Plymouth
Area Problems									
No Industrial Park or Sites	X			X	X				X
Obsolete Industrial Buildings	X				X	X	X	X	X
Poor Transportation Connections to the Outside							X		
Poor Access Roads								X	
Lack of Vocational Education	X	X	X		X	X	X		X
Lack of Higher Education			X				X		
Poor Municipal Services		X				X		X	
Obsolete and Dilapidated Municipal Buildings			X						
Lack of Sewer and Water Facilities	X	X	X	X	X	X		X	X
Deteriorated and Dilapidated Housing		X			X				
No Industrial Development Group with Financing		X		X		X			
Tourist Development Needed			X	X				X	
Poor Reputation			X						
Area Goals									
Create Industrial Jobs Through More Industrial Loans			X	X		X	X	X	
More Tourism and Conventions				X					X
More Citizen Participation and Leadership		X		X	X				X
More Federal Funds for Area Development						X			X

*Data given here were presented in Overall Economic Development Program and were submitted to the Economic Development Administration.

Source: Summarized from Overall Economic Development Programs (OEDP's) submitted to the Area Redevelopment Administration 1963-64.

only partially related to a shortage of adequate jobs. The table suggests that a number of long-standing environmental deficiencies have been identified as critical problems by the areas. With more outside aid available and federal and state pressures for remedial action increasing, they are anxious to proceed with action to remedy the lack of adequate sewer and water facilities as well as to move ahead with urban renewal and improvement of educational facilities.

In some respects, the OEDP's reflect a fundamentally changed climate. For example, the Merrimack and Taunton rivers have been polluted for generations by textile mills and communities alike. Every attempt to upgrade the status of these streams that flow through distressed areas in northeastern and southeastern Massachusetts has been resisted on the ground that such moves jeopardized the local economy. In the mid-1960's, however, stringent laws relating to water pollution, public education, and federal-state financial aid have materially weakened the local resistance movement. Whereas, in past years, dumping of raw sewage and industrial waste into open streams was considered both an inalienable right and an inescapable by-product of modern urban development, now the level of tolerance has been reduced, and esthetic and olfactory standards have been raised. A long-standing nuisance, with the solution hitherto appearing too costly and disruptive to the local economy, has been redefined as a soluble problem.

It is interesting to note the large number of areas that identify vocational education as a special need. This emphasis seems to reflect the changing industrial base in these areas which calls for new skills. Subsequent progress reports from the OEDP committees indicated some advances in this direction, but they also suggested that the scale of retraining for older workers was still inadequate. It is also of interest to note that only one complaint was registered in regard to access to other areas, a problem that arises so frequently in Appalachia and other regions.

The new EDA legislation is likely to improve area-development operations. The so-called dedesignation of some distressed areas and the grouping together of most of those that remain will permit EDA to undertake more rigorous examination of district program design and operations. The product emanating from the areas is also likely to improve in quality: EDA funding of 75 per cent of staff costs will enable the districts to employ professionals to prepare plans and programs. Other benefits available to districts also have been expanded. Nevertheless, even when all of these factors are taken into consideration, it must be remembered that the state of the art in area economic development planning is still relatively primitive, and the degree of public acceptance is unpredictable. Partly for this reason, gaining requisite political support and securing implementation of economic development plans will continue to present special difficulties. To begin with, their large size may have certain drawbacks. The grouping of additional areas may increase the complex task of reconciling objectives for competing areas and interests.[11] It is probably realistic to anticipate that purely technical considerations in district plans will not automatically be translated into consensual programs. They will probably be strongly influenced by a process of intradistrict bargaining and maneuvering and perhaps most of all by the availability of out-of-area funding and/or regulatory pressures for specific programs and proposals.

While predictions are hazardous, it seems likely that much of the future work of the districts will undoubtedly involve a refinement of past efforts rather than breakthroughs in area-development programing. Much more can be done in training manpower, particularly among the disadvantaged segments of the population; air, water, and noise pollution problems remain to be analyzed and remedied; the need for training and encouraging more effective civic leadership and local entrepreneurship could be high on the agenda. Human resource planning on an area basis, especially in health services, deserves much closer attention than it has been given in the past. But these are extremely complicated programs in themselves, and any attempt to coordinate them on a district level is likely to run into trouble. As a result, with respect to most programs, the districts will probably serve as a stimulator and catalytic agent identifying deficiencies and accelerating remedial action by others. [12]

In addition to its formal functions, the districts can serve as a clearinghouse for information available to local communities, outside investors and outside agencies. They can play an effective liaison role in helping federal and state agencies by representing the district and its component areas in improving the quality of local and program decisions. Technical assistance to local governments to help them in applying for federal assistance and in designing and implementing local programs can be a particularly useful function. While communities are too small to employ their own full-time staff, the districts can also supply supplementary expertise to the central cities, particularly in helping them to cope with the problems of slum neighborhoods.

It can be predicted that the term "area development" will be interpreted as encompassing most programs involving the well being of people within the district. This interpretation is consistent with federal directives and inescapably will plunge the district organizations into complex, challenging relationships with federal, state, and local agencies, and vested interests of all types. An early example of such a struggle involved the traditional regional agencies in Massachusetts which feared that the new turn toward economic development threatened their present role and future prospects. Planners attuned to the aims and operations of the federal Department of Housing and Urban Development clearly regarded the entrance of the federal Economic Development Administration into area planning as an unwelcome intrusion. It is possible that this suspicion is associated with previous, unhappy interagency experiences between the Bureau of Public Roads and its state highway counterparts. Thus, even in their formative stage, the districts began to arouse considerable controversy of a type that is likely to become all too familiar as they grapple with other problems.

Before embarking on the mainstream of broad program activities, there is a preliminary problem to resolve in aligning EDA borders and programs with the boundaries and functions of other types of regional agencies. In September, 1966, a Presidential directive required federal agencies to avoid duplication and overlapping and, if possible, to adopt consistent regional alignments in establishing regional planning areas. Directives and administrative regulations requiring each regional operation to take full cognizance of other programs are also being more strictly enforced. Achieving this worthwhile objective, however, poses some serious problems.

There can be no quarrel with the objective of preventing district proliferation, and, as far as is practicable, of avoiding program duplication through dissolution of redundant organizations or negotiation of effective interorganization treaties. It must be recognized, however, that this objective may be difficult to achieve. Federal and state planning activities that cover relevant portions of the districts can not only be expected to continue but are likely to intensify. Similar activities can be anticipated for other supradistrict organizations, including the New England Regional Commission and federal transportation, water resource, and other agencies. For this reason, complete prevention of duplication and overlapping between programs is probably unobtainable.

As was suggested earlier, critical problems may arise with respect to the relationship of districts funded by EDA and regional planning agencies operating largely with funds supplied by the U.S. Department of Housing and Urban Development (HUD) and occasionally by HUD and the U.S. Bureau of Roads (BPR). Although there is a growing convergence in program rhetoric, the framework of regional research and program objectives of these agencies differs substantially from the blueprint required by the Economic Development Administration. Furthermore, the citizen commission members and staffs in such area planning agencies differ sufficiently in outlook and training from those involved in economic development organizations so that problems in communication are created, let alone arriving at firm agreements on substance. Area transportation studies and regional planning organizations have developed a methodology, a timetable, and a vocabulary that reflect highway and land use planning objectives and techniques far removed from most economic development endeavors. The same observation can be made of natural resource agencies. Each agency serves a different clientele with quite definite ideas on what it expects from its own version of area planning; in consequence, regardless of preliminary verbal agreement, no guarantee of interagency harmony, oral or written, may be fully honored. These difficulties would not be so troublesome were they not compounded by the lack of a strong administrative framework to force a swift resolution of area interprogram conflicts; none of the regional planning agencies operate through a district government or a district executive with broad powers.

As the powers of area planning organizations are augmented, as their functions are elevated from research and advisory operations to agencies possessing critical decision-making authority over local capital improvements and other types of investments, they become increasingly subject to the political pressures and harassments leveled at organizations that can confer or withhold significant benefits. As has previously been the case with metropolitan and city-planning agencies, the district organizations are likely to be involved in politicized interagency power struggles that tax the ingenuity and persistence of the participants.[13] Districts may increasingly become arenas in which contenders possessing autonomous powers vie for influence and funds within a very broad framework of federal directives. Moreover, federal agencies that cannot fully reconcile their own conflicts will nevertheless exhort the area gladiators to cease and desist from battle and to work in concord.

As in the case of the model cities program, which involves much interagency integration in slum neighborhoods, many potential frictions could be avoided if there were closer interagency alignment at the federal level. It would be highly desirable if EDA, HUD, BPR, and other agencies developed an effective federal framework not only to make district boundaries coterminous, but to create a single, multipurpose federal organization to work with a district counterpart agency in dealing with a great variety of programs. Although the creation and implementation of this type of federal interagency treaty poses formidable problems, they are probably less severe than those involved when the burden of coordination is relegated to the local level, where there is no equivalent of the U.S. Bureau of the Budget or a Presidential directive to compel consistency.

Along with model cities, the Economic Development Districts are in the forefront of the struggle in federal and state government to impose effective, horizontal coordination over deep, vertical patterns of agency-client relations. This battle has been won in the U.S. Department of Defense, but it remains to be seen if such wide-angle efforts as model cities and the districts manage to escape the onus of single-agency sponsorship and embrace a variety of agencies in integrated programs.

The selection of economic growth centers as required by the EDA legislation is probably the most serious immediate obstacle in initiating an effective development program. Choosing economic growth centers would appear to present few insuperable problems in areas consisting primarily of marginal farms or mining hamlets where a single urban community has clearly emerged as the economic focal point for the surrounding territory. The growth center concept can therefore be easily applied to the rural South, to much of Appalachia, and generally, to sparsely populated areas dominated by widely separated trading centers. In such areas, the creation of districts and growth centers can be considered official recognition of an existing pattern. Even where the situation is more complex, as in France where the concept emerged during the 1950's, a strong central government can enforce the choice of one community over reasonably comparable competitors.

In New England and much of the Northeast, the problem of selection is more difficult, as suggested by an examination of the Economic Development Districts in northeastern and southeastern Massachusetts. There are neither clear-cut growth centers within the districts nor an available mechanism to force a readily acceptable choice of centers.

The grouping of redevelopment areas into Economic Development Districts has not resulted in the creation of economic areas in which a single urban center has emerged as the outstanding growth focus for the surrounding communities. Each of the Massachusetts Economic Development Districts exhibits a number of similar characteristics in terms of problems and performance. Their redevelopment areas have experienced long-term distress as a result of the decline in certain dominant industries such as textiles, leather, and fishing. In each case, the addition of nondesignated areas such as Taunton, Lawrence-Haverhill, and the Massachusetts fringe communities of the Providence-Pawtucket area increases the number of communities afflicted with a persistent hangover from the decline of a vulnerable industry--textiles in Lawrence, leather in Haverhill. The addition of one new element--the low-wage jewelry industry centered in Attleboro and North Attleborough, does not materially alter the fact that in size, economic problems, and past growth trends, the new geographic arrangements resemble the existing redevelopment areas. The creation of the districts, therefore, represents a territorial expansion rather than a change in character; it has expanded the existing pattern of moderate income suburbs surrounding low-wage manufacturing cities found in most urbanized redevelopment areas, without a basic alteration in the existing development context.

Given this situation, there appear to be several alternatives. The first is to make further EDA assistance contingent on a local choice of one or two growth centers. This tactic could force a selection at the cost of considerable resentment from the runners-up who would undoubtedly feel that they had been awarded a booby prize as potential losers, i.e., as candidates for stagnation or decay, the obverse of growth.

A second choice would involve redrawing the district boundaries to include a segment of suburban Boston containing a population of less than 250,000, i.e., within the statutory maximum established by EDA legislation. Areas located on circumferential Route 128 around Boston have demonstrated substantial growth capacity in electronics, research and development, as well as in business services and commerce, and each is within easy commuting distance of a proposed development district.

Another possibility is to designate a "new town," presumably a development in a suburb or rural territory, as a growth center. New-town criteria, however, have not been well defined by the Department of Housing and Urban Development. For example, it is not clear if a very large subdivision, a regional shopping center surrounded by apartments and industrial parks, or a large university with adjoining research and development activity and other installations can be considered a new town.

A final possibility is the adoption of a multiple growth center concept in which each of the principal areas within the districts is designated as a growth center. This approach has the immediate benefit of avoiding potential intradistrict friction. The major drawback is that this might be a step backward because it could appreciably dilute the intentions and potential benefits of the 1965 EDA legislation by increasing the number of beneficiary areas.

If these complexities were not enough of a challenge, there is also the possibility that continued decreases in unemployment may lead to dedesignation of one or more of the district redevelopment areas, a move that would result in loss of district classification. Thus, there is the prospect that the new economic districts which were organized with such difficulty in 1966-67 might lose their official status within a year or two. The question of redrafting the criteria for redevelopment area eligibility may therefore assume a certain urgency in Economic Development Districts whose eligibility rests on the continued designation of a minimum of two redevelopment areas.

A further complication in the growth center concept arises in developing programs to cope with the special problems of intown slum areas. Proposals for creating government centers and light industrial parks have been advanced in Harlem and the Bedford-Stuyvesant areas of New York City. In 1967, EDA engaged in full-scale core-city demonstration programs in five cities and subsequently launched technical assistance efforts in a number of others. One problem with core-city populations, particularly Negroes, is their relative immobility, which appears to be the result of a combination of adjustment to traditional barriers and the extreme difficulty in commuting to distant jobs in some large metropolitan areas. As much time may be required to traverse thirty blocks in a large city via public transportation or automobile as it takes to drive thirty miles in a rural or small-town setting. EDA may have to evolve an elastic concept of growth centers that encompasses a wide variety of ecological conditions and may have to enter the field of public-transportation planning in relation to the slum dweller's journey to work.[14]

THE STAFFING PROBLEM

A discussion of the operational problems of the Economic Development Districts must include at least a brief sketch of the difficulties likely to be encountered in locating and retaining suitable staff. There is little reason to suppose that the current supply of senior-level talent can be easily stretched to man the ramparts of perhaps a hundred or more new districts.

Another problem involves the role of the district administrator. The controversy raging in planning and public administration circles over the neutrality, advocacy, continuity, and political role of the appointed upper-echelon bureaucrat is equally applicable to the staff of the EDD.[15]

Problems in program continuity may arise when a dominant faction is replaced along with an administrator closely identified with its policies. It is also conceivable that disputants may elevate argument into a species of technical warfare, employing economists and planners as advocates as they now employ lawyers and engineers. As the rewards for winning official approval become more enticing, it becomes increasingly probable that distributing a limited supply of benefits among competing applicants represented by eloquent, reputable professionals will generate conflicts among alternative development plans and programs. Once competing interests have advanced beyond the stage of proposing obviously indefensible approaches, the task of selecting from among equally plausible choices will become increasingly vexing. Economic development and planning are not sufficiently exact sciences to permit an administrator to assume unchallenged authority in rejecting the claims of rival areas and interest groups.

The rapid rise in the level of technical sophistication among laymen will make the administrator's job simpler in one sense because he will be spared the boring and time-consuming job of conducting elementary development courses for his constituency. On the other hand, he will probably regret the unhappy day his employers, newspaper reporters, and other area residents learned the ABC's of economic development. He may be pleased to conduct stimulating graduate seminars, but there is a growing danger that the administrator will be monitored to the point of harassment, constantly second-guessed, and frequently overruled on technical as well as policy questions. In brief, the audience may be harder to please, and the administrator's tenure may thereby be curtailed. For this, among other reasons, the Economic Development Districts will generate the materials for a new chapter on the problems of pioneering public administration and planning.

NOTES TO CHAPTER 8

1. For opposing views, see Roscoe C. Martin, *The Cities and the Federal System* (New York: Atherton Press, 1965); Norman Beckman, "For a New Perspective in Federal-State Relations," *State Government,* Autumn, 1966; Daniel Elazar, *American Federalism: A View from the States* (New York: Thomas Y. Crowell Company, 1966).

2. The material in this section is derived in part from the author's review of Sar Levitan's *Federal Aid to Depressed Areas: An Evaluation of the Area Redevelopment Administration* (Baltimore: Johns Hopkins Press, 1964). The review appeared in the *Journal of the American Institute of Planners,* February, 1965.

3. Sar Levitan, *op. cit.*

4. *Hearings* before the Committee on Public Works (Senate) and Committee on Public Works (House of Representatives), "Public Works and Economic Development Act of 1965," 89th Cong., 1st Sess., 1965.

5. David A. Grossman and Melvin R. Levin, "The Appalachian Region, A National Problem Area," *Land Economics*, May, 1961.

6. This discussion is based in part on a review article by Lawrence D. Mann and George J. Pillorge, "French Regional Planning," *Journal of the American Institute of Planners*, XXX, 2 (May, 1964), p. 64; and U.S., Area Redevelopment Administration, *Area Redevelopment Policies in Britain and the Countries of the Common Market* (Washington, D.C.: U.S. Government Printing Office, January, 1965). See especially preface and introduction, Frederick Meyers and Pierre Bouchet, "Regional Development Policies in France," pp. 111-28.

7. Stanislaw Chelstowski, "Deglomeration," *Polish Perspectives, Monthly Review* [in English], Warsaw, Poland, November, 1966.

8. L. Needleman and B. Scott, "Regional Problems and Location of Industry Policy in Britain," *Urban Studies*, Glasgow, Scotland, I, 2 (November, 1964), 153-69. For a discussion of British distressed-area policy, see also Benjamin Chinitz, "Regional Economic Policy in Great Britain," *Urban Affairs Quarterly*, Vol. I, No. 2 (December, 1965), and Vol. I, No. 3 (March, 1966).

9. "Back-Into-Balance Britain," *London Sunday Times*, London, November 5, 1967, p. 34.

10. *American Community Development* (New York: Ford Foundation, 1964), pp. 2-3.

11. Contrary to the trend in area-development legislation, greater political mileage--but not necessarily economic efficiency or administrative ease--can often be secured by moving in the other direction, i.e., by breaking large projects into a multitude of small projects. The Soil Conservation Service which was running into serious controversy in securing Congressional support and local consensus on eleven major watershed projects achieved a major breakthrough by shifting emphasis to a small watershed program. See Aaron Wildavsky, "The Political Economy of Efficiency: Cost-Benefit Analysis, Systems Analysis and Program Budgeting," *Public Administration Review*, XXVI, 4 (December, 1966), 297-98.

12. This combination coordinative and advisory-catalyst role has been recommended in guidelines prepared for the districts by the EDA. See Economic Development Administration, *Handbook for Economic Development*

(Preliminary Draft) (Washington, D.C.:   U.S. Government Printing Office, December, 1966).

13. For an analysis of metropolitan, state and interagency problems, see Chapter 6.

14. Senator Ribicoff has proposed the addition of a new Title VIII, "Urban Redevelopment Areas" to the Public Works and Economic Development Act of 1965. The amendment would enable EDA to provide financial assistance and business-loan projects under Title II of the act to create new jobs in core-city slum areas. Senator Abraham Ribicoff, "The Competent City: An Action Program for Urban America," *Congressional Record,* 89th Cong., 1st Sess. (January 23, 1967), pp. S709-S721.

15. For various and conflicting views on this topic, see Norton E. Long, "Politicians for Hire--The Dilemmas of Education and the Task of Research," *Public Administration Review,* XXV, 2 (June, 1965), 115-20; Benjamin Walter, "Political Decision Making in Arcadia," in Stuart F. Chapin and Shirley F. Weiss (eds.), *Urban Growth Dynamics in a Regional Cluster of Cities* (New York: John Wiley and Sons, Inc., 1962); Alan A. Altshuler, "Rationality and Influence in Public Service," *Public Administration Review* (September, 1965); and Paul Davidoff, "Advocacy and Pluralism in Planning," *Journal of the American Institute of Planners,* XXXI, 4 (November, 1965) reprinted in H. Wentworth Eldredge (ed.), *Taming Megalopolis: Vol. II, How to Manage an Urbanized World* (Garden City: Anchor Books--Doubleday and Co., Inc., 1967), pp. 596-615.

9

POOR NO MORE?
UNEMPLOYMENT RATES AND
CONVALESCING AREAS

INTRODUCTION

The 1965 Public Works and Economic Development Act and related programs of federal assistance have attempted to close the gap between redevelopment areas and the economically flourishing parts of the nation in three ways: They offer technical expertise that distressed areas have proved unable to supply for themselves, special incentives for firms to expand into areas that they have hitherto avoided or would otherwise find unappealing, and they have augmented financial aid to undertake urban renewal and manpower training efforts. The major deficiency in an otherwise useful piece of legislation was its failure to recognize that 1965 was not 1961. By the mid-1960's, it had become apparent that national prosperity was helping to reduce unemployment in many of the traditional distressed areas based on the national rates of the late 1950's and early 1960's. Since the 1965 act retained the eligibility criteria of the 1961 Area Redevelopment Act, the result is that many of these areas are being declared ineligible for further aid.

The causative factors underlying the creation and persistence of redevelopment areas are complex and poorly understood, although certain stigmata are found in all of them: Civic business and leadership in such areas is often inadequate, heads of local financial institutions and other entrepreneurs are often timid and shortsighted and, in general, the psychological and physical environment is unfavorable to modernization. Out of this tangle of causes and effects, the 1965 act selected a single index--unemployment rates--as the sole criterion to determine if an area should remain eligible for special federal assistance.

The author contends that when most of the readily employables in distressed areas have found work, this should not in itself justify eliminating eligibility for distressed area benefits. It is particularly important that a decline in unemployment should be linked to a termination of intensive development efforts, especially programs that attack root causes underlying the emergence of distressed areas. To begin with, the decline in joblessness may be transitory, or the major source of new employment may be low-wage industries. The removal, perhaps on a temporary basis, of one primary surface manifestation of economic distress may leave untouched the basic problems that may either drag the area under at some later date or at best will assure it a permanent place at the lower end of the nation's economic and social ladder.

What alternative is available instead of using unemployment rates to measure distress? It would seem far more reasonable to adopt entirely new standards for distressed area designation. For example, in northern urban areas, indices used for classification could include such social indicators as the proportion of the total population receiving public assistance and wage and income differentials, in addition to unemployment rates. A disparity of perhaps more than 20 per cent in key statistical indices, using the state or the largest proximate metropolitan area as a yardstick, would be more realistic than simply calling it a day when the unemployed find jobs in apparel plants or other low-wage industries. This method would be simple enough, since data on average wages and public assistance are regularly obtained. They are also accurate, because they are gathered for closely supervised, federally financed activities. Moreover, they come closer (particularly the wage criterion) than unemployment rates in underscoring a key feature of the distressed area problem, the continuing income differential with flourishing metropolitan areas. This income gap may be reinforced rather than removed after the distressed areas settle into roles as cheap labor markets.

However, we must go beyond simple statistics. The absolute necessity of also taking intangible factors into account both in area designation and in the design of remedial strategy cannot be stressed too strongly. Despite political and other hazards that may be encountered by treading on sensitive and arguable ground, a realistic yardstick for redevelopment area designation must also consider the unquantifiable elements which play a major role in the cause and cure of the distressed area problem. Purely statistical indices may be highly indicative as well as conventionally defensible, but numbers are insufficient in themselves to portray the special political, social, and economic climate of the distressed area; these qualitative characteristics cannot be ignored in developing realistic remedial programs.

Background of the Problem

In 1965 and 1966, it became increasingly clear that new criteria were needed for the designation of redevelopment areas. Between 1962 and 1965, the total number of areas in the nation exhibiting chronic and substantial unemployment declined by almost 200, falling from 748 to 555 in the three-year period. Nationwide manpower shortages in 1965 and 1966 penetrated even into the most prosperity-resistant redevelopment areas, with the result that their unemployment rates declined to near national levels. Thus, if finding jobs for the readily employable is to be the sole criterion of economic distress, the redevelopment area problem, at least in northern urban states, is approaching a solution. However, it can be reasonably argued that this is far too optimistic a view. Some hard-core areas are still plagued with high unemployment and a multitude of other problems. The intractable human resources problems in the central city slums, in the marginal rural areas, and in the Indian reservations remain acute. In other chronically depressed areas, unemployment has been rapidly declining, but this has not permanently removed fundamental, lingering social and economic ailments. The decrease in jobless has revealed to all what some observers had suspected: Whether our concern is the urban slum or the traditional redevelopment area, putting people to work or providing minimal family incomes provides only part of the answer. Underlying the unemployment and poverty indices that have so long claimed our attention are much more difficult obstructions to progress. Many poor families contain a tangle of pathological ailments for which money alone is not the answer. The chronic alcoholic, the gambler, the drug addict, the mentally unstable are not likely to change their ways if more cash becomes available. The drunkard may switch from wine to whisky, the gambler may transfer his attentions from the $2 window to the $5 window, the addict may increase his consumption of heroin, and the mentally ill may find more scope for bizarre behavior. This is an extremely important point: The multiproblem family as identified by social workers has a close parallel in the multiproblem area.

In any event, the recent downturn in distressed area unemployment indicates that there is little time to lose in developing a more sophisticated yardstick than unemployment rates to delineate redevelopment areas. The concept of differentials may be retained to measure relative distress, but the basis of comparison should be changed from a national to a metropolitan regional yardstick. Furthermore, the focus of the differentials should be broadened to include gaps in living standards and in other measures of economic and social progress. Designation should be primarily based on an examination of historic patterns, including differences in such quantifiable indices as wage rates, incomes, housing, school achievement rates, and unemployment rates. It should also take into account the intangible and unquantifiable elements that tend to be responsible for measurable symptoms of distress. Moreover, whatever its applicability to the rural South or to Indian reservations, a national yardstick is clearly inadequate and misleading. For example, conditions in such chronically depressed Massachusetts areas as Fall River, New Bedford and Lowell should more properly be measured in comparison with the nearby Boston area than with a national standard that includes Appalachia and the South. Similar commonly accepted regional centers exist as bases of comparison in most distressed urbanized areas. In short, regional standards are not only more commonly used and understood by local residents but may also be more realistic.

Although most of the recent upturn in redevelopment districts is primarily attributable to national economic trends rather than to local action, there is still a need for area development program planning based on new, broadened concepts. The time has come for a reappraisal of redevelopment-area strategies and goals. Now that the solution to the problem of chronic unemployment is within reach, other basic issues need more attention, especially a basic upgrading of human resources and modernization of obsolescent physical environments and deteriorated public services.

The period of national prosperity that began in the early 1960's and that showed no immediate sign of ending can be used to secure permanent gains in redevelopment areas. Area development can now go beyond limited economic objectives to include programs that will upgrade the quality of life, will effect improvements to enhance the total environment, and that will encompass programs which will provide competitive training for persons who remain in their communities as well as those who migrate to other areas. A special problem also requires action; particular attention must be given to the doubly handicapped, the disadvantaged residents of central city slums located in the midst of long-distressed areas.

There is a time factor involved as well: Unless a more accurate measure of distress is quickly developed, there is a danger under present legislation that a reduction in high-unemployment rates will be construed as a signal to terminate an area's status as a distressed territory. This would be most unfortunate as it is apparent that distressed areas require help in remedying basic social and economic ailments far transcending the immediate problem of finding jobs for the readily employable. It is likely that an economic development program comparable to the U.S. Department of Housing and Urban Development's model cities program, which attempts to link an area's physical and human resource development in slum neighborhoods, may be in order. The EDA has already moved some distance in this direction through pilot projects in Oakland and other cities, and the agency is beginning to initiate economic development programs in other slum areas in the nation. In December, 1966, EDA found only four large cities eligible for distressed area designation: Oakland, Newark, San Diego, and Miami. EDA may be able to carve out and designate another 70 sizable slum areas, each containing over 50,000 population.[1] The entrance into urban slums has its advantages for an agency that is confronted with the loss of its clientele; HUD, EDA, and other government agencies involved in slum problems will not find it difficult to justify their existence; the slums are likely to be around a lot longer than the traditional distressed areas.

The model cities approach may be directly applicable to the new Economic Development Districts that EDA is establishing under provisions of the Public Works and Economic Development Act of 1965. It must be recognized that there is a critical obstacle to developing a meaningful approach in such districts, namely the absence of a single, legally responsible public executive: no district mayors or governors. Nevertheless, much can probably be accomplished by working through existing political machinery to achieve significant progress on area problems.

BASIC PROBLEMS UNRESOLVED

The distressed area problem can best be examined by considering a specific example, the ten redevelopment areas in Massachusetts. It may be profitable for the seven distressed urban redevelopment areas in Massachusetts (as distinct from the three, small, distressed resort areas) to use the Boston area as a basepoint for comparison of economic and social conditions. Development and related programs in the seven urban areas should try to narrow the gap with the Boston area in family incomes, unemployment rates, housing quality, educational standards, per capita inputs of federal urban renewal funds, and other sources of outside capital. By early 1968, the impact of the current economic recovery in these areas effectively reduced local unemployment to the 6 per cent level, and the downward trend is continuing. Under these circumstances, most of the available surplus labor has been absorbed, but deep-rooted human and environmental problems remain. Unless effective remedial action is undertaken, the redevelopment areas are likely to remain specialized low-wage pockets, vulnerable to economic recessions, and subject to continuing losses of a disproportionate share of their talented young people for want of challenging local career opportunities, partly because they offer an environment unattractive to advanced industries.

The data in Table 2 indicate the extent of the gulf that separates Massachusetts redevelopment areas from metropolitan Boston. Moreover, it reveals that with such important criteria as wages and educational levels the gap has by no means narrowed in past years.

It is much easier, of course, to discuss area needs than to bring about meaningful cures; it takes a good deal of sophistication to formulate and implement new, integrated programs. For this reason, the future of redevelopment areas will depend to a great extent upon their ability to secure the expert skills needed to use expanded federal legislation effectively. Considerable talent is required to assemble, from a number of potential sources of federal and state aid, a program suitable for the special requirements of each area. Narrowing the gap with metropolitan Boston partly depends on the ability to secure a proportionate share of federal grant-in-aid assistance now available to all urban areas that are capable of meeting complex program standards.

CHARACTERISTICS OF MASSACHUSETTS REDEVELOPMENT AREAS

Even in a small state like Massachusetts, redevelopment areas are by no means a simple, all-of-a-kind phenomenon. They differ substantially in history, location, and prospects. In 1964, approximately 600,000 persons lived in ten Massachusetts redevelopment areas. Another 80,000 lived in nine Massachusetts towns on the outer fringes of the Providence-Pawtucket labor-market area. Thus, roughly one seventh of the commonwealth's population (a figure equivalent to the population of the city of Boston) lived in areas of substantial, per-

TABLE 2
Economic and Social Indices—
Boston vs. Massachusetts Redevelopment Areas, 1950-66

SMA's, SMSA's	Median SMSA School Years Completed by Adults (persons over 25)*		Median Family Income		% of Sound Housing^a		Unemployment Rates		Average Weekly Manufacturing Earnings	
	1950	1960	1949	1959	1950	1960	1956	1966d	1958	1965
Community										
Boston^f	(11.9)	(12.1)	($3,516)	($6,687)	(87.8)	(83.9)	(2.7%)	(3.6%)	($95)	($124)
Fall River	71%	71%	83%	78%	46%	82%	252%	122%	63%	64%
Fall River (city)	70	70	84	74	42	76	b	b	63	63
Lowell	82	88	88	90	78	92	248	156	76	83
Lowell (city)	81	82	87	85	80	89	b	b	76	82
New Bedford	70	71	84	78	53	84	230	133	71	70
New Bedford (city)	69	69	84	75	51	80	b	b	69	69
Selected Communities										
Bourne-Wareham (town)	b	102	b	77	b	b	b	211	58	67
Gloucester (city)	83	88	89	79	72	83	b	211	75	81
Newburyport (city)	90	89	86	84	79	88	b	158	72	83
North Adams (city)	75	76	87	85	86	82	226	94	85	85
Plymouth (town)	b	91	b	83	95c	103c	b	267	83	88
Provincetown (town)	82	87	b	69	b	97c	b	b	72	66
Dukes County	102	96	69	71	71	89	b	b	b	b
Massachusetts	92	96	95	94	90	97	b	117	92	92
United States	78	88	87	85	72	88	156	111e	87	87

* Boston SMSA = 100%

a Structurally sound with all plumbing facilities and hot water.

b Not available.

c Unincorporated place.

d Data for May.

e Data for July.

f Numbers in parentheses indicate actual figures; Boston equals 100.

Sources: U.S. Bureau of the Census and Massachusetts Division of Employment Security (unemployment rates and earnings).

sistent unemployment. This is a significant proportion of the state total, yet it
is a percentage that places Massachusetts well below such seriously distressed
states as Alaska or West Virginia, where unemployment is so high and so widespread that virtually the entire state is EDA-designated. But Massachusetts is
still somewhat above neighboring states such as New York and Connecticut,
where unemployment in the early 1960's was under one in fourteen. In early
1965, however, an additional 1.3 million persons lived in areas of high unemployment, including Springfield and Brockton, which were classified as eligible
for federal assistance under the Accelerated Public Works Program. In effect,
much of Massachusetts, with the exception of the Boston Standard Metropolitan Statistical Area and a number of outlying rural communities, was eligible
for aid under one or both programs.

In Massachusetts redevelopment areas, limited population gains have
been the rule since the 1920's. Modest population growth in some of the distressed areas clearly reflects the long-term impact of declining employment in
soft-goods industries without compensating expansion in local growth industries. Since 1940, population growth in the Fall River and New Bedford areas
has been only about one half the state average, while in smaller areas such as
Provincetown, Martha's Vineyard, Newburyport, Gloucester, Plymouth, and
North Adams, year-round population levels have either remained stable or have
actually declined. Martha's Vineyard had roughly as many year-round residents at the time of the American Revolution as it does today, and Provincetown has decreased in population by one third since the early 1920's. Exceptions to the pattern may be explained by unique phenomena; the Lowell area,
lagging between 1940 and 1950, gained substantially with suburban inmigration from Boston during the 1950's; the fast-growing Bourne-Wareham district
became a residential site for Otis Air Force Base personnel during the same
decade.

In addition to the three economically troubled metropolitan areas, the
Massachusetts list of distressed areas included two small industrial centers
(North Adams and Newburyport), two small fishing and resort centers (Provincetown and Gloucester), a small industrial-residential area (Plymouth), a small
resort-service-industrial area (Bourne-Wareham), and a very small resort community (Martha's Vineyard). Also on the list were nine distressed communities
on the fringe of the Providence-Pawtucket labor-market area. These ranged
from small industrial centers such as Attleboro and North Attleboro to residential suburbs such as Seekonk. With three small exceptions, all the areas are
located within an hour's drive of Boston.

Area Differences

For some years, the standard image of a Massachusetts redevelopment
area was that of a grimy, backward, mill city. This portrait in decay has created
problems for local economic- and industrial-development organizations which
have been confronted with the task of proving to potential industrial and other

prospects that their areas offer high-quality amenities, i.e., that they contain attractive sites for factories, commercial establishments, and executives. In many cases, the outsider's belief that the environment is uniformly depressing, a point of view traceable to sporadic newspaper accounts of mill closings and other difficulties, is quickly dispelled by careful, guided tours of the areas. In every case, investigation discloses that designation as an EDA area is by no means an indication either of homogeneity or of substandard living conditions.

Many of the suburban towns surrounding redevelopment area central cities offer living conditions similar to those found in many Boston suburbs. Recruitment of faculty for Southeastern Massachusetts Technological Institute, for example, has been greatly facilitated by the availability of relatively low-cost housing on ocean-front locations. (This approach has had great success with parched, land-locked Midwesterners.) It may be noted, with the exceptions of Lowell and North Adams, that all of the Massachusetts redevelopment areas are coastal communities which can satisfy a widespread craving for proximity to the open sea. For these reasons, the distressed areas in Massachusetts are able to offer favorable environmental conditions for new industries and potential inmigrants for certain suburbs.

Geographic location is important in another sense. In the eastern portions of Massachusetts, for example, a key element in determining economic patterns seems to be commuting distance to Boston. In some areas, including Fall River, New Bedford, Martha's Vineyard, and North Adams, reasonable time-distance to New York City is a critical factor. In terms of intrastate-travel times, Massachusetts is very compact; for example only 3½ hours of driving separates North Adams, the most distant redevelopment area, from Boston.[2] Perhaps the key distinguishing feature in recent economic history is relative closeness to metropolitan Boston, the state's major source of jobs as well as its major research and educational center. Areas closest to Boston, such as Lowell, have benefited substantially from this proximity, while areas on the outer periphery, Plymouth, Gloucester, and Newburyport, may be expected to feel an increasingly greater impact in future years.[3] In some respects, Fall River, New Bedford, and the small resort areas also fall within the Boston orbit. Both of these communities already lay great stress on the fact that only about an hour's driving on high-speed expressways separate them from MIT and Boston's Logan Airport.

In summary, Massachusetts distressed areas are hybrids. While the central cities and much of the population experience chronic economic distress in varying degress, their suburbs offer the attractive living conditions traditionally associated with New England mountain, coastal, and quasi-rural communities. Second, most Massachusetts redevelopment areas are located sufficiently close to Boston, the state's major urban center, to reap some benefit from its growth.

UNEMPLOYMENT CAUSES AND TRENDS

It may be useful to sketch the economic background of the Massachusetts distressed areas, particularly the extent and characteristics of their unemployment problems.

By definition, the central distinguishing characteristic of a redevelopment area is chronically heavy unemployment; as is true in most of the nation's redevelopment areas, none of the Massachusetts distressed areas are late bloomers; substantial economic distress began to afflict the state's textile areas early in the present century, while the resort and fishing areas experienced serious difficulties decades earlier. Thus, the territorial units fated to be officially recognized as redevelopment areas in the 1960's were subjected to many decades of accumulated problems.

As currently defined, the state's redevelopment areas are by no means the only concentrations of low-income families and unemployed. In 1965, for example, the ten redevelopment areas of Massachusetts contained one sixth of the state's total jobless. In terms of sheer numbers, the urban slums of metropolitan Boston's core communities and the Springfield and Worcester areas contain many more of the state's unemployed. Moreover, the redevelopment areas are virtually lily white. Massachusetts Negro population is concentrated in Boston, Cambridge, and Springfield.

While the distressed areas do not constitute the state's most serious current economic and social problem, over the years they have been sorely tried. Unemployment rates in the Fall River, New Bedford, and Lowell areas in the 1930's at times exceeded 25 per cent, more than double the statewide average. Moreover, because of special reliance on the weakened textile industry, these three major redevelopment areas, which contain most of the state's distressed area population, had unemployment rates exceeding 12 per cent for a time during the late 1940's and early 1950's. By the mid-1960's, however, textile employment was sharply reduced in the three areas, and each had been able to make good use of some of the vacant, solidly constructed mill buildings. Apparel, electronics, and especially nonmanufacturing industries had become dominant elements in their economies, many of the new industries locating in vacated textile factories.

A special problem confronting Massachusetts redevelopment areas is the presence of large amounts of vacant floor space in industrial mill buildings. In 1963, over 3 million square feet of vacant industrial space was listed for sale or rent in Massachusetts redevelopment areas, almost two thirds of which was located in New Bedford and Fall River.

Since the 1950's, millions of square feet of abandoned mill space throughout Massachusetts and New England has been adapted for other uses (as noted above). For example, 8 million square feet of textile space has been converted to other uses in the Lawrence area alone.[4] Now, however, industrial realtors maintain that the desirable space has already been sold or rented and that for the most part only marginal vacancies remain. As a consequence of poor planning and minimal investment in renovation, a number of converted mill buildings resemble industrial slums. This led one study to suggest that mill structures are an esthetic blight and a stimulus to wasteful industrial sprawl.[5] Furthermore, a 1962 New Bedford survey revealed that on a per-employee basis, New Bedford manufacturers use more space than manufacturers in cities outside of New England.[6]

The same process of job gains and losses has been at work in the state's smaller distressed areas. The importance of leather and shoe production had greatly diminished in Newburyport, fishing in Provincetown and Gloucester, and textiles in North Adams. The basic shift in the economy was not accomplished without cost, nor was the recovery rapid. Up through the early 1960's, unemployment rates in Massachusetts redevelopment areas occasionally ranged as high as 10 per cent, reaching up to 20 per cent during the off-season in resort communities like Provincetown. Prosperity was late in coming to these areas, but in 1965 and 1966, unemployment rates decreased to the 6-7 per cent range and continued downward through 1966 and 1967.

Averages in annual unemployment rates for Massachusetts redevelopment areas for the period 1949-66 are presented in Table 3. To show the extent and location of seasonal unemployment, this table includes data for January, 1944, and May, 1964.

Unemployment in redevelopment areas has consistently ranged from a minimum of 50 per cent above the national unemployment rate, the level required for EDA designation as a depressed area, to more than double the annual rates of Boston and the nation. The disparity is even wider during the winter months, when seasonal industries lay off workers. Data for January, 1964, indicate that unemployment rates were two to almost four times greater in some redevelopment areas than in the Boston labor-market area and the nation.

Wide year-to-year fluctuations characterize unemployment in redevelopment areas as compared to areas possessing greater economic strength and resilience. For example, as Table 3 indicates, unemployment rates in Massachusetts and the nation varied by only 2 per cent in the selected years between 1949 and 1966, while in metropolitan Boston, the range was less than 2 points. By contrast, in the three principal redevelopment areas, the average year-to-year fluctuations were much larger; in Fall River it was 4 percentage points; in Lowell and New Bedford, about 3 points.

Between 1950 and 1964, total employment increased in three of the areas, remained stable in a fourth, and declined by varying amounts in five others. Substantial job gains registered in many nonmanufacturing industries tended to replace and (in some cases) to overshadow declines in manufacturing

TABLE 3
Massachusetts Unemployment Rates 1949-66
(in per cents)

	1966[d]	1961	1956	1949	1964[e]	1964[f]
Massachusetts Redevelopment Areas						
Bourne-Wareham	7.6	13.5	a	a	22.1	7.1
Fall River	4.4	9.4	6.8	12.0	13.7	13.5
Gloucester	7.6	13.0	a	a	21.5	7.1
Lawrence-Haverhill[b]	4.4	7.6	9.9	26.0	7.5	7.5
Lowell	5.6	9.2	6.7	12.0	10.8	8.1
New Bedford	4.8	9.8	6.2	18.3	9.8	7.3
Newburyport	5.7	11.9	a	a	15.4	9.7
North Adams	3.4	9.4	6.1	a	8.7	5.7
Plymouth	9.6	9.6	a	a	18.3	10.6
Providence-Pawtucket[c]	3.4	7.1	6.0	13.0	7.7	6.4
Boston	3.6	4.8	2.7	7.7	5.8	5.0
United States	3.9[f]	6.7	4.2	5.9	5.4	5.0

All figures are annual averages except where indicated. Data are not seasonally adjusted.

a Not available.

b The Lawrence-Haverhill area was never officially designed as a redevelopment area, but it has been eligible under the Accelerated Public Works programs as an area of substantial unemployment.

c Rhode Island's Providence-Pawtucket area includes approximately 80,000 Massachusetts residents (10 per cent of the population total) in its labor-market area.

d Data for May.

e Data for January.

f Data for July.

Sources: Federal Reserve Bank of Boston, New England Business Review, April, 1962, and Massachusetts Division of Employment Security, unpublished materials.

197

employment. The major sources of manufacturing job losses were the decimation of the textile industry and losses in other soft-goods industries such as leather and shoe production. Smaller areas experienced decreases in employment related to the fishing industry. Within the manufacturing category in most of the industrial redevelopment areas, job decreases in the principal industry, textiles, accounted for a loss of at least three or four jobs for every two jobs gained in expanding nontextile industries.

The apparel industry has been the major growth industry in two of the state's larger distressed areas, Fall River and New Bedford. In 1964, over one third of the state's total number of apparel jobs were concentrated in these two southeastern Massachusetts areas, which contain only 5 per cent of the state population. Massachusetts redevelopment areas as a group contain a relatively small share of electronics employment. Although the redevelopment areas contain 14 per cent of the population, they have little more than one tenth of total employment in this major growth industry. Moreover, most of the electronics plants in the state's distressed areas are the lower-wage, assembly operations of the industry.

In evaluating employment changes, it is necessary to recognize that jobs differ by industry, hours, wages, and seasonality. For example, the shift in employment emphasis in Fall River and New Bedford from textiles to apparel resulted in an increasing proportion of females employed in manufacturing plants. Apparel manufacturing uses a labor force that is about 85 per cent female as compared to about 60 per cent for the textile industry. In addition, apparel workers tend to be more affected by seasonal factors and short work weeks than textile employees because the industry is geared to preholiday peak periods, and average wages in the apparel industry are lower than in textile manufacturing.[7] Expansion of the recreation industry also tends to increase the number of low-wage, seasonal workers, although some recreation employees may be students earning supplementary family income. By contrast, the increase in government and finance employment that has occurred in all redevelopment areas has expanded the number of year-round jobs paying relatively good wages. Nevertheless, the drag of the low-wage manufacturing industries has proved too great to overcome. In 1965, the spread between redevelopment area wages and metropolitan Boston was roughly as great as it was in the 1950's--from 15 per cent to 30 per cent below the Boston area level.

It can be seen that one ancient problem, unemployment, has been reduced to manageable proportions in the redevelopment areas. The trouble is that some of the factors associated with chronic distress are still important obstacles to progress. The redevelopment areas are confronted with one series of problems related to the deteriorated physical environment, including decrepit public facilities, substandard services, and substandard housing. While the response to these problems is by no means a simple matter, it is much easier to make tangible physical improvements than to attack social problems. The most serious handicap of the distressed area is the accumulation of social problems relating to health, education, and welfare, and the even more subtle but extremely troublesome problems relating to attitudes, innovation, and leadership capacities. All of these are difficult to solve, particularly in the face of a decline in the local tax base and a state and local fiscal system that places disproportionately heavy burdens for public school support on financially weak communities and on low-income families. In short, adequate numbers of jobs may resolve one current problem, but more employment in itself may not penetrate much below the surface. This is as true of distressed families as it is of distressed areas. The family whose breadwinner has been unemployed for years tends to develop special problems that do not quickly disappear when the family head finds a job.

NEW TARGETS FOR REDEVELOPMENT AREAS

If the mid-1960's serve as an indication, national prosperity will relieve many of the redevelopment areas' quantitative employment problems, particularly in areas located in intermetropolitan-urban complexes. Surplus labor will be siphoned off, and with the help of some outside inputs of capital, enough local expansion will occur to provide needed jobs and to smooth off the rougher edges in the commercial and services sector. Furthermore, federal and state programs of assistance will help to alleviate social problems such as substandard schools, neglected medical care, and other social needs. Yet, while long-standing defects such as these may be ameliorated with outside financial assistance, the basic problem of qualitative differences in living conditions and family income patterns between areas will not disappear. Furthermore, we have belatedly begun to recognize the existence of other types of distressed areas, the urban slums which pose even more complex problems. Over and above the difficult problems of the traditional distressed areas, even greater obstacles confront efforts to increase the income levels of their central-city slum areas. There are frequently serious health problems and a lack of literacy training. Motivation is often weak and work discipline of the many "subemployed" is feeble. These problems are also prevalent and are probably much more intensified in slum areas of the larger central cities in redevelopment areas. The broad interprogram efforts called for in removing or at least reducing the medical, educational, and psychological handicaps of the subemployed far transcend in complexity and magnitude the traditional economic development operations aimed at creating jobs for the readily employable.

Unfinished business confronting the redevelopment areas clearly requires priority efforts to attack the lingering problem of hard-core unemployment and subemployment. But equally important, it must be recognized that it is vital to achieve a profound transformation in redevelopment areas of physical and cultural patterns. Unless this is done, the distressed area problem will remain a permanent affliction. Although interarea production costs are similar, there will remain wide and persisting differentials in family incomes and industrial wages between distressed areas like Fall River and New Bedford and thriving areas like Boston. It is apparent that the redevelopment area often suffers a self-reinforcing pattern of substandard education, substandard wages, and substandard physical environment. There is a danger that persistent economic, social, and cultural disparities will create a geographical split into "two societies," with one type of area enjoying the full benefits of technological and cultural progress while the disadvantaged area lumbers along in the rear, only very slowly reducing the gulf that separates it from its neighbors.[8]

The marked downturn in unemployment rates in 1965-68 confronts some newly created Economic Development Districts with the possibility of their early removal from areas designated as qualifying for EDA assistance and other forms of federal aid. In areas such as New Bedford, establishment of an Economic Development District under 1965 legislation has postponed the loss of designation status and will permit undesignated areas like Lawrence-Haverhill to share fully in EDA and other benefits, provided that they are selected as district growth centers.

Unless the present rules are altered (or the economy takes an unexpected dip) the annual review of unemployment rates by the U.S. Department of Labor may find one or both distressed areas in some Economic Development Districts no longer eligible for continued designation. They may no longer contain the minimum of two labor-marked areas of substantial and persistent unemployment required by the 1965 Public Works and Economic Development Act. The continued use of unemployment rates among the readily employable as the only standard of measuring distress may help to defeat the promises and purposes of major innovative legislation. Clearly, special legislative provision to help distressed areas complete the transition from convalescence to health is needed. Obviously, prerequisite to the solution of distressed area problems is a foundation of national prosperity upon which local leadership can construct meaningful renovation programs. Assuming that such leadership is on hand, which it is in some areas, it makes no sense at all to deprive such leaders of special distressed area tools to assist them in their painfully difficult task.

NOTES TO CHAPTER 9

1. John H. Nixon, Director, Economic Development Administration, Office of Technical Assistance, United States Department of Commerce, "Jobs for Low-Income Areas of the Inner-City," *Economic Development*, III, 12.

2. North Adams was no longer designated as a redevelopment area by 1967.

3. A recent, unanticipated example of economic fallout is the decision of the Boston Edison Company to construct a major (650 megawatt) atomic energy plant in Plymouth. Because of safety regulations, the Atomic Energy

Commission prohibits construction of such installations in major metropolitan areas; Plymouth, near but not *in* metropolitan Boston, was the beneficiary.

4. Melvin R. Levin and David A. Grossman, *Development Trends in the Central Merrimack Valley* (Cambridge, Mass.: The Planning Services Group, 1961).

5. *The Economy of Metropolitan Fall River, Massachusetts* (Fall River: Hammer and Company Associates and the Fall River Planning Board, December, 1963).

6. *A Study of the Economic Base of the City of New Bedford* (Cambridge: Arthur D. Little, Inc., 1962).

7. For example, in the Fall River area, where the apparel industry provides the largest segment of the manufacturing economy, almost 40 per cent of the females working in 1959 worked less than 40 weeks. The comparable proportion for the Boston area was about one third. *United States Census of Population 1960: Massachusetts Detailed Characteristics* (U.S. Department of Commerce, Bureau of the Census, 1960), Table 118, pp. 353-54.

8. The gulf widened or remained constant between 1940 and 1962. Personal income data indicate a nationwide reduction in interarea disparities between 1929 and 1940. A number of low-income areas made little or no progress in reducing the income gap between 1940 and 1962; they include Mobile and Montgomery, Alabama; Lewiston-Auburn, Maine; Fall River-New Bedford, Massachusetts; Atlantic City, New Jersey; Wilmington, North Carolina; Altoona, Erie, Johnstown, Scranton, and Wilkes-Barre--Hazelton, Pennsylvania; Charleston and Columbia, South Carolina; Chattanooga, Tennessee; and Wheeling, West Virginia. U.S. Department of Commerce, *Survey of Current Business* (Washington, D.C.: U.S. Government Printing Office, May, 1967), Table 1. The survey covered only 97 of the nation's 212 Standard Metropolitan Statistical Areas, and many redevelopment areas were omitted.

10 PUBLIC ENTREPRENEURSHIP
IN
DISTRESSED AREAS

INTRODUCTION

In much of the discussion preceding the enactment of the 1961 Area Development Act and its successor, the Public Works and Economic Development Act of 1965, there seemed to be an implicit assumption that there was a direct parallel to beleaguered England in 1940. "Give us the tools," Winston Churchill assured America, "and we will finish the job." In actual fact, the full resources of two great allies were needed for victory, in addition to Churchill's remarkable talents. Appealing political rhetoric has its limitations; it is apparent that Britain's power was inadequate for the task.

The same Churchillian claim was advanced repeatedly in the hearings preceding the passage of federal distressed area legislation. Based on experience in selected industrial areas, it was suggested that a sizable input of federal funds would generate sufficient private investment to create first- and second-round jobs for a large proportion of the unemployed in redevelopment areas. The ability to make effective use of these funds was taken for granted, perhaps because the mayors and governors testifying in favor of the legislation were so articulate and persuasive.[1] In practice, however, the experience has been closer to wartime Britain. The problems of the redevelopment areas are being met and to some extent, mastered, largely with the help of powerful outside forces. At this point, however, the parallel lines diverge: Many of the redevelopment areas lack inspired leadership.

Overall national prosperity and the intervention of federal resources have accounted for most of the impressive recent progress in reducing unemployment in distressed areas. Even by a generous self-estimate, for example, the Area Redevelopment Administration claimed credit for only a modest share of the impressive job gains in redevelopment areas between 1961 and 1965.[2] The pattern in 1965 and 1966 is more of the same: Nationwide manpower shortages have reduced unemployment rates in most urban distressed areas to the 5-6 per cent level, an improvement that has brought them roughly to the national unemployment rate of prosperous 1963.[3]

The leadership factor is critical because solutions to the problems of unemployment--and, specifically, the uses to which inputs of outside resources to assist redevelopment areas can be put--take many different forms and can have very different consequences. Progress in tackling redevelopment problems is hampered and in some cases is jeopardized by the fact that the quality of redevelopment area political and business leadership is unequal to the task of internal change, upgrading, and renovation. The net result is the widening rather than the narrowing of the gap that separates the redevelopment areas from the flourishing metropolitan areas. They can easily become--or in some cases, remain--Caliban territory, suitable only as sources of low-grade labor and low-grade enterprise with social and political outlooks to match.

Many of these areas are sadly deficient in the critical elements of redevelopment area programs that cannot be imported from Washington--vigorous, inspiring, and effective political and business leadership, backed up by significant technical expertise to implement local programs. The immediate need for jobs is being met through a combination of outmigration and creation of low-wage, local, employment opportunities. Abject poverty is met by direct federal aid to needy persons, but without the combination of better public and private local leadership to improve school systems, housing, physical facilities, and public services to lay the groundwork for higher types of private business and industrial development, many distressed areas will be reduced to a marginal social and economic role. They will provide a pool of undereducated migrant labor for low-wage jobs located in the large metropolitan areas and attractive sites for poorly paid, labor-intensive industry. They will also tend to choose legislators to serve in Congress and in state legislatures, as well as mayors and city councilors, from among the supply of residual talent attuned to an environment consonant with substandard intellectual quality.

The explicit assumption in this gloomy forecast is that a combination of outstanding political and business leadership and technical expertise is required to reduce the accumulated social and economic problems that distinguish the distressed areas from flourishing metropolitan areas. It is also assumed that area initiative may yield fruitful results under almost any general economic conditions, but area progress can be rapid and lasting in a period of national prosperity, particularly when there is a strong federal commitment to assisting needy areas and needy people.

As a rule, each of the essential elements in the leadership-technical-expert pattern tend to be relatively weak in distressed areas. The political leadership is often inbred, weak, and factionalized to the point of near paralysis. A dearth of alternative opportunities combined with decades of selective outmigration have removed young, dedicated, well-educated, and well-motivated men and women whose views extend beyond limited local horizons. In job-hungry redevelopment areas, there is a parallel to underdeveloped nations. In both situations, most personal advancement is feasible only through inheritance, a rich marriage, or securing a niche on the political ladder. Setting aside a possible military career as a means of upward mobility, poor boys in either society tend to engage in fierce competition for the few lucrative local political openings available and to indulge in extensive private use of political office. As a result, local politics tends to revolve around personal cliques and petty scandals rather than public issues.

The business leadership in redevelopment areas has been diluted over the years by the dissolution or relocation of stronger local firms that, whatever their faults in "milking" their business and community, nevertheless retained strong local ties and supplied civic direction at critical junctures. The business newcomers tend either to be branch plant managers whose brief tenure permits little but noncontroversial, charitable activities or marginal operators, often of an alien, suspect background, in a backwater economy. The latter group depends heavily on the favor of local politicians and tends to remain aloof from political controversy. Excluded from the area's inner social circles, the newcomers often strive to retain their ties to other areas. Like the branch managers, they are more often found in useful but noncontroversial civic ventures rather than in party caucuses.

Technicians employed by redevelopment areas are often underpaid, substandard professionals more akin in quality and outlook to local civil servants than to professional staff found in metropolitan communities. The occasional capable elected official finds himself seriously handicapped by the absence of technicians qualified to seek out federal and private outside capital and to design and implement effective programs. When a well-qualified technician is hired, he is usually a bird of passage whose term of service is brief; he is often repelled by local living conditions, especially by pay scales geared to poverty-level local standards rather than to inducement "combat pay" for services rendered under unfavorable conditions.

THE LOST GOLDEN AGE

Before proceeding to examine the indices of defective leadership, it may be worthwhile to sketch some of the history that preceded and helped to create the problem.

Redevelopment areas have been subjected to decades of economic travail so that, not unexpectedly, many residents have developed a special outlook. The struggle over thirty or forty years to preserve their economic base has caused some residents to feel that history has put them through the wringer. Although past records indicate that, even in their heyday, mill towns offered grim living conditions for most of the residents, jobs were nonetheless plentiful. Thus, while their inequality with large metropolitan areas was established virtually from their inception, a persistent nostalgia prevails among older redevelopment area residents, including most of the fifty- to sixty-year-old leadership group, based on the supposition that conditions were far better in some bygone, almost mythical golden age. Against this glowing tapestry, present successes may appear hollow and trivial.

A persistent sense of having been bypassed by events has important implications. Residents in redevelopment areas and their elected officials tend to view themselves as the neglected orphans of the state and federal government. Often they nourish grievances that provide fertile soil for conflict. From the viewpoint of out-of-area officials, redevelopment area leaders seem exclusively preoccupied with continually demanding more local aid for *ad hoc* projects to the detriment of overall program planning. However, what to an outsider may appear to be merely local overreaction to outside proposals for reform or allocation is often traceable to the deep-rooted suspicion of state and federal governments growing out of local interpretations of past history. If redevelopment area officials display the "startle reflex" of a Maine jumper, lashing about in all directions to an unexpected tap on the shoulder, they have good cause. History for such areas has consisted of a series of plant closings and other nasty surprises, disasters that seemed to have grown up overnight from brief announcements on the back pages to banner headlines edged in black.

In addition to the myth of the lost golden age, one frequently encounters a remarkable amount of back biting. There are many legends in distressed areas concerning the large manufacturing plant (often a branch of the Ford Motor Company) that was discouraged from locating by a key local firm which wanted to keep labor cheap and docile. There is also alleged to be an enormous amount of grafting among local officials, although on closer inspection, these venomous stories usually involve such piddling sums as to seem more closely related in scale if not reprehensiveness to robbing the poor box. On occasion, local businessmen are free with comments illustrative of the backwardness and laziness of the local labor supply that is alleged to prefer leisure and low pay to hard work at good wages. Beneath this underbrush of scurrility is a kind of chronic despair and a feeling of impotence in the face of the insoluble. To a great extent, the prevailing attitude is not that of the mainstream of our society; in fact, it is closer to what Americans have come to regard as the alien passivity that once seemed to characterize most underdeveloped nations in Asia, Latin America, and Africa.

The delusion which contrasts a happy, distant past with a difficult present and which tends to regard state and federal governments as insensitive to local needs makes it difficult to develop a reasonable, long-term strategy. Immediate problems seem so overwhelming that most areas tend to proceed from one fragmented effort to another, responding to transient local circumstances and to federal and state initiatives. There is continued frustration and partly concealed conviction that local efforts are doomed by overwhelming historic forces, and that, consequently, current and future action will prove no more effective in reducing persistent problems to a tolerable condition than did the exhausting campaigns of the past. The result is a widespread feeling of running full speed on a treadmill. In addition, there tends to be mounting antipathy to perpetual mobilization for economic and/or industrial development: Many residents and their leaders are tired of never-ending contributions, speech making, publicity, meetings, and committees. Wearied by years of campaigning, at the first sign of a swallow (e.g., a drop in unemployment rates), they are often only too ready to proclaim the advent of summer and to terminate further economic development operations.

New Bedford, one of Massachusetts' three larger (population 125,000) redevelopment areas, in the 1928-38 decade, provides a good example of the magnitude, character, and unrealized hopes that were generated by past economic development programs.[4] In 1928, an Industrial Development Division was established in the city's Board of Commerce to seek out new industry and to assist existing firms. The spring of 1929 saw the inauguration of a "Help New Bedford Plan," involving a public exposition of local products. This was followed in 1930 by the "New Bedford Forward" movement, also initiated by the Board of Commerce to bring together suggestions on attracting specific industries.

In 1938, the mayor created a new organization, the Industrial Development Legion. Following the example of the AEF (or the Salvation Army), he designated himself Commander in Chief, issued a declaration of war against unemployment, and appointed a chief of staff and a number of colonels. These field-grade officers were in turn empowered to appoint captains and lieutenants. A two-year enlistment term was established, corps designations were assigned, military reviews conducted, and distinguished community service medals awarded.

Most of the new plants induced to settle in the city in response to this offensive were low-investment, low-wage, light industries. The city offered the manufacturer 10 million square feet of vacant textile mill space at 10-12 cents per square foot. One firm was provided with free heat, free repairs, and a nightwatchman; free boiler facilities were offered to another, and the city sold a $750,000 mill to a third for $500. In another instance, workers employed by a failing cotton textile plant agreed to take a voluntary 10 per cent cut from their weekly wages to pay the company's creditors: Four months later, the mill closed. Textile employees also contributed part of their slender earnings in vain attempts to save two other mills. The American Legion paid most of the moving costs for another manufacturing plant. Yet, despite these valiant efforts, by 1938, New Bedford's nontextile industries had provided employment for only one fifth as many workers as had been displaced by the employment losses in the city's cotton textile industry over the previous decade.

New Bedford's experience was shared by other cities. The Committee on the New England Textile Industry appointed by the New England Governors concluded, as recently as 1952, that it was "imperative" to maintain the textile industry in New England. The committee's study of seven textile towns showed what happens when a mill closes or migrates. Community depression tends to persist even in years of national prosperity; tax rates rise; skills are lost, and the new industries that come into the depressed town are usually lower wage industries.[5]

The committee reported that all seven communities tried vigorously to find substitute employment offering subsidies such as free space, financial aid, and tax favors. Another study noted that Fall River, another textile city, granted major tax concessions in an attempt to retain remaining textile firms. Not only was there an adverse immediate fiscal impact, but the attempt was a failure: In 1950, textiles, which provided 44 per cent of total manufacturing jobs in Fall River, contributed only 5 per cent of the city's property taxes.[6]

At that time, Fall River's major industry "appeared to be reasonably well stabilized" in the committee's view. However, an earlier research study included a pessimistic but more accurate prognostication: "It seems unlikely that a period of [postwar] readjustment would pass without further reduction in the city's textile capacity."[7] And so it was. Like the fruitless efforts to save jobs in the coal industry and in marginal agriculture in other distressed areas, time, energy, and money were sacrificed with little measurable result aside from fiscal disaster and a residue of suspicion, civic exhaustion, and pessimism.

The result of decades of only partially rewarding struggles is, in some cases, a weakening of resilience and apathetic acquiescence rather than an eager response to outside stimuli and opportunity. Moreover, there is a growing belief that solutions, if these are to be forthcoming, will emerge from new federal programs rather than from local initiative. To a considerable extent, this supposition is well grounded on the fiscal facts of life. A number of areas clearly cannot afford to pay for many of the public improvements they obviously need. But surrender to passivity is also based upon a misconception of the nature of state and federal programs. Although it is true that most of the new investment funds pouring into the areas may be federal (or, less commonly, state) in origin, both their magnitude and their use depend largely upon the locality and its initiative. As a result, enormous interarea differences occur in the size, nature, and impact achieved by urban renewal, public works, manpower training, and antipoverty programs. The funds may be largely external in origin, but local use thereof and the impact created are largely determined by the sophistication and vigor of local leadership.

Local action is particularly vital. The practice of channeling large-scale economic development to redevelopment areas that is operative in parts of Europe is not now and is not likely to be adopted by the United States. In the United States, general grant-in-aid programs (such as urban renewal), which are also available to and usually more heavily utilized by flourishing areas, far overshadow special programs to aid distressed areas. Area development, therefore, involves the task of sharpening area and community skills in securing and implementing aid from the federal and state governments, a technique that can be described as "public entrepreneurship."

It has been suggested that the major problems of distressed areas are (1) their inability, or sometimes unwillingness, to invest in high-quality education and (2) their participation in proportion to their needs in federal programs.

A region which is economically anemic is likely to underinvest in education; not necessarily in relation to its resources, but in relation to the social return and the private return to the clientele. Moreover the institutional fabric is such that one cannot assume that it will upon its own initiative take full advantage of generalized programs of assistance, especially if they require local financial participation.[8]

THE SCHOOLS: COMMUNITY MIRROR

If there is a single criterion that can be used as a faithful reflection of community leadership it is the quality of the public-school system. Despite outside prodding and financing, the schools remain uniquely local, mirroring and perpetuating suburban affluence and central city squalor impartially and accurately.

As is the case in most urban centers, the redevelopment areas are characterized by a wide divergence between core city and suburban educational patterns. The most serious social and economic problems are concentrated in the central-city slum neighborhoods where schools are particularly bad. However, scholastic inbreeding and substandard techniques are found throughout the central-city school system, defects that are related only in part to a persistently inadequate level of expenditures. Before considering the problem of local leadership as it impinges on the schools, it may be well to review a few salient statistics.

An examination of educational indices in the 1960 census reveals that in Fall River, New Bedford, and North Adams areas, one half of the adult population had completed only about eight or nine years of schooling, roughly equivalent to elementary school graduation. This level contrasted sharply with that of the state's largest area, metropolitan Boston, where the median level of educational achievement was over twelve years.[9] In most parts of Massachusetts, the educational level was somewhere between these extremes, with one half of the adults having completed two or three years of high school.

The pattern was similar with respect to other educational indices. In the Fall River and New Bedford areas, only about one quarter of the adults had completed four years of high school or more. In Boston, the proportion was over one half. Furthermore, in Fall River and New Bedford, one out of every eight or nine adults had less than a fifth-grade education in 1960. This compares to a ratio of only one in twenty with less than a fifth-grade education in the Boston area.

One statistic requires special comment. In 1960, only one adult in twenty-five in the Fall River and New Bedford areas had completed four or more years of college, a percentage that had not risen appreciably between 1950 and 1960. By contrast, not only was the 1950 proportion of college graduates more than twice as high in the Boston area than in the two southeastern Massachusetts areas, but the percentage in metropolitan Boston increased markedly between 1950 and 1960. Some of the retrogressive atmosphere in many redevelopment areas is clearly associated with the scarcity of college graduates.

The lack of adequate numbers of jobs for graduates is reflected in labor-mobility patterns. Generally, migration and education are closely correlated: Evidence exists to support the view that in redevelopment areas a high school diploma is equivalent to a passport for migration.

Statistical data fail to illuminate qualitative differences in educational systems. It is apparent, however, that there is a reasonably close link between expenditures per pupil and educational standards. For this reason, the fact that per pupil elementary and secondary expenditures in Massachusetts redevelopment area central cities are in the $400-$500 range rather than the $700-$800 level characteristic of Boston suburbs is a matter of extreme significance.[10]

Newspaper stories have revealed the lack of supplementary educational services in redevelopment area schools. This is reflected, for example, in inadequate health and remedial reading instruction in Fall River.[11] Reports indicate that in Fall River an unusually large proportion (18-20 per cent) of Title I grants under the Federal Elementary and Secondary Education Act of 1965 was used to provide supplementary nutrition for students from poor families. ESEA was designed to help local systems expand and renovate their schools, and wealthier communities have been able to devote their entire allocations to this purpose alone.

In summary, the critical deficiencies in educating redevelopment area children is partly due to a lack of funds. However, there is some evidence that the horizons and talents of public and civic leadership, including school administrators, are extremely limited; they are incapable of closing the gap, even if funds can be made available. Statistical measurements of poor administration and substandard teaching are unavailable, and the observer is forced to rely on subjective comments. Nevertheless, there is fire as well as smoke in the charges of backwardness that have been leveled at many central city school systems, not only in southeastern Massachusetts, but elsewhere in the state and nation.

TABLE 4
Selected Data for the Thirteen Largest Cities in Massachusetts, 1955-65

City	(a) Total 1965 Population (nearest 1,000)	(b) % of Population Change 1955-65	(c) % of Families With Income Under $3,000 in 1959	(d) Total Dwelling Units (nearest 1,000)	(e) % of Substandard Housing in 1960	(f) % of Adults Who Completed High School or More by 1960	(g) Per Capita Commitments for Urban Renewal, Through 1965 Federal	State
Boston	616,000	-15.0	16.7	239,000	26.7	44.6	$254	$64
Brocton*	83,000	33.3	12.6	24,000	18.4	43.9	30	8
Cambridge	93,000	-6.3	15.3	35,000	21.1	49.7	61	15
Fall River†	98,000	-6.8	20.0	34,000	36.6	20.5	6	2
Lawrence*	69,000	-9.2	18.5	24,000	26.3	33.2	128	32
Lowell†	87,000	-7.8	15.5	30,000	25.5	35.6	37	9
Lynn	100,000	-5.0	15.0	33,000	18.0	42.3	26	7
New Bedford†	93,000	-6.4	22.4	37,000	32.5	20.3	80	20
Newton	90,000	2.3	6.0	26,000	5.7	71.7	**	**
Quincy	87,000	3.2	9.4	27,000	10.7	53.5	**	**
Somerville	86,000	-11.0	11.9	29,000	17.2	40.1	6	1
Springfield*	166,000	-0.3	14.6	59,000	22.2	41.8	51	13
Worcester	180,000	-11.3	15.4	59,000	22.2	39.9	17	4
State	5,295,000	9.5	12.4	1,961,000	18.9	47.0	**	**

** Not available.
* Cities in areas eligible for accelerated public-works assistance during 1961-65.
† Cities in designated redevelopment areas.
Source: Division of Urban Renewal, Massachusetts Department of Commerce and Development.

Table 4 Sources

Columns (a) and (b) *Massachusetts State Decennial Census* (Boston: Office of the Secretary of State). The state census is not entirely comparable to the federal census since it omits "temporary" and institutionalized persons. Community totals presented in the state census tend to understate population totals in areas containing appreciable numbers of military personnel, dormitory students, or hospitals.

Column (c) *U.S. Census of Population, 1960, Massachusetts, General Social and Economic Characteristics* (U.S. Department of Commerce, Bureau of Census, 1960), Table 33, pp. 23-121. The data were obtained from respondents and are not wholly reliable. Income from public assistance, social security, and unemployment compensation is included (p. xxiv) and the figure refers to gross income, i.e., before deductions for social security, income taxes, etc.; the $3,000 family level is generally considered the poverty line.

Columns (d) and (e) *U.S. Census of Housing, 1960, Massachusetts* (U.S. Department of Commerce, Bureau of Census, 1960), Table 1. The total in column (d) includes units occupied or intended for occupancy as separate living quarters, e.g., exclusive use of a kitchen and direct access to the outside. Hotel rooms with cooking facilities, trailers, and vacation cottages are included (pp. xiv-xv). The criteria for sound, substandard, deteriorating, and dilapidated housing, and for plumbing facilities are based on observable structural characteristics (e.g., foundation and wiring deficiencies are excluded). Information on plumbing facilities is derived from respondents. In 1960 enumerators were given "improved training techniques," but the figures must be used with caution, especially for small areas (pp. xxii-xxiii).

Column (f) *U.S. Census of Population, 1960, Massachusetts, General Social and Economic Characteristics* (U.S. Department of Commerce, Bureau of Census, 1960), Table 32, pp. 23-119. "Adults" are persons 25 years or older in 1960.

Column (g) Massachusetts Division of Urban Renewal (unpublished statistics). The data include the total federal and state amounts earmarked for specific, approved projects. The per capita calculation is based on the last state census (1959).

URBAN RENEWAL EXPENDITURES: A MEASURE
OF PUBLIC ENTREPRENEURSHIP

Assuming that the problems are roughly uniform and that all large communities are theoretically capable of conducting programs to deal with their physical and social deficiencies, one would expect that there would be no major disparity in the scale of their problem-solving, federally aided operations. However, as columns (e) and (g) in Table 4 suggest, this is not the case: On a per-capita basis, Boston is by far the leader in urban renewal funding in Massachusetts. Why is this pattern so lopsided? Smaller communities receive their proportionate share of public assistance and unemployment compensation, funds allocated by the government directly to the individual recipient. But funds for renewal and poverty are forthcoming only on a community basis to municipalities that can pass a number of tests of skill and endurance. A desperate need for assistance is not enough. The community must have an effective organization, must be capable of satisfying complex and rapidly changing federal criteria, and must be able to compete for funds against rival claimants in regional and federal offices and in the state house. Moreover, if it wishes to receive further allocations, it must exhibit some evidence of performance. In short, the community must be able to operate like a large, efficient corporation with substantial government contracts.

An examination of federal antipoverty grants points up the consequences of differences in the ability of local, public entrepreneurs. While cities like Boston in fiscal 1966 received almost three times the amount per capita stipulated in OEO guidelines, many communities received only one sixth of the guideline figure. The successes (such as Boston) were due to municipal aggressiveness and technical preparedness to make use of all the types of projects available.[12]

As in the case of business corporations, perhaps there is a critical-size factor involved in attracting federal money: Smaller Massachusetts cities do not carry the political weight of Boston, nor do they have Boston's special potential for expansion, as shown in the development of a major Government Center, a Prudential Insurance Center, or a medical complex. Even allowing for their smaller size, they lack a proportional potential for expansion in government, finance, business services, medicine, and higher education, all of which are among the nation's key growth industries. But other compensating factors work in favor of the smaller communities in securing government aid. Federal and state agencies are normally reluctant to concentrate disproportionate amounts of their funds in a few large cities. Agency survival and expansion require a broad base of political support and this, in turn, depends upon practical demonstrations of their concern for districts that contain no metropolises. For this reason, federal and state agencies are often more than eager to channel some of their largesse into the needy smaller cities. But they cannot respond without an effective local stimulus, and many smaller cities are unable to generate approvable applications for funds. Thus, whatever the federal hesitations, an undeniable tendency exists to continue pouring large amounts of money into the same handful of cities. It is partially the result of momentum; once begun, programs cannot be choked off in midstream. Furthermore, as the large city increases its technical abilities, it is able to keep abreast of rapidly changing, extraordinarily complicated criteria for new types of programs.

To get down to first causes, however, the comparative grant-in-aid starvation of the small- and medium-sized city in redevelopment areas is primarily a consequence of a deficiency in the combination of expertise and leadership.[13] There is apparently a shortage of specialized skills--those needed to qualify for funds in programs requiring substantial public entrepreneurship. Yet, some small cities have shown that size is not an insuperable handicap. New Haven, with a population of about 150,000 in receipt of per-capita federal renewal and antipoverty funding larger than Boston, is one nearby example. Close at hand is Lawrence, the smallest of the cities listed in Table 4, but second only to Boston in per-capita federal renewal commitments.

The example selected for purposes of comparison, the urban renewal program, is only a sample of a wide range of government assistance available to the active city. In passing, in view of the harsh criticisms leveled at urban renewal and other programs, it may be in order to remind ourselves that these are voluntary programs; the community has to exert considerable effort to participate at all. The undeniable hardships that were perpetrated in the 1950's when poor families were displaced as a result of badly conceived renewal projects represent, one would hope, both a deficiency in the state-of-the-art of redevelopment planning and an inability of the disadvantaged to swing much political weight. The grant-in-aid program is an instrument: The community, in its wisdom or lack thereof, and through its political leadership, can use it well, or badly, or leave it alone.

There is no conclusive evidence to explain why the smaller Massachusetts cities, particularly central cities in redevelopment areas, have been less successful in securing federal and state grants-in-aid than Boston. But three hypotheses can be offered.

1. *Redevelopment areas tend to be provincial.* In an era of instant communication via mass media, it seems ridiculous to suggest that municipal officials can be unaware of the ground rules of applying for, receiving, and implementing federal aid, yet this is the case. The new programs are complicated, and a mayor's two-year term can slip by before he has found the time to comprehend the paper work involved in these new programs. Moreover, there are sometimes lingering pockets of hostility to federal aid reminiscent of the 1930's, residual attitudes to big government that predate the Eisenhower era.

2. *Local bureaucracies are often weak.* Mayors would find life easier if they could rely on a cadre of vigorous, flexible, and imaginative civil servants. Too often, they inherit instead an aging bureaucracy, barely capable of coping with routine operations and sometimes unable to select reputable consultants.

Cities in redevelopment areas are simply not attracting their share of the available young talent, for, by and large, they offer neither inspiring nor remunerative employment for ambitious youth. The occasional, outstanding civil-servant-in-residence is often lured away by talent scouts from the federal agencies, larger cities, or private enterprise.

3. *"Little league" criteria are used as the basis of self-evaluation.* Too many redevelopment areas seem willing, even anxious, to settle for less in achievement, in salaries, and in aspirations. The local leadership is often inordinately proud of what exists, and it tends to be fearful of urging innovation lest calls for reform be construed as denigration of friends and neighbors. Thus, the smallness in scale and the closeness of personal ties tend to mute needed criticism and mitigate the dissatisfaction that must precede progress. To cite a specific example, salary levels for planning and redevelopment directors are often pegged to the level of that of the mayor despite the fact that (1) the mayor is considered a part-time functionary who usually has a supplementary income from a business or law firm, and (2) redevelopment areas that possess few intrinsic nonmonetary attractions for professional staff (e.g., major universities) must offer more rather than less cash to lure scarce talent.

It would be a gross error to suggest that problems of urban development are confined to cities located in redevelopment areas. Up to the spring of 1965, only 28 Massachusetts communities, roughly 1 in 12 in the state, had embarked on urban redevelopment programs. A glance at housing data reveals that the proportion might be at least 1 in 4 if the presence of slum housing proportionate to that of Boston is used as a criterion.

The case is not entirely hopeless, however. It would not be accurate to imply that Massachusetts redevelopment areas have not managed to secure substantial inputs of federal and state capital. Each of the seven redevelopment areas has benefited from the federal-state highway program, each has antipoverty operations in progress, each has urban renewal projects in various stages of execution, and all contain, are within easy commuting distance of, or are scheduled to receive regional vocational schools, community colleges, state teachers colleges, and medical-care institutions. New Bedford is the site of a large federally constructed hurricane barrier, and its airport has been the recipient of considerable federal funds. Fall River will be the site of a new federal-state financed regional vocational high school and a new community college. In combination, the two southeastern Massachusetts areas have succeeded in gaining major state and federal commitments for the technological institute under construction between them. Lowell has received federal funds for its industrial park, and other areas have gained other benefits from the various programs.

However, as the data on urban renewal expenditures suggests, the amounts received are not proportional to the population of the redevelopment areas, and they are even less commensurate with their relatively greater physical and human resource problems. Most have experienced frustrating difficulties in the application and implementation stage of these programs. For this reason, it is proper to identify public entrepreneurship as a distinct problem in Massachusetts redevelopment planning.

There are major differences between areas: For example, while Fall River and Lowell have succeeded in pumping into their depleted economies roughly one fortieth as much federal renewal funds as Boston, Lawrence is up to one half the Boston level. It seems clear that the city which is willing and able to act can secure a proportionate share of federal aid. On the whole, however, it appears unlikely that the imbalance can be corrected solely through local efforts. The cycle of inadequate skills and outlooks that traps poor families in poverty seems to apply equally to distressed cities and others not as destitute. What is apparently needed is a combination of outside technical assistance from state and federal sources and a greater local willingness to play by "big league" rules and standards.

Unless both are forthcoming--and soon--the skill gap between "haves" and "have nots" will grow wider. Just as the ill-trained poor find it increasingly difficult to advance in an education-oriented career structure, so will the poorly staffed city find it harder to qualify for the large amounts of federal and state aid that are available only to the sophisticated public entrepreneur.[14]

Dennis O'Harrow, Executive Director of the American Society of Planning Officials, has summarized the trend toward complexity in government programs.

> In the beginning [back in 1954] you got your workable program accepted merely by professing good intentions. . . . Now a dozen years later, you have to deliver on your promises, or the purse out of which urban renewal grants are paid is closed to you. . . . The next step beyond urban renewal . . . is called the comprehensive city demonstration program. . . . The rules will be proof of financial ability, proper administration . . . modern building code[s] . . . will be some of the prerequisites . . . some day the federal coordinator will say you get no money for urban renewal until you clear up the pollution in your river, until you stop pouring guck into the air, until you set up a decent education system, until you build adequate medical facilities . . . we can be sure that he who pays the piper is readying up some new tunes to call.[15]

New tunes are already a reality. The model cities program is a good example of a new, major source of funds that many distressed communities will find difficult to tap. The program is designed to provide special grants amounting to 80 per cent of all nonfederal costs of an array of federal grant-in-aid programs for the purpose of rebuilding the total environment of entire neighborhoods. In effect, qualifying for a large-scale model cities program multiplies a community's financial resources by restricting its investment in its future to perhaps 5-10 per cent of program cost. However, President Johnson has warned that:

> It will not be simple to qualify for such a program. We have neither the means nor the desire to invest public funds in an expensive program whose net effects will be marginal, wasteful, or visible only after protracted delay. We intend to help only those cities who help themselves. . . . There must be a high quality of design in new building . . . The demonstration proposal should offer proof that adequate municipal appropriations and services are available and will be sustained throughout the demonstration period.[16]

THE IMPROVING CLIMATE

The question of solutions now arises. In the past, the tendency was either to ignore the problem or to hope that a temporary injection of consultant expertise would be sufficient, assuming the presence of capable political and business leadership. More recently, federal agencies have attempted to fill the expertise gap. The Economic Development Administration has been empowered to assist Economic Development Districts, groups of two or more redevelopment areas, and possibly adjoining territory, in hiring technical staff. Under the Public Works and Economic Development Act of 1965, EDA can pay 75 per cent of the staff and administrative costs for the districts. It is probable that such aid will be extremely welcome, but it should be remembered that since 1954 the Department of Housing and Urban Development has been empowered to pay for a large proportion of planning and renewal staff costs in redevelopment areas and, in comparison to large metropolitan communities, the results have ranged from modest to negligible.

The chief difficulty appears to lie in the political and business sphere. Leadership is hard to come by in such areas. There are, however, a few hopeful signs. With the passage of time, the older leaders who still bear the scars of past failures are leaving the scene. In their place is emerging a new, more hopeful breed of better educated, more widely traveled leaders whose horizons and aspirations are more comparable to flourishing areas. In some areas, including New Bedford, Plymouth, Lowell, and North Adams, a smaller former textile area, some of the more adaptable older leaders have worked with young leaders who have emerged in businesses and in the political arena to achieve significant successes in urban renewal and economic development programs. In other cases, leadership has developed in significant nonpolitical projects such as the successful effort to move the battleship U.S.S. Massachusetts to Fall River and to develop the vessel and its surrounding area into a major tourist attraction. Thus, there is tangible reason to anticipate improvement in this vital prerequisite and to hope that some of this talent will concentrate on making a success of the newly created Economic Development Districts.

A second source of optimism is the potential technical expertise that can be tapped in the universities and colleges located in redevelopment areas. Growing community colleges, state colleges, and technical institutes can be found in or near the smaller Massachusetts redevelopment areas. In addition to the possibility of using regular faculty, it may be possible to attract and retain competent technicians who might otherwise prove unreceptive, particularly if close linkages can be forged with major out-of-area universities. Here again, local initiative is essential: Title III of the 1965 Higher Education Act provides federal funds to assist small colleges in developing and maintaining quality standards through working arrangements with universities, but securing such funds requires aggressiveness and sophistication. The promise of a college environment--insulation from the political hurly-burly and faculty status--can be powerful lures for the professional who might otherwise be repelled by the prospect of a career in a redevelopment area.

CONCLUSIONS

If the redevelopment area is not to evolve into a fully employed but low-wage area, providing resident strong backs and migrant strong minds for the nation, it must attempt to convert its specialized role into a more balanced replica of the great metropolis. This is an elaborate way of saying that the southeastern Massachusetts and Lowell areas are eminently correct in trying to rebuild area educational systems ranging from pre-kindergarten, through the public and vocational schools, to community colleges and technological institutes. The efforts of these and other urban-redevelopment areas in Massachusetts to conduct extensive urban renewal and antipoverty programs and to expand outdoor recreation facilities and other amenities can also be viewed as steps in the direction toward being able to offer on a modest scale the range and quality of facilities and services provided in the Boston area. Fortunately, there are clear signs of an improvement in the leadership picture.

What of the communities in which leadership was, is, and will probably remain incompetent, corrupt, or simply inadequate? The question arises as to the degree that the unfortunate citizenry, especially nonvoting children, should be penalized by a geographic accident. In such cases, the only answer seems to be an increased reliance on direct federal government-to-individual and federal-to-family programs that do not have to filter through the local government structure. Scholarships, welfare allowances, medical grants may provide the prototype family allowances; relocation grants and other district forms of aid unrelated to the quality of local government may help to compensate for some of the disparity in public entrepreneurship.

An important objective in formulating area development programs should be the improvement of the environment and the quality of human resources, including the strengthening of local pools of talent that should be the sources of political leadership. Under the American political system, the local political candidate is usually a long-term area resident. A look at the congressional and senatorial pattern often discloses a reasonably close relationship between a backward economy and a retarded political outlook on the part of elected representatives, even to the point of being a retrogressive influence in national legislation. Politics in a long-distressed area often revolve around bread-and-butter patronage topped with emotional rhetoric that capitalizes on local sentiments of estrangement from national patterns. It is to the national interest, therefore, that strenuous efforts be made to augment the intellectual resources of the redevelopment area. A flourishing metropolis, being the host of a steady stream of distressed area migrants, therefore has a strong interest in the educational and medical backgrounds of these people as well as in their willingness and ability to perform as productive citizens.

NOTES TO CHAPTER 10

1. See, for example, U.S. Senate, 86th Cong., Area Redevelopment Act, Subcommittee of the Committee on Banking and Currency, *Hearings,* 1st Sess., Pt. 1, February 25-27, 1959.

2. ARA claimed that it helped to create 115,000 jobs in distressed areas between 1961 and early 1965. Statements of Congressman John A. Blatnik on H.R. 6991 and related bills, House of Representatives, *Hearings* Before the Committee on Public Works, 89th Cong., 1st Sess., p. 23.

3. The 1963 United States rate was 5.7 per cent. However, pockets of poverty persisted in Indian reservations, in Negro slum areas, particularly among Negro adolescents, and in the form of underemployment in many rural areas. See U.S. Department of Labor, *Manpower Report of the President,* March, 1966, Table 19, p. 89; and George Iden, "Industrial Growth in Areas of Chronic Unemployment," *Monthly Labor Review,* May, 1966, pp. 485-90.

4. Information on New Bedford's depression-era economic development efforts is taken from Seymour Wolfbein, *Decline of a Cotton Textile City: A Study of New Bedford* (New York: Columbia University Press, 1944).

5. Committee Appointed by the Conference of New England Governors, Seymour Harris, Chairman, *Report on the New England Textile Industry* (Boston: New England Governors Council, 1952), p. 4. Four of the seven textile communities were in Massachusetts--Lowell, Lawrence, Fall River, and New Bedford.

6. Thomas Russell Smith, *The Cotton Textile Industry of Fall River, Massachusetts* (New York: Kings Crown Press, 1944), p. 162.

7. *Ibid.,* p. 163.

8. Benjamin Chinitz, "Appropriate Goals for Regional Economic Policy," *Urban Studies,* Glasgow, III, 1 (February, 1966), p. 5.

9. The Boston area figure, however, is affected by the presence of tens of thousands of college and university students who are counted as residents by the Census Bureau.

10. Massachusetts Department of Education, *Annual Report for the Year Ending June 30, 1963.* Figures have been updated on the basis of more recent data.

11. *The Boston Herald,* "The Rich Get Richer," Editorial, January 3, 1967.

12. Joseph A. Loftus, "City Poverty Grants Linked to Aggressiveness," *The New York Times,* August 18, 1966, p. 12.

13. For an insightful analysis of the role of leading public entrepreneurs in large-scale, community, urban renewal programs, see Jewel Bellush and Murray Hausknecht, "Entrepreneurs and Urban Renewal," *Journal of the American Institute of Planners,* Vol. XXXII (September, 1966), pp. 289-97.

14. Since there are almost 300 federal programs dealing with education, environment, and community development, involving more than 100 departmental subdivisions in 18 different federal agencies, a major manufacturer of business machines has established a subscriber-information service on federal programs. Their first directory, *Directory of Federal Programs for Schools and Communities* (Washington, D.C.: Xerox Corporation, Education Division, 1966), covering programs for schools and communities, is over 600 pages.

15. Dennis O'Harrow, "A New Tune for the Piper," *American Society of Planning Officials Newsletter,* XXXII, 3 (March, 1966), pp. 21-22.

16. U.S., President's Message, "City Demonstration Programs," H.R. Doc. No. 368, 89th Cong., 2nd Sess., January 29, 1966, pp. 4-5.

CHAPTER 11
TALENT MIGRATION: DISTRESSED AREA DILEMMA

MIGRANT TYPES AND MIGRANT PROBLEMS

In the past three centuries, the United States has been the recipient of millions of foreign immigrants. Between 1820 and 1965, 43 million immigrants, primarily from Europe and for the most part unskilled or poorly skilled, came to settle throughout the nation. Most tended to concentrate in urban areas in the nation's northeastern quadrant. The process continues with an estimated 1 million entering the country between 1965 and 1968, most of them locating in cities.

While this process is well known, the process of internal migration has-- at least until recently--been the subject of much less attention. Only one type of internal migrant, the Negro, has become an object of concern; 3.7 million Negroes moved out of the South between 1940 and 1966[1] and this trend shows every sign of continuing and perhaps even increasing. Similarly, migration of Latin Americans, poor white southerners and Indians is proceeding. Increasingly, as these disadvantaged groups become urban residents, the migration involves movement from small to large cities, a trend which tends to diminish some of the culture shock attendant on relocation from farms to urban slums. For the most part, the great historic migrant stream of white migrants from the rural areas and small towns to the city has been welcomed. The farm boy, with little education but alert and eager, who rises rapidly in the world, is a major theme in American legend. The problems of rural migrants have only begun to cause major concern when the movers have been black, brown or bleached Appalachian.

A third type of migrant, the relocatee from urban redevelopment areas, is the subject of this chapter. Usually Caucasian and fairly well educated, this type of migrant is warmly welcomed by employers in large metropolitan receiving areas. Unfortunately, he also represents a serious loss to his home area.

The American metropolis is the meeting place of these distinctive types of migrants. In order to understand the role of the urban relocatees, it is desirable to examine briefly the role of the immigrant from abroad, the migrant Negro, and the rural small town migrants attracted to the big cities.

TALENT MIGRATION: DISTRESSED AREA DILEMMA

In legend and often in fact, foreign immigrants were displaced peasants and impoverished urban workers fleeing poverty and often persecution for a land of opportunity. Adrift in strange surroundings, the newly arrived immigrant was often forced to accept a life of menial, low-paying employment and prolonged self-deprivation. As a rule, he labored in the confident hope and expectation that he, or more likely his children, would reap the harvest of his toil (in perhaps twenty or thirty years). Each nationality disembarked, became acclimatized, and regrettably but understandably rejected succeeding arrivals as "alien riffraff." The children of the Europeans, currently the dominant population component of the large metropolitan areas, are now coping with the transition associated with Negro migration whose travails and adjustments resemble, to a great extent, those encountered by their forefathers.

The integration of Negroes into the mainstream of the nation's life has aptly been termed America's principal urban problem during the last third of the twentieth century. Various social, economic, and historic arguments have been advanced to explain the frictions and continuing disequilibrium of the Negro ghettos. It can be argued that migration is not so much responsible for creating new difficulties as it is for bringing hidden problems into public visibility. Although there is little consolation in recognizing the fact, it would appear that the same family, employment, and social strains that cause such concern in the cities existed in pretty much the same form in the rural areas and small towns, in overt or latent form. Concentrated by the pressures of the urban slums, the transfer of Negro populations to the larger cities has brought neglected social maladies to public attention in a way that was never possible in the rural South. Generations of accumulated misery have been brought within the scope of systems of welfare, health services, and police that do not exist in the same form in areas like rural Mississippi.

Although analogies have been made with the nineteenth century Irish and Italian migrants, it is apparent that some old assumptions are invalid; a mood of antipathy and despair, reinforced by substandard environmental and familial patterns and historic traditions have combined to render many Negro migrants not only incapable of securing and retaining gainful employment but assuring that many of their children will follow in their unfortunate footsteps.[2] While remnants of the early waves of European immigrants remain near the bottom of the social and economic pyramid, the proportion is diminishing; the sense that caste barriers condemn ethnic groups to economic and social immobility is much weaker if not wholly absent. As a result, there is a general conviction that time will provide solutions as the enclaves age and new generations develop wider horizons, the educated children leave, and only the ethnic remnants remain. In the case of the Negro immigrant, this happy anticipation is much less prevalent. While signs of progress are much in evidence, the ghettos are growing rather than shrinking. In addition, it is apparent that expectations have outrun the genuine progress which was achieved in the 1950's. The eruptions of violence and looting in Negro slum districts since 1966 indicate a difference between the population of the poverty-ridden ghettos as compared to the response of the traditional, ethnic slum populations. In past generations, with the special exceptions like the depressed mining counties and the Irish draft riots in New York City during the Civil War, there have been no large-scale outbreaks of violence against the established order in the nation's distressed areas.

Negro migration differs substantially from another great historic migrant stream. For many decades, rural areas and small towns in the United States provided a domestic supply of labor that did not differ substantially in education or training from the urban, old settler group. Many a farm boy, hard-working, lucky, devoted to his employer, and possessed of native shrewdness rose to eminence and wealth. Horatio Alger heroes were not entirely creatures of mythology.

Rapid upward mobility for a farm boy was, of course, exceptional. More frequently, there was a slower, generation-to-generation social and spatial mobility similar in many respects to most of the foreign immigrant groups. There was, however, this important difference with the Negro and indeed with some foreigners: By and large, the rural white migrants to the cities did not experience prolonged prejudicial treatment that relegated them as a group to the lower rungs of society. On the contrary, they were viewed in popular ideology as unalloyed assets, infusing decadent metropolitan melting pots with health, vigor, and morality. In many respects, they tended to be--and still are--invisible immigrants vanishing almost instantly into the main body of the population. Moreover this observation not only applies to native WASPS but also to English-speaking Canadians. For example, migrants from the Maritime Provinces are an important component of the New England population, but this comes to light only through an examination of census data.

Not all members of the rural-small town stream have been greeted in the cities with warmth and enthusiasm. California's reaction to the dust bowl refugees of the 1930's is similar to the sentiments expressed in Chicago and other Midwestern cities with respect to the Appalachian hillbillies, migrants of the 1950's. This less benign outlook on internal migration is reflected even more strongly in areas where Mexicans and Puerto Ricans have been imported for menial labor and subsequently treated as less-than-equal aliens after decades of residence. It should be noted that education combined with law-abiding industriousness does seem to melt away some of the caste barriers. For example, since the postwar period, the nation has had a relatively good record with the absorption of our relatively small Oriental population. By 1960, the income and occupational distribution of Japanese Americans was similar to Caucasian Americans.

The Negro migration, and to a much smaller extent the rural small town migration, have clearly created many critical problems. This is suggested by the fact that proposals to slow rural migration by stimulating area development in farm areas have become increasingly respectable.[3] But what has been called "the urban relocatee" creates a different sort of vexation. This outward flow from small, urban distressed areas may have numerous unpleasant side effects, not on the "receiving area" which is happy to welcome young, ambitious, and reasonably well-educated people who make up the bulk of the migrants, but on the "sending area" which each year loses a vital component of its population. The attractiveness of redevelopment areas for new economic growth is thereby diminished, further darkening the dim outlook for the remaining population. For this reason, a type of migration that is barely noticed in our larger urban centers requires careful study because it can do lasting damage to the social and and economic structure of urban distressed areas.

Migration Trends in Redevelopment Areas

Certain parts of the nation have long served as breeding grounds for the production of workers for larger industrial centers because a sizable segment of the population continues to reside in economic backwaters, unable to provide enough jobs for their labor force. As long as this pattern persists (and it will, unless there is a totally unforeseen reallocation of economic development), there will remain definable and identifiable areas where outmigration can be expected to be a way of life.

Outmigration tends to be one of the more sensitive issues among community leaders in redevelopment areas. Some meet the problem by refusing to discuss it; others deny that it exists at all or suggest that the very next census will see an upturn in population; still others call for major federal efforts to reverse the tide by stimulating the growth of the local economy to the point where it can provide jobs for its young people. It would be fair to say that few have faced the prospect with candor and realism. Many distressed areas have been particularly remiss in failing to prepare the majority of their young people to be fully competitive in out-of-area labor markets; they tend to be recruits for the lower end of the employment spectrum, not management trainees. In part, this failure in education is due to a consistent pattern of investment choices in distressed areas that favors allocations for construction over investments in human capital as the major strategy for area renewal. The redevelopment area leadership tends to opt for physical investments that generate visible campaign material, construction contracts and jobs, and promise the area future economic growth. On the other hand, investments in human resources, as experience demonstrates, involve sizable allocations to highly portable assets. Poor areas see no reason to beggar themselves in educating their children only to have their graduates pick up and leave; the harvest of investment in human resources may be reaped by other areas in the form of migrating skilled workers. There was also the tendency in past years to regard under-educated, low-wage labor as a major asset in attracting new industry, and it was believed by some that too much education spoiled a docile, hard working (and inexpensive) labor force. It is only relatively recently that the need for first-rate schools and well-educated workers was recognized by local development organizations which discovered that an adequate school system was a prerequisite for advanced types of industry. In earlier years, all the stress was on the eagerness and trainability of a willing, energetic labor force, grateful for any regular job at improved wages.

There are, however, a number of more basic reasons for resistance at facing the prospect of continued outmigration and of designing programs associated with the process. Many redevelopment area leaders sincerely believe that their people are better off at home, low wages or no. There are numerous studies (some of them vividly portrayed in fiction and nonfiction) devoted to the plight of the newly arrived migrant. The easily fleeced rubes, greenhorns, and yokels caught in the snares and ground to dust by the callous environment of the big town are still a topic of concern in fact as well as fiction. Clearly, the wrenching apart of family ties, the loss of an accustomed place in a stable social order, the exposure to debilitating slums, and the sometimes disastrous effects to the health of those relocating in the big cities can be very real threats to the well being of the migrant.

Much time, effort, and money will be allocated to the problems created by the adjustment of the migrant in the next generation; the hardships encountered by earlier generations of migrants in the city slums are also still very much with us. As far as urban distressed areas are concerned, however, the adjustment problems caused by immigration are relatively minor. The social and economic strains on the big city or on the migrant himself are very much reduced when the migrant from the "sending" distressed area is white, has an urban background, and has completed two or more years of high school. Certainly any problems that may arise in the "receiving" area are susceptible to relatively simple solutions as compared to the complexities involved in facilitating a smooth integration of a rural, racially different, or non-English speaking population.

SKIMMING OFF THE CREAM

In a highly mobile society like the United States, where one person in five changes his residence each year, the decision to pull up stakes often is far from a matter fraught with trauma or drama. Migration is a matter of fact, concomitant with a variety of high-status occupations. This generalization concerning the ease of migration is by no means applicable to a very large proportion of the population. While restlessness affects the young, there is a strong homing instinct at work that makes for powerful attachments to one's home area. Furthermore, many parents regard rapid modern communications as no substitute for close physical proximity to their children and grandchildren.

This chapter is not concerned with the personal strains and hardships linked to migration of the young but with its long-term effects on the future and on urban distressed areas. Migration from distressed areas may lead to deterioration of leadership, leaving such communities "abandoned to their own incompetence."[4] Moreover, the process in time may be almost irreversible if the labor force loses most of its attraction for new investments. If the migrant is young, well trained, and currently employed, as a large proportion of them are, the "sending" area's economic potential may thereby be diminished. A loss of skilled and enterprising persons may render an area less capable of reviving itself than before the migration took place.[5]

A research study on distressed area problems in Western Europe concluded that

> as virtually all studies show, voluntary migration is selective and greatly reduces the quality of the labor force remaining in redevelopment areas. With its age distribution becoming progressively poorer, the labor force degenerates into a pool of obsolete skills. . . . Full employment by itself cannot solve these problems [of the redevelopment areas]; indeed, it may well aggravate them by the progressive deterioration resulting from selective mobility.[6]

These observations are also fully applicable to urban redevelopment areas in the United States. For example, research studies show that in 12 chronically depressed areas in Pennsylvania, migration in the 1950's was concentrated in the prime working ages, ages 25 to 44.[7]

On the basis of past performance, it can be expected that many youths will leave redevelopment areas after completing six to twelve years of public education. One report concluded that "the more a depressed region aids in the education of an individual, the greater the probability that the particular individual will leave the region of his education."[8] Since public and private family costs involved in nurturing and training children are quite heavy, the strain on family and local government finances in redevelopment areas is a major argument for increased contribution from outside sources to assist in child rearing. The plea for outside aid for child development seems particularly appropriate because many of these children represent part of the future labor force for more wealthy, economically expanding areas.

A disproportionate number of migrants from most distressed areas are young people--family heads under age 35 and college graduates. Only a small proportion of the family heads in redevelopment area cities were under 35 as compared to their counterparts in the suburbs, and slightly over 1 in 4 adults in the nation have had some college training compared to only 1 in 7 in United States redevelopment areas.

A special sample survey of distressed areas in 1962-63 indicated that of the heads of families under 35 years of age in redevelopment areas, 9 per cent moved away, as compared to only 1 per cent of the family heads over 55. Less than 2 per cent of the family heads with a grade-school education migrated, compared to over 10 per cent of the family heads who went to college. The result was to drain away the people who had any substantial education. Only 1 out of 7 adults in redevelopment areas have had some college training as compared to 1 in 4 in other parts of the nation.[9] Migration has also drained away the young; 1960 population data for 14 chronically depressed urban areas indicates that 20-34 year olds comprised only 16.6 per cent of their aggregate population. This compares with 19.2 per cent for the urban United States and 18.6 per cent for the nation.

To develop more information on distressed area migrants and, specifically, to assess the size of the talent drain, the Area Development Center of Boston University sponsored a research study in the North Adams area, a relatively small, isolated area in the Berkshires of western Massachusetts.[10] The survey revealed a startling statistic: Almost 40 per cent of the area's high school honor graduates had left the area in the 1950-60 decade. Less unexpectedly, it was found that attendance at an out-of-area college was closely correlated to a permanent departure.

A survey of the graduating classes of high schools in the North Adams area from 1951 to 1960 with a total sample of about 200 graduates yielded two major findings. First, 38 of the 100 honor graduates, and 19 of the 100 "representative" graduates had left the area; 11 of the honor graduates and 31 of the control group appeared to retain some roots in the area (in the armed forces, away at school, away on a temporary job, and so forth), and might or might not return; 20 of the first group and 17 of the second, primarily young women who might have been married, could not be traced. This meant that 31 of the honor graduates and 33 of the "representatives of the average" graduates could be readily located in the area.

Second, college enrollment was an important factor in migration. Most of the honor group went on to college. Those students attending North Adams State College (a former state teacher's college) were more likely to remain in the area than those who went elsewhere, but many of them also left the northern Berkshires, although they were more likely to remain in Massachusetts. In contrast, a majority of those who attended the University of Massachusetts, Williams College, and other institutions appear to have left the area.

There has been a small amount of inmigration of talent to the North Adams area to compensate for the talent drain. A large, expanding electronics firm has brought in engineers and technicians, and a significant upgrading of the area economy has occurred with the replacement of the long-dominant, low-wage, low-skill textile industry with this and other electronic firms. (North Adams, it may be noted, was the state's first redevelopment area to be removed from the Economic Development Administration's list of high-unemployment areas.) The situation in North Adams, therefore, while symptomatic, is probably far less serious than in other redevelopment areas.

Lingering Impact of Migration

One result of migration is the creation of an "hourglass effect" in the age-distribution pyramid. This means that fewer working-age people are available to support a larger proportion of dependent children and older people.[11]

Of the two types of dependents, it is the elderly who seem to be dominant in the outlook of urban redevelopment areas. The heavy outmigration of the younger, restless, ambitious, and articulate population leaves the social and political orientation to reflect the conservative patterns associated with a pessimistic older population whose outlook is conditioned by generations of failure.

The impact of this selective migration on smaller communities is reflected in the inability of local and state governments to keep up with the times.

The cream of small-town creativity has soured as small-town vitality has diminished . . . . by the end of World War II, these places consisted mainly of those who did not want to try to advance under the new rules . . . state government is suffering from an overdose of the small-town political ideology . . . . a querulousness about government "frills" is almost all that remains of the once-proud doctrine of small-town individualism. . . . Small-town morality finds no place for suspected academic or intellectual dreamers. . . . The trained specialist is regarded as a "fuzzy-minded" idealist, an overeducated fool.[12]

There are other more mundane side effects of the swelling numbers of an aging population. As the number of older persons increases, public welfare costs rise, and the pressure on limited family income grows more burdensome.

Family incomes in redevelopment areas also feel the impact of demands from another quarter. The redevelopment area is a nursery as well as an old-folks home; the base of the age pyramid is relatively larger in relation to working-age population. The costs of educating and rearing the young can be ill afforded by areas in which wage levels are low and the tax base grows slowly, if at all.

Migration and Unemployment Rates

It would be unreasonable to dwell wholly on the unfavorable impact of migration. Of all the alternative manpower strategies open to distressed areas, the most disastrous is to encourage a deceleration in migration if enough jobs cannot be provided for their labor force. The obvious consequences of such a policy are rapidly mounting unemployment, welfare rates, and social unrest.

There is a long-standing tradition for ambitious young people in stagnant areas to pull up stakes for greener pastures. De Toqueville indicated that:

in 1830 thirty-six of the members of Congress were born in the little state of Connecticut. The population of Connecticut, which constitutes only one forty-third part of that of the United States, thus furnished one eighth of the whole body of representatives. The state of Connecticut of itself, however, sends only five delegates to Congress; and the thirty-one others sit for the new Western states. If these thirty-one individuals had remained in Connecticut, it is probable that, instead of becoming rich landowners, they would have remained humble

laborers, that they would have lived in obscurity without
being able to rise into public life, and that, far from becoming
useful legislators, they might have been unruly citizens.[13]

In contrast to potential negative, long-term effects, there can be a positive, short-run impact from outmigration of the working-age population. In the
case of the city of New Bedford, a backup in the migration stream during the
Great Depression had disastrous effects on local unemployment rates.[14] In
1937, unemployment reached 32.3 per cent for the "gainful workers" in the
city, as compared to 18 per cent in the state and 16 per cent in the nation. In
February, 1939, approximately one quarter of the city's population was dependent on public assistance.[15]

All indications are that through the mid-1960's, migration (or commutation) has been a major factor in declining unemployment rates in the Fall
River and New Bedford areas. In 1962, unemployment rates averaged over 10
per cent in the two areas, but by mid-1967, unemployment had declined to the
6 per cent level. This improvement was achieved despite the fact that there was
no employment gain in the New Bedford area between 1961 and mid-1966,
while total employment actually decreased in the Fall River area. Thus, with
the aid of net migration, the unemployment rolls decreased by almost 3,000 in
both Fall River and New Bedford, although one area showed no gain at all in
Division of Employment Security recorded employment, and the other area actually lost 1,700 jobs. Clearly, one helpful result of migration is to produce a
more reasonable balance between the size of the labor force and employment,
both in the depressed area left behind and in the receiving areas in which the
migrants relocate.

If the migrant is one of the long-term unemployed for whom local job
prospects are poor, the area--and the nation--clearly benefits from his leaving if
he can find work elsewhere or if his children can eventually find work of a quality that is simply not available in the distressed area. Some retailers and land-
lords may suffer, congressmen may complain about the loss of seats when the
population diminishes, and many canons of American "growthmanship" may
be violated, but most will agree that productive employment is preferable to
stagnating idleness. In the absence of a very heavy, continuing outmigration
from rural areas with high birth rates, the "sending" areas would be faced with
extremely serious social and economic problems. The scale is much larger than
may appear on the surface: One study found that in Alabama, a movement of
465,000 people from agriculture in the course of a decade reduced the farm-
labor force by only 127,000. The reason: In the same period, 338,000 new
farm workers entered the labor force.[16]

There is a direct parallel between the relocation from domestic urban
redevelopment areas and the "brain drain" in the United States and Western
Europe that has been the subject of much complaint among the drainees. In
both cases, the principal beneficiaries are the nation's thriving metropolitan

areas. The migrants are enthusiastically welcomed and rapidly assimilated, particularly in hospitals and research laboratories, but the "sending" areas lose a significant share of their expensively trained, better-educated, and most productive talent.[17]

In fiscal 1966, more than 300,000 immigrants came to settle permanently in the United States, 44 per cent of them professional people. This selective migration was accelerated by the 1965 Immigration Act that ended the "national origins" quota system, giving priority to skills instead of ancestry. For example, it is estimated that less than 10 per cent of the Taiwan students studying in the United States will return to their country.

In 1966, 6,000 students from developing countries graduated from American colleges and universities, but 4,400 remained in the United States, leaving a net gain of only 3 in 10 new graduates for the developing nations.[18]

Unlike migration of unskilled or semiskilled labor, brain drains are often based on courtship rather than accident. In addition to their domestic recruiting programs, American firms have assiduously advertised in European newspapers for technical manpower. A British observer writes:

> The Americans do not look for our selling or marketing men . . .
> it is our Ph.D. and M.Sc. rather than B.Sc. men, that the
> Americans want--and get . . . our most sophisticated technolo-
> gical skills are drawn to the super-civilization, with California
> at the heart of the brain drain area . . . almost as many of our
> physicists go into American industry as into our own.[19]

WHY THEY LEAVE

There has been much emphasis on the impact of financial incentives as a determining factor in migration. Certainly if a job opening is available in one area and there is no comparable employment in the home community, there is an obvious incentive to move on. But moving is expensive, particularly if a family is involved, and transfer costs may easily absorb the first year's pay differential. The reason for migration of better-qualified people clearly involves more than an immediate increase in pay scales.

To begin with, there is professional pride. In many respects, the nation's smaller urban areas function as class B, C and D leagues in baseball. Talent is discovered and the small-town star is only too happy to make his way up from the minors to the major ball clubs. Similarly, every profession has a hierarchical system of spatial promotion in which small-town talent is promoted to larger areas and larger firms that offer prestige among one's peers as well as greater financial remuneration. But there is often a push factor involved as well. Younger, ambitious people tend to be innovative and impatient; they are often repelled by conservative outlooks and the lack of prospects for rapid promotion in the narrow world of the distressed area. Unless his interests lie in politics or unless he is somehow connected with one of the area's narrow business or financial circles, the young man's prospects are not likely to be as favorable as in the more fluid society of a larger urban center. This is surely one factor in the self-reinforcing leadership problem of redevelopment areas. The departure of each wave of potential innovators leaves decisions to the less imaginative, and this stultifying atmosphere helps to speed another wave of bright young people outward.

It would not be accurate to suggest that backward, distressed area leadership is solely to blame for this selective outmigration. Most redevelopment areas are also handicapped by their relatively small size. To a degree, modest size in itself can be a serious handicap; much of the nation's scientific talent, for example, is concentrated in a handful of large metropolitan areas. The relationship between large populations and such expensive cultural installations as opera houses, symphony halls, and commercial theaters is well known. Corporate and government headquarters, banks and insurance companies, and many other types of development also tend to cluster in larger centers. In a direct sense, the problem of the urban redevelopment area is the problem of the small city: How is it to maintain first-rank quality when its size alone seems to place it squarely in the minor leagues?

Some redevelopment areas have attempted to counter this trend by moves in the direction of "decentralizing excellence." They are hoping to create or to build a broad cultural and economic base on existing or new local institutions of higher learning. Others are attempting to construct new centers of the performing arts, to develop diversified economies emphasizing advanced industries and high-quality medical and recreational services.[20] The growth-center concept contained in the Public Works and Economic Development Act of 1965 may offer a number of possibilities in this direction. The legislation assumes that potential growth centers either exist or can be created within each Economic Development District embracing two or more distressed areas, that these centers can serve as a focus and magnet for public and private investment, and that, consequently, commutation to the center rather than relocation out of the area will become an increasingly feasible alternative for the redevelopment area's labor force.

Commutation a Solution?

There is another method of attacking unemployment problems without depending either on local growth or outmigration--namely, commutation from redevelopment areas. Redevelopment areas located near flourishing metropolitan areas can make use of the larger metropolis as a cultural magnet to help in hiring and retaining professional and managerial talent. In Massachusetts, for example, some residents of the Fall River and New Bedford areas travel from 30 to 40 miles or more to work in communities on the fringe of the greater Boston area or in metropolitan Providence. Some North Adams area residents commute to the Pittsfield and Schenectady-Albany-Troy areas, 20 to 30 miles distant. It is conceivable that through intensified, carefully designed education and training programs, which would improve the competitive characteristics of the labor force of these areas, and with the help of modern highways, a larger proportion of the distressed area's labor pool may be able to commute to job centers within relatively easy driving distance. While expanded commutation will not help much to alleviate local tax-base problems, commuting is probably preferable (from a redevelopment area standpoint) to outright migration and is clearly more desirable than a slowdown or backup in migration that might increase area unemployment and public welfare rates such as occurred during the Great Depression.

There is another overlooked benefit from commutation. Well-educated executives and professionals employed in larger, nearby metropolitan areas have purchased homes in distressed area fringe suburbs. While they retain their occupational ties to their place of employment, in time the executives (and their wives) become increasingly involved in local affairs. To date, their influence has been most in evidence in community rather than area concerns, particularly in the improvement of the public schools. This influx of resident-commuter talent can have a significant impact on area standards and programs. It is particularly difficult to involve outcommuting suburban residents in the severe problems of central cities in which they have no visible ties. A commitment to area civic and development programs can serve as a useful substitute and possibly as an entree into the more vexatious problems of the core neighborhoods.

Below the Talent Stratum: Are Migrants Ready?

The lower educational levels in redevelopment areas raise certain questions regarding not only the welcome that many migrants are likely to receive in the competitive labor markets of larger areas but also their ability to make the move at all. An examination of key educational indices in the 1960 census reveals that the Fall River, New Bedford, and North Adams areas fell far short of metropolitan Boston.

The pattern was similar with respect to other educational indices. In southeastern Massachusetts (the Fall River and New Bedford areas) and North Adams, only about one quarter of the adults had completed four years of high school or more. In Boston, the percentage was over one half, while in other areas it was about 40 per cent.

The summary of the data in Table 5 shows the disparity that existed in 1960 between various parts of Massachusetts in adult educational levels. In the Fall River and New Bedford areas, for example, one out of every eight or nine adults had less than a fifth-grade education in 1960. This compares to a ratio of only one in twenty with less than a fifth-grade education in the Boston area. Other distressed areas in Massachusetts are close to the one-in-twenty Boston level. On the other side of the ledger, in 1960, only one adult in twenty-five in the Fall River and New Bedford areas was a college graduate, a proportion that did not rise appreciably between 1950 and 1960.

It is clear that much remains to be done in providing children in all areas of the state (and of the nation) with a solid educational foundation.

Jobs for Low-Skill Migrants?

The trend toward increasing formal education and training for many occupations has led some to believe that while earlier immigrant groups could easily be absorbed in unskilled jobs, the current crop of migrants from distressed areas are difficult to integrate into the economy.

There is one distinction that must be clarified. Despite the evidence that migrants from redevelopment areas tend to be young, well motivated, and fairly well educated,[21] there is a considerable body of public and professional opinion that seems to confuse these relocatees with ill-prepared, rural migrants. Much of the public apparently believes that most migrants are more interested in access to welfare payments than in available jobs. This dim view of the migrant stream has ancient roots; each ethnic group has been scorned by its predecessors, who, forgetful of their chilly initial reception, maintain that the newcomers represent the dregs of humanity. This is not solely a matter of lay opinion. Some serious students of migration suggest that many migrants represent an inferior labor-force component and hence make only a marginal contribution to the economy to which they relocate.[22] The result, they maintain, is a decline in per capita income and other adverse consequences in the receiving area. There are those, including the author, who see redevelopment area migration as a help to receiving areas but a diminution of attractions and talent to the redevelopment areas. On the other hand, some have adopted a rosier viewpoint, suggesting that such migration benefits both sending and host areas.

Perhaps the cautious answer is that the impact depends on circumstances, that, depending on employment conditions and prospects in the redevelopment areas, migration may be a help or hindrance to sending areas, to receiving areas, and to migrants themselves. At the present time, for example, there can be little reason to suggest that migrants from any type of area who will accept previous unfilled, low-wage service jobs are a drag on the area's economy. The difficulty is that migration is associated with the relocation of a demoralized rural population rather than the sober, industrious, and thereby virtually invisible migrants who staff a sizable proportion of the jobs in growing areas in the early 1960's.

In Massachusetts, earlier generations of migrants were welcomed as a source of casual labor in mills and service industries to perform a variety of other tasks calling for muscle power rather than schooling. It is pointed out that while previous generations picked up most of their training on the job, this is no longer the case. Over two thirds of the nation's workers aged 55-64 did not receive formal vocational training, while almost the reverse was true of persons in the 22-24 age bracket.[23]

TABLE 5

Educational Statistics in Massachusetts Areas, 1950 and 1960

| Area | % of 16 and 17 Year Olds Enrolled in School† | | Persons 25 Years of Age and Over | | | | | | | |
| | | | % With 4 or More Years of College | | % With 4 Years of High School | | % With Less Than 5 Grades Completed | | Median School Years Completed | |
	1950	1960	1950	1960	1950	1960	1950	1960	1950	1960
SMA's, SMSA's*										
Boston	82.2	83.4	8.8	11.2	30.8	31.7	6.8	5.2	11.9	12.1
Fall River	59.0	67.6	3.6	3.8	13.1	14.6	14.9	11.0	8.4	8.6
Lowell	71.7	71.9	4.6	5.2	23.1	26.7	7.5	5.2	9.8	10.6
New Bedford	60.8	70.1	3.0	3.7	14.1	15.6	15.9	12.4	8.3	8.6
Selected										
Gloucester	79.8	77.6	3.8	5.2	25.2	26.9	8.7	6.7	9.9	10.6
Newburyport	88.9	82.4	5.9	5.3	24.2	27.6	3.9	4.7	10.7	10.8
North Adams	72.3	96.3	4.2	4.6	17.2	19.9	8.4	5.0	8.9	9.2
Massachusetts	78.6	80.7	7.4	8.8	27.9	28.8	8.1	6.0	10.9	11.6
United States	74.5	80.9	6.2	7.7	20.7	24.6	11.1	8.4	9.3	10.6

* The 1950 data for metropolitan areas are for SMA's; the 1960 figures are derived from the 1960 census and are adjusted to SMSA's.

† Figures for 16 and 17 year olds enrolled in school for both 1950 and 1960 were calculated from the raw data, using the appropriate population figures for 16 and 17 year olds in U.S. Census, 1960, General Population Characteristics, Massachusetts, Tables 16, 20, and 27; and U.S. Census, 1960, General Population Characteristics, United States Summary, Table 46. These figures do not always agree with the already calculated census percentages of 16 and 17 year olds enrolled in school and are therefore not comparable with same.

Sources: U.S. Census of Population (Washington, D.C.: U.S. Government Printing Office, 1950 and 1960).

This is a matter of direct concern to redevelopment areas as well as to receiving areas. Is a significant amount of formal schooling and occupational training really required to qualify local labor for available jobs within redevelopment areas or as migrants to other areas? If a high school education and several years of formal training are actually prerequisites for all occupations, the chances of reducing distressed area unemployment would be substantially decreased, and receiving areas would have some justification for the jaundiced view they sometimes adopt toward inmigrants. Fortunately, the problem seems to be overstated. Good motivation combined with modest basic schooling and good health is still the key to employment. Many white-collar as well as blue-collar occupations require only a limited amount of formal education in combination with on-the-job training or short-term vocational courses.

There are many examples of migrants with modest education but good motivation who have made a highly successful adjustment to modern urban conditions. It would appear that, despite the gloom over the disappearance of jobs for unskilled laborers and domestics, there is an adequate quantity of low-paying job openings each year. If the migrant is steadily employed, is respectful of home and property, and sends his children to school, he is quickly assimilated into metropolitan areas and is nobody's problem. This description applies to most of the present migrant stream from redevelopment areas and to a large and overlooked proportion of Negro migrants from rural areas.[24]

Surveys among large employers lend further support to the belief that lack of occupational training or formal vocational training is not a major obstacle to hiring. Many prefer to hire well-motivated individuals and to train them in company techniques and methods. Efficient, short-term training programs in these companies have produced better results than have been obtainable through less-concentrated and less-tailored manpower programs conducted with state and federal assistance.

This tendency to bypass formal occupational training is apparently confirmed by the U.S. Department of Labor which shows that the majority of workers in most nonprofessional occupations either learned their trade on the job or picked it up through "casual" means. In 1950, the data indicate that three fourths of the nation's labor force had received less than six months of training for their present job,[25] a pattern which did not change materially in the 1960 census. This accounts, in part, for the success of a number of public and employer short-term (less than 12-month) manpower training courses. In most instances, there has been no difficulty in locating employment for graduates of short-term courses designed to meet manpower needs in growth sectors of the economy.

Furthermore, it has been suggested that the possibilities of using poorly educated labor have not yet been fully explored. Aside from the development of "new careers for the poor" as subprofessional aides, there is the possibility of expanding a variety of public services to create hundreds of thousands or even millions of jobs in periods of recession. Twice-a-day mail deliveries, day nurseries for working mothers, the development of home health aide programs, foster grandparent programs, conservation and beautification programs could absorb large quantities of such labor. The recommendation that government assume the role of "employer of last resort" for the jobless could be adopted in an era of increasing public revenues and rising demand for an improved environment and better public services. There was an encouraging move in this direction in the 1966 Amendments to the Economic Opportunity Act.[26]

In recent years, there has been much criticism of vocational training programs[27] and job locating services for the poor, particularly minority groups. Charges that past employment efforts were excessively concentrated on "dead-end," low-wage, low-status occupations have led to demands for programs aimed at providing job opportunities within the mainstream of the labor force. It has been urged that jobs and training for the disadvantaged be restructured to offer the possibility of upgrading and advancement based on merit, training, and application.

Substantial resistance to employment in low-paying, menial jobs in the underside of the economy is a new phenomenon. Negro and white teen-agers who choose unemployment or street-corner hustling in preference to employment as hospital attendants, kitchen help, stock room workers and carwashers stigmatize such jobs as slave labor, unacceptable for modern youth. This represents a significant change from immigrant generations who shouldered pick and shovel, shoved pushcarts and wheelbarrows, and generally, willingly or not, took whatever jobs were available. The new careers approach is based in part on questionable premises regarding occupational trends, but it accurately reflects a widespread, overt distaste for jobs that carry neither prestige, money, nor hope for the future. Moves to develop career continuums are not only desirable but may be inescapable if the street-corner youth is to be attracted into the mainstream of society. Experience may suggest, however, that the new careers approach may benefit those who would have done fairly well in its absence, among them the migrants from urban distressed areas.

EMPLOYMENT BARRIERS AND MIGRATION

One reason for resistance to inmigration of poorly educated labor is empirical evidence that more schooling is a characteristic of the persons employed in an increasing number of occupations. Even for jobs in which no change in skills was involved (e.g., glaziers and railroad switchmen), median school years completed by job holders rose by roughly one year between 1950 and 1960. However, it is often not recognized that this trend is largely a function of generally rising levels of education rather than the imposition of stiffer educational prerequisites by employers or unions.

Inflated educational prerequisites may range from requiring high school graduation to advanced degrees. Close examination would reveal no rational need for such levels of education in a wide variety of occupations that now require the symbolic parchment. Remedial action to remove or at least reduce job discrimination practices along with the fraudulent inflation of job prerequisites would appear to deserve high priority. They not only contribute to making life more difficult for the less educated migrants from redevelopment areas but also create unnecessary trouble in providing adequate jobs for all types of disadvantaged workers, including rural migrants.

AUTOMATION AND FUTURE MANPOWER NEEDS

An issue that has generated considerable discussion is the impact of automation on future demand for poorly educated workers of the type available in large numbers in distressed areas and in slum areas of large cities.[28] During the 1950's and early 1960's, some scholars predicted that many industries would follow the lead of mining and agriculture (i.e., manufacturing output would increase with a smaller work force as a consequence of heavy capital investments in labor-saving machinery).

Some of the popular publications in the 1960's suggested that the new jobs opened up by an increasingly complex technology would tend to be restricted to holders of college degrees or at least to persons with substantial post high school training. However, experience seems to indicate that, while in its early, pioneering stages, a new process requires highly trained staff. In time, routinization leads to job simplification, opening up the field for less well-educated and less-expensive personnel. To take one striking example, computer programming was at first restricted to college graduates and included many Ph.D. mathematicians, but by the mid-1960's, high school graduation followed by short-term specialist training was an acceptable background for a new programmer.

Without delving into the detailed reasoning underlying these persuasive, conflicting scholarly works, it may be noted that if the gloomier predictions had proved accurate, the market for distressed area labor in the 1960's would be considerably smaller than it actually is, and fewer migrants could anticipate successful relocation. To date, however, automation has not had this type of impact: In most areas, aside from special cases (e.g., Negro teen-agers), manpower shortages rather than surpluses of employable workers have been the troublesome labor problems of the mid-1960's. This does not mean that automation may not have a depressing effect on future demands for labor, especially in some areas that may experience severe employment cuts without compensating job gains. Dozens of dying mining communities testify to the fact that automation can have a crippling impact on a vulnerable local economy. However, up to the present time and perhaps over the next decade, automation seems not to have dehydrated overall manpower demand in large metropolitan areas, nor has it eroded the numbers of jobs for which modest skills are enough for entry.

NOTES FOR A GOVERNMENT POLICY

From the viewpoint of governmental policy, there are at least two ways of looking at the problems of distressed areas. The first is to decide that their problems are largely beyond their control and that what is needed is federal policy. This approach would aim at allocating regional investment in order to maximize national economic growth and only secondarily to maintain "a certain interregional balance in levels of living, at least sufficient to preserve political stability in support of the drive to national growth."[29] Under this policy, the role of distressed areas would be extremely circumscribed; they could engage in "adaptive" planning of a "limited kind to exert a modest influence on improving their economy and their environment."[30]

A second approach to area development is implicit in federal distressed area legislation and allied federal programs. It assumes that national patterns and trends offer considerable room for local initiative, particularly because deliberate federal policy to write off the distressed areas in favor of flourishing metropolitan areas is not politically realistic.

These positions are obviously simplified. The polarity that has been indicated is actually more of a continuum because few specialists hold extreme views. Nevertheless, the difference in approach is a crucial one, as one or the other basic assumption colors entire sets of policies and investment patterns.

On the whole, it may be concluded that the redevelopment area can do a great deal to influence its environment and its economic future. We hasten to explain that this by no means suggests that there is no need for national policies. Redevelopment areas lack both money and talent, and unless there is federal aid to help fill these deficiencies, they are not equipped to do very much to improve their social and cultural base and will continue to do an inadequate job of preparing many of their future migrants.

Some of the programs related to a national policy for redevelopment areas were mentioned earlier. The Economic Development Districts, with their growth centers, may help to create more attractions for bright, well-educated people. Federal-aid programs for institutions of higher learning have helped to strengthen cultural facilities. Assistance for public-school systems, urban renewal, manpower training, health services, industrial parks, and other aspects of urban life are all available, often on preferential terms for redevelopment areas, and these, too, have been helpful in modernizing areas with weak financial resources. At present, however, the nation does not yet have either a policy or a comprehensive program for interarea migration. In this final section, we will discuss some of the elements that might be included in a national approach toward this problem.

It is often easier to visualize and to market a product if one like it has already been successful. In the case of relocation programs, one of the most desirable products seems to be manufactured in Sweden. That country may offer the United States useful clues on how families of semiskilled and unskilled workers can be assisted to relocate with minimal hardship. Broadening the population stream relocating from distressed areas could be a useful contribution to their future development; a planned relocation program would help more marginal workers to leave.

Long recognized as being far in advance of the United States in many social welfare programs, Sweden has had notable success in its efforts to help poorly educated migrant families relocate under a comprehensive program dating back to the mid-1950's. The program includes medical examinations, aptitude tests, vocational guidance, training, family allowances, and payment of transportation and moving costs.[31] The cost per family may run as high as $2,000, but officials feel that these are one-time expenses and that the large initial sum may prevent far costlier, long-term social problems.

It is clear that it is much easier to effectuate this type of program in Sweden than in the United States. The nation's small size, the homogeneity of its population, and the government's experience in national planning are significant and perhaps unique advantages. Furthermore, the Swedish program is part of a long-range national planning effort designed to correct both temporary imbalances in the labor market, and more important, to follow a well-defined and clearly directed path toward flexibility in restructuring the economy as the needs of the nation seem to dictate. This is one of the critical differences: The task of moving a tenant farmer and his family to the city, finding him a home, giving him training and a job can all be accomplished entirely within the context of labor-market demands. What Sweden is attempting is far more significant. By ensuring that the working man is not adversely affected to any significant extent by structural changes in the economy, Sweden may be able to counter worker resistance to progress. There are fewer anguished cries of dismay on the part of a work force that is guaranteed that its livelihood is not threatened. Such pressures in the United States have been one factor in generating powerful protectionist pressures to shield and subsidize inefficient industries--and to decelerate entry of minority groups into skilled jobs. Unless some method is found to remove labor's fears, the nation may well be faced with an unending series of political obstacles to the process of economic rationalization. Surely there are enough barriers to progress without adding to them unnecessarily.

The Swedish experience suggests two prerequisites for maximum effectiveness in relocation programs: (1) nationwide coverage, and (2) a broad national policy in which relocation is only one important component.

This obviously suggests that relocation programs should be operated by the federal government or at the very least should be designed, coordinated, and evaluated within a controlling national framework. Action on the part of individual redevelopment areas, the states, or even large regional commissions such as New England and Appalachia would be most effective when linked closely to other areas. Financing and integration would clearly have to be a federal responsibility.

Would a relocation program be horrendously expensive? On the basis of cost-benefit analysis, probably not. Total expenditures for poverty and welfare programs in the United States can be reduced appreciably by a workable relocation program. Subsidized relocation is undoubtedly less costly than supporting idled, redundant workers and their dependents. If the balance sheet were longer (i.e., if long-term national goals or intangible social benefits were included), the results are even likely to be conclusively in favor of a major federal relocation program. Unfortunately, neither the Swedish nor other Europeans nor Americans have developed adequate data on the process. One United Nations report on the relocation of rural manpower to industry indicated that:

> There is practically no information available concerning the costs and benefits of the adjustment process. Some concepts and tools have been developed to tackle the problem of the costs involved in migration, but as a recent publication states "provide only a sketchy framework for further empirical study of labor movement. Measures of the psychic cost of migration, for example, are hard to come by." The most essential conclusion, however in this context is that "the relation between private and social costs of, and returns to, migration at best depends on market structure, resources, mobility in general, and revenue policies of state and local governments."[32]

In the United States, we have witnessed the consequences of a mélange of inconsistent development and manpower programs. But it would be more accurate to recognize that most relocation takes place with little reference to government policy. Government has not taken special action relating to manpower requirements. Changes in agricultural technology, distasteful environmental conditions, and a hope of betterment in the cities have sent millions of Negroes and whites to large urban areas. Their past experience has poorly prepared rural migrants for new challenges, and they have experienced enormous difficulties in adjusting to urban conditions. On the other hand, to their detriment, migration from urban redevelopment areas has been heavily concentrated among the relatively well educated.

As was suggested, a rational national policy should aim at broadening the base of migration from redevelopment areas. It is likely that encouraging greater numbers of the less-educated workers and their families to relocate would doubtless require better communication linkages with the low-income population. As we know from recent experience with the urban ghettos, neither physical proximity nor exposure to the mass media is any guarantee that the poor will be drawn into the mainstream of the labor market or the available network of social services. However, because the distressed area population tends

to be better educated and motivated than are the hard-core unemployed in the
large city ghettos, the task is not likely to be as difficult or frustrating.

BROADENING THE TALENT BASE

Broadening the migrant stream attacks only half the problem of selective migration from distressed areas. What is also needed is an incentive system
to enlarge the shallow pools of local talent. This suggests a need for a policy
that might include, among its other components, relocation allowances "to
move *into* the redevelopment area the labor force ingredients in terms of skill
and age, necessary to maximize its usefulness."[33] This suggestion, which has
been recommended for the relatively small Benelux countries, applies with even
greater force in the United States. In a sense, public and private incentives are
already available in the form of job opportunities, enticing promotion of recreational facilities, and company relocation allowances. But it would appear that
this is not enough. It would be helpful if incentive pay and career opportunities
could be offered as the Russians do in attracting migrants to Siberia, as the
Israelis do in luring migrants to the desert, and as American construction firms
offer in recruiting skilled labor for overseas hardship posts. A federal system of
executive relocation allowances or bonuses could conceivably be part of a national relocation policy.

The problem of talent migration may involve even more sweeping federal action including some controls over the distribution of economic growth.
The brain-drain dilemma raises a number of fundamental questions involving
national policies that are barely embryonic. For example, medical concentration in major metropolitan areas has resulted in physician-to-population ratios
two to three times higher than the ratios in underdeveloped areas.[34]

Should the federal government take action to strengthen the talent base
in redevelopment areas? If the answer to this question is yes, this raises a series
of subsidiary issues. How far are we to go in this direction? How much federal
incentive should there be to locate advanced types of development in such areas
to provide jobs for college graduates? Would interference with the traditional
flow of talent to large metropolitan areas, the "Class A League," eventually be
harmful to national interests? Is there danger of parochialism and inbreeding if
large-scale movement of talent is diminished?

Clearly, more than the future of a redevelopment area or even a metropolis is at stake. Can the nation afford to permit a continuing, possibly widening
gulf between a relative handful of large metropolitan areas and the remainder
of the nation? What would be the long-term consequences of such divergence
in terms of leadership, culture, politics, and national progress? These are basic
questions that need more than hasty answers. At present, we would be wise to
limit ourselves to indicating the existence of a talent migration problem and
probably remain content with modest measure to reduce its impact. But the

problem is not temporally finite; it must be regarded as permanent, and thus it requires long-term policies and programs built into the governmental fabric.

It may be noted that this is not solely an American problem. For a number of years, a growing concern with overconcentration of talent in capital cities had led many European nations to adopt active policies aimed at devolution (i.e., building up provincial centers and restricting growth in the capital). French data for 1962 revealed that the Paris region contained a seventh of that nation's population, a quarter of its government employment, a third of its college and graduate students, two thirds of its artists and writers, and almost two thirds of its corporate headquarters. The government aims at creating a new balance through an environment plan that visualizes equipping cities in large "provincial urban complexes [so that they] can be real economic and social leaders in their regional spheres of influence and can in general be free from complete dependency on Paris."[35] It was estimated that by 1985, eight urban complexes with populations ranging from 360,000 to 1.5 million would be ready to play this autonomous role.[36] It is entirely possible that European successes and failures can be helpful in developing a sound policy suited for the American landscape.

NOTES TO CHAPTER 11

1. U.S. Department of Labor, Report No. 332, Current Population Reports Series P-23, No. 24, *Social and Economic Conditions of Negroes in the United States* (Washington, D.C.: U.S. Government Printing Office, October, 1967), p. 6.

2. See Daniel P. Moynihan, "Poverty in Cities," *The Metropolitan Enigma: Inquiries into the Nature and Dimensions of America's "Urban Crisis,"* Volume II (Washington, D.C.: Chamber of Commerce of the United States, 1967), pp. 300-317.

3. See Economic Development Administration, "Creating Alternatives to Urban Migration," *Economic Development,* V, 1 (January, 1968), 6-8.

4. John Friedmann and William Alonso (eds.), *Regional Development and Planning* (Cambridge, Mass.: M.I.T. Press, 1964), p. 11.

5. See John B. Parr, "Outmigration and the Depressed Area Problem," *Land Economics,* May, 1966, p. 158.

6. U.S. Area Redevelopment Administration, *Area Redevelopment Policies in Britain and the Countries of the Common Market* (Washington, D.C.: U.S. Government Printing Office, January, 1965), p. 6.

7. J. J. Kaufman, "Labor Mobility, Training, and Retraining," *Studies in Unemployment,* U.S. Senate Special Committee on Unemployment Problems (Washington, D.C.: U.S. Government Printing Office, 1960), pp. 343-65.

8. University of Wisconsin, Industrial Relations Research Institute, *Retraining and Migration as Factors in Regional Economic Development* (Madison: University of Wisconsin, 1966), p. 2.

9. U.S. Area Redevelopment Administration, *The Propensity to Move* (Washington, D.C.: U.S. Government Printing Office, July, 1964), pp. 7-8.

10. George Blackwood, "The Northern Berkshire Area and Its Future," (unpublished manuscript, Area Development Center, Boston University, 1965), pp. 10-14.

11. U.S. Area Redevelopment Administration, *Population, Labor Force and Unemployment in Chronically Depressed Areas* (Washington, D.C.: U.S. Government Printing Office, October, 1964), pp. 12-13.

12. Charles Press and Charles R. Adrian, "Why Our State Governments Are Sick," *The Antioch Review,* Summer, 1964, pp. 156-57.

13. Alexis de Toqueville, *Democracy in America,* Vol. I (New York: Vintage Books, 1954), p. 304.

14. This is not to suggest that during the 1930's there was a deliberate policy in New Bedford aimed at discouraging outmigration. There were, however, a series of futile attempts to resuscitate dying textile mills which nourished illusions of an imminent economic revival. A frank recognition that the situation was hopeless might have led to an "Okie"-style abandonment, i.e., a difficult transitional period for the migrants followed by successful integration into the more resilient economy of another area.

15. Seymour L. Wolfbein, *Decline of a Cotton Textile City: A Study of New Bedford* (New York: Columbia University Press, 1944), pp. 34-35, 37.

16. In underdeveloped countries where this scale of farm migration to productive urban jobs is not feasible, conditions approach the catastrophic.

17. *The Christian Science Monitor,* January 31, 1968, p. 11.

18. *The New York Times,* August 27, 1967, p. 15.

19. "Careers 67," *London Times,* August 27, 1967.

20. See Oliver C. Winston, "An Urbanization Pattern for the United States--Some Considerations for the Decentralization of Excellence," *Land Economics,* February, 1967, p. 1.

21. Unlike other groups this is not the case with respect to Puerto Rican immigrants, a fact which may account for the impression fostered by news media centered in New York City, the primary receiving area for Puerto Rican migration. Stanely L. Friedlander, *Labor Migration and Economic Growth: A Case Study of Puerto Rico* (Cambridge, Mass.: The M.I.T. Press, 1965).

22. See Bernard Okun, "Regional Income Inequlaity and Internal Population Migration," *Economic Development and Cultural Change,* January, 1961, pp. 128-43; and Stefan Robock, "Strategies for Regional Economic Development," *Regional Science Association Papers,* XVII, 1966, pp. 129-42.

23. Formal vocational training refers to training provided through school, apprenticeship, or the armed forces. The data obtained are from "Statistical Tables on Manpower," a reprint from U.S. Department of Labor, *Manpower Report of the President* (Washington, D.C.: U.S. Government Printing Office, March, 1964), Table F-8.

24. See the perceptive comments in Irving Kristol, "The Negro Today Is the Immigrant of Yesterday," *The New York Times Magazine,* September 11, 1966, pp. 50-51. See also Charles Till, "Migration and Negro Relocation," *The Metropolitan Enigma, op. cit.*

25. R. S. Eckaus, "Economic Criteria for Education and Training," *The Review of Economics and Statistics,* May, 1964, pp. 181-90.

26. See "Comments" in *Economic Opportunity in Cities* (Chicago: U.S. Conference of Mayors, January, 1966), especially pp. 44-45.

27. A major shift in the MDTA program which had hitherto concentrated on training the readily employable occurred in fiscal 1967. A fourth of the trainees were to be disadvantaged young people and another two fifths, disadvantaged adults. U.S. Department of Labor, *Manpower Report of the President* (Washington, D.C.: U.S. Government Printing Office, March, 1966), pp. 3, 69-74.

28. Edward K. Kalachek, "Automation and Full Employment," *Trans-Action,* March, 1967. The threat and promise of automation has occasioned considerable research and controversy: *Automation,* American Academy of Political and Social Science, March, 1962; Report from the President's Advisory Committee on Labor Management Policy, *The Benefits and Problems Incidental to Automation and Other Technological Advances* (Washington, D.C.: U.S. Government Printing Office, January, 1962); U.S. Department of Labor, *Manpower Implications of Automation,* 1964; U.S. Senate, Committee on Labor

and Public Welfare, 1964, 1965, *Selected Readings in Employment and Manpower*, 6 Vols.; and *Technology and the American Economy*, Report of the National Commission on Technology, Automation, and Economic Progress, I (Washington, D.C.: U.S. Government Printing Office, February, 1966).

29. Friedmann and Alonso, *op. cit.*, p. 5.

30. *Ibid.*

31. "How Sweden Keeps Them Working," *Business Week*, July 15, 1967, pp. 100-102.

33. G. Beijer, *National Rural Manpower: Adjustment to Industry* (Paris, OECD, 1965); quotation from L. A. Sjaastad, "The Costs and Returns of Human Migration," *The Journal of Political Economy*, LXX, 5(2) (1962), 80-93.

33. U.S. Area Redevelopment Administration, *Area Redevelopment Policies in Britain, op. cit.*, p. 7.

34. Accurate figures for the domestic brain drain are unavailable, but there is much data on international migration of talent. It is known that in 1966, immigrant scientific manpower added nearly 10 per cent to the supply of newly graduated engineers and 26 per cent of its new physicians. *The New York Times*, August 27, 1967, p. 12. Of U.S. scientists, engineers, and physicians, 5-10 per cent "are apparently of foriegn origin in the sensè of foreign birth and training." Thomas J. Mills, "Scientific Personnel and the Professions," *The Annals*, issue entitled *The New Immigration*, Vol. 367, September, 1966, pp. 33-42.

35. *France, Town and Country Environment Planning* (New York, N.Y.: 927 Fifth Avenue, Service de Presse d'Information, December, 1965).

36. *Ibid.*

CHAPTER 12 THE BIG REGIONS

THE BIG REGIONS AND AMERICA'S FUTURE

By the mid-1970's, Americans may well take for granted a new level of government--a region that covers several states or includes portions of several. In some instances, these will be traditional or "natural" regions; in most, their boundaries will follow relatively predictable lines based on unifying socio-economic factors operating in a plausible geographic area.

These so-called big regions will assume increasing importance in the lives of the people of the United States during the last quarter of the twentieth century. Created as a "new dimension of federalism," an entity to operate between the states and the federal government, they will gradually develop clear-cut identities based on their special problems and interests.

The new regionalism is one side of a developmental coin that, when turned over, reveals model cities legislation. Both are aimed at helping to relieve intolerable social headaches--the persistence of gnawing poverty, stubbornly high unemployment rates, inadequate education and skills, racial and ethnic tensions, shabby housing, serious transportation needs, and, in general, wretched misuse of human- and natural-resource potential. Both stress the role of planning and impatience with existing governmental inadequacies; both stress massive, planned investment and new types of social and economic accounting.

Yet, clearly the new regionalism departs from the analogy in at least one major respect: It does not focus primarily on poverty. Rather, the states involved--some of whom are relatively opulent--are engaged in an experiment in Creative Federalism: as an expression of a new posture of cooperation. They will use their political strength within the federal government to solve the problems of backward areas within their states which reach across boundaries to neighboring states. But there will be more emphasis on working with their neighbor states to secure the federal help needed to solve problems which are beyond the unaided capacities of even the wealthiest states.

This chapter, therefore, explores the status of the newly evolving regional commissions and speculates on their future possibilities.

The New Dimension

From 1965 through 1967, six massive new regional commissions were formally created under federal legislation and embraced approximately 40 million people. These include Appalachia with 15.3 million; New England, 10.5 million; Ozarks, 2.5 million; Upper Great Lakes, 2.7 million; Four Corners, 1.8 million; and Atlantic Coastal Plains, 4.5 million (see Table 6). Furthermore, in 1967, plans were underway to designate three other regions, the Upper Great Plains, Pacific Northwest, and Mississippi Delta. By 1970, perhaps a third of the nation's land area and a quarter of its population may be included within new regions.

The primary vehicle for the establishment of the new regional agencies was the Public Works and Economic Development Act of 1965 passed in late August, although Appalachia, the forerunner and model for PL 89-136, had been established some months earlier in separate legislation.[1]

In some respects, the new regions are direct descendants of the regionalism theory of the 1930's as outlined in studies by the National Resources Planning Board (NRPB)[2] and continue the strong emphasis of the NRPB programs dealing with resource depletion, misuse, and economic development. However, there is less attention to another, later type of regionalism, the urban regions; a child of the 1950's, it represents an attempt, mostly unsuccessful but still in progress, to deal with metropolitan problems.

Raising echoes of the New Deal, the new regions ostensibly are an economic response to area poverty. In fact, however, they are in the process of becoming organizations with far broader interests and concerns. In a sense, they are political regions; most owe their establishment to a *quid pro quo* for the support of their congressional delegations in the designation of Appalachia. They are also political in another respect: Their predecessors, operating in a climate of opinion in which violent hostility to government intervention and planning was commonplace, laid heavy stress on attempts to develop plausible proof of their profitability. In contrast, the new regions have departed both from the cost-benefit analysis of the river-basin variety and the seed money, investment-job generation formulae used in securing passage of area redevelopment legislation in the early 1960's. The new political and environmental dimensions reflect adjustments to an affluent, more sophisticated society, as evidenced by the regions' substantial attention to human resources and to physical environment. This redirection is not totally divorced from sound investment principles; it can be and has been explained as belated pragmatism, as an attempt to modernize their defective infrastructure to compete for sound economic development. In the poor regions, social overhead facilities and services tend to be neglected and rundown, although they have been found to be indispensable prerequisites for modern economic growth.

TABLE 6
Appalachia and EDA Regions, 1967

	Area in Square Miles (nearest 000)	Population in 1960 (nearest 000)	Net Civilian Migration, 1950-60 (nearest 000)	Median Family Income, 1959 (in dollars)	% of Families With Incomes Below $3,000 in 1960	Median School Years Completed, 1960 (persons over 25)
Appalachia	165,000	15,328,000	-2,014,000	*	30.7	9.1
Four Corners	288,000	1,758,000	-11,000	5,080	25.1	10.9
Atlantic Coastal Plains	79,000	4,487,000	-571,000	3,459	44.8	9.0
Ozarks	89,000	2,495,000	-431,000	3,492	44.4	9.3
Upper Great Lakes	116,000	2,694,000	-253,000	4,735	26.8	9.7
New England	67,000	10,509,000	+31,000	6,128	13.6	11.2
Total Regions	804,000	37,271,000	*	*	*	*
United States	3,549,000	179,323,000	+2,973,000	5,625	21.4	10.6

* Not available or not given.

Source: Letter from Robert Murphy, Economic Development Administration, from U.S. census data. Article published May 15, 1967.

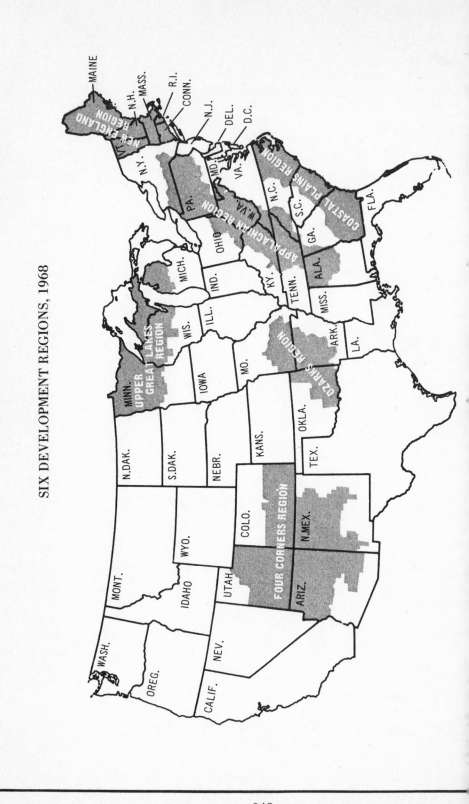

SIX DEVELOPMENT REGIONS, 1968

There is clearly another assumption involved in the inclusion of public schools and public health in regional development programs that once riveted their energy on industrial parks or flood problems. The people who live in distressed regions, like other disadvantaged segments of the society, are no longer satisfied merely with basic shelter and steady, low-wage jobs in territorial or racial enclaves. The cries for redress of grievances for the underdogs of society-- the poor, the minority groups, and the backward areas--can no longer be stilled by providing unskilled jobs or freedom from periodic flooding. Their aspirations are now much more ambitious and involve rapid movement into the mainstream of society.

While past approaches were by no means as simple minded as some critics have charged, they are dwarfed by the new, broader focus that has cut loose from the familiar landmarks of cost-benefit irrigation projects and economic development promotion linked to public bonds for industrial parks. It is also noteworthy that it is no longer necessary to display the beggar's sores. The underdog argument has lost much of its force compared to political considerations when applied to areas such as New England, where incomes have been higher and living conditions have been more favorable than in most parts of the nation. In short, although some of the rhetoric of the 1930's has been disinterred, the examples of Appalachia and New England suggest that in the past few years, large-scale regional development programs in the United States have been profoundly altered in character and concept.

HISTORIC ROOTS

There is no clear agreement on what constitutes regional planning and development either as a field of study or a field of operations. To a considerable extent, John Friedmann's caustic observation to the effect that regional planning has usually involved much research but little implementation in a "rather ill-defined combination of physical, economic, human resource and natural resource concerns" is clearly correct.[3] But the field is so amorphous that it defies even the loosest parameters. Even Friedmann's extremely wide definition for regional planning as the "ordering of human activities in supra-urban space"[4] seems too narrow to encompass all of the operations of the new regions, particularly the administrative, lobbying, investment, and organizational issues that occupy so much time and effort. The new regions are political entities with responsibilities that include but far transcend the economists' and planners' tasks of developing a technical framework and priorities for intraregional choices and allocations determined at the federal level.

Another major problem in developing a suitable definition is pinning down the slippery term "region." There is, for example, a great variation in size. The entire Southeast of the United States has been defined as a region in some studies, while miniscular "regions" with populations of less than 10,000 have been organized, recognized, and subsequently funded with federal assistance.

Until recently, smallness seemed to be winning out; the "urban regions" of the 1950's were in most cases roughly equivalent to standard metropolitan areas, and most were geographically small, with populations well under a million. The redevelopment areas of the early 1960's were even smaller; a number of designated rural and resort areas had populations of only a few thousand. This was in distinct contrast to the practice of the 1930's and 1940's, when regional activity was focused on vast river basins like the Tennessee,5 the Missouri, and the Columbia. These watersheds of the Depression decade were always sizable in territory if not always large in population. Similarly, the identification of the economically and physically distressed Appalachian, Ozark, and Cutover areas in the 1930's also involved boundaries encompassing parts of a number of states. However, the total population involved was smaller than in the nation's leading states.

By the end of World War II, the always loosely defined term "region" had lost almost all relevance except as a convenient geographic expression. The one experiment that seemed to point hopefully to the future (and perhaps the point is that it was a generation before its time) was the brave new world of the Tennessee Valley Authority (TVA). In original concept, this was to be the source of a great transformation for millions of America's poorest people. A central argument for support of TVA by taxpayers from Bangor to San Diego was that the growth of a market in the Tennessee Valley would benefit everybody; the rising tide of prosperity along the Tennessee would help to lift all American boats.

This has been a salient point made by proponents of aid to depressed regions (and poor people) ever since--that they were simply bad business for a prosperous society. And certainly the economic development of northern Alabama and southern Tennessee provided testimony to the significance of the pioneering experiment in that region. But the danger with the river basin approach is its unsuitability for an urbanized nation. Water resources do not appear to be useful for organizational and program orientation in the present era. It seems questionable that a region created on the basis of its natural resource needs and problems can readjust its main thrust to focus adequately on urban problems. An organization's initial orientation, supporters, and staff place a permanent stamp on its subsequent conduct.

TVA also ran into another basic problem. The realities of political survival in the 1930's and 1940's dictated an agency emphasis narrowed to the simple production of electric power, with only limited side activities including flood control and recreation development. In the climate of state and local hostility to planning that existed in the 1930's and 1940's, TVA found itself forced to operate within these parentheses, largely as a matter of realistic accomodation with the land-grant colleges and their clientele, area businessmen, and other components of the local establishment. As compared to the programs in Appalachia and those likely to emerge from new regions, for example, TVA's direct involvement with human resource development will seem rather minimal. Had it been otherwise, TVA might well have succumbed to its enemies and exist now only as a brave wraith, extinguished in a premature, losing battle for the tenant farmer and the poor.

Although the new regions more closely resembled the districts of the 1930's in size, they have clearly been influenced by the experience of the 1940's and 1950's. Two divergent trends were apparent in the 1950's. The first involved the transformation of the 1930's state research-planning agencies into industrial and tourist promotion organizations, usually with limited state planning responsibilities. The second was the previously mentioned focus on urban regions, reflecting the philosophies and policies of the U.S. Housing and Home Finance Agency (now the Department of Housing and Urban Development). Since these metropolitan areas were generally smaller in both territory and population, as compared to the mammoth regions of the previous two decades, the new EDA regions represent a return to the scale of the 1930's.

With the exception of weak, privately sponsored regional advisory agencies and public river-basin commissions that have only a tenuous hold on political loyalties and power, the new multistate regions operate in a *tabula rasa* situation: The regional territory has not been as thoroughly staked out by strong rivals. It is likely that their confrontations and dissensions will result from internal fractionalism among governors, senators, and clientele groups rather than from head-to-head battles among regional contenders with overlapping spheres of activity. The only potential rivals on the horizon are the interstate river-basin commissions being created under the Water Resources Act of 1965. However, in an urbanized society, river basin agencies do not appear to have the political resources necessary to equip them for serious fratricidal battle.

APPALACHIAN ANALOGUE

Charting the probable direction of evolution for large EDA regions could conceivably be a difficult task because the enabling legislation is so broad that it offers adequate authority for an enormous variety of programs. Consider, for example, the research and advisory functions enumerated in Section 503 of the 1965 legislation based on its predecessor, the Appalachian Act. The new regions are empowered to assist regional development by undertaking research, initiating and coordinating long-range development plans, promoting increased private investment, preparing legislative recommendations, and conducting research on resources. Given this broad mandate, the limitations are so vague that they are nonexistent.

- While they are kissing cousins with respect to research, there is one vital difference between Appalachia and the new regions. From an organizational standpoint, Appalachia is a relatively robust relative. From its inception, Appalachia has received federal assistance for conducting programs as well as for research and advisory activities. Thus, it has had real muscle to ensure that recommendations were carried out. Under Title II of the 1965 legislation, the Appalachian region was allocated over $1 billion. This included $840 million for a development highway system, $69 million for demonstration health facilities, $63 million for various natural-resource programs, $16 million for vocational education facilities, and $90 million to increase the normal federal matching share for a broad range of federal grant-in-aid programs. In combination, these funds gave the Appalachian organization substantial and sustained political leverage. Evidence of its strength was the passage in 1967 of a congressional appropriation for the region virtually identical with the President's requests. This was somewhat unusual, coming at a time when appropriations for other great-society programs like model cities were subjected to major cutbacks. The fact that Appalachia has program funds of its own to distribute helps the region to achieve budgetary immunity reflecting substantial grass roots support.

It can be predicted that the new regions will follow Appalachia's lead and not be content to remain restricted to research and advisory roles. Before much time has passed, the multistate regions will undoubtedly attempt to emulate Appalachian autonomy and move toward separate funding, independent of EDA control. However, EDA is not entirely prepared to let its children go without a struggle. In early 1968, a Presidential executive order designated the Secretary of Commerce to provide effective liaison between the federal government and the regional commissions (Appalachia excluded), assisted by an advisory committee composed of representatives of other agencies.[6] This role as compulsory intermediary--the Department of Commerce is EDA's parent agency--may tend to circumscribe the autonomy of the new regions, but the thrust toward secession is inevitable.

It is striking that both of the nation's large, autonomous regions have been established in southern or border state territory. Despite violent attacks on TVA as a dangerous venture into socialism, the Tennessee Valley Authority has been fervently embraced by area politicians, many of whom tend to be highly conservative on other domestic matters. Often, elected officials in the South reserve ideological warfare for Communism and the race issue and are otherwise supremely effective pragmatists (i.e., lobbyists for their constituents). TVA may have looked like creeping socialism to northern conservatives, but in much of the South it has been considered an effective vehicle for pumping federal investment and payrolls into the area--an asset similar to the costly military installations and federal public-works projects that freckle the Southland. By and large, it has been the North and Midwest that rejected, on ideological grounds, proposals to create similar regional river basin authorities on the Missouri and other rivers.

By the time the Appalachian region was created, much of the political controversy over TVA had dissipated, despite an occasional nostalgic flicker of hostility from private power companies. Even more important, perhaps, the Appalachian Commission, from its birth, was in reality the "establishment" creature that critics of TVA claimed it had become by the late 1930's--an administrative vehicle closely tied to the local power structure.[7] This stance has certain political advantages. Largely controlled and operated by state governments, the new regions do not provide a vulnerable target to a conservative opposition that has proclaimed itself the champion of states rights. Furthermore, within the states, the new regions are creatures of the governors; they in no way resemble the community-action organizations that the U.S. Office of Economic Opportunity has financed to mobilize the poor and forsaken to do battle with city hall.

Perhaps the dichotomy between the establishment and the poor is not entirely meaningful. Governors are popularly elected, and the programs that help them to achieve and retain power are directed toward securing support from all segments of the electorate, including the poor. With some exceptions, mainly in the South, the poor are making greater use of their franchise and the difference in program orientation between underdogs, many of whom are moving out of poverty, and larger middle-class electorates has become increasingly blurred. The Appalachian precedents suggest, setting aside the continuing commitment to highway construction, that the regions' growing concentration on human-resource programs has resulted in a focus which is probably reasonably close to that likely to be demanded by spokesmen for the disadvantaged. This is not to say that there is complete harmony between the middle class, the "interests," and the poor in Appalachia. The administration of these programs and their efficacy in meeting the needs of the hard-core poor can become the subject of bitter controversy. It is probable that a maximum, feasible-participation requirement in policy-making similar to OEO legislation would result in significant revisions in administration, program content, and outlook. This raises some interesting questions. While, at first blush, the vast territory of a multistate region seems an improbable arena for the kind of protest groups that have developed in slum neighborhoods, the creation of antiestablishment organizations on a regional scale is by no means inconceivable.

Once again, Appalachia may point the direction--the demand of an Appalachian citizens' group for public control of the coal-mining industry [8] is an example of the kind of dissidence that could develop within the regions. In New England, a primary issue for dissent may be the public power question, while other regions find controversy arising from poverty or natural resource programs. Thus, Appalachia may be the prototype in experiencing the onslaught of a pioneering, regional-gadfly organization that attempts to enlist large segments of the population in efforts to force the official regional commission to give early battle to vested interests.

Human Resource Programs

The 1960 research study upon which much of subsequent Appalachian action was based recommended more emphasis on "portable investments" such as education and manpower training and less stress on costly highways and headwater dams.[9] The study also suggested that primary efforts be concentrated on developing urban areas of demonstrated growth potential. In part, the approach was based on this author's conclusions from research in southern Illinois, an area of marginal farming, declining employment in the coal industry, and shabby mining hamlets similar in many respects to Appalachia.[10]

Neither concept met with the complete approval of the governors assembled at the 1960 Governor's Conference on Appalachia. Some of the governors argued that acceptance of these human resource recommendations would be tantamount to adopting a policy of accelerating depopulation for much of the region; they were not receptive to programs that called for expending much of Appalachia's limited resources on education and training activities which amounted to a subsidy of the well-off regions receiving Appalachian migrants. Moreover, they were not enthralled with the idea of ploughing most of their scarce development and promotion money into a few, obviously thriving, urban areas at the risk of alienating most of the dying small towns.

An idea that found greater favor was the development highway. A mountain region that possessed little but coal and timber to attract outside investors, Appalachia had been bypassed by the main thrust of national economic growth, partly because of its isolation. The governors suggested that new roads would open the region to the mainstream of the nation's economic expansion. However, they recognized that these new highways would never be built unless new criteria for road construction were created; they were to be "development highways" to generate future traffic. Current criteria for highway construction are grounded primarily on an extrapolation of present traffic volumes, a premise that usually discriminates against the underdeveloped region. The governors complained that the extensive federal interstate highway system and the ABC system[11] would link the region's major urban centers with first-class routes, but they were obviously not going to penetrate into many mountain areas.

The Appalachian Governors' orientation was fully reflected both in the 1964 report of the President's Appalachian study commission[12] and in the three annual budgetary allocations of the Appalachian Regional Development Commission through fiscal 1968. For fiscal years 1966 and 1967, total appropriations amounted to $282 million for a start on 2,350 miles of development highways and $18 million for local-access roads.[13]

The commission had continued its stress on highway construction, which it regards as a vital prerequisite for development. Despite the care that had gone into program design, some of Appalachia's other original programs did not live up to advance billing. Two notable examples are the timberland and pasture operations. There had been much needless worry on the part of western cattle interests fearful of grassy, eastern valleys swarming with near-to-market beef, but for a variety of reasons, neither effort produced the type of early payoff that some had anticipated. In contrast, one of Appalachia's significant successes was financial matching to help impoverished areas take advantage of federal grant-in-aid programs. These supplementary grants-in-aid constituted a powerful weapon in helping the commission develop a strong, local power base and enabling it to attack a variety of problems along a broad front. To cite one example, progress is being made on the desperate problem of substandard rural housing. The commission found that it could make good use of technical-assistance funds in helping farm areas complete complicated application forms required to qualify for grants and low-interest loans available from other federal agencies.

In passing, it may be noted that TVA also claimed that its free technical assistance helped to invigorate local communities.[14] While this is undoubtedly accurate, it has its ironic aspects. Roughly two thirds of the TVA area is included in the Appalachian region and its commission staff allege that many of the TVA communities are a mess. The TVA, it is suggested, has remained a hydrology-oriented agency rather than having evolved into a comprehensive planning operation, and Appalachia has inherited some of the consequences of TVA's failure to broaden its horizons. In time, the Appalachian Regional Development Commission too may be attacked for not dealing effectively with the poverty problem. It is likely that the assault will not be as concerned with the nature of the commission's program mix as with the organization's inability to secure larger amounts of federal money for poverty-oriented activities.[15]

Unmistakable signs of a change in program emphasis--if not monetary allocations--quickly became apparent as the commission went into action. A preliminary report, financed by the U.S. Office of Regional Economic Development, the EDA branch responsible for regional programs, took account of the contribution of human resource development to the growth of the economy as an "implicit" factor in the economic analysis. In accordance with the terms of the research contract which called for a delineation of subregions, the report placed much stress on the urban growth-center concept.[16] A year later, in 1966, the commission reported that it was moving "toward comprehensive programs for helping develop the Region's manpower . . . a detailed assessment of the educational needs and potentials of the region"[17] and toward a new-towns policy to regroup the dispersed population living in central Appalachia.[18] Most supplemental grant funds--82 per cent of $13.7 million--were approved for higher education and hospital facilities, nursing homes, mental-health centers, and libraries. In early 1967, the executive director reported that the commission had approved over 400 school and hospital projects, community colleges and graduate research facilities, and that plans were being completed for a series of comprehensive health-service facilities in several parts of the region.[19] The commission quickly discovered, however, that the more serious problem was not providing bricks and mortar but the shortage of trained people. Commission programs in the health field, for example, were subsequently modified to reflect the need for augmenting the supply of qualified staff.

One of the central themes that runs through the Appalachian commission's study, as indeed through the hearings conducted on the 1965 EDA legislation, is the concept of social disadvantage as reflected in indices comparing the region to the nation. The Appalachian commission reports included data showing that the infant mortality rate in Appalachia was double the national average, that the region had a 50 per cent deficiency in long-term health care facilities compared to the nation, that the region's per capita ratio of physicians and nurses was much lower, that the proportion of high school and college graduates in the population was considerably smaller, and that housing conditions were relatively worse.

In interpreting its mandate to further economic progress in this liberal fashion, the Appalachian commission is increasingly grappling with a broad spectrum of social problems. While the commission's efforts in this direction would not have been possible on any substantial scale were it not for great-society legislation and national prosperity, the Appalachian programs clearly reflect a sensitive awareness not only to the human needs of the region but also to the fact that action to meet these needs has become politically advantageous.

HOW TO RUN A SURPLUS: THE CASE OF NEW ENGLAND

The designation of New England as a development region raises a number of pertinent questions. Some are related to the applicability of the Appalachian criteria used as a yardstick for delineating the new regions, and others clearly suggest that, in future years, the creation of new multistate organizations will not be associated with a response to poverty or alleged lag relative to the nation but will be a pragmatic approach to resolving multistate problems. In this sense, New England, like Appalachia, is a national prototype.

For a number of years, states in the Northeast and Midwest have registered complaints concerning alleged federal favoritism toward the South and West. In New England, the southern states in particular were visualized as the beneficiaries of a vast outpouring of federal expenditures for military installations and public works because of powerful southern influence operating through the congressional committee seniority system. The federal government was believed to be highly effective in the role of equalizer, taxing wealthy states in New England and elsewhere for the benefit of the needy, politically influential South and West.

Some who believed that this federal redistribution was a reality argued that it was all a mistake; a larger share of federal funds should be channeled to expanding states rather than be poured into rural sinkholes. Others, after discovering that in reality the rich states were getting richer via a disproportionately large share of federal expenditures, also suggested that it was a matter for concern. They argued that a larger share of federal aid should be given to the poor, if only to help them improve the health and education of future migrants.

As the focus of regional development broadens to include the better-off regions--led by New England--the problem of interregional and interstate allocation of federal funds will emerge as an increasingly crucial issue. It is useful, for this reason, to examine how the system works, especially how and why wealthy regions manage to secure a larger share of federal allocations than poor regions.

Evidence that the federal role in channeling relatively larger amounts of federal funds to poor regions was not particularly effective came to light in a study published in 1966. Analyzing the pattern of federal expenditures to states and regions between 1957 and 1963, the study concluded that "greater amounts of federal expenditures in the period of this study tend to go to states with higher levels of per capita income."[20] The persistence of this pattern is attributable to the fact that most of the nation's spending for defense procurement and for NASA is allocated to states that have a strong urban-industrial-research base and that these states use a substantial part of their wealth for public assistance and other federally aided programs as matching money to bring in additional federal allocations.

Data for the New England region show this process in action. Between 1957 and 1963, the region increased its percentage share of national expenditures. On a per-capita basis, New England's 45 per cent growth was slightly greater than the 43 per cent national increase; its gains in federal expenditures outstripped its modest population increase. In practice, this meant that New England continued to receive about 35 per cent more federal expenditures per capita than the national average. As a region, it was exceeded only by the Far West, which was 44 per cent over the national level in 1963.[21] (In passing, the $570 in per-capita federal allocations received by New England in 1963 and its $175 per-capita increase between 1957 and 1963 may be compared to proposals to expend an additional $50 to $100 per capita annually to accelerate progress in dealing with the region's unfinished business, most notably to cleanse its polluted rivers and shore areas.)

An examination of the statistics indicates how this feat was accomplished. In 1963, New England, with 5.8 per cent of the nation's population, received almost 9 per cent of United States defense and NASA expenditures; by allocating large amounts of money to federally matchable public assistance programs, the region proceeded to secure almost 8 per cent of U.S. expenditures for transfer payments. As Table 7 indicates, despite New England's smaller share of civilian military wages, the third component of the "big three" in federal expenditures, all states in the region were above the national level with the exception of Vermont.

Connecticut and Massachusetts are clearly the regional leaders. The disparity between these two states and the remainder of the region is particularly marked with respect to the vital research and development function. An examination of 1963 allocations of the $12.7 billion spent for federal and corporate

TABLE 7
The New England States'
Shares of Major Allocated Federal Expenditures* 1957 and 1963

	% of Population in 1963	Per Capita Allocations in Dollars		% of Total Allocations		% of Civilian and Military Wages		% of Transfer Payments		% Defense Procurement	
		1957	1963	1957	1963	1957	1963	1957	1963	1957	1963
New England	5.8	388	565	6.9	7.0	5.2	5.1	7.8	7.9	8.6	8.4
Massachusetts	2.8	372	592	3.2	3.5	2.6	2.6	4.4	4.8	3.2	3.7
Rhode Island	0.5	372	502	0.6	0.6	0.9	0.7	0.6	0.6	0.2	0.3
New Hampshire	0.3	297	452	0.3	0.3	0.3	0.4	0.4	0.4	0.2	0.2
Connecticut	1.4	503	649	2.1	2.0	0.6	0.7	1.5	1.4	4.6	4.0
Vermont	0.2	239	346	0.2	0.2	0.1	0.1	0.2	0.2	0.1	0.1
Maine	0.5	322	403	0.5	0.5	0.6	0.6	0.6	0.6	0.4	0.2
United States		329	470								

* Includes almost 87 per cent of total 1963 federal allocations as follows: civilian, military wages, salaries ($23.9 billion, 27.0 per cent of $88.6 billion allocated in 1963; transfer payments $24.6 billion, 27.8 per cent of total) and defense, NASA, procurement ($28.4 billion, 32.0 per cent of total).

Source: U.S. Senate, 89th Cong., 2nd Sess., Subcommittee on Intergovernmental Relations, Committee on Government Operations, Federal Expenditures to States and Regions (Washington, D.C.: U.S. Government Printing Office, June 29, 1966), pp. 109, 113, 126, 130.

Research and Development funds revealed that the region accounted for 8 per cent of the nation's total R & D expenditures, roughly a billion dollar input to the economy.[22] Massachusetts and Connecticut contain three fourths of New England's total population and accounted for virtually all R & D activity. Although the disparity is not quite as serious as it appears, Rhode Island and the three northern New England states are clearly not securing a proportionate regional share of R & D operations. This and other factors may suggest that one of the reasons for designating wealthier regions is that a regional approach may enable them to deal more effectively with their economically lagging states and subareas.

It is not suggested that New England has adopted a cold-blooded policy of increasing its public assistance expenditures in order to maximize federal contributions. Unlike states in some parts of the nation, relative generosity to the poor in the New England states extends to all forms of public aid, including the general assistance program for which no federal matching funds are made available. Thus, while per-person Massachusetts payments for old age assistance (for which federally matching funds are available) are almost double the level in West Virginia, the average per-case payment for general assistance (for which no federal funds are available) is also more than twice that of West Virginia.[23]

EIGHT CRITERIA: A BAD FIT?

The eight criteria for designation of the new EDA development regions clearly are based on the Appalachian precedent. They include major deviations from national rates of population growth, income levels, housing quality, industrial expansion, unemployment rates, threats to the economy from automation, contractions of major industries from defense-plant closings, serious natural-resource problems, and a common bond of regionality.[24]

Several difficulties with the criteria as stated are obvious. They do not take into account the different stages of economic development from region to region that range from explosive growth to stagnation--senescence or an almost total lack of development. They fail to make sufficient allowance for variations within a region that cover the same broad spectrum; they apply a narrow type of slide-rule mathematics--a heritage of the rather questionable idea that industrial growth somehow equals economic and social progress. But as the five designated regions come into full operation (and if the other three presently contemplated also become realities), the criteria will doubtless be expanded and made more meaningful. The new regionalism can therefore provide a rich diversity of experiences on which to base experiments elsewhere in the country. New England is a case in point.

In terms of geography and historical tradition, regional designation is particularly appropriate for the six-state New England region (some analysts would exclude western Connecticut, or at least Fairfield County, as more logically associated with the New York Metropolitan Region). New England is comparable in total size and population to Illinois and other sizable states, and, unlike Appalachia, whose boundaries have contracted and expanded like an accordion, New England possesses a genuine demarcated, historic identity.

In recent years, there has been considerable improvement in the region's economy, with the result that a number of its redevelopment areas have been dedesignated. By mid-1967, unemployment rates in all but a few of the region's labor-market areas were down below 6 per cent (vs. 3 to 4 per cent for the nation); in Boston, Providence, and the Connecticut Valley, which contain most of the region's population, jobless rates ran below or near the national level. Furthermore, New England's per capita income has remained substantially above the national level; the percentage of substandard housing is appreciably lower; and the problems posed in some areas by cutbacks in military installations are apparently being mastered.

However, while the data reveal that New England is by no means another Appalachia, the region nevertheless faces a number of significant challenges that demand interstate action. Water pollution and transportation problems, especially those of the railroads, are two examples. Net outmigration of better-educated young people has depleted some area labor markets and local-leadership strata.

The current rosy economic picture must also be viewed in historic perspective. In much of the region, the recent improvement is superimposed on decades of economic distress and neglect that has resulted in cities plagued by rundown public buildings, antiquated schools, and difficult human resource problems. The massive urban renewal and antipoverty programs in New Haven and Boston, which have so far gone only part way in attacking this accumulation, provide some indication of the kind of action and the scale of expenditures likely to be required to rectify past neglect, particularly in the small- and medium-sized cities that have barely managed to launch renewal programs. Moreover, a realistic water pollution program and transportation improvements will call for massive expenditures far in excess of regional and local resources.

Thus, when everything has been said in favor of designation on the basis of the 1965 EDA criteria, the fact is that New England is truly a region but represents a departure from past practice in that it owes its current status primarily to factors other than economic deprivation. In a real sense, this is a pioneering step. It is now possible to visualize a nationwide pattern of regions covering the Middle Atlantic, Middle West and Far West states, designated not because they are poor and economically distressed but because they have multistate problems, because they wish to create a regional voice to deal with these problems, and because they have the political strength to secure federal aid to support regional programs.

OUTMIGRATION AND THE REGIONS

The same observations on relative regional disadvantages compared to national criteria found in Appalachia were offered with respect to the Ozarks region, the Upper Peninsula of Michigan, and portions of the Four Corners region. A principal, common symptom advanced to justify federal aid in Congressional testimony on the 1965 EDA legislation was outmigration. On this proposition, the Upper Great Lakes and New England were in full agreement--heavy, net outmigration of better-educated young people from certain regions constitutes an obstacle to economic growth, a drain on local resources, and a subsidy to the regions that receive the migrants.

The migration argument possesses obvious merit when applied to most of the new regions. Net outmigration occurred on a huge scale in the Ozarks, Atlantic Coastal Plains, Upper Great Lakes, and Appalachian regions. In contrast, as Table 6 indicates, the Four Corners region experienced a very small net outmigration while New England received a minor influx of migrants. However, most of New England's net gain can be attributed to suburbanization in western Connecticut. Connecticut gained almost a quarter of a million migrants in the 1950-60 decade, more than compensating for the 130,000 loss in Massachusetts, Maine, Vermont, and Rhode Island.

Outmigration is perhaps one of the most realistic arguments for seeking federal aid to subsidize distressed areas. However, migration is not a simple phenomenon, and, consequently, arguments involving cross movements of population must be used with caution. It is true that a considerable amount of impressive data and fearsome comparisons can be developed from migration statistics. In the Senate, *Hearings* testimony on net migration from the state of Montana suggested, in terms of dollars, that the estimated annual net loss from the migration of 5,000 high school and college graduates each year amounted to over a third of the state's combined average sales of livestock and wheat.[25]

There is no obvious method of determining how the costs and benefits of this interregional migration of young people balances out. For example, no wholly satisfactory technique has been devised to determine if the economic and social contribution of a dozen inmigrant scientists and engineers more than compensates for the losses in public and private investment accruing through the loss of 100 or 200 miners and farmers; this is in fact the West Virginia pattern. To cite other examples, if migrants return "invisible imports" in the form of cash contributions to their families, or if the alternative to migration were public subsidy on the welfare rolls, there is room for arguing, in the first instance, that not all of the local investment has been lost, and, in the second, that the economy benefited rather than suffered from outmigration. On the other hand, if migrants are troublesome or of marginal quality, the receiving areas can reasonably claim that they are also net losers by the transfer. In connection with the problems generated by migrants, in an off-the-record talk, a prominent authority on regional problems suggested that northern cities would find it cheaper to subsidize his unruly, ill-educated neighbors to stay home. In short, cost-benefit calculations to determine net beneficiary areas from migrant cross-currents are difficult to determine or to defend.

Nevertheless, even when all of these caveats are taken into consideration, the migration argument has substantial merit. Persistent poverty in migrant-sending areas is partly attributable to the burden of childrearing and public education on poor families and financially weak state and local governments. While it is true, as in the underdeveloped nations, that past failures in family planning are partly responsible for these areas' current problems, control of conception is a complex phenomenon which tends to follow rather than precede economic progress.

Allocations of federal funds to distressed regions can be viewed in a more realistic perspective by examining some pertinent migration data. An analysis of migration statistics comparing the number of residents aged 25-29 with the number aged 15-19 a decade earlier is revealing. It is assumed that the death rate in this age bracket is extremely small (i.e., consistent with national rates).[26] It is also assumed that persons aged 25-29 are not likely to be in the armed forces or attending school; the figures are presumably not affected by the presence of universities or military installations.

Table 8 presents a comparison of statistics for the two age categories. It reveals that New England lost only 2 per cent of its young adults between the 1950 and 1960 censuses; there were about 621,000 residents aged 15-19 in the region in 1950 compared to 606,000 persons aged 25-29 in 1960. As might be expected, the pattern in the New England states was extremely uneven, with a substantial gain in Connecticut, and significant losses in Vermont, Maine, and Rhode Island. By way of a yardstick, the loss in Oklahoma was 23 per cent and in West Virginia, a very high 40 per cent. In Montana, a state proposed for inclusion in a new Upper Great Plains region, the figure was approximately equal to Massachusetts--5 per cent.

Carl F. Kraenzel's data prepared for Montana suggest that the per person rearing cost to "parents and citizens" is $19,000 for high school graduates and $32,000 for departing college graduates. If these figures can be accepted as reasonably accurate and applicable, the loss in New England, excluding Connecticut, through net outmigration of young people was probably well in hundreds of millions of dollars annually between 1950 and 1960. In West Virginia and Oklahoma, the annual figure probably exceeded $100 million.[27]

That some correlation between heavy net migration and income levels exists is suggested by the fact that Vermont, New England's high migration state, has the lowest per capita personal income in New England while Connecticut, the inmigrant state, has the highest. This is a national pattern. States like California and New York, which receive large numbers of migrants, exhibit high per capita incomes associated with an expanding economy, while net loss

TABLE 8

Outmigration of Youth in
New England and Selected States, 1950-60
(nearest 000)

| | Number of Persons Aged | | | |
	15-19 in 1950	25-29 in 1960	Net Loss	% of Change
Connecticut	122,000	150,000	+ 28,000	+ 23
Maine	70,000	56,000	- 14,000	- 20
Massachusetts	309,000	298,000	- 11,000	- 4
New Hampshire	37,000	34,000	- 3,000	- 8
Rhode Island	54,000	47,000	- 7,000	- 13
Vermont	29,000	21,000	- 8,000	- 28
New England (Total)	621,000	606,000	- 15,000	- 2
Montana	41,000	39,000	- 2,000	- 5
Oklahoma	179,000	137,000	- 42,000	- 23
West Virginia	166,000	100,000	- 66,000	- 40
United States	10,671,000	10,869,000	+ 198,000	+ 2

Sources: U.S. Census of Population, 1960 (Washington, D.C.: U.S. Government Printing Office), Tables 47-52; Statistical Abstract of the United States, 1965 (Washington, D.C.: U.S. Government Printing Office), Table 22.

states like West Virginia and Oklahoma have lower per capita incomes. There are exceptions like Pennsylvania (high outmigration--average incomes) and Florida (large inmigration--low incomes), but the trend is clear even in these instances; Pennsylvania incomes have declined relative to the nation, while per capita incomes in Florida have at least kept pace with the national growth rate despite the continuous influx of retirees, many of whom have comparatively little income.

Measured against an apparent annual subsidy of human capital to other areas on the order of $100-$200 per capita in certain states located in development regions, such as West Virginia, Montana, and Oklahoma, proposals to expend perhaps an extra $3-$4 billion dollars a year in the nation's new development regions do not appear wildly out of line. Spread out over a total combined regional population of perhaps 40 million, this huge sum amounts to only $100 per capita annually. Viewed as an incremental amount over and above normal governmental expenditures, it can be seriously argued that areas which rear much of the nation's labor force at great expense and which demonstrably do not share fully in national prosperity deserve considerable assistance, if only to improve the quality of the migrants they ship out each year to work in other regions. It can be noted that increased educational expenditures alone could easily absorb much of this new money. Public school per-pupil allocations in Appalachia, the South, and Ozark states in some cases are $200-$300 below levels in progressive northern states.

This help-for-the-deprived argument runs into trouble in regions like New England, characterized by pockets of poverty rather than pockets of prosperity, as is the case in the other new regions. The migration argument is even tenuous in such states as Connecticut and Massachusetts, both relatively successful in exchanging young high school graduates for older executive and professional workers--although Maine and Vermont obviously share in some of the problems found in the poverty-ridden regions.

CONCLUSION: NEW REGIONS EQUAL NEW ARENAS

It is possible to discern the faint outlines of a national regional policy since the late 1960's, partly with the help of the Appalachian and New England bellwethers. It can be predicted that considerable attention will be given to problems of defining regional goals and objectives. Under the prodding of the U.S. Bureau of the Budget and the adoption of PPBS, we can anticipate embarrassing, intensive, and useful efforts in developing performance standards to measure the efficacy of various regional programs. Much time will be devoted to identifying that elusive element, the public interest, after the regions begin to tackle (or attempt to avoid) controversial, divisive issues. A sophisticated form of technical warfare will probably develop as planners, economists, sociologists, and other professionals are mobilized to present, defend, or attack alternative plans and programs.

Unlike the urban (i.e., metropolitan) regions that remain federally sponsored clients with weak political roots, the new regions were politicized from their inception; they will undoubtedly develop into active political arenas, creating an interesting fourth dimension in the present federal-state-local system. However, there are several foreseeable problems in playing this role effectively. The first involves organization. Three southern states, the Carolinas and Georgia, are members of two regions, Appalachia and the Coastal Plains. Other states with varied territory and characteristics are likely to be confronted by the same challenge. It is extremely difficult to allocate limited staff resources and gubernatorial attention to two or more regional organizations, aside from the work entailed in dealing with metropolitan areas, Economic Development Districts, and other units. Whatever the violence to economic logic, whole-state membership in a single region may be highly desirable. Also, Appalachia simply may be too large. Breaking that region into at least two smaller regions may be in the cards.

A second problem concerns the level of public interest in regional problems and the activities of an interstate organization. Both of the burning issues of the latter third of this century, violence at home and abroad, come under the jurisdiction of the federal government, while cities are on the firing line of domestic disorder.

Similarly, other critical problems like taxes, schools, and employment are in the federal and local domain although the state role is being enlarged. Regional organizations are left with significant functions in such matters as air and water pollution and open space issues that apparently arouse little sustained public interest, secondary roles in research, and roles as political intermediaries and financial conduits in human resource and transportation development.

As research, lobbying, and troubleshooting organizations, the big regions will have more than enough to keep them occupied for their first few years. Subsequently, the regional commissions may find themselves grappling with some of the basic, unresolved issues in our society.

One such issue involves "overdevelopment," the point at which a national policy decision must be made between permitting population, economic and other types of growth to continue to flow to one or two major centers as compared to deliberate policies of redirecting the stream of growth to other, smaller centers and new towns.[28] Many European nations have adopted this second alternative even at the risk of running counter to broad, deep, and historic trends toward centralization. The time may not be far off when the United States will no longer be able to avoid a similar confrontation between powerful, natural forces moving toward a continuing concentration and demands for effective action to stimulate decentralization. Beginning with research and policy recommendations and following through to attempts to influence national policy on resource allocation and development incentives, the big regions will surely be closely involved in this controversial issue.

The efficacy of the new regional agencies will depend to a great extent on the quality of their staff. A well-balanced, well-led research team, trusted by the states and federal agencies, can play an important part in broadening the focus of government operations and making programs more meaningful. The ability to perform sound, broad-gauge, action-oriented research rapidly can be a great strength. Conversely, a feebly led technical staff is not likely to have much impact.

There will obviously be a wide gulf between a high-powered regional-research team, the states that tend to lack impressive planning and research capacity, and the public whose attention is focused elsewhere and has insufficient understanding of the issues and complexities. Commissions are obviously faced by a great task in assisting the states to improve their capabilities and in helping to educate the public concerning their activities and decisions.

Finally, one can hazard the prophecy that interregional clashes are likely to provide additional stimulus for national planning. The new regions can conceivably play a significant role in recapturing some of the ground lost under the ideological onslaughts of the 1930's and early 1940's which killed the National Resources Planning Board.

On the whole, however, the regional commissions will open up new roles and new challenges for the existing cast of characters rather than bring in "new faces of 1970." Existing state and federal agencies will take on new tasks, and governors and senators will respond to new opportunities for achievement and maneuver. Finally, the road ahead is likely to be rocky: There seems to be a rule of governmental, academic, and military bureaucracy that each new coordinative mechanism further complicates the difficulties of coordination. It has been wisely said that a coordinator is a man who sits between two expediters. A remarkable combination of managerial and planning talent will be required to measure up to the challenges generated by the new regionalism. Despite Appalachia's reputation as a habitat for political sharks, the Appalachian regional commission has been ably commanded and staffed. There are disquieting signs of trouble in some of the newer EDA regions which seem to be much weaker in terms of leadership and technical personnel. It appears that some key positions have been used to repay minor political debts and are occupied by amiable and personable lightweights lacking in both background and in educability.

One obstacle will probably be removed in fairly short order: The new regions will all follow Appalachia's lead in opting for independent status. Any attempt to integrate interagency programs on a comprehensive basis is doomed, if it is mounted by an organizational component of a weak federal agency. The departure of regional commissions out of EDA's embrace may have implications for model cities in which HUD-sponsored organizations will attempt to reshape programs operated by local police departments, school boards, vocational-education boards, and other agencies.

In conclusion, one thing we can count on in the future is that, while Americans commemorate the Revolution and the writing of the Constitution, they will not revolutionize their governmental structure or discard the Constitution for a new one. The states will have the same boundaries in 1988 as they now have. But on the most sophisticated maps there will be a new feature--regions reaching across state lines, united by common economic and social interests. The experiences of TVA, Appalachia, and the New England region all point to this conclusion.

NOTES TO CHAPTER 12

1. U.S. Congress, Public Law 89-4, "Appalachian Regional Development Act of 1965," 89th Cong., 1st Sess., March 9, 1965.

2. See National Resources Planning Board, *Security, Work and Relief Policies,* a report of the Committee on Long-Range Work and Relief Policies, (Washington, D.C.: U.S. Government Printing Office, 1942). The cutover region (Upper Great Lakes) boundaries are similar to those delineated in the NRPB research, but the Appalachian and other EDA regions are substantially different.

3. See John Friedmann, "Regional Planning as a Field of Study," *Journal of the American Institute of Planners,* XXIX (August, 1963); and his "The Concept of a Planning Region--The Evolution of an Idea in the United States," *Land Economics,* February, 1956. See also Howard W. Odum and Harry Estill Moore, *American Regionalism* (New York: Henry Holt and Co., 1938).

4. Friedmann, *op. cit.,* "Regional Planning as a Field of Study," p. 63.

5. The example of the Tennessee Valley was frequently cited in the Senate and House hearings on 1965 EDA legislation. See *Hearings* before the Committee on Public Works (Senate) and Committee on Public Works (House of Representatives), "Public Works and Economic Development Act of 1965," 89th Cong., 1st Sess., 1965.

6. U.S. Economic Development Administration, *Economic Development* (Washington, D.C.: U.S. Government Printing Office, February, 1968), p. 3.

7. Philip Selznick, *TVA and the Grass Roots* (Berkeley: University of California Press, 1949).

8. *The New York Times,* March 26, 1967, p. 14. A new organization, The Congress for Appalachian Development, approved the summoning of an "Appalachian Peoples Congress" in the summer of 1967 to rally support for a new plan to transfer ownership of control over company-owned coal resources to a new authority modeled on the Tennessee Valley Authority.

9. David A. Grossman and Melvin R. Levin, "The Appalachian Region: A National Problem Area," *Land Economics,* May, 1961, p. 140.

10. Melvin R. Levin, *The Depressed Area: A Study of Southern Illinois* (Unpublished Ph.D. Dissertation, University of Chicago, 1956).

11. The ABC system refers to highways financed on a 50-50 basis by the federal and state governments. The smaller, generally higher quality, interstate system is 90 per cent financed by the federal government.

12. U.S., A Report by the President's Appalachian Regional Commission, *Appalachia* (Washington, D.C.: U.S. Government Printing Office, 1964).

13. The Appalachian Regional Development Commission, *Executive Director's Semi-Annual Report,* Table, "Status of Program Funds Through Fiscal Year 1967," Washington, July 1--December 31, 1966.

14. Charles McKinley, "The Valley Authority and Its Alternatives," *American Political Science Review,* September, 1950; included as Chap. 28 in John Friedmann and William Alonso, *Regional Development and Planning: A Reader* (Cambridge, Mass.: M.I.T. Press, 1964), p. 556.

15. An opening salvo in this campaign was fired by Senator Robert F. Kennedy. See Ben A. Franklin, "Kennedy Calls Antipoverty Program a Failure," *The New York Times,* February 15, 1968, p. 1.

16. Litton Industries, *Preliminary Analysis for Economic Development Plan for the Appalachian Region,* Prepared for the Area Redevelopment Administration (Washington, D.C.: Appalachian Regional Commission, 1965), pp. 259-60.

17. A proposal for creating new towns in eastern Kentucky had been recommended in 1960. See University of Kentucky, Department of Architecture, "A Case Study Located in Eastern Kentucky," *New Towns: A Proposal for the Appalachian Region* (Lexington: University of Kentucky, 1960). The proposal was stimulated by Grady Clay, editor of *Landscape Architecture* magazine, who served on the advisory committee.

18. *Executive Director's Semi-Annual Report, op. cit.,* Letter of Transmittal, Ralph R. Widner, Executive Director.

19. *Hearings, op. cit.*, see statements of Dr. John Peterson, University of Arkansas, pp. 226-27.

20. U.S. Subcommittee on Intergovernmental Relations of the Senate Committee on Government Operations, *Federal Expenditures to States and Regions* (Washington, D.C.: U.S. Government Printing Office, June, 1966), p. 6.

21. *Ibid.*, Table C-6, p. 130.

22. "Geographic Distribution of Funds for Research and Development, 1963," *Reviews of Data on Science Resources* (Washington, D.C.: National Science Foundation, August, 1965).

23. U.S. Bureau of the Census, *Statistical Abstract of the United States* (Washington, D.C.: U.S. Government Printing Office, 1966), Table No. 431, p. 305. The average per-case pyament for December, 1965, in Massachusetts was $74 vs. $36 in West Virginia.

24. Boston University, Area Development Center, "A Brief in Support of the Designation of New England as an Economic Development Region," unpublished manuscript, 1965.

25. *Hearings, op. cit.*, statement by Carl F. Kraenzel, Department of Agricultural Economics and Rural Sociology, Montana State College, p. 192.

26. As a result of net immigration, as noted in Table 8, in the U.S., the number of persons aged 15-19 in 1950 was 2 per cent smaller than the number aged 25-29 in 1960. In the nation, the death rate per 1,000 population between ages 15 and 29 ranges between 0.6 per cent at age 15 and 1.3 per cent at age 29. *Statistical Abstract of the United States, 1965, op. cit.*, Table 60.

27. These calculations are based on data prepared by Carl F. Kraenzel, Department of Agricultural Economics and Rural Sociology, Montana State College, as presented in Exhibit VIII, *Hearings, op. cit.*, p. 192. Kraenzel's figures are based on data developed by James D. Turner and Theodore Schultz. Schultz estimates the cost through completion of high school at $19,600, and $32,800 through four years of college. These are inclusive of foregone earnings in high school and college. See Theodore Schultz, "Investment in Human Capital," *American Economic Review*, March, 1961; his "Capital Formation in Education," *Journal of Political Economy*, December, 1960; and his "Education and Economic Growth," *1961 Yearbook of the National Society for the Study of Education* (Chicago: National Society for the Study of Education, 5835 Kimbark Avenue), Chapter 3.

28. See Myles Wright, "Regional Development: Problems and Lines of Advance in Europe," reprinted in H. Wentworth Eldredge (ed.), *Taming*

Megalopolis, Vol. II (Garden City: Anchor Books--Doubleday and Co., Inc., 1967), pp. 1119-1142.

CHAPTER **13** SUMMING UP:
ONE SMALL
CANDLE?

BACKGROUND INFORMATION

The preceding chapters have constituted a guided tour around some of the perimeters of the great society. As the discussion of policies and programs has suggested, there has been no shortage of new ideas to deal with old problems. The trouble is that bold, imaginative concepts call for remarkable people to translate dreams into reality, and this is precisely where cutting edges of the great society have become dulled and chipped. PPBS, the poverty program, metropolitan area planning, Economic Development Districts, and the big regions not only require first-quality staff at the top but also competent staff in the middle and lower echelons. While not many additionally trained people are required in global terms--perhaps only five thousand--we simply do not have them. This may neither be the first nor the last time in history that noble concepts and imaginative plans were degraded by faulty execution, but there is something rather odd in the spectacle of major programs in a major nation faltering for want of a few thousand trained professionals.

There are other difficulties beyond the people shortage: Events moved so fast in the 1960's that ideas and assumptions could become obsolete in a matter of a few years. On the whole, our programs tend to be mood pieces reflecting a transient consensus. They may crystallize years of awakening and discussion, but the actual legislation is essentially a response geared to handle a current crisis. A significant and unexpected trend like the decline in unemployment in redevelopment areas calls for a rethinking of criteria for eligibility for continued federal aid. The Black Power movement in the central cities has led to new thinking on the future of the ghettos, and prospective Negro political domination of many central cities will undoubtedly render metropolitan government more popular among suburbanites who scorned the idea in past years. On the other hand, to the surprise of some within and without the federal agencies, the states are beginning to react strongly against the metropolitan ministates that are being created by federal fiat; contrary to early, sanguine hopes, the poverty program has been in a continuing condition of bloody plasticity. Consequently, one sensed less of an air of finality about government programs in the mid-1960's. Modesty and humility were less uncommon virtues than in past eras of self-righteous moralizing.

271

This chastened outlook is due to a variety of exogenous forces, not the least of which is a forceful, albeit unsystematic battering from Congress and the press. But internal pressures are also at work in this direction. PPBS, a delightful concept to the professional administrator, is revealing in a systematic fashion that many programs rest on brittle, terra-cotta foundations, partly because of the persisting talent shortage but also because we have discovered, despite all our research, that we know little about many basic aspects of our society. Government agencies are being exposed to a pitiless analysis that shows just how deep is our ignorance about the processes of economic development, manpower training, education and health programs, and, indeed, in what ways our various efforts affect client groups and the larger society. We are equally feeble in the vital field of projections; planning ahead is often an exercise in poor judgment. Even that basic building block for long-range plans, population forecasting, has repeatedly been shown to be the most inexact of sciences.

New approaches like PPBS are not likely to eliminate uncertainty over ends, means, goals, and consequences. In fact, it is much more probable that PPBS will be as vulnerable as cost benefit to charges that its basic assumptions are mostly unproved, that it can work only by screening out most of the real world, and that it can easily be manipulated to yield any desired result.

In a way, a series of chapters of this character functions as a dual Rorschach Test and reveals as much about the outlook of the commentator as about the programs he studies and dissects. The author pleads guilty to having begun with a mild skepticism that has been further strengthened by his research. It appears to him that bureaucracies find it difficult to reshape their policies without an externally originated galvanic shock and that their perceptions seem limited to the acquisition of sanctioned, generally favorable information which reaches headquarters through approved channels.

Insulated Agencies

This unwillingness or perhaps incapacity to assimilate embarrassing facts pointing to program weaknesses probably accounts for agency slowness in responding to criticisms of urban renewal programs and other domestic endeavors. Bureaucracy's capacity for self-delusion seems limitless, and, unfortunately is far from unknown in other, more dangerous areas. The second-ranking embassy official in South Vietnam in the early 1960's wrote:

> The root of the problem was the fact that much of what the newsmen took to be lies was exactly what the U.S. Mission genuinely believed, and was reporting to Washington. Events were to prove that the Mission itself was unaware of how badly the war was going, operating in a world of illusion. Our feud with the newsmen was an angry symptom of bureaucratic sickness.[1]

The inability of the bureaucracies to assess the impact of their programs and to make appropriate, timely adjustments related in part to an obvious unwillingness to hear bad news. This deficiency is closely related to a built-in tendency to exaggerate successes--each bureaucrat passes reports upward that cast his operation in a rosy light. Even a shaky program, crumbling around the edges, is bathed in radiance by the time the successive layers of bureaucracy have done their work, partly as a justification for enlarged appropriations. Often there is also a professional reluctance to expose dirty linen to public view. Further, there is a tendency for programs to be captured by educators, generals, highway engineers, physicians, welfare workers, and other professionals. This leads to situations in which criticisms from laymen (i.e., nonmembers) are usually resented as ignorant meddling, events are interpreted, problems are screened, and solutions are circumscribed by the narrow scope of professional ideology and practice.

Smith Simpson, in his trenchant examination of the ills of the Department of State, lays much of the blame on the inertness and incapacity of the "pyramidal mass" and on the built-in resistance to even the best-intentioned criticism. During most of the career officer's working life:

> He has been excessively bothered by suggestions of better policies and performance, and has joined with his colleagues in attributing criticism from without to obtuseness and general myopia and criticism from within to unspeakable treachery. So keenly resented has criticism been over the years that its points have been rarely deemed worthy of serious consideration and its factual validity has been generally dismissed disdainfully without examination.[2]

The failure to receive accurate information exacerbates inherent tendencies toward insulating top officials from the outside world. Deeply involved in day-to-day activities and minor crises, living in a closed, two-dimensional world of internal operations and interagency relations, the upper-echelon executive is barraged by huge, undigestible amounts of conflicting information; consequently, his span of attention for upsetting criticism tends to be abbreviated. The world, however, is not hermetically sealed, and client and legislative feedback often exercises a salutary influence in adding flesh to this skeletonized, abstract environment. But outbursts by Congress and the pickets and the press are symptoms of the disease rather than a remedy.

Anthony Downs[3] discusses a distortion arising from "noise" and semiautonomous, hierarchial screening processes inherent in bureaucracies as large quantities of program information are received, condensed, and transmitted up the hierarchy. He recommends a number of antidistortion methods that may be used by top executives to arrive at an accurate assessment of the situation, including deliberate injection of counter biases, reduction in the number of middlemen filters, introduction of intra-agency competition to provide overlapping information, and use of out-of-agency sources.

The fact is that the programs have grown so vast and so complex as to defy the casual investigation, the sporadic outbreak, and the one-shot committee grilling. The trend toward comprehensiveness in planning, toward creation of Byzantine interagency arrangements, and toward proliferation of agency guidelines and regulations has led to a situation in which many programs have grown harder to comprehend, much less to control. There are masses of data and piles of reports, but basic questions involving the effectiveness of enormous, expensive programs go unanswered. Moreover, over and above internal agency problems, any serious attempts at program evaluation run the danger of falling afoul of the interstices between agency responsibilities. It has become terribly difficult to assign blame and credit to particular agencies and agency components when responsibilities are fragmented, causes and effects are imperfectly understood, and values and goals are conflicting and/or poorly articulated.

Arthur Schlesinger's version of the "pyramidal mass" is the "permanent government." In his opinion, it represents an awesome barrier to executive control over a mammoth establishment. President Kennedy's methods of manipulating this leviathan included the appointment of his own trusted, highly efficient executives to head key agencies and a practice of shaking up the departments through direct, out-of-channels contact with lower echelons. Both approaches have their limitations: The bureaucracy does not take kindly to winds of change:

> though a valuable reservoir of intelligence and experience as well as a valuable guarantee against presidential government's going off the tracks, the permanent government remained in bulk a force against innovation with an inexhaustible capacity to dilute, delay and obstruct presidential purpose. Only so many fights were possible with the permanent government. The fighters--one saw this happen to Richard Goodwin when he went over to the State Department--were gradually weakened, cut off, surrounded and shot down, as if from ambush, by the bureaucracy and its anti-New Frontier allies in Congress and the press. At the start we had all felt free to "meddle" when we thought that we had a good idea or someone else a poor one. But, as the ice began to form again over the government, freewheeling became increasingly difficult and dangerous.[4]

Some help for the chief executive with the stumbling agency may be available if continuing, inhouse program analysis can be successfully institutionalized. PPBS and related techniques hold considerable promise, at long last, that basic questions will be asked about program objectives, inputs, and consequences. Getting defensible answers is, of course, another matter. At the end of the road, questioning and research may lead not to the solution of basic problems but simply to their being better understood. Moreover, because goals are elusive and the measurement techniques are primitive, PPBS also raises less attractive possibilities. It may generate endless turmoil or bitter technical disputes over the value judgments and techniques that provide yardsticks for performance measurements. There is much room for argument between agency staff, legislative investigators, and advocate technicians to plead their respective cause in assigning priorities and formulating criteria for measurement of program impact.

The fact that an increasing number of clever people inside and outside the agencies will be embroiled in technical guerrila warfare in disputes over means and ends is by no means an alarming prospect. A little violence is needed to break through the hardened surface that seals off agencies from the sulfurous but bracing atmosphere of the outside world. Perhaps, at some later stage, much of the new look can be made routine and tucked away in standard manuals suitable for technicians of modest abilities. This is not the case at present, either at the federal level or in the states and localities.

The Prime Prerequisite: Staff Capability

One primary thrust in this work has been to underscore the need for qualified staff at all levels of government, but, especially, in the states and localities. The analogy between the states and underdeveloped foreign nations, neither properly equipped to run their own affairs efficiently nor to absorb outside assistance, is perhaps harsh. It will certainly be disputed by those fortunate persons whose experience has brought them into contact with the minority of progressive states and cities in the United States.

There are, of course, compensating benefits that offset administrative deficiencies at the state and local levels. Granting the weaknesses of extreme decentralization during the 1830's, Alexis de Toqueville maintained that Americans derive political advantages from localism, from smallish governments organized on a human scale. Many will argue that a little anarchy has its benefits and that stimulating local initiative at the cost of some corruption, some unfairness to minorities, and substantial inefficiency is a price worth paying. The tendency to develop an abundance of private associations and to rely on the powers of the ordinary citizen, alone and in combination, has accounted for much of the strength, growth, character, and stability of the nation. De Toqueville's comments on the consequences of centralization could well be taken as a text by those who wish to see the states and localities stronger, more capable of asserting rights and assuming responsibilities.

> The partisans of centralization in Europe are wont to maintain that the government can administer the affairs of each locality better than the citizens can do it for themselves. This may be true when the central power is enlightened and the local authorities are ignorant; when it is alert and they are slow; when it is accustomed to act and they to obey. Indeed, it is evident that this double tendency must augment with the increase of centralization, and that the readiness of the one and the incapacity of the others must become more and more prominent. . . . However enlightened and skillful a central power may be, it cannot

of itself embrace all the details of the life of a great nation. Such vigilance exceeds the powers of man. And when it attempts unaided to create and set in motion so many complicated springs, it must submit to a very imperfect result or exhaust itself in bootless efforts.[5]

De Toqueville's mistrust of powerful central government may have had its origins in royal and imperial France, but in the late 1960's, one sensed a growing body of opinion in the United States that had tasted the fruit of the federal tree and found it bitter. Interestingly enough, the critics include many liberals who have become disenchanted with the cyclical pattern characteristic of a number of promising programs--innovation degenerating into suspended animation. Daniel Moynihan's gloomy chronology portrays this sentiment vividly.

the pattern persists: the bright new idea, the new agency, the White House swearing in of the first agency head followed by a shaky beginning, the departure eighteen months later of the first head to be replaced by his deputy, the gradual slipping out of sight, a Budget Bureau reorganization, name change, a new head, this time from the civil service, and slow obscurity covers all.[6]

Some social scientists, despairing of efforts to improve sprawling bureaucracies, suggest that the answer may lie in dismantling the complex apparatus and shifting the primary emphasis to government-to-people programs like social security. Their recommendations include guaranteed annual incomes, rather than poverty or housing programs, and family tuition allowances to permit parents to send their children to private schools. There are also increasing numbers of suggestions aimed at turning over to private enterprise the operation of some government functions and responsibilities in attacking unsolved social problems. This can be achieved in a number of ways, including subcontracts to private corporations, as is the case with Job Corps camps, Rand Corporation research for the Air Force, and through government guarantees and incentives, as with the quasi-private corporations being formed to undertake new housing and economic development programs in big-city ghettos. If supplements were adopted for family income, some of the elaborate bureaucratic apparatus of poverty, urban and welfare programs would be eliminated and replaced by government checks for the poor, covering the difference between their present income and some desirable income level. The assault on the federal bureaucracy would also include a final weapon--block grants to local governments, because it is argued, de Toqueville style, that if government must do the job, it is preferable to assign the task to localities and possibly to states.

Dangers of Decentralization

In some ways, it is strange that so much recent criticism has focused on relatively better manned federal bureaucracies rather than on states and cities,

despite the latters' well-documented weaknesses. This is evidenced in the growing sentiment for the federal government to distribute no-strings-attached grants
to replace the present complex structure of 170 federal grant-in-aid programs to
state and local governments.

While it is difficult to quarrel with the concept of individual and family
allowances or with a wider use of corporate skills and organization, the trouble
with block grants to lower-echelon governments as a method of curing the ills
of the large federal bureaucracies is that state and local bureaucracies may be
smaller, but they are also much more feeble. One not only finds at least a similar fog of confusion in program impacts and conflicting ends and means in state
and city government but also much less in the way of average competence in
dealing with the confusion. The current dismal situation is succinctly stated by
Senator Edmund S. Muskie, who concluded:

> The primary need of state and local governments is to attract
> and retain quality personnel. . . . Unfavorable working environ-
> ments and inadequate personnel systems discourage both pros-
> pective employees and careerists. Too often, administrative
> personnel are given assignments without clear objectives, are
> frustrated by complicated intergovernmental structures, and find
> that the public holds them in low esteem. Compensation is sub-
> stantially below industry standards. Career development pro-
> grams, including opportunities for job mobility, in-service train-
> ing and promotions are minimal except in some of the larger
> jurisdictions. Lack of effective merit systems permits the loading
> of agencies with incompetent, uninspiring and often indifferent
> personnel. Responsible administrators are often frustrated by
> inflexible rules and regulations dictating whom they may hire;
> whom, when, and how they shall promote; and whether, if at
> all, they may discipline or fire the incompetent or insubor-
> dinate.[7]

Admittedly, the talent problem is not confined to state and local agencies. As one observer indicates with respect to the federal government:

> The supply of able, experienced executives is not increasing
> as fast as the number of problems being addressed by public
> policy. . . . Everywhere, except in government, it seems the
> scarcity of talent is accepted as a fact of life. . . . The govern-
> ment--at least publicly--seems to act as if the supply of able
> executives were infinitely elastic, though people setting up new
> agencies will often admit privately that they are so frustrated
> and appalled by the shortage of talent that the only wonder is
> why disaster is so long in coming. . . . "Talent is scarcer than
> money" should be the motto of the Budget Bureau.[8]

Unfortunately, one can see only painfully slow progress even at the federal level in enlarging the supply of talent. And so far as state and local governments are concerned, unless their currently limited attractions for professionals can somehow be augmented, there seems to be little hope of achieving a more effective federalism. All their responsiveness and closeness to the voter, all their potential for experimentation and innovation will be of little use unless these governments can be ably staffed.

At best, we probably can look forward to a decade of federal leadership with other governments limping along in the rear, responding as well as they can to federal initiatives and incentives. The handful of states and localities that have demonstrated significant capabilities will continue to complain of confinement to program straitjackets apparently designed for potentially dangerous criminals and cretins. Short of a near revolution in staffing patterns, however, it is hard to see how program guidelines can be made sufficiently flexible to combine discretionary block grants for Wisconsin, with tightly supervised grants-in-aid for Mississippi.

To summarize, a working system of federalism requires a realistic ability to diffuse power. At present, most states and localities, because of their lack of competent staff, are having more than enough trouble in keeping abreast of existing programs, let alone taking on new responsibilities. To some extent, the problem can be bypassed by placing increasing emphasis on personal choice through direct cash grants to individuals. The extent to which a combination of federal cash transmitted through government-to-people programs and massive injections of private enterprise in helping to attack urban problems can be combined to dehydrate government bureaucracy has yet to be tested. Nevertheless this concept seems to be winning a surprising number of followers all across the political spectrum. If, however, it is conceded that this approach has its unspecified but definite limits, we are still left with the problem of weak states and weak localities.

What may be needed is some method of injecting more intelligence into state and local government on a nationwide, continuing basis, through infusions of new staff and consulting capabilities. The method should include, if possible, a means of upgrading the cultural and physical environment and of establishing higher standards of excellence. There should be direct economic gains for the local economy and at least the possibility of generating additional economic growth. Hopefully, no great increase in the size of government bureaucracy should be required, and there should be considerable room for experimentation and innovation.

Obviously, this is a tall order, and perhaps the best we can do is to meet most, if not all, of the criteria. The answer, so far as one is available, seems to lie in exploiting the latent possibilities of the vast network of public and private universities, colleges, and community colleges that presently exist in state capitals and in many other localities, including the distressed areas.

THE UNIVERSITIES AND THE FUTURE OF FEDERALISM

It is almost a cliche to remark that the university is assuming a pivotal position in economic development. The growing emphasis on resource allocation and priorities now primarily involves human resources; concentrations of scientific ability and the migration of professional and technical personnel have in recent years deservedly received more attention than proximity to coal or iron ore as key economic determinants. One of the major roles of the university is this direct and indirect spillover of economic vitality into its surrounding area. This role involves assemblage of a creditable, sizable faculty, close relations with the corporate and government worlds through off-campus research activities, and training of bright young people. In this manner, dozens of colleges and universities have blossomed into major components of their area economy.

This potential economic role is one reason for the recommended expansion of higher educational facilities in state capitals, in distressed areas, and, for that matter, in the small and medium-sized cities throughout much of the nation.

The nation's major metropolitan areas doubtless will continue to skim off the cream of the backwoods talent, although, doubtless, a national manpower and migration policy to encourage more bright people to locate in small cities and distressed areas would be helpful. It does appear, however, that one way of attacking the problem is to concentrate on developing the capabilities of local universities and colleges as a critical point in strengthening economic and cultural development and the injection of nationally recognized professional standards in lagging areas. Unless action of this type is pursued, what we seem to be headed for is an era of cultural and economic polarization, in which a relatively few metropolitan areas (and a few balmy Riviera recreation areas along the coasts)[9] wind up with brain-oriented activities, and the remainder of the nation is relegated to routine, colonial type operations, supervised by a thin layer of imported transients.

State and local governments can profitably be viewed as underdeveloped territories that lack the technical capacities and continuing, institutional structures to keep abreast of advanced areas. The problem of standards is crucial because the talent drain has acted to reinforce tendencies toward parochialism. It may be suggested that many of the small institutions could be adopted by or otherwise integrated within a high quality state system or, alternatively, could simply develop symbiotic relations with first rank, out-of-area institutions. This might well embrace arrangements for exchange of faculty, student transfers, and graduate study. In particular, this technique might help in augmenting the leadership stratum in redevelopment areas; many of them have seen generation after generation of their bright young men depart in search of economic opportunity and wider horizons.

The university can also play a useful role in improving the general quality of its environment in several ways. Normally, a higher educational institution of any size represents a significant environmental factor. It creates an oasis attractive to outside talent; professors and their wives become involved in local schools, planning boards, and other civic endeavors. There is also a bread-and-butter contribution to the local economy that is of special interest to redevelopment areas. The university is a substantial source of jobs, retail and service sales, and construction activity. Moreover, there is always the prospect that professorial research and related attractions will bloom into smaller-scale versions of the Cambridge-Route 128 complex associated with M.I.T. and other Boston area institutions. In short, a growing university can make depressing areas reasonably attractive to outside talent. This is extremely important because only to a degree does the yawning gulf in bureaucratic quality between the federal establishment and most state and local agencies relate to differential agency pay scales, recruitment policies, and career opportunities.

Environmental factors tend to be overlooked in discussions of remedial measures. With some remarkable exceptions like Madison, Wisconsin, Boston, and Minneapolis, state capitals and many cities are grim, intellectually barren places, without major universities or other attractions that would render them habitable to high-quality professional staff. The same observation is even more applicable to redevelopment areas. A national policy aimed at strengthening state and local government must include some attention to upgrading their qualitative social and cultural aspects because of the increasingly migratory propensity of talent. In the 1960's, a good professional could shop around for a community that offered much more than simply a paying job. Obviously, his preferences pose difficult problems because not much can be done to moderate the magnetic attractions of the larger metropolitan areas on the nation's periphery or the California or Florida coastal plains. Fortunately, much can be achieved in enhancing the attractiveness of the enormous number of territories that are being consistently bypassed by first-quality people. A key role in this endeavor clearly belongs to the local colleges and universities. For example, one of their special, and thus far, largely unexploited potentials is the luring of otherwise unapproachable public officials by offering them part-time faculty appointments. This can be an extremely powerful incentive; American professional men seem to be divided into two broad categories, the professors, and the remainder, who apparently yearn for faculty status.

The foregoing is not to suggest that the university no longer retains a primary role as an educational institution. Here, too, there is a special potential that is only beginning to be realized, namely, training large numbers of practitioners for service with state and local government and other area organizations. Provided the danger of inbreeding can be avoided, the natural ties of the student to his university environment can help an area meet its needs for trained professionals. It need hardly be said, however, that supply must be matched by demand. As has been indicated at some length, the townie-run states and localities have not been overly hospitable to university intellectuals in past years.

Unless this situation changes and the states and localities become more attractive, there is reason to suppose that, as in past years, a diploma from a local university for ambitious youth will continue to serve as a passport for migration to a more promising area.

The same observation is equally valid for the professors. Professors have traditionally played a number of roles in government. They are a potential source of new bureaucratic appointments, adornments for administrations anxious to show off to the intelligentsia, and a problem-solving lifeline for the permanent staff that must devote virtually all of its time to wrestling with routine agency functions. The university can play significant roles as a repository of consulting talent in helping to solve urgent problems and in continuing basic inquiries into fundamental governmental maladies. If the academicians are not employed by state and local governments in applied and basic research and advisory capacities, outstanding professorial talent will continue to commute to Washington. Under these circumstances, the gap between the federal establishment and the neglected lower echelons of government will remain.

THE UNIVERSITIES AND THE EVALUATION
OF GOVERNMENT PROGRAMS

As has been suggested, one of the more depressing patterns of the past few decades is the recurrence of troublesome situations in which skilled newspapermen know much more about the impact of government programs than bureaucrats who run them. Time and again, there have been foreign and domestic debacles in which the failure of an agency's hierarchical structure to transmit accurate information to the decision-makers was a significant factor. If this distortion is an inherent defect of bureaucracy, as it appears to be, the question arises as to possible methods of securing valid intelligence. A third role for the university might be found in this area.

Given the current state of affluence in available research funds and the capacities and orientation of most academicians, it is probable that this latter function--hired men for the agency--will continue to be the principal relationship between government and the professors. This is a useful role, but if the government agency's weak evaluative potential and its early-warning radar screen are to be strengthened, it is fairly clear that something more is required.

One approach to this problem is suggested by Clark Kerr in his proposal for a system of urban-grant universities in large cities that would parallel the traditional pattern of land-grant colleges.[10] These universities would, in Kerr's view, concentrate on urban-slum problems and assume major responsibilities for such functions as public-school systems, medical, welfare, and public-safety needs, and planning. This would involve faculty in "grubby, practical issues" far removed from the posture as critical observers of the urban scene that has been adopted by many academicians.

Robert Wood has classified two principal types of professorial approaches to urban problems as a debate among "Cassandras and the Urban Standpatters--between those who see the city as beyond redemption and those who feel it needs none."[11]   The Rorschach factor is very much in evidence among observers of the urban scene. One can be rather cheery about a society that has made enormous progress in providing most of its citizens with a remarkable standard of affluence and culture, in which a rough but effective system of political and economic priorities operates to offer most of the citizenry comfortable, pleasant lives. Or one can just as easily take the opposite tack and concentrate on unsolved and perhaps insoluble problems of the slums, the Negroes, and foreign affairs, to conclude that the nation is gravely and perhaps fatally afflicted.

What Wood failed to mention is that although each school of intellectuals may be bitterly opposed on substantive issues, they are united in blasting government agencies. Whether hawkish or dovish on matters of policy, they are united in agreement that current programs are faulty in conception, weak in administration, and barren of favorable consequences. Much of the growing body of political science literature concerns deficiencies in government programs, and many of the studies tend to be scathing denunciations. The impact of these publications on government agencies can be likened to a blowtorch that burns off the outer layers of insulated bureaucratic complacency. Because the government agency often resembles the legendary army mule whose attention could not be gained until he was whacked with a baseball bat, past experience indicates that there is a role for forceful academicians who awaken agency interest in an irritating and usually unappreciated manner.

This is, however, a brutal, costly, ex post facto way of going about the business of program evaluation and revision. What seems to be needed is preventative medicine. One approach is the pilot study that tests a program on a small scale before it becomes national policy. This technique has its advantages, although small, carefully planned pilots have a strange propensity to fly while their larger and more expensive successors remain earthbound. Regardless of whether this trial-balloon method is used, there appears to be a place for friendly academics, or more accurately, constructive professorial evaluators. Outside academicians can be employed by central headquarters, by foundations, or by publishers, to examine agency programs. The question is: Can the agencies act on information that is not wrapped around a baseball bat? The answer must necessarily be tentative, although some agencies have certainly arrived at the state of maturity and competence where friendly critics are welcomed instead of lacerated. The intelligent agency can help to establish a continuing, institutionalized critique, a mechanism that draws on the academic community to act as a combined, distant, early-warning system, an evaluative laboratory, and an idea factory. Certain federal agencies, including the Department of Defense and the Department of Housing and Urban Development, have already made some progress in this direction. Whether state and local governments can follow suit is another matter, but even there the ground has been broken by a few of the more sophisticated agencies.

It should be made clear that state and local governments are not wholly responsible for neglecting near-at-hand academic resources; the available institutions are not presently organized to provide substantial, usable assistance. There are several ways in which this deficiency can be corrected. The universities can probably enlarge their role as agency critics through improved consultation arrangements, particularly by encouraging academic departments to crossbreed with government officials. The "in-and-outer," as Richard Neustadt terms him, the academic who from time to time serves in government and the executive who occasionally serves on the university faculty, is fairly common at the upper echelon of the federal establishment. What is needed is a lot more of this mutual pollenization at other government levels.

This central focus can be developed under a variety of titles--an urban-studies center, an urban-extension program,[12] a metrocenter, or an urban observatory. The important ingredient is a concentration of productive, pragmatic talent in the university that shares a common outlook and retains a noble and unshakable faith in the perfectability of government, whatever evidence to the contrary.

In summary, the university comes about as close as any existing institution to meeting the critical needs of underdeveloped states and localities. The reshaping of the physical environment, narrowing of the cultural gap, training administrators and technical staff, and providing a continuing, local professional consulting resource will become a major responsibility for the universities and colleges, or the outlook for creative federalism is likely to be on the dim side.

NOTES TO CHAPTER 13

1. John Mecklin, *Mission in Torment* (New York: Doubleday, 1965), pp. 100-101.

2. Smith Simpson, *Anatomy of the State Department* (Boston: Houghton Mifflin Co., 1967), p. 9.

3. Anthony Downs, *Inside Bureaucracy* (Boston: Little, Brown and Company, 1967); see his "Communications Bureaus," pp. 112-31 and "The Fragmentalized Perception of Large Organizations," pp. 188-99.

4. Arthur Schlesinger, *A Thousand Days: John F. Kennedy in the White House* (Boston: Houghton Mifflin Co., 1965), p. 683.

5. Alexis de Toqueville, *Democracy in America*, Vol. I (New York: Vintage Books, 1954), pp. 93-94.

6. Daniel P. Moynihan, "You Can't Run the Nation from Washington," *Boston Globe*, October 28, 1967, p. 43.

7. Senator Edmund S. Muskie, "The Challenge of Creative Federalism," *Congressional Record*, March 25, 1966. See also: Committee for Economic Development, *Modernizing State Government* (New York: Committee for Economic Development, July, 1967); and Terry Sanford, *Storm Over the States* (New York: McGraw-Hill Book Co., 1967). Governor Sanford points to danger from another quarter: overprofessionalization in which health, welfare, education, and other agencies become closed agencies run by and for professional cliques and shielded from "the hand and eye of the public."

8. James Q. Wilson, "The Bureaucracy Problem," *The Public Interest*, No. 6 (Winter, 1967), 3-9.

9. See Jean Gottmann, "The Rising Demand for Urban Amenities," in Sam Bass Warner (ed.), *Planning for a Nation of Cities* (Cambridge, Mass.: M.I.T. Press, 1966).

10. Fred M. Hechinger, "Call for the 'Urban-Grant' College," *The New York Times*, October 22, 1967, p. 73.

11. Robert Wood, "Government and the Intellectual: The Necessary Alliance for Effective Action to Meet Urban Needs," *The Annals*, issue entitled *New Scientific Approaches*, Vol. 371, May, 1967.

12. There is considerable literature on this subject. See, in addition to the Hechinger article, *op. cit.*, Kirk R. Petshek, "A New Role for City Universities--Urban Extension Programs," *Journal of the American Institute of Planners*, November, 1964; Senator Abraham Ribicoff, "The Competent City: An Action Program for Urban America," *Congressional Record*, 89th Cong., 1st Sess., January 23, 1967; J. Martin Klotsche, *The Urban University and the Future of our Cities* (New York: Harper and Row, 1966).

SELECTED BIBLIOGRAPHY

BOOKS

Abrams, Richard M. *Conservatism in a Progressive Era: Massachusetts Politics, 1900-1912.* Cambridge, Mass.: Harvard University Press, 1964.

Adams, James Truslow. "The Historical Background," in *New England's Prospect: 1933.* Edited by J. T. Adams *et al.* New York: Little, Brown and Company, 1931.

Adrian, Charles R. "Metropology and the Planner," *Planning 1962.* Chicago: American Society of Planning Officials, 1962.

Altshuler, Alan A. *The City Planning Process, A Political Analysis.* Ithaca, N.Y.: Cornell University Press, 1965.

American Society of Planning Officials. *Nursing Homes.* (Information Report Number 185.) Chicago: American Society of Planning Officials, 1964.

Banfield, Edward C. *Political Influence.* Glencoe, Ill.: The Free Press, 1961.

_____, and Wilson, James Q. *City Politics.* Cambridge, Mass.: Harvard University Press and M.I.T. Press, 1963.

Bauer, Raymond A. (ed.). *Social Indicators.* Cambridge, Mass: M.I.T. Press, 1966.

Boston Chamber of Commerce. *New England, What It Is and What It Is To Be.* Edited by George French. Cambridge, Mass.: University Printing Press, 1911.

Brunner, John. *Squares of the City.* New York: Ballantine Books, 1965.

Cahn, Anne H., and Parthasarathi, Ashok. *The Impact of a Government-Sponsored University Research Laboratory on the Local R & D Economy.* Cambridge, Mass.: Massachusetts Institute of Technology, 1967.

Cater, Douglass. "The Fourth Branch," in *Power in Washington.* New York: Vintage Books, 1965.

285

Chase, Edward T. "The Trouble with the New York Port Authority," in *Urban Government*. Edited by Edward C. Banfield. Glencoe, Ill.: The Free Press, 1961.

Clark, Kenneth. *Dark Ghetto: Dilemmas of Social Power*. New York: Harper and Row, 1965.

Comay, Eli. "How Metropolitan Toronto Government Works," *Planning 1965*. Chicago: American Society of Planning Officials, 1965.

Committee for Economic Development. *Modernizing State Government*. New York: Committee for Economic Development, 1967.

Committee of New England of the National Planning Association. *The Economic State of New England*. New Haven: Yale University Press, 1954.

Council of State Governments. *Planning Services for State Governments*. Chicago: Council of State Governments, 1956.

Croly, Herbert. *Progressive Democracy*. New York: The Macmillan Company, 1914.

_____. *The Promise of American Life*. Edited by Arthur M. Schlesinger, Jr. Cambridge, Mass.: The Belknap Press of the Harvard University Press, 1965.

Dimock, Marshall E. "Expanding Jurisdictions: A Case Study in Bureaucratic Conflict," in *Reader in Bureaucracy*. Edited by Robert K. Merton, *et al*. Glencoe, Ill.: The Free Press, 1951.

Doody, Francis S. *The Immediate Economic Impact of Higher Education in New England*. (Education Studies, No. 1.) Boston: Bureau of Business Research, College of Business Administration, Boston University, 1961.

Downs, Anthony. *Inside Bureaucracy*. Boston: Little, Brown and Company, 1967.

The Economy of Metropolitan Fall River, Massachusetts. Fall River, Mass.: Hammer and Company Associates and the Fall River Planning Board, 1963.

Elazar, Daniel. *American Federalism: A View from the States*. New York: Thomas Y. Crowell Company, 1966.

Eldredge, H. Wentworth (ed.). *Taming Megalopolis*. Volume II. New York: Anchor Books--Doubleday and Co., Inc., 1967.

France, Town and Country Environment Planning. New York: Service de Presse d'Information, 1965.

Freedman, Ronald, Whelpton, Pascal K., and Campbell, Arthur A. *Family Planning, Sterility and Population Growth.* New York: McGraw-Hill Book Company, 1959.

Friedlander, Stanley L. *Labor Migration and Economic Growth: A Case Study of Puerto Rico.* Cambridge, Mass.: M.I.T. Press, 1965.

Friedmann, John, and Alonso, William (eds.). *Regional Development and Planning.* Cambridge, Mass.: M.I.T. Press, 1964.

Galbraith, John K. *American Capitalism.* Boston: Houghton Mifflin Co., 1952.

Gans, Herbert. *The Levittowners.* New York: Pantheon Books, 1967.

_____. *The Urban Villagers: Group and Class in the Life of Italian-Americans.* Glencoe, Ill.: The Free Press, 1962.

Gaus, John M., White, Leonard D., and Dimock, Marshall E. *The Frontiers of Public Administration.* Chicago: The University of Chicago Press, 1936.

Gottman, Jean. "The Rising Demand for Urban Amenities," in *Planning for a Nation of Cities.* Edited by Sam Bass Warner. Cambridge, Mass.: M.I.T. Press, 1966.

Greer, Scott. *Urban Renewal and American Cities: The Dilemma of Democratic Intervention.* Indianapolis: Bobbs-Merrill, 1965.

Grodzins, Morton. "The Federal System," in *Democracy in the Fifty States.* Edited by Charles Press and Oliver P. Williams. Chicago: Rand McNally Co., 1966.

Hofstadter, Richard. *Anti-Intellectualism in American Life.* New York: Vintage Press, 1963.

Hunter, Floyd. *Community Power Structure.* Chapel Hill, N.C.: University of North Carolina Press, 1953.

Jacobs, Jane. *The Death and Life of Great American Cities.* New York: Random House, 1961.

Klotsche, J. Martin. *The Urban University and the Future of Our Cities.* New York: Harper and Row, 1966.

Levin, Melvin R. "Planning Component Study," in *Master Plan Study.* Commonwealth of Massachusetts: Massachusetts Board of Regional Community Colleges, 1966.

_____, and Grossman, David A. *Development Trends in the Central Merrimack Valley.* Cambridge, Mass.: The Planning Services Group, 1961.

Levitan, Sar A. *Antipoverty Work and Training Efforts: Goals and Reality.* Washington, D.C.:   Joint publication of the Institute of Labor and Industrial Relations and the National Manpower Policy Task Force, 1967.

_____. *Federal Aid to Depressed Areas: An Evaluation of the ARA.* Baltimore: The Johns Hopkins Press, 1964.

Lewis, Hylan. *Poverty's Children.* Washington, D.C.:   Cross-Tell (Communicating Research on the Urban Poor), Health and Welfare Council, National Capital Area, 1966.

Markfield, Wallace. *To An Early Grave.* New York: Pocket Books, 1965.

Marris, Peter, and Rein, Martin. *Dilemmas of Social Reform.* Institute of Community Studies. London: Routledge and Kegan Paul, 1967.

Martin, Roscoe C. *The Cities and the Federal System.* New York: Atherton Press, 1965.

Mecklin, John. *Mission in Torment.* New York: Doubleday, 1965.

Miller, Herman P. "The Dimensions of Poverty," in *Poverty as a Public Issue.* Edited by Ben B. Seligman. Glencoe, Ill.: The Free Press, 1965.

Miller, William Lee. *The Fifteenth Ward and the Great Society.* New York: Harper and Row, 1966.

Mills, C. Wright, *The Power Elite.* New York: Oxford University Press, 1956.

Monsen, R. Joseph, Jr., and Cannon, Mark W. *The Makers of Public Policy.* New York: McGraw-Hill Book Company, 1965.

Morris, Robert, and Binstock, Robert H. *Feasible Planning for Social Change.* New York: Columbia University Press, 1966.

Mowitz, Robert, and Wright, Deil S. *Profile of a Metropolis, A Case Book.* Detroit: Wayne University Press, 1962.

Moynihan, Daniel P., "Poverty in Cities," in *The Metropolitan Enigma: Inquiries into the Nature and Dimensions of America's "Urban Crisis."* Volume II. Washington, D.C.: Chamber of Commerce of the United States, 1967.

Myrdal, Gunnar. *An American Dilemma, The Negro Problem and American Democracy.* New York: Harper and Bros., 1946.

Odum, Howard W., and Moore, Harry Estill. *American Regionalism.* New York: Henry Holt and Co., 1938.

Organski, A. F. K. *The Stages of Political Development.* New York: A. A. Knopf, 1966.

Polenberg, Richard. *Reorganizing Roosevelt's Government.* Cambridge, Mass.: Harvard University Press, 1966.

Rainwater, Lee, and Yancey, William. *The Moynihan Report and the Politics of Controversy.* Cambridge, Mass.: M.I.T. Press, 1967.

Sanford, Terry. *Storm Over the States.* New York: McGraw-Hill Book Company, 1967.

Schlesinger, Arthur. *A Thousand Days: John F. Kennedy in the White House.* Boston: Houghton Mifflin Co., 1965.

Selznick, Philip. *TVA and the Grass Roots.* Berkeley: University of California Press, 1949.

Simpson, Smith. *Anatomy of the State Department.* Boston: Houghton Mifflin Co., 1967.

Smith, Thomas Russell. *The Cotton Textile Industry of Fall River, Massachusetts.* New York: Kings Crown Press, 1944.

A Study of the Economic Base of the City of New Bedford. Cambridge, Mass.: Arthur D. Little, Inc., 1962.

Till, Charles. "Migration and Negro Relocation," in *The Metropolitan Enigma: Inquiries into the Nature and Dimensions of America's "Urban Crisis."* Volume II. Washington, D.C.: Chamber of Commerce of the United States, 1967.

Toqueville, Alexis de. *Democracy in America.* Volumes I and II. New York: Vintage Books, 1954.

University of Kentucky, Department of Architecture. "A Case Study Located in Eastern Kentucky," in *New Towns: A Proposal for the Appalachian Region.* Lexington: University of Kentucky, 1960.

University of Wisconsin, Industrial Relations Research Institute. *Retraining and Migration as Factors in Regional Economic Development.* Madison: University of Wisconsin, 1966.

Walker, Robert. *The Planning Function in Urban Government.* 1st ed. Chicago: University of Chicago Press, 1941.

Walter, Benjamin. "Political Decision Making in Arcadia," in *Urban Growth Dynamics in a Regional Cluster of Cities.* Edited by Stuart F. Chapin and Shirley F. Weiss. New York: John Wiley and Sons, Inc., 1962.

Whelpton, Pascal K., Campbell, Arthur A., and Patterson, John E. *Fertility and Family Planning in the United States.* Princeton, N.J.: Princeton University Press, 1966.

Wingo, Lowden, Jr. "Urban Renewal: Objectives, Analyses and Information Systems," in *Regional Accounts for Policy Decisions.* Edited by Werner Z. Hirsch. Baltimore: The Johns Hopkins Press, 1965.

Wise, Harold F. *Planning 1965.* Chicago: American Society of Planning Officials, 1965.

Wolfbein, Seymour L. *Decline of a Cotton Textile City: A Study of New Bedford.* New York: Columbia University Press, 1944.

Wood, Robert C. "A Federal Policy for Metropolitan Areas," in *Metropolitan Politics: A Reader.* Edited by Michael N. Danielson. Boston: Little, Brown and Co., 1966.

_____. *1400 Governments, New York Metropolitan Region Study.* Cambridge, Mass.: Harvard University Press, 1961.

ARTICLES AND PERIODICALS

Adrian, Charles R. "State and Local Government Participation in the Design and Administration of Intergovernmental Programs," *The Annals,* Vol. 359 (May, 1965).

Altshuler, Alan A. "Rationality and Influence in Public Service," *Public Administration Review* (September, 1965).

"Back-Into-Balance Britain," *London Sunday Times,* November 5, 1967, p. 34.

Ball, Claiborne M. "Employment Effects of Construction Expenditures," *Monthly Labor Review,* LXXXVII (February, 1965).

Banfield, Edward C. "The Political Implications of Metropolitan Growth," *Daedalus* (Winter, 1961).

Barnes, Ralph M., and Raymond, George M. "The Fiscal Approach to Land Use Planning," *Journal of the American Institute of Planners* (Spring-Summer, 1955).

Beckman, Norman. "For a New Perspective in Federal-State Relations," *State Government* (Autumn, 1966).

_____. "The Planner as a Bureaucrat," *Journal of the American Institute of Planners,* XXX (November, 1964).

Beijer, G. *National Rural Manpower: Adjustment to Industry.* (Paris: OECD, 1965). (Quoted in Sjaastad, L. A., "The Costs and Returns of Human Migration," *The Journal of Political Economy,* LXX, 5 [2] [1962].)

Bellush, Jewel, and Hausknecht, Murray. "Entrepreneurs and Urban Renewal," *Journal of the American Institute of Planners,* XXXII (September, 1966).

Benson, George C. S. "Trends in Intergovernmental Relations," *The Annals,* Vol. 359 (May, 1965).

Bogue, Donald J. "The End of the Population Explosion," *The Public Interest,* VII (Spring, 1967).

The Boston Herald, April 3, 1938, and January 3, 1967.

The Boston Post, September 4, 1937.

Business Week (July 15, 1967).

Chelstowski, Stanislaw. "Deglomeration," *Polish Perspectives Monthly Review* (Warsaw, Poland) (November, 1966).

Chinitz, Benjamin. "Appropriate Goals for Regional Economic Policy," *Urban Studies* (Glasgow, Scotland), Vol. III, No. 1 (February, 1966).

_____. "Regional Economic Policy in Great Britain," *Urban Affairs Quarterly,* Vol. I, No. 2 (December, 1965), and Vol. I, No. 3 (March, 1966).

The Christian Science Monitor (Boston), March 8, 10, 1966, and January 31, 1968.

Cohen, Wilbur J. "Education and Learning," *The Annals,* issue entitled *Social Goals and Indicators,* Vol. 373 (September, 1967).

Colman, William G. "The Federal Government in Intergovernmental Programs," *The Annals,* Vol. 359 (May, 1965).

Congressional Quarterly Weekly Report, March 13, 1965; XXIV, No. 5 (February 4, 1966); XXIV, No. 14 (April 8, 1966); XXIV, No. 42 (October 21, 1966).

Davidoff, Paul. "Advocacy and Pluralism in Planning," *Journal of the American Institute of Planners,* XXXI (November, 1965).

Dorfman, Robert. "Measuring Benefits of Government Investments," Edited by Robert Dorfman. Washington, D.C.: Brookings Institution Studies in Finance, 1965.

Duhl, Leonard J. "Planning and Predicting: Or What to Do When You Don't Know the Names of the Variables," in *Daedalus,* issue entitled *Toward the Year 2,000: Work in Progress* (Summer, 1967).

Dyckman, John. "Social Planning, Social Planners, and Planned Societies," *Journal of the American Institute of Planners,* XXXII (March, 1966).

Eckaus, R. S. "Economic Criteria for Education and Training," *The Review of Economics and Statistics* (May, 1964).

Franklin, Ben A. "Kennedy Calls Antipoverty Program a Failure," *The New York Times,* February 15, 1968.

Freeman, Howard E., and Sherwood, Clarence C. "Research in Large Scale Intervention Programs," *Journal of Social Issues* (January, 1965).

Friedmann, John. "The Concept of a Planning Region--The Evolution of an Idea in the United States," *Land Economics* (February, 1956).

_____. "Planning as Innovation: The Chilean Case," *Journal of the American Institute of Planners,* XXXII (July, 1966).

_____. "Regional Planning as a Field of Study," *Journal of the American Institute of Planners,* XXIX (August, 1963).

Glazer, Nathan. "The Grand Design of the Poverty Program," *The New York Times Magazine* (February 27, 1966).

Goodwin, Richard N. "The Shape of American Politics," *Commentary* (June, 1967).

Gorham, William. "Notes of a Practitioner," *The Public Interest,* issue entitled *PPBS, Its Scope and Limits,* VIII (Summer, 1967).

Gross, Bertram M., and Springer, Michael. "A New Orientation in American Government," *The Annals,* issue entitled *Social Goals and Indicators in American Society* (May, 1967).

Grossman, David A., and Levin, Melvin R. "The Appalachian Region: A National Problem Area," *Land Economics* (May, 1961).

Hechinger, Fred M. "Call for the 'Urban-Grant' College," *The New York Times,* October 22, 1967.

Horowitz, Irving Louis, and Rainwater, Lee. "Social Accounting for the Nation," *Trans-Action* (May, 1967).

Iden, George. "Industrial Growth in Areas of Chronic Unemployment," *Monthly Labor Review* (May, 1966).

Kalachek, Edward K. "Automation and Full Employment," *Trans-Action* (March, 1967).

Keyserling, Herman. "Genius Locii," *Atlantic Monthly,* CXLIV (September, 1929), 302-11. (Quoted in Odum, Howard W., and Moore, Harry Estill, *American Regionalism.* New York: Henry Holt and Company, 1938).

Kifner, John, *The New York Times,* June 14, 1966.

Kristol, Irving. "The Negro Today Is the Immigrant of Yesterday," *The New York Times Magazine* (September 11, 1966).

Levin, Melvin R. "Planners and Metropolitan Planning," *Journal of the American Institute of Planners* (March, 1967).

_____. "Review of *Federal Aid to Depressed Areas: An Evaluation of the Area Redevelopment Administration,* by Sar Levitan," *Journal of the American Institute of Planners* (February, 1965).

Lewis, Anthony. *The New York Times,* June 21, 1961, the last of a series of articles on Massachusetts.

Loftus, Joseph A. "City Poverty Grants Linked to Aggressiveness," *The New York Times,* August 18, 1966.

Long, Norton E. "Citizenship or Consumership in Metropolitan Areas," *Journal of the American Institute of Planners*, XXXI (February, 1965).

_____. "Politicians for Hire--The Dilemmas of Education and the Task of Research," *Public Administration Review*, XXV, 2 (June, 1965).

McKinley, Charles. "The Valley Authority and Its Alternatives," *American Political Science Review* (September, 1950). (Included as Chapter 28 in Friedmann, John, and Alonso, William, *Regional Development and Planning: A Reader*. Cambridge, Mass.: M.I.T. Press, 1964.)

Mann, Lawrence C., and Pillorge, George J. "French Regional Planning," *Journal of the American Institute of Planners*, XXX, 2 (May, 1964).

Mao, James C. T. "Efficiency in Public Urban Renewal Expenditures Through Benefit-Cost Analysis," *Journal of the American Institute of Planners*, XXXII (March, 1966).

Mills, Thomas J. "Scientific Personnel and the Professions," *The Annals*, issue entitled *The New Immigration*, Vol. 367 (September, 1966).

Moynihan, Daniel P. "The Moynihan Report and Its Critics," *Commentary* (February, 1967).

_____. *The Public Interest*, V (Fall, 1966).

_____. "Urban Conditions: General," *The Annals*, 371 (May, 1967).

_____. "You Can't Run the Nation from Washington," *Boston Globe*, October 18, 1967

Muskie, Edmund S., Senator. "Manpower: The Achilles Heel of Creative Federalism," *Public Administration Review* (June, 1967).

Needleman, L., and Scott, B. "Regional Problems and Location of Industry in Britain," *Urban Studies* (Glasgow, Scotland), I, 2 (November, 1964).

The New York Times, March 26, 1958; January 16, and 23, 1966; February 10, 1966; March 6, 13, 25, 1966; March 26, 1967; June 22, 1967; August 27, 1967; January 13, 1968; February 2, 1968.

Nixon, John H. "Jobs for Low-Income Areas of the Inner-City," *Economic Development*, III, 12 (December, 1966).

O'Harrow, Dennis. "A Broad Brush With A Sharp Edge," *American Society of Planning Officials Newsletter* (June, 1967).

_____. "A New Tune for the Piper," *American Society of Planning Officials Newsletter*, XXXII, 3 (March, 1966).

Okun, Bernard. "Regional Income Inequality and Internal Population Migration," *Economic Development and Cultural Change* (January, 1961).

Orshansky, Molly. "Who's Who Among the Poor: A Demographic View of Poverty," *Social Security Bulletin* (July, 1965).

Parr, John B. "Outmigration and the Depressed Area Problem," *Land Economics* (May, 1966).

Petshek, Kirk R. "A New Role for City Universities--Urban Extension Programs," *Journal of the American Institute of Planners* (November, 1964).

Population Reference Bureau. "Boom Babies Come of Age: The American Family at the Crossroads," *Population Bulletin*, XXII, No. 3 (August, 1966).

Press, Charles, and Adrian, Charles R. "Why Our State Governments Are Sick," *The Antioch Review* (Summer, 1964).

Pynchon, Thomas, "A Journey Into the Mind of Watts," *The New York Times Magazine* (June 23, 1966).

Rein, Martin, and Miller, S. M. "Poverty Programs and Policy Priorities," *Trans-Action* (September, 1967).

Robock, Stefan. "Strategies for Regional Economic Development," *Regional Science Association Papers*, XVII, 1966.

Rossi, Peter. "Evaluating Social Action Programs," *Trans-Action* (June, 1967).

Schick, Allen. "The Road to PPBS: The Stages of Budget Reform," *Public Administration Review* (December, 1966).

Schultz, Theodore W. "Capital Formation in Education," *Journal of Political Economy* (December, 1960).

_____. "Education and Economic Growth," *1961 Yearbook of the National Society for the Study of Education*, Ch. 3.

_____. (ed.). "Investment in Human Beings," *The Journal of Political Economy*, LXX (October, 1962).

Sheehan, Neil. "You Don't Know Where Johnson Ends and McNamara Begins," *The New York Times Magazine* (October 22, 1967).

Shorr, Alvin L. "Program for the Social Orphans," *The New York Times Magazine* (March 13, 1966).

Shriver, Sargent. *The New York Times,* March 9, 1966, p. 24; November 6, 1966, p. 6E.

The Wall Street Journal, March 7, 1966, p. 1.

Wildavsky, Aaron. "The Political Economy of Efficiency: Cost-Benefit Analysis, Systems Analysis and Program Budgeting," *Public Administration Review* (December, 1966), pp. 297-98.

_____. "The Political Economy of Efficiency," *The Public Interest,* 8 (Summer, 1967), 30-48.

Wilson, James Q. "The Bureaucracy Problem," *The Public Interest,* VI (Winter, 1967), 3-9.

Winston, Oliver C. "An Urbanization Pattern for the United States--Some Considerations for the Decentralization of Excellence," *Land Economics* (February, 1967).

Wirtz, Willard, "War on Poverty," *Congressional Quarterly,* XXIV, No. 11 (March 18, 1966), p. 603.

Wood, Robert. "Government and the Intellectual: The Necessary Alliance for Effective Action to Meet Urban Needs," *The Annals,* issue entitled *Governing Urban Society: New Scientific Approaches,* Vol. 371 (May, 1967).

PUBLIC DOCUMENTS

Boston College. *Fact Finding Survey of Nursing Homes.* Boston, 1963.

Committee Appointed by the Conference of New England Governors. *Report on the New England Textile Industry.* Boston, 1952.

Kaufman, J. J. "Labor Mobility, Training, and Retraining," *Studies in Unemployment.* U.S. Senate Special Committee on Unemployment Problems. Washington, 1960.

Landis, James M. *Report on Regulatory Agencies to the President Elect.* Washington, 1960.

Levin, Melvin R. *Toward A State Plan for Nursing Homes.* Prepared for the Division of Adult Health. Boston, 1966.

Litton Industries. *Preliminary Analysis for Economic Development Plan for the Appalachian Region.* Prepared for the Area Redevelopment Administration, Washington, 1965.

Maine. Office of Health Education, Department of Health, Education, and Welfare. *Nursing Home Patient Care.* Augusta, 1965.

Massachusetts. Board of Regional Community Colleges. *Access to Quality Community College Opportunity: A Master Plan for Massachusetts Community Colleges Through 1975.* Boston, 1967.

Commonwealth of Massachusetts. *The Commonwealth Service Corps News,* Vol. 2, No. 2, March, 1966.

_____. Department of Education. *Annual Report for the Year Ending June 30, 1963.*

_____. Governor's Management Engineering Task Force. *Survey Report and Recommendations.* Boston, 1965.

_____. Special Commission on Audit of State Needs. *Needs in Massachusetts Higher Education.* Boston, 1958.

_____. State Planning Board. *Progress Report.* Boston, 1936.

Moynihan, Daniel Patrick. *The Negro Family.* Washington: U.S. Department of Labor, 1965.

Ribicoff, Abraham, Senator. "The Competent City: An Action Program for Urban America," *Congressional Record,* 89th Cong., 1st Sess., January 23, 1967.

U.S. Advisory Commission on Intergovernmental Relations. *Factors Affecting Governmental Reorganization in Metropolitan Areas.* Washington, 1962.

_____. The Appalachian Regional Development Commission. *Executive Director's Semi-Annual Report.* Washington, 1966.

_____. Area Redevelopment Administration. *Area Redevelopment Policies in Britain and the Countries of the Common Market.* Washington, 1965.

_____. Area Redevelopment Administration. *Population, Labor Force and Unemployment in Chronically Distressed Areas.* Washington, 1964.

_____. Area Redevelopment Administration. *The Propensity to Move.* Washington, 1964.

_____. Bureau of the Budget. *Bulletin No. 66-3, Planning-Programming-Budgeting.* Washington, 1965.

_____. *Supplement to Bulletin No. 66-3.* Washington, 1966.

_____. Bureau of the Census. *Census.* Washington, 1960.

_____. Bureau of the Census. *1963 Census of Transportation.* "Home-to-Work Travel." TC63 (a)-P5.

_____. Bureau of the Census. *Current Population Reports, Population Estimates.* Series P-25, Nos. 326 and 347. Washington, 1966.

_____. Bureau of the Census. *Statistical Abstract of the United States.* Washington, 1965-67.

_____. Committee on Government Operations. Subcommittee on Intergovernmental Relations. "Federal Expenditures to States and Regions." Washington, 1966.

_____. Committee on Government Operations. Subcommittee on Intergovernmental Relations. "The Federal System as Seen by Federal Aid Officials." Washington, 1965.

_____. Congress. Public Law 89-4, "Appalachian Regional Development Act of 1965," 89th Cong., 1st Sess., 1965.

_____. Department of Commerce. *Survey of Current Business.* Washington, 1967.

_____. Department of Health, Education and Welfare. *Nursing Home Standards Guide.* Publication No. 827. Washington, 1961; reprinted 1963.

_____. Department of Labor. *Manpower Implications of Automation.* Washington, 1964.

_____. Department of Labor. *Manpower Report of the President.* Washington, 1964 and 1966.

_____. Department of Labor. *Projections 1970, Interindustry Relationships, Potential Demand, Employment.* Bulletin No. 1536. Washington, 1966.

_____. Department of Labor. *Social and Economic Conditions of Negroes in the United States.* Bureau of Labor Statistics Report No. 332. Washington, 1967.

_____. Economic Development Administration. *Economic Development.* Washington, January and February, 1968.

_____. *Hearings* before the Committee on Public Works (Senate) and Committee on Public Works (House of Representatives). "Public Works and Economic Development Act of 1965." 89th Cong., 1st Sess., 1965.

_____. *Hearings* before the Subcommittee of the Committee on Banking and Currency. "Area Redevelopment Act." 86th Cong., 1st Sess., 1959.

_____. *Hearings* before the Subcommittee on Intergovernmental Relations. "Creative Federalism." 90th Cong., 1st Sess., 1967.

_____. Joint Economic Committee. Subcommittee on Economic Progress. *Federal Programs for the Development of Human Resources.* Washington, 1966.

_____. National Aeronautics and Space Administration. *Electronic Research Center.* Washington, 1964.

_____. National Commission on Technology, Automation and Economic Progress. *Technology and the American Economy.* Washington, 1966.

_____. National Resources Planning Board. Committee on Long-Range Work and Relief Policies. *Security, Work and Relief Policies.* Washington, 1942.

_____. National Science Foundation. "Geographic Distribution of Funds for Research and Development, 1963," *Reviews of Data on Science Resources.* Washington, 1965.

_____. Office of Economic Opportunity. *Community Action Program Guide.* Washington, 1965.

_____. Office of Economic Opportunity. *Office of Economic Opportunity Memorandum.* Nos. 23 and 28. Washington, 1966.

_____. President's Advisory Committee on Labor Management Policy. *The Benefits and Problems Incidental to Automation and Other Technological Advances.* Washington, 1962.

_____. President's Appalachian Regional Commission. *Appalachia.* Washington, 1964.

_____. President's Commission on National Goals. *Goals for Americans.* Washington, 1960.

_____. President's Committee on Administrative Management. *Report of the Committee.* Washington, 1937.

_____. President's Message. "City Demonstration Programs." 89th Cong., 2nd Sess., 1966.

_____. Senate. Committee on Labor and Public Welfare. *Selected Readings in Employment and Manpower.* 6 Vols. Washington, 1964 and 1965.

Wheaton, William L. C., and Schussheim, Morton J. *The Cost of Municipal Services in Residential Areas.* Prepared for the Housing and Home Finance Agency. Washington, 1955

Wolfle, Dael. "Can Professional Manpower Trends Be Predicted," *Seminar on Manpower Policy and Program.* Prepared for the U.S. Department of Labor, Manpower Administration. Washington, 1967.

REPORTS

Action for Boston Community Development. *Community Action Program 7-30.*

_____. *A Report on ABCD Activities.* Boston, September, 1963 - August, 1964.

_____. *Staff Memoranda.* Boston, February, 1966.

_____. *Staff Reports,* Community Action Program. Submitted to Robert Coard, Director, CAP-ABCD. Boston, December, 1964 - January, 1966.

American Institute of Planners Committee on Metropolitan Planning. *Workshop Report. Proceedings of the 1964 Annual Conference.* American Institute of Planners, 1964.

Fischer, Victor A. *Proceedings of the 1964 Annual Conference.* American Institute of Planners, 1965.

Hayes, Frederick O'Reilly. *Urban Planning and the Transportation Study. Proceedings of the 1963 Annual Conference.* American Institute of Planners, 1964.

Lepawsky, Albert. *State Planning and Economic Development in the South.* Report No. 4. Washington: National Planning Association, Committee of the South, 1949.

Loeks, C. David. *Where Metropolitan Planning Stands Today. Proceedings of the 1958 Annual Conference.* American Institute of Planners, 1959, pp. 31-33.

UNPUBLISHED MATERIAL

Blackwood, George. "The Northern Berkshire Area and Its Future." Unpublished manuscript, Area Development Center, Boston University, 1965.

Boston University, Area Development Center. "A Brief in Support of the Designation of New England as an Economic Development Region." Unpublished manuscript, 1965.

_____. "State Agencies and Regional Development: A Study Prepared for the Massachusetts Department of Commerce and Development." Unpublished manuscript, Boston University, 1966.

Levin, Melvin R. "The Depressed Area: A Study of Southern Illinois." Unpublished Ph.D. dissertation, University of Chicago, 1956.

Abrams, Richard M., 96-97
Adrian, Charles R., 53, 129, 131, 135, 142, 143
Alinsky, Saul, 56, 89
Altshuler, Alan A., 45, 138
Atlantic Coastal Plains, 261

Banfield, Edward C., 11, 45, 111, 131, 136
Bauer, Raymond A., 69
Beckman, Norman, 138
Benson, George C. S., 53
Biderman, Albert D., 70
Birkhead, Guthrie S., 130
Brownlow, Louis, 4, 6

Cambridge, Mass., 154
Cater, Douglass, 53
Churchill, Winston, 202
Clark, Kenneth, 28
Comay, Eli, 131
Connecticut, 257
Croly, Herbert, 3
Cutover Area, 250

Davidoff, Paul, 137
Delaware, 136
Douglas, Senator Paul, 9, 171-73
Downs, Anthony, 273
Duhl, Leonard J., 55
Dyckman, John, 55

Fall River, Mass., 133, 149, 198, 207, 209, 214, 228
Fischer, Victor A., 128
Four Corners, 261
Friedmann, John, 56, 249

Gans, Herbert, 67
Glazer, Nathan, 93
GOVERNMENT AND NON-GOVERNMENT AGENCIES: Action for Boston Community Development, 83, 87-88, 90-93; Advisory Commission on Intergovernmental Relations, 127, 130, 140; American Insti-

tute of Planners, 5, 128; American Nursing Home Association, 161; American Society of Planning Officials, 109, 161-162; Appalachian Regional Development Commission, 10, 48, 254; Area Planning Action Council, 94-95; Area Redevelopment Administration, 173, 202; Board of Economic Advisers (Mass.), 79; Board of Trade Incentives and Regulations, 175; Boston Chamber of Commerce, 114; Boston Redevelopment Authority, 92; Boston Regional Planning Project, 134; Bureau of the Budget (U.S.), 7-8, 52, 134, 137, 181, 264; Bureau of Building Construction (Mass.), 76; Bureau of Labor Statistics (U.S.), 98; Bureau of Public Roads (U.S.), 128-129, 179; Census Bureau (U.S.), 119, 122; Committee for Economic Development, 8; Council of Economic Advisers, 7, 68; Department of Defense, 40, 42, 45, 134, 140, 282; Department of Health, Education, and Welfare, 92, 100, 129, 140, 157; Department of Housing and Urban Development, 139, 179-180, 216, 251, 282; Department of Labor, 92, 100, 173, 234; Department of Public Health (Mass.), 150; Division of Adult Health (Mass.), 162; Economic and Youth Opportunity Agency (Los Angeles), 83; Economic Development Administration, 140, 179, 216; Executive Office for Administration and Finance (Mass.), 75; Federal Aviation Administration, 129, 140; Ford Foundation, 88; Governor's Management Engineering Task Force, 77; Hoover Commissions, 8, 75; Housing and Home Finance Agency, 128; Joint Economic Committee, 52, 68; Kestnbaum Commission, 8, 72; Massachusetts Bay Transportation Authority, 76, 130; Massachusetts Board of Regional Community Colleges, 149;

Massachusetts Port Authority, 130; Massachusetts Turnpike Authority, 76, 130; Metropolitan District Commission (Mass.), 130; National Academy of Science, 117; National Aeronautics and Space Administration, 116-117, 257; National Opinion Research Center, 29; National Resources Committee, 6; National Resources Planning Board, 7, 246, 266; New England Regional Commission, 180; New York Department of Health, 159; New York Port Authority, 130; New York Regional OEO Office, 84, 86, 91; New York Regional Plan Association, 127; Office of Economic Opportunity (U.S.), 26, 84, 88, 90, 100, 253; Office of Education (U.S.), 86; Office of Regional Economic Development (U.S.), 255; President's Appalachian Study Commission, 254; Public Administration Clearing House, 4; Public Health Service (U.S.), 162; Rand Corporation, 276; Social Science Research Council, 4; Southern Massachusetts Technological Institute, 194; Tennessee Valley Authority, 5, 250, 255; United Nations, 239; United States Employment Service, 92

GOVERNMENT LEGISLATION: Appalachian Regional Development Act of 1965, 10, 251; Area Redevelopment Act of 1961, 170-171, 202; Economic Opportunity Act of 1964, 10, 98, 1966 Amendments, 235; Elementary and Secondary Education Act of 1965; 86, 209; Federal Aid Highway Act of 1962, 110; Higher Education Act of 1965, 217; Highway Act of 1956, 8; Housing Act of 1949, 8; Housing Act of 1954, 8; Immigration Act of 1965, 229; Intergovernmental Personnel Act of 1967, 52; Manpower Development and Training Act of 1962, 9, 92; Public Works and Economic Development Act of 1965, 9, 169, 175, 187, 202, 216, 230, 246, 252, 261; Social Security Amendments of 1965, 158; Water Resources Act of 1965, 251

GOVERNMENT PROGRAMS: Automatic Data Processing, 77-79; bureaucracy, 213, 273; Community Action Program, 83, 93, 139; Community Renewal Program, 10; cost-benefit analysis, 40, 44, 46, 64-68,

72, 246; education and training, 150-152, 108, 231, 235, 277, 281; evaluation, 27-28, 41-42, 53, 59, 274, 281; expenditures, 118, 257-258, 276; Federalism, 245, 254, 256; goals and values, 43, 49-50, 54-55, 110, 134, 138, 239, 264, 274; impact, 277; interagency and intergovernmental coordination, 129, 134, 139, 141, 179-181; Job Corps, 66, 90, 100, 276; Medicaid, 157-158; Medicare, 157-158, 165; metropolitan government, 129-130; Model Cities, 31, 48, 139, 190, 267; Neighborhood Youth Corps, 60, 85, 87; New Deal, 5, 246; Operation Headstart, 85, 89, 99-100; Peace Corps, 89; planning, 9, 45, 136-137, 148-149, 166, 237, 271; Planning Programing Budgeting System, 39-53, 55, 57-58, 60, 64, 72, 74, 76, 79-80, 100, 264, 271-272, 274; protectionist pressures, 239; "pyramidal mass," 273-274; river basins, 250; social indicators, 68, 71-72, 80; staff capability, 24, 32-37, 271, 275; state government, 74, 275, 279; Work Horizons Program, 95; Youth Employment and Training Program, 84

Greer, Scott, 11, 49, 83
Gross, Bertram M., 66

Harlem and Bedford-Stuyvesant, 183
Harris, Fred, 70
Hurley, Governor Charles F., 6

Jacobs, Jane, 67
Johnson, Lyndon Baines, 10, 40, 74, 215-216

Kafka, Franz, 17, 84
Kennedy, John F., 9, 172, 274
Kerr, Clark, 281
Kestnbaum, Meyer, 8
Keynes, John Maynard, 7
Kraenzel, Carl F., 262
Kuznets, Simon, 7

Landis, James M., 7
Lawrence, Mass., 213
Levitan, Sar A., 100, 173
Lewis, Anthony, 96
Lincoln, Abraham, 42, 45
Loek, C. David, 142
Long, Norton E., 129, 144
Los Angeles, 117
Lowell, Mass., 214, 216

McNamara, Robert, 21, 25, 41-42, 134, 140
Mao, James C. T., 67
Marquand, J. P., 113
Marris, Peter, 27-28
Massachusetts, 75, 111, 118, 150-151, 156, 176, 257
Merriam, Charles E., 4, 6
Metropolitan Boston, 111-112, 133, 151, 154, 208, 212
Meyerson, Martin, 131
Miami, 130, 190
MIGRATION: aspects, 224, 229, 232, 261-262, 264, 272; beneficial impacts, 228; European patterns, 220-222, 240, 265; national policy, 279; Negro, 221; relocation problems, 203, 223; "sending" and "receiving" areas, 228, 261; statistics, 262
Miller, S. M., 67
Miller, William Lee, 29
Mondale, Senator Walter F., 68
Montana, 262
Moynihan, Daniel Patrick, 11, 28, 89, 276
Muskie, Senator Edmund S., 52, 74, 127-129, 277
Myrdal, Gunnar, 48

NEGROES: Black Power movement, 101, 271; conflict with community, 86, 94-95; ghetto, 50, 59, 132; job discrimination, 236; population, 132, 153, 195, 220, 235; status, 57, 69, 94
Neustadt, Richard, 9, 283
Newark, 190
New Bedford, Mass., 198, 206, 214, 216, 228
New England, 111, 174, 222, 239, 249, 256, 262-263
New Haven, 213
New York, 84, 94, 117, 183
North Adams, Mass., 216, 226
North End (Boston), 94, 96

Oakland, 190
Ogburn, William Fielding, 4
O'Harrow, Dennis, 109-110, 215
Organski, A. F. K., 2
Ozark, 250, 261

Parratt, Spencer, 9
Pennsylvania, 225
Plymouth, 216

Population, 120-123, 225, 227, 272
Powell, Adam Clayton, 89

REDEVELOPMENT AREAS: Appalachia, 10, 174, 178, 222, 239, 246, 250, 254, 261; Caliban Territory, 203; "combat pay," 204; distressed area, 71, 170, 172, 191, 195, 227; distressed area, foreign, 175, 225, 238; distressed areas, textile industry, 112, 195-196, 198, 203, 206; Economic Development Districts, 169-170, 173, 181, 183-184, 216, 230, 238, 271; EDA development regions, 259, 266; eligibility criteria, 187, 259; job gains, 202; "little league" criteria, 214; "Lost Golden Age," 205; scarcity of college graduates, 209
Reed, Thomas H., 131
Rein, Martin, 27-28, 67
Rhode Island, 136
Ribicoff, Senator Abraham, 70
Roosevelt, Theodore, 3
Rossi, Peter, 26, 28-29

San Diego, 190
Schick, Allen, 75
Schlesinger, Arthur, 274
Shriver, Sargent, 59, 92
Simpson, Smith, 273
Smith, Governor Alfred E., 5
Southern Illinois, 171
Springer, Michael, 66

Tennessee, 136
Toqueville, Alexis de, 18, 227-228, 275-276
Truman, Harry S., 7

Upper Peninsula (Mich.), 261

Vermont, 257

Walker, Harvey, 132
Walker, Robert A., 4, 138
Ward, Lester Frank, 3
Washington, D.C., 96, 133
West Virginia, 171
Wharton, Edith, 113
Wheaton, William L. C., 130
Wingo, Lowden, Jr., 11
Wise, Harold, 127
Wood, Robert C., 11, 131, 139, 142, 282
Woodbury, Coleman, 130-131

ABOUT THE AUTHOR

Melvin R. Levin is Professor of Government and Lecturer in the Urban Affairs program as well as Director of Research at Boston University's Area Development Center. Since 1957 he has been a consultant in planning and administration specializing in problems of redevelopment areas and state government in the Midwest, South and New England. Among his early experience was his service on project staffs replanning coastal areas of Rhode Island and North Carolina after the hurricane tidal floods of 1954 and 1955 and in Eastern Kentucky after the 1957 river floods. Between 1955 and 1957 he was a senior economist at Midwest Research Institute engaged in area studies (e.g. the Northern Plains) and in community and market research.

In recent years he has been a consultant to the Department of Housing and Urban Development for which he has recently completed a major research report on intergovernmental relations in five area transportation studies. A member of the Triton Foundation, he collaborated with R. Buckminster Fuller in a study of proposed floating communities and a major urban design project for the city of Toronto. Dr. Levin's wide range of consulting experience is reflected in the various chapters of this book: He was involved in the conceptual planning which led to the formation of the Appalachian Regional Commission, has prepared statewide plans for nursing home facilities and regional community colleges, and studies for regional planning agencies, transportation commissions, and distressed areas.

Dr. Levin received an M.A. in Sociology and a Ph.D. in Planning from the University of Chicago. He has been Director of Research at Boston University's Area Development Center since 1964. In this capacity he directed a study of the impact of Massachusetts state agencies on metropolitan Boston and conducted research which provided the technical rationale for the creation of the New England Regional Commission. Among his major research studies are *The Boston Region*, and *Models for Code Administration* which he co-authored with Joseph Slavet for the National Commission on Urban Problems.